"Disassembled" Images
Allan Sekula and Contemporary Art

The Lieven Gevaert Series is a major series of substantial and innovative books on photography. Launched in 2004, the Series takes into account the ubiquitous presence of photography within modern culture and, in particular, the visual arts. At the forefront of contemporary thinking on photography, the books offer new insights on the position of the photographic medium within art historical, theoretical, social and institutional contexts.

The Series is produced by the Lieven Gevaert Research Centre for Photography, Art and Visual Culture (www.lievengevaertcentre.be) and covers four types of approaches: publication of outstanding monographic studies, proceedings of international conferences, book length projects with artists, translations and republications of classic material. The Lieven Gevaert Series is published by Leuven University Press, and distributed in North America by Cornell University Press.

"Disassembled" Images
Allan Sekula and Contemporary Art

Edited by Alexander Streitberger and Hilde Van Gelder

Leuven University Press

Contents

Acknowledgements

The present publication is one of the outcomes of a long-term research project entitled "Art Against the Grain of 'Collective Sisyphus': The Case of Allan Sekula's *Ship of Fools | The Dockers' Museum* (2010–2013)," supervised by Hilde Van Gelder. Jointly pursued by the Lieven Gevaert Research Centre for Photography, Art, and Visual Culture (LGC) and M HKA, Museum van Hedendaagse Kunst Antwerpen between 2014 and 2019 it has received funding by the Research Council of the University of Leuven and by the Research Foundation-Flanders (FWO). While conducting our activities we have received the invaluable support of Sally Stein, who granted permission to reproduce numerous illustrations from the works of Allan Sekula. Ina Steiner, the Allan Sekula Studio manager, provided essential research materials and information in relation to image captions and collections. Further permissions were kindly granted by Victor Burgin, Chris Larson, Martha Rosler, Alamy, Getty Images, Royal Museum of Fine Arts of Belgium, Brussels, The British Museum, The State Hermitage Museum in St. Petersburg, The Warburg Institute, and Museum der Moderne Salzburg.

The large majority of the essays included in this book were first presented as papers at the conference *"Disassembled Images": Contemporary Art After Allan Sekula* (Antwerp, 2–4 March 2017). Key members of the research team who contributed to the initial conception of this conference were the project's co-supervisors Mieke Bleyen and Edwin Carels, its postdoctoral researcher Nicola Setari, its two PhD-students Anja Isabel Schneider and Jeroen Verbeeck, and our first project assistant Katelijne Lindemans. We thank Bart De Baere, director of M HKA, for having hosted this three-day long event. Federica Mantoan, our second project assistant, expertly coordinated the conference, helped by Zeynep Kubat. Federica Mantoan also assisted with the editorial work in the early stages of this manuscript, for which we sincerely thank her. In the run-up towards making this publication we received additional support from Marie Verreth and Erien Withouck. Thomas Desmet designed the conference materials, of which the reader will find a trace in the illustrations accompanying our introduction to this volume. We thank all of them for their precious contributions leading up to the book's production. We also thank the authors for their challenging and thought-provoking essays, as well as Ton Brouwers who meticulously copy edited each and every word of the manuscript. Finally, we want to express our sincere gratitude to the two anonymous reviewers of the manuscript, who provided invaluable feedback.

— Alexander Streitberger and Hilde Van Gelder

Introduction

Alexander Streitberger and Hilde Van Gelder

> I go back to a portrait made back in 1994. A Greek ship is carrying parts of a disassembled American steel mill to China. The electrician aboard, Marek, a Pole from Warsaw, shares his profession with the then-president of Poland, hero of the Gdansk shipyard. Marek has no clue where the ship is going after the stop in China, since it is an unscheduled tramp steamer, picking up cargo charters as opportunities arise. He is very curious about the exchange rate for the dollar, a curiosity he no doubt shares with the ship's owners. (Sekula, 2009: 62)

These enigmatic lines figure in Allan Sekula's autobiographical essay "Polonia and Other Fables 2007–2009." Sekula inserts them toward the end of a section entitled "'**PRELIMINARY NOTES' (Or How Not To Get a Grant From the NEA)**" [original emphasis]. He refers to a particular photograph he most likely made while working on *Fish Story* (1989–1995). As mentioned elsewhere in the same text, this image is now part of "the chaos of [his] non-archive." (Sekula, 2009: 57) He dryly points out that he managed to locate it amidst the enormous quantity of pictures produced over the years. Yet instead of sharing the photograph, he only provides the above-quoted short description. The reader understands it to be a portrait of a Polish seafarer aboard a cargo ship sailing under Greek flag. It is unclear whether or not the photograph shows parts of the disassembled steel mill in the ship's hold.

Sekula was born in Erie, Pennsylvania, in 1951. At that time this city—located on the likewise named Lake and as such a perfect place for industrial activity—was still considered a beating heart of American steel manufacturing. Although his parents moved West when Sekula was still a child, the artist remained mildly attached to his native region. As he outlines in the same text from which the above quotation is taken, his paternal grandparents—immigrants from Polish Galicia—lie buried in nearby DuBois, PA. In our view, this seemingly random excerpt from an essay by Allan Sekula well exemplifies his working method. Central to his body of work, we believe, is the idea of disassembling items or elements in order to reassemble some of them in a varied or alternative constellation. He engages in this very operation, however, only to disassemble a few (other) elements once again. To characterize this process, Sekula fondly referred to "poor Jerry Lewis" as protagonist of the movie *The Disorderly Orderly* (1964), in whom he recognized a role model, perhaps for his way of wreaking havoc in a hospital that turns the established order of things and hierarchies upside down. (Sekula, 2009: 58)

For this book we propose to take Sekula's vaguely identified photograph as motto. We did not put any effort in trying to find the photograph. Our motto refers to an invisible and as of yet slightly mysterious object. It is quite possible that one day this particular image will be recovered from his archive, now preserved at the Getty Research Institute in Los Angeles. Sekula explicitly wished his oeuvre to be as complex as the worldly reality he kept relentlessly investigating. Deliberately creating such blind spots was an integral part of the artistic game he played. In the introductory note to an early work, *Aerospace Folktales* (1973), he explained that he originally conceived of its installation in terms of a "disassembled movie." (Sekula, [1984] 2016: 106) By this he meant that he brought together in the same space the "separate narrative elements" of spoken sound, images, and written commentary—if in a rather unexpected and unpredictable way. (106)

He would further develop and sustain this strategy throughout his career, as much later he clarified in an interview with Katarzyna Ruchel-Stockmans. Referring to both Bertolt Brecht's concept of the "*Lehrstück*" and to Samuel Beckett's theatrical pieces, he indicated that it was possible to understand some of his works in terms of a "philosophical play." (Ruchel-Stockmans, 2006: 141) What he had in mind was actually a very specific idea of atypical play. The "cast of characters" was intended to remain "offstage." (141) As an example, Sekula referred to the two panels he produced for an outdoor placement at the STUK theater in Leuven, part of *Shipwreck and Workers* (2005–07). Constantin Meunier and Alberto Giacometti, two artists Sekula was fond of, were invited on stage by means of two "sculptures of the human body" (*The Puddler* and *The Hand*). (141) The other photographic panels from *Shipwreck and Workers* with which they interacted were positioned "elsewhere in (or, rather 'on') the building and its immediate environs." (141) For Sekula, this way of proceeding with the installation amounted to a form of "exploded or disassembled play." (141)

As an artist, Sekula challenged his audience to make a major investment in order really to engage with his work. One among many possible explanations for his fondness of playing the hide-and-seek game with his public is that he felt this to be the only way to make them feel the absurdity of how on a worldwide scale human life became organized in the post-Cold War era. Elsewhere in his writings he described this mechanism as that of the "Collective Sisyphus." (Sekula, 2003: 324) An American steel mill in parts is moved to China, Sekula informs us, where it is likely to be rebuilt for the purpose of being restarted with cheaper laborers. He portrays one of the workers performing this dismal operation. Then he decides not to publish the picture, while still making a quick reference to Lech Walesa, then-president of Poland and a recurrent protagonist in Sekula's body of work.

About the Gdansk Solidarity Union he concludes sharply in the same text that it was

> the workers' movement to end all workers' movements, in the gleeful private fantasies of Margaret Thatcher and company, who paid an immediate visit to an obsequious Lech Walesa, who, for all his valor, may be said to have had no idea what he was getting into, that Poland was about to endure a version of the "shock therapy" that had been visited on Chile by Friedman's "Chicago Boys." (Sekula, 2009: 63; original typesetting)

From the 1950s on, members of the Chicago School developed the clear mission to liberate the market from unwelcome interferences such as fixed prices, minimum wages, and access to public education systems. What is contemporary visual art to do in the light of the omnipresent reality of a neoliberal market "purism" that feeds as a drip the "disaster capitalism complex," as Naomi Klein calls it? (Klein, 2007: 53 and 281) How can visual art relevantly contribute to creating radical democratic awareness and provoke humane thought? These were fundamental questions that preoccupied Allan Sekula during his entire career.

The present volume is the published outcome of a conference that took Allan Sekula's last project, entitled *Ship of Fools | The Dockers' Museum* (2010–2013), as its point of departure. At the very end of his life, Sekula produced this unfinished, multifaceted, and variously installable work of art—which contains some 1250 objects—as a means to pay tribute to all the joint efforts of human labor now irretrievably lost in history. With *Ship of Fools | The Dockers' Museum* Sekula wanted to send out a message of hope. When he died in the summer of 2013 he was leaving behind this vast "disassembled" set of images and objects all focusing on the lifeworld of dockworkers and seafarers. The project was his final contribution to a life-long search for imagining possible forms of solidarity in a globalized economy evermore confronted with its own limitations.

By encouraging others to try to make sense of *Ship of Fools | The Dockers' Museum after* him, Sekula expressed the wish that his own efforts would not have been completely in vain, or "Sisyphean," as he would put it. (Sekula, 2003: 324) *"Disassembled Images": Contemporary*

Art After Allan Sekula took up this challenge. (figs. 1–3) Organized by the Lieven Gevaert Research Centre for Photography, Art and Visual Culture (KU Leuven-Université catholique de Louvain), together with M HKA – Museum of Contemporary Art Antwerp, the conference was held in Antwerp on March 2–4, 2017. It was an intense meeting of researchers, artists, and curators keen to discuss ways and methods for relevantly developing, in the words of Sekula, an "active resistance … aimed ultimately at … the transformation of society." ([1984] 2016: 74–75)

The event was organized around three thematic clusters, entitled "Collecting Folly," "Maritime Failures and Imaginaries," and "Critical Realism in Dialogue." This way of structuring the debate allowed us first to come to terms with today's meaning and significance of compulsively collecting "objects of interest," as Allan Sekula called them. From there on, the talks developed into various directions, all reflecting on the role of contemporary visual art in our society. We also rely on the three sections as a structural framework for this book. "Collecting Folly" departs from Sekula's representation of the universe and imaginary of dockworkers in *Ship of Fools | The Dockers' Museum*. Far from being a pastime, this unfinished project is the culmination of long-term research into the lives and maritime labors that have been exploited in order for global capitalism to strive and create its seamless flow and circulation of goods. The act of collecting the metonymical objects that compose Sekula's museum was largely carried out by the artist through online platforms such as eBay, thus ironically and virtually simulating and retracing on a miniature scale the processes his very collection puts into question.

The section on "Collecting Folly" intends to capture a twofold inquiry exploring the act of collecting through the lens of folly and madness, as well as the 'collection' of actual representations of fools and madness. From the perspective of contemporary art, the section centers on the following questions: which particular strategies and intuitions do contemporary artists mobilize in their collections, and how do they differ from those of private and public collections? How is collecting transformed into a tool for contemporary artists, and toward who or what is it directed? What is the critical potential of representations of folly and madness in contemporary art? Do they destabilize normative understandings of production, including artistic production?

W.J.T. Mitchell's keynote essay immediately precedes this section to open its discussion, as well as to set the parameters of the concerns of this volume as a whole. As such his argument offers a subtle and insightful reflection on the "Ship of Fools" as a metaphor for what he calls the "Planetary Madness" of the global system of deregulated capitalism. Sekula's *Ship of Fools | The Dockers' Museum*, he argues, has to be understood as a critical project that explores maritime space

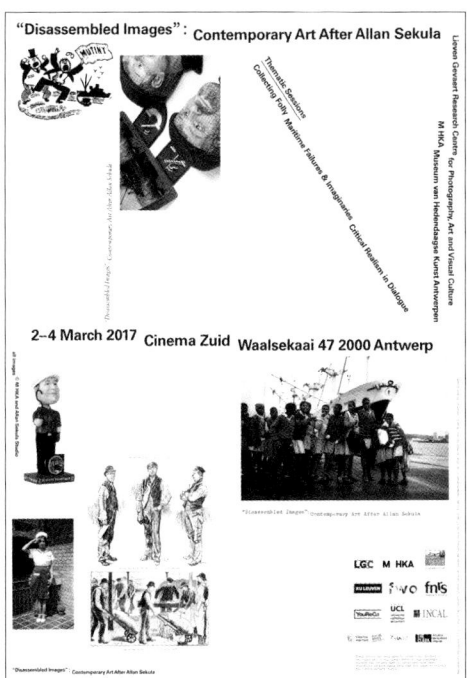

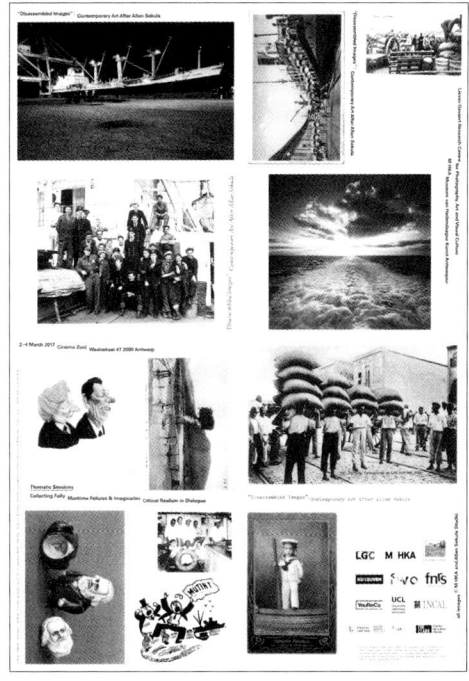

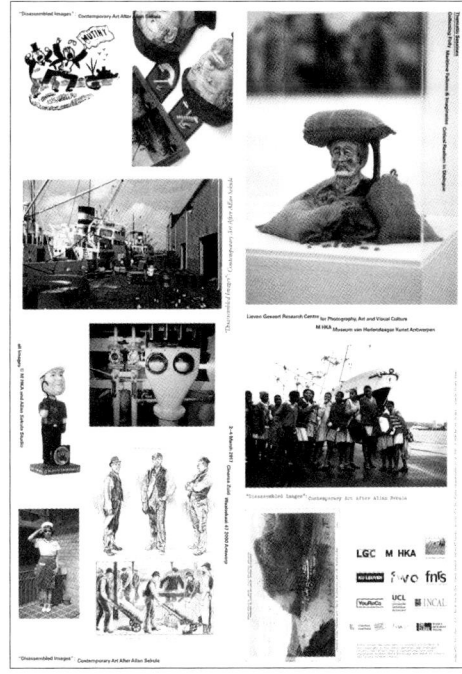

Figs. 1–3

Conference poster *"Disassembled Images": Contemporary
Art After Allan Sekula*, Antwerp, 2–4 March 2017. Page design
Thomas Desmet. © Allan Sekula Studio. Courtesy м нка,
Museum van Hedendaagse Kunst Antwerpen. Courtesy Lieven
Gevaert Research Centre for Photography, Art and Visual Culture.

as a major concern in the light of the destruction of our planet in the wake of neoliberal processes of globalization. Proposing "a provisional *Bilderatlas* of planetary madness," Mitchell describes Sekula's project as an "exhibitionary archive from below," an open constellation that invites us "to make sense of it."

Next, the section on "Collecting Folly" opens with Bart De Baere and Anja Isabel Schneider's thoughtful discussion of *The Dockers' Museum* from a curatorial perspective. According to the authors, Sekula's project takes the form of the "Double Helix of an Activist Stance and of Curating." Oscillating between a socio-political critical approach and a propensity for concrete narratives, *The Dockers' Museum* aims at the creation of what Sekula himself called "a sort of imaginary or phantasmatic collective lifeworld (*Lebenswelt*)." As an activist Sekula takes into account the mediatized outcomes of his activities in order to address public opinion, while his curatorial approach leads him to include his "objects of interest" in the structural set-up of the gallery space. De Baere and Schneider conclude their essay with the observation that it is precisely this double move between the positions of the activist and the curator that defines Sekula's approach as a "practice of transformative worldmaking."

Likewise, Stefanie Diekmann's essay focuses on the transformative aspects of a collection of objects. Departing from considerations on the classical collection of material, individualized objects, of which Sekula's *The Dockers' Museum* would be an example, Diekmann wonders if there "is a way to pay homage to objects while not holding on to them?" Chris Larson's *Land Speed Record* (2016), she suggests, could provide an answer to this question. Conceived as a "temporary showcase," as an assemblage of obsolete objects passing by the eyes of the spectator, Larson's sound-video work stages not the objects themselves but their state of "moving on towards oblivion." This sharply contrasts with both early cinema's staging of objects and the art collection's insistence on the material or emotional value of the individual artifact.

Ronnie Close uses Sekula's term "objects of interest" as a springboard for his own considerations on visual image politics in today's Egypt. Close examines two sets of photographs that represent different forms of censorship: his own collection of photographic artbooks bought in Cairo bookstores and a series of female fashion images from a message board website operated by conservative Islamic women. While in the first example, reflecting a case of state censorship, the images of photo-books are doctored with the purpose of concealing the erotic effect of the body, the second set of images represent a form of auto-censorship in which fashion photographs from Western culture are Photoshopped in order to adapt them to a conservative Islamic audience. Close critically links these forms of censorial practices to the history of Orientalism, revealing the complexity and the contradictions at play when Western image culture encounters conservative Middle-East contexts. As parts of an archive of censorship, the photographs examined in this article become "objects of interest" for how they represent and mediate the image politics in many countries in the Middle East.

Departing from reflections on media archaeology as both a theoretical approach and a practice, Edwin Carels zooms in on the private collection of analogue audio-visual equipment of Samuel Verstraete, which resulted in an exhibition project shown in Ghent and Eeklo in 2016 and 2017. After the death of Verstraete, who was called "Vava" (meaning "grandpa" in Flemish-Dutch), a VHS tape was found among his belongings on which he had recorded all the old analogue equipment he collected—radios, televisions, amplifiers, tape recorders, antennas, and all kind of electronic devices—thus producing both a visual archive of the analogue world and a narrative of the collector and his private domain. This doubling of the assembled objects through the video tape, Carels argues, reveals the collection's character as an "archive of intensities," a term he borrows from Georges Didi-Huberman's study on Aby Warburg's *Mnemosyne Atlas*.

In the final essay of the section, Barbara Baert also draws on Warburg's *Mnemosyne Atlas* when she defines *The Dockers' Museum* as an empathic collection driven by pulsations of desire and sensuality while at the same time constituting a dynamic thought-space (*Denkraum*). Using an original hermeneutical approach, Baert suggests to understand Sekula's archival project less in terms of rational knowledge than in terms of sensorial experiences. Associating *The Dockers' Museum* with notions of empathy and *Besonnenheit* (temperance, thoughtfulness), Baert certainly meets Mitchell's considerations on the openness of Sekula's "archive from below" and, referring to the latter as a "radical descent into the world of the wound," gives it both a visceral and instinctive turn.

At least since *Fish Story* (1989–1995), Allan Sekula has conceptualized, through his art and writings, the maritime sphere as a way to explore novel epistemological questions with regard to the increasingly opaque nature of globalized capital. Following his cue, the section on "Maritime Failures and Imaginaries" looks at the myriad of ways in which artists have recently explored the imaginaries and materialities of the maritime as a space of disaster and failure. It investigates the possibilities of artists confronting ecological disasters, unbridled supply chain capitalism, violence and death related to migratory crossings, and the fraught histories of imperialism and colonialism. The essays in this section are equally interested in these various forms of solidarity and agency connected to the world of maritime labor: mutinies, piracies, and waterfront insurrections that, although failed, offer alternative models of rupture and contestation for our present predicament.

"Maritime Failures and Imaginaries" opens with a portfolio by Berlin-based artist Marco Poloni. The text begins with a description of the artist's multi-media installation *The Majorana Experience* (2008–2010) as an exploration of the intriguing disappearance at sea of Italian physician Ettore Majorana. By insisting on his interest in the sea "as a space intersected by geopolitical processes," Poloni clearly situates his work in the wake of Sekula. Claiming a politics of representation, Poloni wonders about the possibility of understanding the Mediterranean Sea not as object but as subject. This non-anthropocentric perspective leads him to Timothy Morton's concept of "hyperobjects," entities of extremely long duration or enormous scale which exceed human capacities of comprehension. In the second part of his paper Poloni develops four possible categories of a post-anthropocentric cinema—Scale, Movement, Fragmentation and Suture, and Perspective—and shows how some of them are adapted in his film *Una Cuba mediterranea* (2017).

Next, Clara Masnatta discusses two recent films about the maritime world, Lois Patiño's *Costa da Morte* [Coast of Death] (2013) and *Leviathan* (2012) by Véréna Paravel and Lucien Castaing-Taylor. For their overt rejection of linearity and traditional point of view, both films are related to Sekula's disassembled photo-texts. Masnatta argues that *Costa da Morte* and *Leviathan* represent two ways of "an amphibian cinema of senses at sea," in which a sensual experience of maritime space is created by different means and diverging approaches. On the one hand, *Leviathan* immerses the viewer completely into a tangible experience triggered by surround sound and the proximity of changing cameras simulating the sea's perspectives in a post-human stance. In *Costa da Morte*, on the other hand, sound is used to make the perceptual distance between image and sound palpable. *Leviathan's* voiceless "simulacral plenitude" is rejected in favor of a multitude of interwoven historical, mythological, and vernacular voices in order to activate the viewer's imagination.

Jonathan Stafford provides a thought-provoking analysis of the role of the container in Sekula's *Fish Story* (and other "sea works") regarding maritime labor in the context of global capitalism. Citing Mark Fisher, Stafford, like Mitchell, denounces "the illusion of a 'dematerialized' capitalism." While the capitalist system obfuscates its concrete reality by making it disappear from people's visual field by means of automated container shipping, Sekula's critical project emphasizes the materiality of maritime logistics eliciting thus "an aesthetic charge antithetical to the ideology of 'friction-free capitalism.'" The ship, Stafford further argues against Philip Steinberg, stands for a crisis of capitalism, for it represents capital's contradictions and complexity. In particular the widespread phenomenon of ghost ships or zombie ships, carrying containers full of commodities that are nowhere unloaded, well symbolizes capitalism's inertia and absurdity. Sekula's *Shipwreck and Workers*, finally, features the shipwreck, as a metaphor for the crisis of capital's flow and shifts the perspective to the human, social, and personal narratives of the dockers and sea workers.

The fourth contribution to this section comprises an interview by Hilde Van Gelder with Carles Guerra, conducted at the Fundació Antoni Tàpies in 2016. Based on Guerra's experience of the fieldtrip he made with Sekula to the Galician shore shortly after the *Prestige* oil spill, the interview provides an account of the genesis of the work *Black Tide/ Marea negra* (2002–2003), which the artist conceived as a response to the disaster. In the course of the interview, Sekula's *Black Tide/*Marea negra is described as an example of deconstruction of journalistic and documentary practices. Similar to Stafford, Guerra hints at the contradictory structure of capital and its representation when he establishes an analogy between the flow of the capital stopped by shipwreck and photography's endless circulation arrested by the decisive moment. The interview concludes with some considerations on the predictive character of Sekula's work and its particular, often subtle sense of humor.

The final section, "Critical Realism in Dialogue," departs from Benjamin H.D. Buchloh's productive description of Allan Sekula's artistic approach in terms of "critical realism." (Buchloh, 1995: 191) Realism, when understood this way, is not necessarily an artistic style. It rather points to the research methods of a reflective artistic practice, including—among other elements—high-profile theoretical and essayistic writing, photography, and essay film. Foundational for such a methodology is the dialogue and participatory observation pursued by the artist with workers, activists, and scholars to explore existing and potential models of collaboration (e.g., with ITF trade unionists on the *Global Mariner* ship or with activist organizations during the 1999 WTF protests in Seattle). In the contributions to this section, the authors explore different possibilities for bringing about such critically realist art practices and how they may be changing the stakes within the field of contemporary art production. They address concerns such as the role of skill and/or deskilling as well as the re-distribution of labor in contemporary art, challenges to conventional forms of visual pleasure within contemporary art, and the consequences of selecting the worker as a key visual motif within an artistic practice. Does such "sympathetic materialism," as Sekula called it (Sekula, 2001: 10), perhaps bring about new social agencies among people and new insights with regard to our world's future? How, in other words, as Sekula once defined the problem of critical realism, "do we find the interval within which the idea of freedom resides?" (Sekula, 1998: 26)

In his essay, Alexander Streitberger relates this question to a historical moment of the 1970s when Marxist-oriented artists such as Sekula, Martha Rosler, and Victor Burgin referred to Brecht and Benjamin in order to seek creative freedom in the interval between theory and practice. Based on a thorough comparison of the writings with the artistic practice of these artist-theoreticians, Streitberger shows that each of them subscribes to the socialist project of "cultural work as a *praxis*" in a different way. While Burgin's meta-textual work *VI* (1973) deconstructs advertising photographs by means of an "aesthetics of fragments and cracks" and Sekula's *Aerospace Folktales* of the same year integrates critical and biographical narratives into a "disassembled movie," Rosler's "poetry of drunkenness" resists the classical stance of the documentary genre in favor of a critical practice oscillating between the "possibility of negation and metacommentary."

Stephanie Schwartz takes Sekula's phrasing "the face of protest" as a starting-point to show how the artist undermines the common photojournalistic practice of monumentalizing and isolating a particularly expressive face or gesture in order to produce a pathetic effect on the audience. In *Waiting for Tear Gas*, Schwartz argues, Sekula adopts an alternative perspective that takes into account the fact that protest is always a concern of "multiple faces" located within the space of the relationship between the public and the private. Schwartz points out that Sekula started to use the form of the photo-essay at the very moment of its crisis in the early 1970s caused by the fact that Americans increasingly relied on television rather than newspapers and magazines. Within the context of today's neoliberal media practices, which are largely based on social media accounts and individually customized media platforms, Sekula "re-invented" the photojournalistic essay as a "meta-critical" tool to examine and to counter the way media operate.

Anthony Abiragi shares with Schwartz the insight that a critical realism should not merely be concerned with *what* happens but also with the question of *how* events are mediated and subjected to the logic of visibility and invisibility. "Photography in an Age of Asymmetry" is a stimulating reflection on the *Global Mariner*, an activist ship identified by Sekula as a "*metaship*." (Sekula, 2002: 31; original emphasis) This ship functions as a "contested allegory" that invites us to read the world rather in terms of context than in terms of objects. To reveal Sekula's traffic with abstraction Abiragi further refers to the *Global Mariner* as an exemplar. The exemplar only becomes readable when connected with other sectors of reality. For the exemplar has to be enacted within a given social order. Abiragi finally suggests to understand Sekula's allegorical abstractions as perlocutionary performatives: as "non-sovereign signs," which derive their authority as acts of judgment not through established institutions but through their enactment "in a new, adjacent context."

The volume concludes with Benjamin Young's considerations on "Realism and Humanism in Photography of Israel-Palestine." Referring to the event "Decolonize This Place," organized on May 7, 2016 by activists at the Brooklyn Museum to protest against the exhibition *This Place*, Young argues that the humanist stance of the curators, conceiving their exhibition as an exploration of the human condition in Palestine, was doomed to fail because its essentialist humanism based on the aestheticization of apartheid and settler colonialism excluded and dehumanized Palestinians. Through a subtle analysis of the various works and the exhibition display, Young shows that the claims to universal humanism were sapped by the curators' emphasis on the formal autonomy of the pictures and their aesthetic presentation. This would also explain why the activists were unable to appreciate such highly critical work as Fazal Sheikh's *Desert Bloom*, representing a kind of forensic aesthetics identified by Young as "one of the most important inheritors of Sekula's critique of photographic humanism."

From this we may conclude that Sekula's appeal for a critical realism in terms of "a truly critical social documentary that will frame the crime, the trial, and the system of justice and its official myths" doesn't end with the work's realization. (Sekula, [1984] 2016: 57) It has to be tested over and over again, each time when it is presented within a particular situation and for a specific purpose and public.

Bibliography

Pascal Beausse, "The critical realism of Allan Sekula," *Art Press,* 240 (November 1998): 20–26.

Benjamin H.D. Buchloh, "Allan Sekula: Photography between Discourse and Document," in Allan Sekula, *Fish Story* (Düsseldorf: Richter Verlag, 1995), 189–200.

Naomi Klein, *The Shock Doctrine. The Rise of Disaster Capitalism* (London: Penguin, 2007).

Katarzyna Ruchel-Stockmans, "Interview with Allan Sekula," in *Critical Realism in Contemporary Art. Around Allan Sekula's Photography*, eds Jan Baetens and Hilde Van Gelder (Leuven: Leuven University Press, 2006), 138–151.

Allan Sekula, *Photography Against the Grain. Essays and Photo Works 1973–1983* [1984] (London: Mack, 2016).

Allan Sekula, "Deep Six," in *Calais vu par Allan Sekula* (Calais: Musée des Beaux-Arts, 2001), 10.

Allan Sekula, "Between the Net and the Deep Blue Sea (Rethinking the Traffic in Photographs)," *October*, 102 (Autumn 2002): 3–34.

Allan Sekula, *Performance Under Working Conditions* (Vienna: Generali Foundation, 2003).

Allan Sekula, *Polonia and Other Fables* (Chicago and Warsaw: The Renaissance Society at the University of Chicago and Zachęta National Gallery of Art, 2009).

Planetary Madness: Globalizing the Ship of Fools

W.J.T. Mitchell

Where bodies are buried in secret there must also be a buried archive […] waiting for resurrection. An archive, but not an atlas; the point here is not to take the world upon one's shoulders, but to crouch down to the earth, and dig.
– Allan Sekula

In the destructive element immerse.
– Joseph Conrad, *Lord Jim*

We are like sailors who have to rebuild their ship on the open sea, without ever being able to dismantle it in dry-dock and reconstruct it from its best components.
– Otto Neurath

The theme of the end of the world, and of the great final violence, was also a part of the critical experience of madness.
– Michel Foucault, *History of Madness*

Our attempt to "see madness" has progressed as a series of ever-larger concentric circles, from the "up close and personal" account of a single case of schizophrenia, to the world of the arts and media, to an atlas of the world's images, to the latest outbreak of crazy nationalism I have called the "American Psychosis." But today it looks as if a "planetary madness" is afflicting the world. Reactionary nationalism, authoritarianism, and racism are on the march, and the world's most powerful democracy has elected a lunatic and conman to be its president.

I use "lunatic" in the technical, not the pejorative sense. A lunatic is an *episodic* madman, constantly changing (as the term suggests) with the phases of the moon. He is a person who can sound reasonable one moment, but then give way easily to delusions, lies, and illogic accompanied by impulsive emotional outbreaks. Therefore he can be extremely "high functioning" in any clinical sense of the word. A successful businessman and reality TV star, Donald Trump has a style of brutal frankness and spontaneity that is deeply appealing to people who like to keep things simple, direct, and (by their lights) honest. His riches and celebrity make him admired, and his questionable personal morals can be overlooked, or even chalked up to his credit for living out a certain version of the white male American dream: lots of toys, some of them women. He is thus the perfect demagogue for the moment, what Nietzsche called the "epoch," the moment when history's nightmare flares up in a crazy outburst of populist resentment, rage, and militant ignorance. The ancient trope of the "Ship of Fools," Plato's image of democracy, comes back to life in what Lewis Lapham has called the "Age of Folly," when "America abandons its democracy." (2016)

It is not the first time that a mad sovereign has assumed tyrannical powers. From the Biblical Nebuchadnezzar to King George III to Hitler, the emergence of terrifying authoritarian regimes has punctuated epochs in human history. And democracies, as Plato foresaw, are especially vulnerable to the rise of maniacal despots. Plato's famous metaphor of the Ship of Fools captures perfectly the way populist irrationality can lead the Ship of State, steered by an incompetent, corrupt, and deranged captain, into a catastrophic shipwreck.

But our time is different. Instead of a mad tyrant ruling over a local city-state or (even more ominous) a regional nation-state, the election of Donald Trump to the most powerful position on the planet promises to produce a global calamity. We are no longer in a world where disastrous wars, destruction of the environment, and the immiseration of vast populations can be confined within national borders. In an age of global climate change and a deeply dysfunctional global economy of deregulated capitalism, the risks have taken on a planetary scale. The Ship of Fools is no longer a metaphor for the rogue state. We are now living on a rogue *planet*, inhabited by a species that fits the legal criterion for insanity, namely, that it is a danger to itself and others. The modern cult of the dinosaur is the symbolic recognition of this fact, conveying the inexorable message of Darwinism about the potential for the human race, now the dominant animal group on this planet, to go the way of our Saurian ancestors.[1] Unlike the dinosaurs, who were a durable lot, and found a way to evolve beyond their earth bound status to take flight as birds, the human race is stuck on this planet, the only one we have, and it will be responsible for its own extinction. The Ship of Fools is now a planetary vessel, and the earth can no longer be seen as an island in space. As the etymology of the word "planet" (an errant wanderer—OED) indicates, we now have to catch up with intuition of Walt Disney's Epcot Center, and imagine ourselves realistically as "spaceship earth," a Noah's Ark that may not have any harbor waiting for it.[2]

But exactly what kind of spaceship do we inhabit? Bruno Latour, in a recent *Critical Inquiry* essay, has provided an image of the most urgent way of thinking about this question. He compares the contemporary world to an enormous passenger plane that is running low on fuel. The pilots announce that the long-standing modern destination—modernity, modernization, and "the global"—has just been closed off by the simple fact that the planet cannot possibly sustain modern development as presently envisaged. We would need anywhere from "2 to 5 virtual planets" to accommodate the 8 billion people who will inhabit this orb in the predictable future. Globalization, as an economic and ecological program, has become obsolete.

The passengers on Latour's airplane are understandably concerned. Some of them even stop sipping their whiskeys, and begin looking at alternative destinations. The most popular at this point is the populist, reactionary answer. Let's go back to "where we came from," to our "own country," our nation and our kind of people. Let's return to the Homeland, or just "the Land," whether it is called Fortress America or Little England. Certainly it is not Europe, or any of the global destinations. And most certainly it involves a closing of borders to immigrants, foreigners, aliens, refugees, and outsiders. The passengers tell the pilot, well let's go back, then. Let's go home. Let's make America, or Russia, or France "great again."

The pilots, however, have bad news. The Homeland is no longer reachable either; the borders have already been long since breached, and the spaces promised by neo-nationalists "offer a space much too small for us." (Latour, 2018: 217) The only answer is to "triangulate," to imagine a third destination—Latour calls it "Gaia" or "the Earth"—the actual physical ecosystem in which the species has to come to ground, or risk crashing and burning.

Latour's choice of Earth is, I think, to be taken both literally and metaphorically: literally as the limited amount of solid ground for feeding an out of control population; metaphorically as a figure for ecological balance and harmony, the kind of thing envisioned back in the 1960s by the famous *Whole Earth Catalog*. But there is a fourth possibility that he does not consider, and that is the sea, which covers two thirds of the planet. This is an element that must surely be considered in both its literal and metaphoric terms as well. We need to remember that every plane flight begins with safety instructions that include a short lesson on what to do "in case of a water landing." For one thing, climate change is already producing a rise in sea levels, so the proportion of the planet comprised of earth is going to shrink. The sea is also where all of the planet's life-forms originated, and a major source of its nutrition. It is, despite the dominance of hyper-modern modes of communication and transportation, air travel and the internet, the medium in which most of the world's material commerce is carried on. Speculative finance capital may operate at the blinding speed of computers, but physical commodities still circulate around the world at about the same speed that they did in the late 19th century era of the steamship.

I am invoking here the striking conclusion of the late Allan Sekula's photo essay, *Fish Story*, in which he makes the following point:

> My argument here runs against the commonly held view that the computer and telecommunications are the sole engines of the third industrial revolution. In effect, I am arguing for the continued importance of maritime space in order to counter the exaggerated importance attached to that largely metaphysical construct, "cyberspace," and the corollary myth of "instantaneous" contact between distant spaces. I am often struck by the ignorance of intellectuals in this respect: the self-congratulating conceptual aggrandizement of "information" frequently is accompanied by peculiar erroneous beliefs: among these is the widely held quasi-anthropomorphic notion that most of the world's cargo travels as people do, by air. (1995: 50)

I want to take Sekula's irrefutable argument as a launching point for a reconsideration of the *ship at sea* rather than the airship or airplane as the appropriate metaphor for re-imagining our earthly habitat, and the *sea* as the inevitable image of the element in which that ship lives and moves and has its being. Sekula's last unfinished project, *Ship of Fools | The Dockers' Museum*, already points toward that heading. And it does so with particular emphasis on the question of collective and individual madness as the psychological and political framework within which a critical account of our planetary insanity has to be re-framed. I should say, however, that I don't think this was exactly the direction that Allan himself was heading. He was a hard-headed Marxist materialist, and as an artist-photographer committed to documenting the material conditions of labor. His treatment of madness, or more precisely, folly, was basically pitched toward ideologies such as the metaphysics of cyberspace that he skewers in the passage just quoted, and in the neoliberal processes of globalization that have turned our attention away from maritime space while planting the seeds of destruction for human life on this planet.

My aim here is to emphasize the question of folly and madness, both in the global system that Sekula criticized, and in the heroic, even Herculean effort he waged to bring it all into focus. I want to take seriously the remarks of his widow, photo historian Sally Stein, who saw the wild miscellany of objects in Allan's *The Dockers' Museum* "as a private archive. […] in all the madness of that collecting enterprise" that

Walter Benjamin described: "Every passion borders on the chaotic, but the collector's passion borders on the chaos of memories." (2015: 103) Stein goes one step further to suggest that Allan was risking "immersion" in "a sinkhole of money spent on a folly." (103) He was in the grip of a "mad materialism" that pre-dated the onset of his fatal illness in 2011. (100) Benjamin's hope that a legible "constellation" would emerge from the collector's chaotic passion has yet to happen with Sekula's last project. There is no guarantee that it ever will, and certainly I will not be able to provide one. We are like Walter Benjamin's "revolutionary spy or detective" contemplating a wall of evidence.[3] We are observing a forensic atlas that is either reducible to something like the material conditions of narrative as such, the "ball of string," the *yarn* that connects all the images and objects, or a subjective complex that may turn any perceived order in the array into a case of apophenia, the psychiatric syndrome in which one projects patterns into an array of clues that are not visible to anyone else.[4]

Certainly Allan Sekula would not be the first to succumb to the collector's passion, especially when it seems that the fate of the world somehow hangs in the balance. The founder of modern art history, Aby Warburg, attempted a similar thing with images rather than objects, by creating a *Bilderatlas* that would place in a totalizing perspective all the graphic representations of the human species' expressions of passion, the *pathosformel* that were to complete Darwin's program of cataloging the expressions of emotions in animals and man. Warburg's project occupied a border zone between madness and rationality, folly and encyclopedic knowledge. His earlier project of attempting to compile an atlas of all the images and texts associated with the nightmare of history known as the Great War finally came to nothing. The residue of that project now resides in unsorted archives of the Warburg Institute in London, still waiting after almost a century for the archivist who might be able to see the patterns that Warburg was seeking. Within weeks of the end of World War I, Warburg experienced a psychotic break in which he attempted to murder his own family. Like Hercules, the mythological hero who attempts to civilize the known world, killing monsters and even taking the world on his shoulders while Atlas runs an errand for him, Warburg was broken by the enormity of the task he had undertaken.

When Warburg emerged from the asylum where he was confined for five years, he took up the project of the *Bilderatlas* with a passion. Fortunately for us, he survived long enough to serve as the "archon" or authoritative master of the archive fever he was experiencing.[5] Not that he regarded the *Bilderatlas* as the cure for anything. Warburg declared himself "incurable," a revenant or phantom. And he regarded himself in that sense as a representative man, since in his view "all mankind is everywhere and eternally schizophrenic." Warburg glimpsed the "plan-etary madness" that was being unveiled in his research, and in himself. Allow me to quote once again R. D. Laing's portrait of rare and gifted "schizophrenic seafarers":

> Perhaps we will learn to accord to so-called schizophrenics who have come back to us, perhaps after years, no less respect than the often no less lost explorers of the Renaissance. If the human race survives, future men will, I suspect, look back on our en-lightened epoch as a veritable Age of Darkness. (1967: 129)

Laing is not romanticizing schizophrenia here. He knows very well that it is a malady that produces extreme suffering in its victims. He is speaking of the lucky ones "who have come back to us," the rare souls that are able to work and create some reflection on their condition (see Judge Schreber's *Memoir of My Nervous Illness*). Like Coleridge's Ancient Mariner, some seafarers return as "loons" from the sea with a terrifying story of madness calculated to hypnotize the listener, and to make her reflect on her own condition.

The sea is, of course, the image of madness *par excellence*. Chaotic, ever-changing, in contrast to terra firma, the grounds and stable foun-dations of thought. The boring, vast emptiness of the sea is an invita-tion to madness. Since the 18th century it has been well established that seafaring is one of the professions most conducive to mental illness.[6] To be all at sea is to be confused, disoriented, overwhelmed, as Sally Stein found herself, confronted with Allan's enormous, unreadable archive. If the *Bilderatlas* was Warburg's "art history without a text," Allan's *Ship of Fools | The Dockers' Museum* is an archive without an archon. It is up to us to make sense of it.[7]

I want to come at it via a maritime image that Allan did not collect, namely an interesting 19th-century French print of the mariner/dock-worker astride the globe, that was collected by Sally Stein, and hung in a tableau on the stairs at their home. (fig. 1) I am particularly interested in this one because of Allan's curious behavior around it. He was, Sally tells us, completely indifferent to it. And yet in her eyes, it was precisely a portrait of Allan himself:

> To my surprise, this nineteenth-century French lithograph did not produce much reaction, let alone self-recognition—despite the centrality of a stocky smocked worker (with a markedly re-ceding hairline similar to Allan's) who studies the globe while perched atop it. He simply ignored this one image I considered so emblematic of his insatiable quest to encompass the world and

fathom its linked systems of politics, production, and communication. (Stein, 2015: 99)

I don't think this is a case of "Dorian Sekula," the shameful repression of one's own revelatory portrait. In fact, it seems to me just the opposite, revealing instead an image of a certain political ego ideal, a fantasy of the global working class as the vanguard of world revolution. Instead of the world in the grip of Leviathan, the anarchist dockworker rolls precariously along astride a world he has mastered. Could it have been just a bit embarrassing in its explicit reminder of Allan's own utopian sentimentality about the lost world of maritime space during the industrial revolution, the site of the IWW (Industrial Workers in the World) and international workers solidarity? In today's maritime space, the disastrous underbelly of Leviathan is hidden from view, as national flags are rented out by multi-national corporations to evade regulations, with disastrous consequences. Allan was constructing his "archive from below," in the otherwise invisible spaces of the everyday in contemporary maritime space. The Atlas-like dockworker surveying the world from above might have been a bit too grandiose for Allan's temperament.

Fig. 1

Anon. (probably French artist). Untitled chine-collé lithograph, ca 1870s, 16,2 × 11,5 cm. © Photo: Mary Reinsch Sackett. Collection of Sally Stein.

I do think he should have looked longer at this picture, where he could have seen in it a compelling portrait of his own paradoxical task. For it is undeniable that he was trying to "take it all in," to collect *everything*.[8] He had seen the planetary madness, and now he had caught it, and was riding it like a runaway horse. The French worker is not securely positioned above the globe in the position of an unmoved mover or detached surveyor. He seems to be rolling atop it, and could be tossed off any moment, as indicated by the way his hat is flying off. His left hand is spread out in a measuring gesture, as if he is estimating distances, while his right hand grips the edge of the world to keep him from falling off. The globe is advancing into a perilous fjord, a chasm between two steep cliffs—perhaps an echo of Atlas at the pillars of Hercules. The left

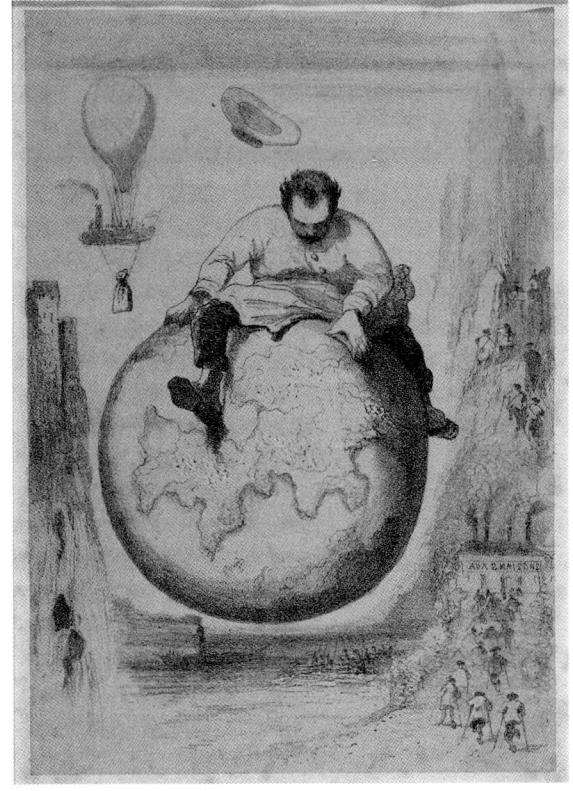

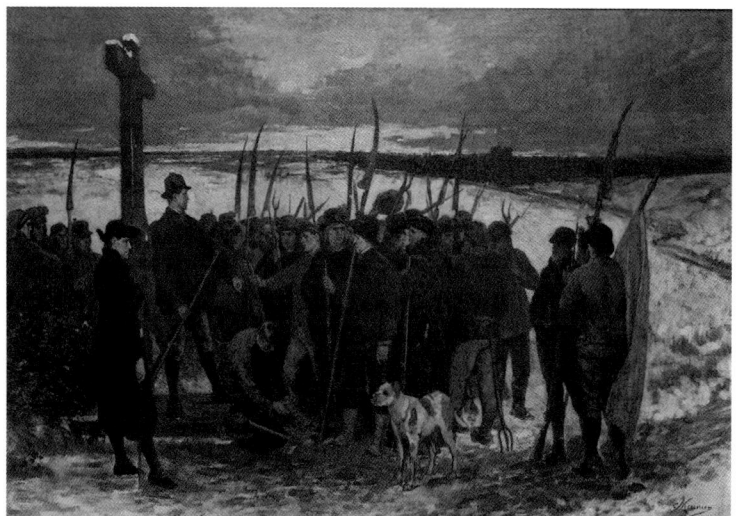

Fig. 2

Constantin Meunier,
*La Guerre des paysans
1798–1799 (le rassem-
blement)*, ca. 1875, oil on
canvas, 114,5 × 176 cm.
© Royal Museums of Fine
Arts of Belgium, Brussels
/ photo: J. Geleyns
– Ro scan.

side is surmounted by a castle, the other with a procession of crippled workers marching uphill to a smoking factory called "Aux 2 Maisons." Above on the right, mountain climbers are clambering up the rock face, perhaps to join their globe-riding comrade, while on the left, three ghostly figures ascend the rock face toward the medieval castle at the top, perhaps echoing the theme of ascent to the heavenly city. Out in the harbor the vague outline of a steamship is on the horizon, and a body of men seems to be advancing down the beach brandishing pikes, perhaps an echo of Constantin Meunier's painting of Belgian peasants resisting the French invasion in 1798–99. (fig. 2) Meunier's monumental sculptures of 19th-century workers are a crucial inspiration for Sekula's project; a portrait of the great Belgian realist appears in *The Dockers' Museum*.[9] And in the sky in the background, the new mode of planetary transport hovers a hot air balloon, anchored by a sandbag, carrying, not the expected gondola, but a steamship.

The airship is the ironic punctum complicating Allan's project of an "Atlas from below." Cyberspace and air freight are the communication and transportation media that made his *The Dockers' Museum* collection possible. In the long, boring stretches of seafaring, Allan spent a lot of time ordering "objects of interest" on eBay. Cyberspace was taking over his work as a hunter-gatherer of images and objects, leaving behind an amazing variety of objects, from crutches to a soccer ball signed by Pelé—the closest thing I can find in *The Dockers' Museum* to a globe. (fig. 3) I hope that future curators will not be parsimonious about

Fig. 3

Pelé Signed Football
[title given by Allan
Sekula], leather, ø 22 cm.
Producer, production and
signing date with black
alcohol marker by Pelé
unknown. Part of Allan
Sekula, *Ship of Fools /
The Dockers' Museum*
(2010–2013) [TDM 42].
Purchased by Allan
Sekula through eBay on 15
July 2011. Collection M HKA
/ Collection Flemish
Community of Belgium.
© Photo: M HKA, Christine
Clinckx. Courtesy Allan
Sekula Studio.

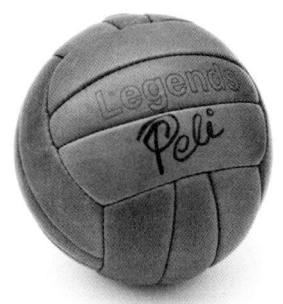

displaying these objects. They should definitely not be treated as auratic singularities. I would try instead to show their abundance and fecundity; and overwhelm the beholder the way Sally was overwhelmed. Keep some of them in packing crates, unopened. There is no need for an exhibition of these objects to look orderly. My sense is that he was trying to bring these things together with the images to produce a kind of exhibitionary archive from below, perhaps a submarine space "below decks," an ark of the history of maritime space.

In a sense, then, the anonymous 19th-century French print plays the role of archon for this archive, showing the worker as a young global knight errant astride his planetary steed. This image builds upon a whole genealogy of planetary, global iconography. And here I have to confess that I have come down with a serious case of the planetary madness that afflicted Allan Sekula, and found myself compiling a boundless archive of "world pictures" that link images of the globe to seafaring, fortune, risk, and work, from the onset of early modern maritime space until the present day. My condition is not nearly as serious as that of Peter Sloterdijk, whose meditation on the philosophical status of the sphere (from bubbles to globes to foams) now occupies three capacious volumes (the *Spheres* trilogy). The following, then, should be taken as a provisional *Bilderatlas* of planetary madness that is purely speculative and improvisatory. Somehow this seems like the right place to take this risk.

We could begin with Warburg himself, and with "Panel B," his "panel of panels," a cosmological tableau linking the early modern seafaring discovery that "the world is round," with the ancient belief that "man is the measure" of that circumference, his body a microcosm of the macrocosm, ruled by the same elementary humors, earth, air, water, and fire.[10] (fig. 4) Leonardo's Vitruvian man might be exhibit A, along with Hildegard von Bingen's and William Blake's *Albion Rising*. Portrayals of the planet as a kind of "hand-held device" in the firm grasp of Christ as *salvator mundi*, the savior of a planet bound together by Christian

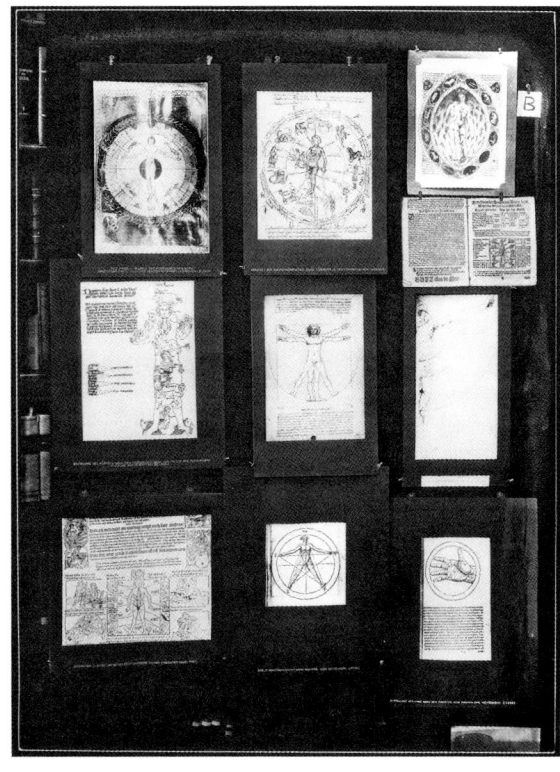

Fig. 4

Aby Warburg, *Der Bilderatlas Mnemosyne*, ed. Martin Warnke, II.1 (Berlin: Akademie Verlag, 2000), Tafel B. © The Warburg Institute, London.

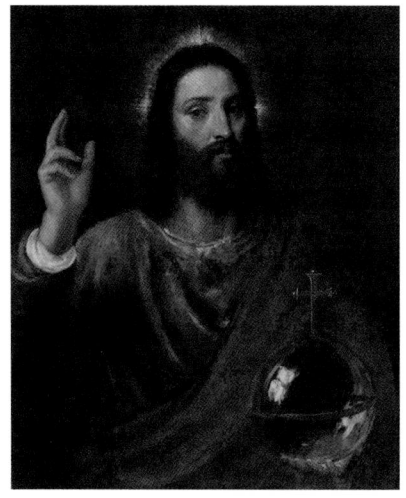

Fig 5

Titian, *Christ Blessing,* Italy, circa 1570. Oil on canvas, 96 × 80 cm. Inv. no. GE-114. The State Hermitage Museum, St. Petersburg. © Photo: The State Hermitage Museum. Photo by Inna Regentova.

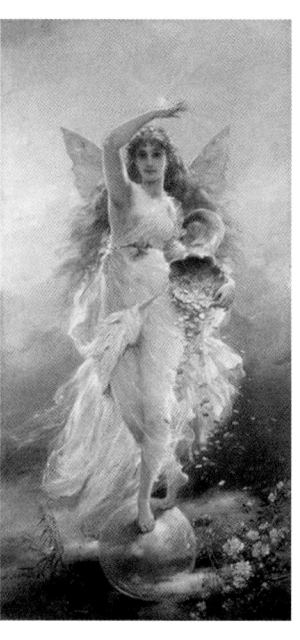

imperialism might serve as exhibit B.[11] (fig. 5) But, aside from Atlas, it is arguably the figure of the Roman goddess Fortuna that is the most apt predecessor for the thoroughly secular world in the French print. Fortuna is frequently portrayed as the goddess of the lucrative but risky world of maritime commerce. She is often shown standing precariously on the globe, buffeted by winds which she catches in her shawl, as if she were herself a sailing ship. (fig. 6) In her positive appearance as "Felicitas" and riches she pours forth an abundance of gold coins, as in Jean Francois Bernard's (1829–1894) *Goddess of Luck and Risk.* She is the keeper of our destiny and the guiding power behind all fortunate and unfortunate turns of events.

Fig. 6

Jean-Francois Bernard, *Fortuna,* date unknown. © Alamy Limited.

In Fortuna's negative role as Tyche or Nemesis, she is a blind goddess who personifies chance, risk, and the ever-present possibility of disaster so central to the world of global commerce conducted in maritime space. (fig. 7) In Tadeusz Kuntze's painting she is seen standing on the globe, oblivious to the catastrophe unfolding at her feet, and the useless appeals of petitioners atop the heap of human bodies. In the background, the citadel seems to be going up in flames, the figure of Victory is mourning defeat at the left, and in the distance we see a ship buffeted by storms. That is why Fortuna is so often associated with the sea, or stands on a globe between the images of a sailing ship and a church, rather like the Ancient Mariner returning to his "home countree."

One of the most interesting troves of "globalizing" or "planetary" images is to be found in a relatively little known *Bilderbuch* by the German artist Andreas Friedrich, the *Emblemata Nova* of 1617. Published at the onset of the first great age of voyages, Friedrich's engravings depict the

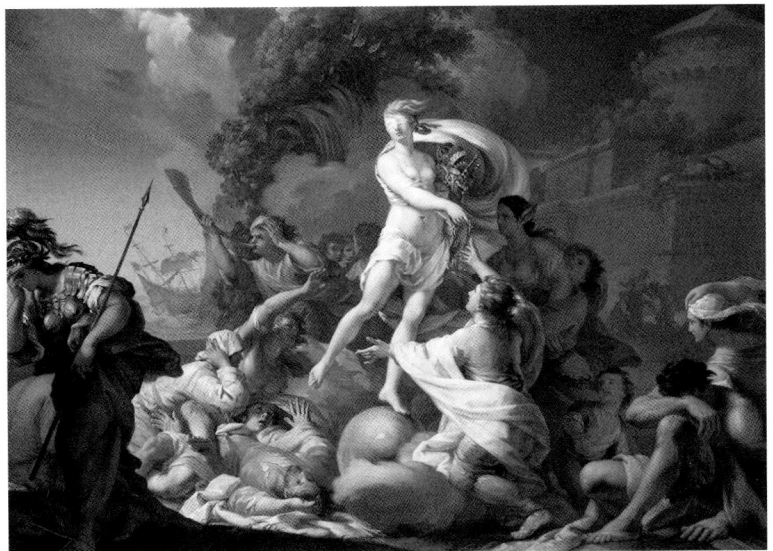

Fig. 7

Tadeusz Kuntze, *Blind Fortuna*, 1754, oil on canvas, 114 × 163 cm. Collection of the National Museum in Warsaw. Photo: the National Museum in Warsaw. Source: https://commons.wikimedia.org/wiki/File:Tadeusz_Kuntze_001.jpg

globe in ways that I think Allan Sekula would have found deeply resonant with his *Ship of Fools* understood as a planetary project. Perhaps most congenial to Sekula's vision would have been this emblem of the globe as itself the cargo on a ship that is being rowed by the devil. (fig. 8) Instead of Fortuna, we find a literal "fortune" atop the globe, in which the symbols of Faith and Justice have been planted. Atop the central pedestal is the Cock who crows the impending dawn of a Divine Providence that will replace the reign of money. The hour-glass on the bowsprit tells the devil that although he is in control at the moment, his time is running out. It is as if the Ship of Fools has been globalized, as if all the world's inhabitants are "in the same boat," an idea that is made explicit in a subsequent emblem, the world as itself a kind of Leviathan comprised of the human multitudes.[12] (fig. 9)

Friedrich's sardonic vision of a world driven by money is made most explicit in this image of the Christian imperial *globus cruciger* resting atop a bag of money, as the prize in a tug of war between the Devil and the Fool. (fig. 10) A blank heraldic shield is topped by a death's head that supports the familiar hour-glass, and beneath the money bag are strewn various objects of interest: a casket with crucifix, a pair of staves, a sword and what might be the notorious torture instrument known as a cat of nine tails. At the bottom center are a pair of dismembered hands, locked in a handshake which I cannot resist reading as an emblem of the "art of the deal." This bleak vision is reinforced by the next emblem, which portrays the world under the sovereignty of the devil, on an altar attended by a pair of burghers, one of whom is drinking to excess, flanked by figures of the Seven Deadly Sins.

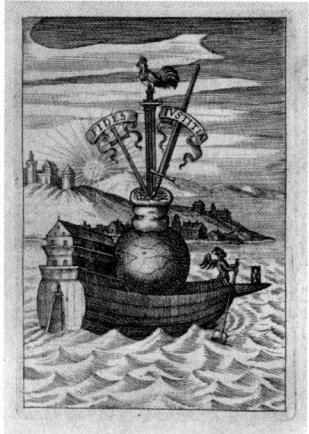 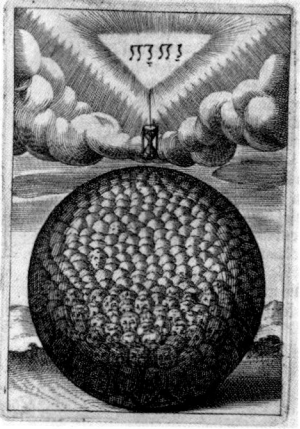 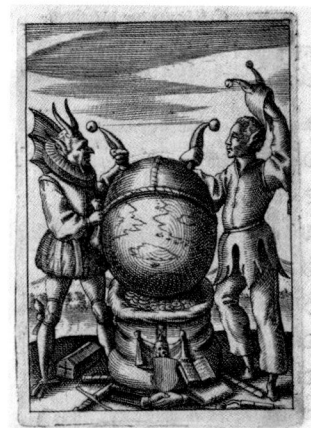

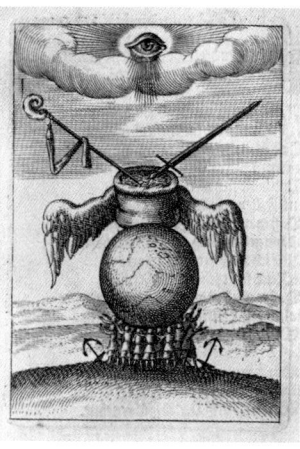 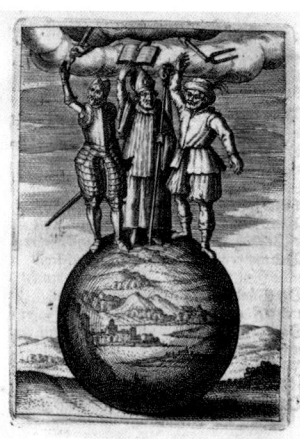

Figs. 8–12

Andreas Friedrich, *Emblemata Nova*,
1617, p. 71, 3, 7, 121 and 5.

What about the great masses of workers who hold up the world? They are shown in this emblem like a crowd of Sekula's dockworkers, anchoring the planet, staggering under its weight, and gesturing for relief. (fig. 11) But the world they support with their labor is itself weighed down once again by the winged curse of money, which serves as the potting soil for a shepherd's crook and a sword, the emblems of Religion and War. This is about as close as Friedrich comes to hinting at an impious message, relieved only by the all-seeing eye of God above, who presumably will set things right. If the masses of proletarian and peasant labor hold up the world in Friedrich's planetary emblem, the figures of the dominant classes are shown in the following image where the soldier, the priest, and (probably) the farmer are shown receiving the instruments of their professions from on high. (fig. 12)

Shortly after *Emblemata Nova*, Michael Maier's *Atalanta Fugiens* appeared, featuring the following image. Instead of the earth as a globe dominated or upheld by men, or ridden by the fickle goddess of Fortune, she appears as what Bruno Latour calls "Gaia," the Mother Earth who is the source of all the life-forms that we know. Peter Sloterdijk reads this as an emblem of Catholic Mariolatry, which places the mother at the center, only to render her subordinate to the divine child that she is nursing. (2014, 102) (pl. 1) I read this quite differently, as Destination Earth, the goal of human flourishing that has overcome both the false destinations of the national homeland and the abstract figure of a globalizing process driven by folly and vice, the madness and greed of neoliberalism. Probably I am being anachronistic; but so is the image. It launches me forward to the period of the French Revolution when William Blake provided his own images of the global imaginary in the form of three figures. Instead of the trio of Warrior, Priest, and Farmer, Blake gives us three planetary deities: the rational Newtonian mathematician who creates the world as a geometric abstraction; the artisan blacksmith, who creates the world out of material labor; and his own version of the *Terra nutrix*, a maternal goddess who is giving birth to a world that is still in its embryonic form, the placenta still attached to the mother. (figs. 13–15)

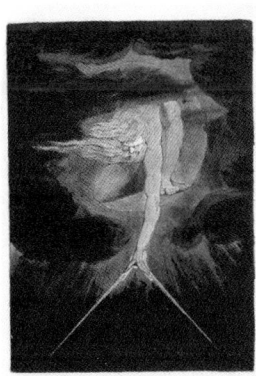

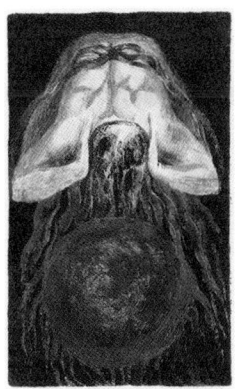

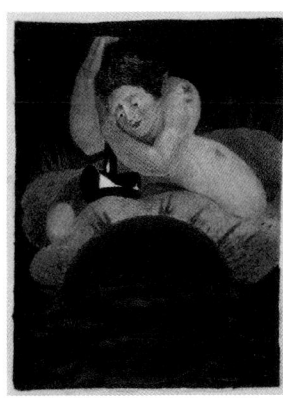

Fig. 13

Print made by William Blake, 1757–1827, British, *Europe. A Prophecy*, Plate 1, Frontispiece, 1794. Color-printed relief etching in dark brown with pen and black ink, oil and watercolor on moderately thick, slightly textured, cream wove paper inlaid to size, Yale Center for British Art, Paul Mellon Collection.

Fig. 14

Print made by William Blake, 1757–1827, British, *The First Book of Urizen*, Plate 16 (Bentley 17), 1794. Color-printed relief etching in orange-brown with watercolor on moderately thick, slightly textured, cream wove paper, Yale Center for British Art, Paul Mellon Collection.

Fig. 15

Plate 8 from Copy A of William Blake, *The Song of Los*, 1795. Color-printed relief etching, hand-coloring added, 23,5 × 17, 6 cm. The British Museum Collection (1856,0209.416). © The Trustees of the British Museum.

Conclusion: Back to Allan Sekula.

I have tried to envelope Allan Sekula's "atlas from below," within a complementary archive launched by reflections on the portrait owned by Sally Stein of the artist as a worker of the world. Sometimes these workers appear as Herculean figures or burdened masses lifting the world on their shoulders; more often, they seem to be ordinary folks—a drunken pilot, a cleaning woman, a coalminer—or ordinary objects: a soccer ball, a crutch, a wrench. At all times, I think, they are parts of what Gustave Courbet called "real allegories," objects and images seized from the world to constitute that world "from below." The presence of allegory seems to me especially undeniable in the explicit moral contrast between the "good" and "bad" ships, the *Salamis Glory*, like the traditional "Ship of Fools" dedicated to nothing but idleness, consumption, and oblivious distraction, and the "good ship" *Global Mariner*, the "wise fools" who carry no commodities around the world, just a body of critical thinking.[13] (pl. 2–3) Sekula did not shrink from vulgar Marxist moralizing, making sure that the modern devils and fools of capital would make their appearance. Andreas Friedrich would, I think, recognize the presence of emblematics in every image and object of *Ship of Fools | The Dockers' Museum*. But he would also understand that this artist has no need to literalize the image of the globe as he did, or as I have done, but can let the smallest detail stand for the totality. Even the simplest part-object—a wrench displaced on a welder's bench—has the effect of putting this tool back to work in service of a photographic revelation of the fossilized detritus of capital. (pl. 4) In place of the eye of God surveying the global ship of fools, Sekula offers his own keen eye, seeing everything through the lens of a critical historical materialism and radically egalitarian politics. One wonders, at what point in his voyage of the discovery, did this artist-mariner begin to notice that some of the ship's equipment was starting to look back at him? (figs. 16–18) Was it before or after he spent a bit too long contemplating the "churn" or wake left by the Ship of Fools, and abandoned himself to the oceanic madness of his final work? (pl. 5)

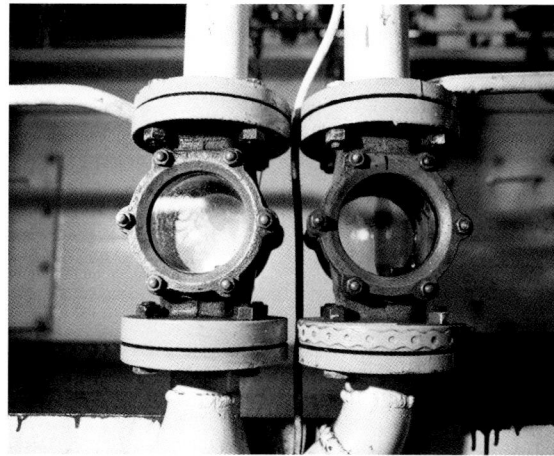

Fig. 16

Allan Sekula, *Engine Room Eyes 1*, 1999/2010. Framed chromogenic print mounted on alu-dibond, part of *Ship of Fools* (2010), 101,6 × 127 cm. Collection M HKA / Collection Flemish Community of Belgium. © Allan Sekula Studio.

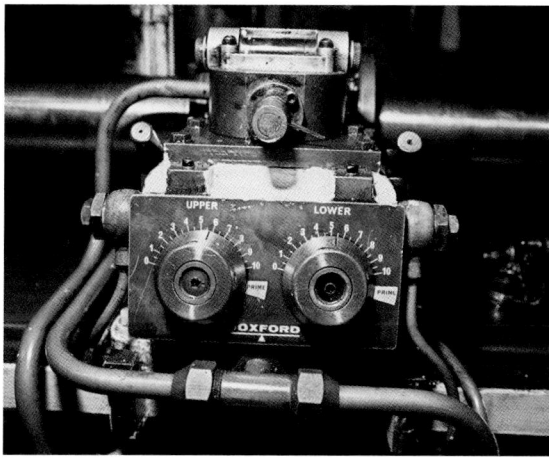

Fig. 17

Allan Sekula, *Engine Room Eyes 2*, 1999/2010. Framed chromogenic print mounted on alu-dibond, part of *Ship of Fools* (2010), 101,6 × 127 cm. Collection M HKA / Collection Flemish Community of Belgium. © Allan Sekula Studio.

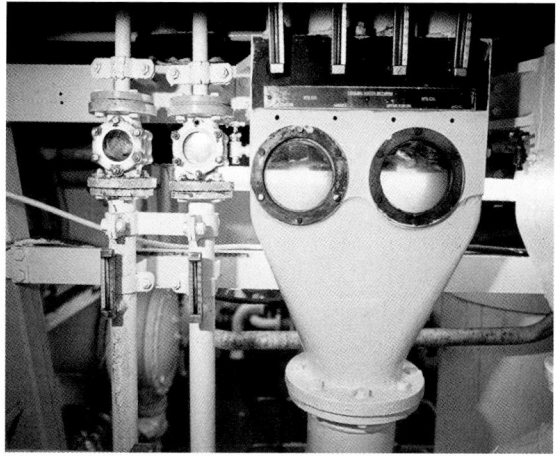

Fig. 18

Allan Sekula, *Engine Room Eyes 3*, 1999/2010. Framed chromogenic print mounted on alu-dibond, part of *Ship of Fools* (2010), 101,6 × 127 cm. Collection M HKA / Collection Flemish Community of Belgium. © Allan Sekula Studio.

Notes

1. See my study of this cultural icon *The Last Dinosaur Book* (Mitchell, 1998).

2. The word "planet" comes from the ancient Greek for "wanderer," applied to wandering stars (cf. classical Latin *stellae errant*—to lead astray [in passive] to wander, of uncertain origin). See my essay, "World Pictures," in *Image Science* (Mitchell, 2015: 97).

3. An imaginary "footnote to come" would consist of notes on Sally Stein's brilliant essay on Sekula: they would include Sekula's remarks on Benjamin on montage and "revolutionary spy or detective," as well as the figure of the "critical journalist," and the mania of collecting. (see Setari, Van Gelder, 2016: 50) For links to Warburg, Snowden, Nash, Blake, see the chapter "Method, Madness, Montage" of my forthcoming book *Seeing Through Madness*.

4. See the discussion of evidence wall, the ball of yarn, and the *New Yorker* cartoons on these topics in the chapter "Method, Madness, Montage" of my forthcoming book *Seeing Through Madness*.

5. I am echoing here Derrida's *Archive Fever*.

6. *"Don't drink the ocean, K'nuckles! Seawater makes you crazy! Look at me! I've been drinking it for hours!!! NYEHAHAHAHAHAHAHA!"* —Flapjack, *The Marvelous Misadventures of Flapjack* incredible animated cartoon series about a boy, a pirate, and a whale. The whale is his mother, a big blue balloon with a Black woman's voice. The pirate, Knuckles, is a picaro, a rogue with a vivid personality. The art is amazing; the stories disturbingly surreal and dark. Fair amount of cruelty, teasing of Knuckles. Related to Space Madness. Being away at sea for a long time seems to take its toll on your mind. Maybe it's the unchanging landscape, maybe it's being away from your loved ones. Either way, in period pieces and even sometimes in modern ones, you can expect any characters away on sea for extended periods of time to go crazy. Historically a Truth in Television. In addition, there's a lot of validity to the "don't drink seawater" idea, since salt water has the nasty effect of making you even *more* dehydrated, which can lead to delirium. And, y'know, death. See http://tvtropes.org/pmwiki/pmwiki.php/Main/OceanMadness (accessed October 19, 2018).

7. A first posthumous attempt was made on the occasion of the exhibition *Allan Sekula: Collective Sisyphus*, curated by Carles Guerra, Anja Isabel Schneider, and Hilde Van Gelder at the Fundació Antoni Tàpies (Barcelona, 2017).

8. The craving for totality, for the entire world that a collection represents, is shared across many disciplines, and even the state. Consider the NSA's mad project of monitoring and archiving all network communication. CIA Director John Brennan's "we want it all." Ironically, Brennan is now a slender line of defense against Trump's treasonous behavior.

9. For a reproduction of Meunier's 1904 portrait by Pierre Vibert, see Van Gelder, 2015: 204.

10. See Spyros Papapetros' commentary on this panel in the Cornell *Bilderatlas*, https://live-warburglibrarycornelledu.pantheonsite.io/image-group/panel-b-introduction-1–3?sequence=944 (accessed October 19, 2018).

11. See my chapter on "World Pictures: Globalization and Visual Culture," in *Image Science* (2015) for further discussion of these images.

12. See "World Pictures" in *Image Science* (2015) on the figure of the globe as etymologically a multitude.

13. See Hilde Van Gelder's essay, "Allan Sekula: Recollections of a 'Sage Fool'" (2018) about his egalitarian, anti-Socratic pedagogy. On p. 101 a statuette of Plato together with a damaged Globe in Allan's back yard is reproduced, a crucial image to further illustrate my present argument.

Bibliography

Ronald D. Laing, *The Politics of Experience and the Bird of Paradise* (London: Penguin Books, 1967).

Lewis Lapham, *Age of Folly: America Abandons Its Democracy* (New York: Verso, 2016).

Bruno Latour, "On a Possible Triangulation of Some Present Political Positions," *Critical Inquiry*, 44 (Winter 2018): 213–226.

W.J.T. Mitchell, *The Last Dinosaur Book* (Chicago: University of Chicago Press, 1998).

W.J.T. Mitchell, *Image Science* (Chicago: University of Chicago Press, 2015).

Allan Sekula, *Fish Story* (Düsseldorf: Richter Verlag, 1995).

Nicola Setari and Hilde Van Gelder (eds), *Allan Sekula: Mining Section (*Bureau des mines*)* (Gent: AraMER, 2016).

Peter Sloterdijk, *Globes*, trans. Wieland Hoban (Cambridge, MA: MIT Press, 2014).

Sally Stein, "Collection & Recollection: Allan Sekula's Nutcracker Suite," in *Allan Sekula.* Ship of Fools / The Dockers' Museum, ed. Hilde Van Gelder (Leuven: Leuven University Press, 2015), 96–106.

Hilde Van Gelder (ed.), *Allan Sekula.* Ship of Fools / The Dockers' Museum (Leuven: Leuven University Press, 2015).

Hilde Van Gelder, "Allan Sekula: Recollections of a 'Sage Fool,'" in *Place.Labour.Capital,* eds Ute Meta Bauer and Anca Rujoiu (Singapore and Milan: Nanyang Technological University, Centre for Contemporary Art and Mousse Publishing, 2018), 94–101.

Part 1
Collecting Folly

Allan Sekula: The Double Helix of an Activist Stance and of Curating

Bart De Baere and Anja Isabel Schneider

And so *[The] Dockers' Museum* is a collection of artefacts. [...]
I wouldn't call these readymades, or even artworks, they're objects of interest. And what I'm trying to construct is a kind of
phantasmatic, or imaginary lifeworld of a phantasmatic collective. And that collective could be all those who labor on the sea,
or who engage in the cargo from sea to shore and shore to sea.
(Sekula, online lecture, 2012, our emphasis)

1. The Double Helix of an Activist Stance and of Curating

Allan Sekula understood the role of the artist as a "critical subject," as
one who finds "a path that is coherent through that incoherence and
aggregation of overloaded meaning." (Sekula, online interview, 2011) If
he expressed discomfort with the role of the "direct agitator" of "com-
manding political speech," his approach is instead grounded in dialogue, in everyday social exchanges—a dialogue that functions critically
with the aim "to transform social conditions." (Sekula, online interview, 2011) This understanding succinctly points to the activist stance
underlying his final project *The Dockers' Museum*, which is part of the
collection of M HKA, Museum van Hedendaagse Kunst Antwerpen.
Conceived as an anti-museum and anti-archive—meticulously set up,
positioned, and unfolded—this project also bespeaks Sekula's unflag-
ging commitment, which informed his life and work—as both an artist
and an intellectual. His breadth of mind is reflected in his personal library, now a research collection, held at the Clark Art Institute.[1]

The artist as "critical subject" may help, according to Sekula, "to
keep the flame of the demos alive." (Sekula, online interview, 2011) It
is the human body asserting "itself against the abstraction of global
capital." (Sekula, 2000: n.p.) He alludes here to his slide piece *Waiting
for Teargas* (1999–2000), in which he presents himself as a supporter

"Disassembled" Images

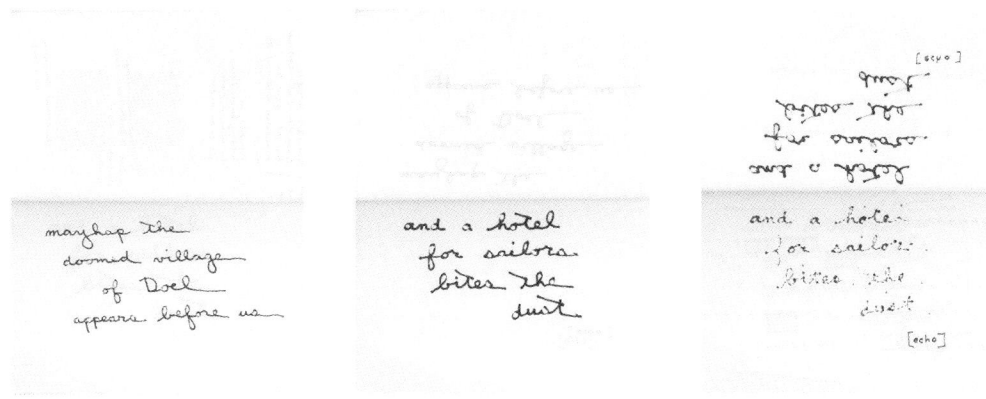

Figs. 1–3.

Allan Sekula, *Notebook #125*, 2010, n.p. © and courtesy Allan Sekula Studio.

rather than a reporter during the 1999 protests against the World Trade Organisation in Seattle. In *Dear Bill Gates* (1999), a "companion piece" to the latter, Sekula even explicitly states that he "stands in for this crowd," aligning himself—in real proximity—with the protest's "more radical groups" of transport and dock workers, who played an essential role in the unfolding of events. (Sekula, online interview, 2011) Yet these are art works, images that aspire to continue rather than document the events, brought together in a specific way to bridge the space between that moment and the art scene. Can we consider curating as the fine-tuning of this position?

This double-sided approach was also present when Sekula would visit Antwerp, one of the cities to which he was attracted. He came quite regularly to this city because of his engagement with M HKA in the context of *Ship of Fools | The Dockers' Museum* (2010–2013). We would work together in the museum, resulting in precious moments of talk and discussion, whereby it also became clear that he related to the city in his own way. When in Antwerp he wouldn't automatically follow all activist narratives, but was interested in topics connected with its port dimension. One was the struggle to save the *Internationaal Zeemanshuis* [International Seaman's House], a hotel and service facility for seamen, including a theater, from the modernist era. The other was the fight to save the nearby polder village of Doel, which was largely destroyed after extensions of the port area.[2] (figs. 1–3) Doel is also the name of the nuclear power station on the Schelde river bank, its containment buildings serving not only as the most important landmark of Europe's second largest port city, but also as a great liability in the midst of its most densely populated area. Sekula knew about this and at times he would even play with the multiple possibilities of translating the village's name in a rather jocular way.[3] His relation with the museum, in other words, was real; it was a museum situated in Antwerp. As such, the idyllic amateur painting in *The Dockers' Museum* of the Three Mile Island reactor before the meltdown was real as well (see pl. 11), as were other objects in the so-called "Bombing Section" of *The Dockers' Museum*, fully named "Bombing Section. Curie-Einstein-Hiroshima-Nagasaki-Three Mile Island-Chernobyl-Fukushima Division."[4] His extra-artistic contacts made up his real network, and these included the autonomous dockers' union *La Coordinadora* (*Coordinadora Estatal de Trabajadores del Mar*) —his reference in Barcelona.[5]

We seek to describe a back and forth movement, with regard to both Sekula's working method and existential understanding, as a double approach that winds around a common axis. To do so, we take recourse to the double helix, the structure of a DNA molecule, two strands that wind around each other like a twisted ladder—an image used by Sekula himself, too. (Sekula, unpublished email, 2011) First, let us further specify Sekula's approach, as one that is "anti-idealist, explicitly materialist, political and paraxial," as aptly described by Gail Day. (Day, 2015: 59) His position in the world, as also expressed in the positioning of his work and achieved through a process of rigorous reflection, precise editing, and curating, is, by extension, a positioning and a sense of the world itself. In our understanding, then, the artist's approach is already double in the locating of his project. "Double" should be understood here as 'multiple' or 'diverse'—not as binary.

If Sekula advocates a multiplication of linkage points, it is to eschew binary thinking. The port, according to the artist, is—as a metaphor of differences—a counter example to the notion of border. (Sekula, online conversation, 2011) This existential understanding is grounded in the relational constellation of ports. As such it is not only demonstrated through the artist's work, but also reenacted/performed and brought into being by it, in this very back-and-forth movement: "a kind of switching," which for Sekula amounts to an "epistemological question." (Sekula, online conversation, 2011) Sekula's double approach of "inclusive differentiation" is further highlighted in *The Dockers' Museum* with its very particular curatorial approach. The curatorial becomes an equivalent of his capacity of editing and, more in general, of reflection as a valid companion of life. An ambitious "museum" structure to house multiple reference points, often—not only in the atomic bomb section—of an explosive nature, was continued through attentive, fragile decisions, focusing on the materiality, scale, and specificity of the objects. This kind of attention moves back and forth between socio-political understanding and hyper-concrete narratives. One may see these as two strands that wind around each other like a twisted ladder, but should then not forget the in-between, which delivers the real motoric energy, creating relays. The Antwerp section, entitled

"Harbors, Antwerp & Santos" opens with Constantin Meunier's "dock-hand" sculpture *Débardeur du port d'Anvers* (1890)—art evoking pride, and doing so in Antwerp, in real space, next to the city hall.[6] The initial Antwerp presentation already included references to Santos; Santos which will end up on a football signed Pelé, another source of pride.[7] *The Dockers' Museum* makes vast leaps, creating high complexity with simple means, in an effort described as "Herculean."[8] Why did the artist feel compelled to realize it? *The Dockers' Museum* offers a radicalization of the process-oriented approach, in works such as TITANIC's wake (2003) or *Shipwreck and Workers* (2007), entailing further, additional levels of articulation. *The Dockers' Museum* focuses not on "art work," but on "worldmaking."[9]

> The idea of the museum is that these are objects of interest that might create the idea of some sort of imaginary or phantasmatic collective lifeworld (*Lebenswelt*). (Sekula, unpublished interview, 2011)

2. *The Dockers' Museum* as Activist

Allan Sekula opened up a singular approach, grounded in the notion of "objects of interest," literally as objects "to be between."[10] When he populates the exhibition space with artefacts, postcards, and graphics, these discrete objects, sourced by the artist via eBay, are not to be understood as works of art. In *The Dockers' Museum*, these objects are nevertheless approached artistically and staged museologically. Yet, it is an anti-museum. What, exactly, does the prefix "anti" entail when addressed in terms of performativity? Revocable rules? A dynamics of variance? A transformative process, a passing from one state of being to another? A going against anything conclusive, fixed? A process of activation through insertion? A move from how it should not be to how it could be otherwise? *The Dockers' Museum* as a space of the elsewhere impossible? In speaking about his final undertaking, Sekula expressed possibilities of future additions to his collection, such as outtakes from his meticulously edited photographic sequences. However, when it came to *The Dockers' Museum*, outtakes resulting from such editing practice would again assume potential relevance. Expanding intensities could then potentially open up a space for "wild installations," including noise terror and the use of red rotary alarm lights as part of the viewing experience.

Sekula once recounted that he initially avoided any art world contact in Barcelona up until 1996, when he stayed frequently in the city. Years later he went to visit his exhibition at MACBA (Museu d'art Contemporani Barcelona) with his friends from *La Coordinadora*. In which sense should we consider Allan Sekula to be an activist? Instead of starting from the generic notion, "one who advocates a doctrine of direct action," we ought to foreground the specific praxis—in scale differentiated from the *Zeemanshuis* to the Seattle WTO protests—that loaded the term in the wake of the counter-globalization movement.[11] If so, activism is not only about direct action. The Direct Action Network was part of Seattle but so were the "teamsters and turtles," an alliance of trade unions and environmentalists. Activism in this vein is about sustained lucid "moves" with mediatized outcomes, targeting cases to address public opinion, opening up space again for alternative thinking, which had been closed through the rise of managerial output-thinking since the 1980s, and reestablishing this reflective space through a topical focus.

The praxis of Allan Sekula does not only accompany this dynamics actively, as a reflective counterpart. He also translated it into an artistic strategy, reenacting its structural set-up. Through his focus on topics, his work becomes both a "medium"—heralding the earlier moment as may television or newspapers—and a "move," a next moment with a position on its own behalf that may in its turn gain wider attention for the reflections surrounding the topic. At the same time, Sekula offered a space for worldmaking indeed. By taking a stand, like Meunier's dock-hand, he becomes part, like this dock-hand, of a multitude, caring and daring. The path that leads to *The Dockers' Museum*, then, builds on the following presuppositions. First, for Sekula, an intervention in the world through reified social relations is only possible in taking recourse to abstraction, as a way to make such relations visible. This entails a movement from the "concrete to the abstract, and back to the concrete." (Day, 2015: 69–70) Secondly, in order to "get out of" the commodity fetishism of the art market economy, economic flows may be interrupted. This implies a twist from the usual dynamics of the acquisition process, with M HKA owning the objects, acquiring them as a supportive producer, and Sekula assuming ownership over his artist museum.

These twists, such as Sekula's "objects of interest" being registered, etc. set in motion a process at once interrogative, i.e. provoking questions, rather than providing answers, and confrontational: how can we do it differently? Consider, for example, all-embracing cultural forms: the structural model of the archive, which is challenged by Sekula's anti-archive. If *The Dockers' Museum* is generative of a differential space within specific, and therefore local context, relations and linkage points, its activist dynamics literally opens the museum toward the world. *The Dockers' Museum* thus calls forth an active spectator. And, thirdly, the notion of reversal of roles and relationships suggests a potential shifting of agencies.[12] From *The Dockers' Museum* we understand how Sekula's double helix is functioning and how it can even be equaled to the specificity of the activism of the past two decades, strangely un-graspable as it has been for traditional politics in its combination of focused topicality, radical rethinking, and fluid operationality. There is no longer a primacy of small over large, of thoughts over actions, as in the conventional ideologies, or of actions over thoughts, as in manage-rialism. Acting and thinking go together in a double helix that may have the most diverse appearances, on a micro level as well as on a macro level. It is the merger of direct action, geared to a concrete topic, and of "deep thinking," the kind of thinking it's all about. The reflective and self-critical turn of *The Dockers' Museum* may be seen as Herculean in-deed, because it opens up both the operating modes of cultural institut-ing and a worldview in which the land is linked with the sea, here with there, then with now, and specificity with holistic understanding. This is a museum about or of dock workers, who represent the in-between. The single items each testify of the same complexity. Time and again, broad human moves become visible through their specificity. *The Dockers' Museum* allows us a multitude of inroads to understand the artist's vision on what an activist stance may entail. The triad editing/curating/reflecting does not have to conclude/be conclusive; it can also open space in a praxis of transformative worldmaking.

> And so *[The] Dockers' Museum* is a collection of artefacts. [...] I wouldn't call these readymades, or even artworks, they're objects of interest. And what I'm trying to construct is a kind of phantas-matic, or imaginary lifeworld of a phantasmatic collective. And that collective could be all those who labor on the sea, or who engage in the cargo from sea to shore and shore to sea. (Sekula, online lecture, 2012, our emphasis)

3. Curating at Large Valued as Activist

How can we sustain the work's interventionist aspirations? Thinking with Sekula necessarily implies engaging in a discourse, one "that is crafted together with others," as Marina Garcés put it. (Garcés, 2012) M HKA as a service provider and hub to *The Dockers' Museum* thus can-not play this role alone, as the close and intense collaboration with the Lieven Gevaert Centre (LGC) attests. If we understand *The Dockers' Museum* as a vital space, the latter necessarily calls for an extension into other kinds of spaces, beyond the physical exhibition space, despite, or perhaps because of the work's pronounced materiality. Hence, this in-tervention should result in different modes of cognition and re-cogni-tion. As part of the challenge presented, we do have to account for the shifting modalities the work underwent during/shortly after Sekula's lifetime. To make sense of Sekula's complex endeavor, unfinished and open-ended, is to embrace these shifts as constituent to the work itself. Precisely because of that, we should interrogate them. The emphasis lies deliberately on the work's unfixed nature, which, by extension contributes to a potentially more precise understanding of the "objects of interest," to be made accessible. A common project, here the "interest" extends and literally translates into a shared concern, and responsibility, both in terms of care and of dissemination, and this very concern is also our point of reference.

What can we learn from the praxis of Allan Sekula for a coming activist turn in curating? In general, the abovementioned aspects provide the possibilities for restructuring, realignment, reintegration; there is not necessarily a binary opposition between person and role or between personal engagement and cultural praxis. Our reflexes of differentiation should not necessarily lead to professionalized separation ($\neq$). Sekula instead uses, so to speak, the approximation symbol $\approx$, through which a sense of difference is maintained, but proximity is stressed for operational purposes. Thus reflecting $\approx$ refusing & resisting $\approx$ editing $\approx$ curating $\approx$ moving autonomously $\approx$ activism. Essentially, thinking and action are intertwined and seemingly diverse operations may come out of that. Apparent opposites are tentatively revealed as emanations of the same intensity in different moments or circumstances, with the core operations ascribed to the one working in the other. Examples of this are the resistance of dissidence/exodus, versus the vitalism of activism, or the doubleness of action on the one hand and reflection on the other. Editing and curating are tools for Sekula to obtain this transformative capacity. Starting with fieldwork, he continues to have an embodied relationship with the items he distills from it. It is therefore not obvious to fix the precise notions that may be derived from his praxis; they rather are in the registers of the situational and provisional, of reciprocity and interdependence, of the subversive and reassertion. The critical freedom to be found in *The Dockers' Museum* is dynamic: it allows a zooming in, i.e. a focus, a zooming out, and back in.

Existing perspectives of curating, from clearly positioned (critique & institutions) to criticality (a reflective position in which to inscribe one's own awareness of relativity), and thematic/political curating out of discomfort are insufficient to validate Sekula's take on it. We have to move from the "curatorial" as mode of reflection to a mode of concern and involvement, in which commitment acts as precondition of the latter. If activist curating operates in the in-between spaces, it is thus as much about a meaningful positioning, positioning including mobility, as it is about relativity, of being related. The turn we are describing here, in which curating at large may be valued as more or less activist, is that of an embodied position. It is therefore a turn, which stresses the situational and provisional. Its dynamic condition of variance is literally turned toward a continuous process, one that is "outward-bound." Sekula might have liked this, the adverbial suffix "-ward" is expressing a direction: "… on a course out from the home port."[13] Activist curating may thus be envisaged as the way to (re)turn to a lifeworld.

Allan Sekula used the notion of "lifeworld" several times discursively, not only in the fragments of his voice we sought to resonate, but also when speaking about the port of Los Angeles he grew up in, and also in a conversation here at M HKA when speaking about it in relation to "the use of human energy and the human intentionality."[14] (Sekula, unpublished conversation, 2012) The notion of lifeworld is used in different sciences, building upon its phenomenological coining by Edmund Husserl. Sekula sees its significance and urgency in highly contemporary terms, of multitudes and specific people, of dockers and a dockhand, of me and all of us at the same time, experiencing, living together, and sharing a consciousness about the world. This consciousness makes the world our world, a lifeworld. That basis, in its turn, allows us to be active and to strive for "objective truth." Is *The Dockers' Museum* not a contemporary iteration of what Husserl describes as "a grand theatre of objects variously arranged in space and time relative to perceiving subjects … the 'ground' for all shared human experience"? (Husserl, 1936/1970: 42) Sekula humbly calls it "a kind of phantasmatic, or imaginary lifeworld of a phantasmatic collective," but it is a lifeworld all the same. For this reason, it is always a matter of yes and no about the topic, beyond the symbolic, beyond concrete social projects, beyond abstract concepts, constitutive of knowledge production, and therefore of a transformative process, renewing points of departure. It is a matter of transforming that which is self-evident or self-given into a process of making everything non-self-evident, turning it into transformative worldmaking.

Notes

1. For more information on the Allan Sekula Library, see http://www.clarkart.edu/rap/library (accessed October 15, 2018).

2. Such as the *Deurganckdock* in the port of Antwerp, the largest tidal dock in the world, geared to container traffic.

3. In an email exchange between January 23, 2006 and February 2, 2006, Hilde Van Gelder informed Allan Sekula that the Dutch name "Doel" translates into English as "aim." Sekula replied: "Does the name 'Aim' make a place a target or a firing position? Strange!" Van Gelder responded that, as a matter of fact the Dutch noun "doel" also, among others, translates as "target."

4. *Romantic Landscape Painting of Three Mile Island Nuclear Reactor, Made Before 1979 Partial Meltdown, Artist Name Indecipherable* [title given by Allan Sekula], oil on canvas, 1974–1975, 61 × 76,2 cm. Purchased by Allan Sekula on eBay on April 10, 2011. See Van Gelder, 2015: 88; 200; 237.

5. *La Coordinadora* supported, for instance, the solidarity movement in Poland, as well as the Liverpool Dockers' Strikes, and related in 2003 to the *Prestige* disaster in Galicia through acts of solidarity. The Barcelona dockers collected money and with that bought protective gear for the volunteers, which they drove to Galicia. Cf. Weir, 2004. See also "Los estibadores catalanes, con Galicia" in *La Estiba. La voz de los puertos*, Boletín de la Coordinadora Estatal de Trabajadores del Mar, 76.IV (March 2003): 15.

6. Constantin Meunier, *Débardeur du port d'Anvers*, bronze, 1980, 48,5 × 22 × 18 cm. Purchased in December 2011 by M HKA for *The Dockers' Museum*, at the request of Allan Sekula. See Van Gelder, 2015: 89–90; 215; 236.

7. *Pelé Signed Football* [title given by Allan Sekula], leather, producer, production, and signing date with black alcohol marker by Pelé unknown, ø 22 cm. Purchased by Allan Sekula on eBay on July 15, 2011. See Van Gelder, 2015: 198; 236.

8. See Bock and De Baere, 2015: 20.

9. The basic reference here to mention is Nelson Goodman, *Ways of Worldmaking* (Indianapolis & Cambridge: Hackett Publishing Company, 1978). We think it is interesting to extend the notion of worldmaking to curating.

10. "to be between" is the etymological reading of the word "interest," "literally 'to be between,' from *inter* 'between' (see inter-) + esse 'to be' (from PIE root *es- 'to be')." See https://www.etymonline.com (accessed October 15, 2018).

11. "activist (n.) 'one who advocates a doctrine of direct action' in any sense, 1915; from active + -ist. Originally in reference to a political movement in Sweden advocating abandonment of neutrality in World War I and active support for the Central Powers. The word was used earlier in philosophy (1907)." See http://www.etymonline.com (accessed October 15, 2018).

12. On the reversal of roles, see Van Gelder, 2015: 75; 76.

13. Cf. http://www.dictionary.com/browse/outward (accessed October 15, 2018).

14. The full quote reads: "It's a lifeworld, and it's a lifeworld that gets forgotten or mis-… the biggest mistake you can make is go by and think it's just automatic, entirely so. The use of human energy and the human intentionality and all of it, all of that has to be brought out, because it feels like a system running on automatic." Cf. Van Gelder, 2015: 84.

Bibliography

Jürgen Bock and Bart De Baere, "Foreword: Pas de deux," in *Allan Sekula*. Ship of Fools / The Dockers' Museum, ed. Hilde Van Gelder (Leuven: University Press, 2015), 19–21.

Gail Day, "Allan Sekula's Transitive Poetics: Metonymy and Metaphor in *Lottery of the Sea, Ship of Fools* and *The Dockers' Museum*," in *Allan Sekula*. Ship of Fools / The Dockers' Museum, ed. Hilde Van Gelder (Leuven: University Press, 2015), 57–70.

Marina Garcés, "Honesty with the Real," *Journal of Aesthetics and Culture*, 4, (Spring, 2012), http://www.tandfonline.com/doi/full/10.3402/jac.v4i0.18820 (accessed October 15, 2018).

Nelson Goodman, *Ways of Worldmaking* (Indianapolis & Cambridge: Hackett Publishing Company, 1978).

Edmund Husserl, *The Crisis of European Sciences and Transcendental Phenomenology* (Evanston, IL: Northwestern University Press, 1936/1970).

Allan Sekula, "Waiting for Tear Gas [white globe to black]," in *5 Days that Shook the World. Seattle and Beyond*, eds Alexander Cockburn, Jeffrey St. Clair, and Allan Sekula (London/New York: Verso, 2000), n.p.

Allan Sekula, unpublished email exchange with Hilde Van Gelder, bearing the subject heading "On Obstructions and the Hand-Held Camera," January 23–February 2, 2006.

Allan Sekula, "RWM SON[I]A: Interview with the artist, writer and critic Allan Sekula," MACBA, January 27, 2011, http://rwm.macba.cat/en/search (accessed October 15, 2018).

Allan Sekula, "Talking Heads. Allan Sekula (Part 1)," [in conversation with Jean Perret and Pascal Beausse]. Head, Geneva, February 23, 2011, https://vimeo.com/78807540 (accessed October 15, 2018).

Allan Sekula, unpublished email to Bart De Baere, June 22, 2011.

Allan Sekula, unpublished interview with Jürgen Bock and Larys Frogier, November 18, 2011, at La Criée, Rennes.

Allan Sekula, unpublished conversation with Bart De Baere and Christine Lambrechts, April 18, 2012, at M HKA, Antwerp.

Allan Sekula, "Lecture at Emily Carr University," October 25, 2012, https://vimeo.com/53897947 (accessed October 15, 2018).

Hilde Van Gelder, "Allan Sekula's Labor of Giants," in *Allan Sekula*. Ship of Fools / The Dockers' Museum, ed. Hilde Van Gelder (Leuven: University Press, 2015), 73–94.

Stan Weir, "Introduction to Coordinadora (1989)" and "Strike in Spain Reveals Sickness and Cure (1986)," in *Singlejack Solidarity*, ed. George Lipsitz (Minneapolis and London: University of Minnesota Press, 2004), 152–155 and 156–159 respectively.

X., "Los estibadores catalanes, con Galicia" in *La Estiba. La voz de los puertos*, Boletín de la Coordinadora Estatal de Trabajadores del Mar, 76.IV (March 2003): 15.

The Stuff in the Studio: On Chris Larson's *Land Speed Record* (2016)

Stefanie Diekmann

Object Lesson 1

Our relations with objects, all objects, are limited. Either the objects will be used, or not. If they are used, they will likely be put out of use and discarded after a certain time. And among those objects that are not (or not immediately) discarded, some are put in storage, some are passed on to other users, and only a very limited number will be kept and raised to the status of collectors' items, museum objects, and exhibits, which experience a different form of use in the context of private and public displays.

However, between the more or less clear-cut options of use, storage, display, or discharge—as one connoisseur of objects has put it, objects are "either admired and preserved or used, broken and thrown away" (MacGregor, 2012: xv)—there is limbo, a stage of uncertainty, often prolonged, in which the object is neither here nor there, between categories, out of use or circulation but not yet reduced to the status of garbage or the more promising status of reusable material. As a matter of fact, limbo, although unattractive, may be the stage that is most prominent in the history of objects; especially personal objects, as these are often kept for no particular reason and stored away long after their usefulness has ended. Objects are stubborn. They have a tendency to remain. Getting rid of them can be a somewhat brutal operation. Again, this is particularly true for personal objects and items, which may be kept for the longest time and then thrown away abruptly in the course of renovation, refurnishing, moving from one apartment to another, or one of those occasional fits that demand *the clutter* (a cruel and final category of objecthood that places the items one step away from garbage) has to go. And a.s.a.p., if possible.

To soften our relations with the many (way too many) objects that there are, there is recycling and upcycling, there is vintage and eBay, and there is collecting. Unlike museum objects, the status of which must be researched and explained, well justified, and well defended, the objects in a collection are permitted a certain degree of implausibility; or, rather, a plausibility that results mostly from the interests of the respective collection and not necessarily from any cultural or market value. Collectors may appear as amateurs, scavengers, fools, and eccentrics and still be regarded as serious collectors: collections themselves can be idiosyncratic and eclectic but for this very reason they have always been recognized as an environment that grants a second life to objects and may even ensure they are treated with respect and attention.

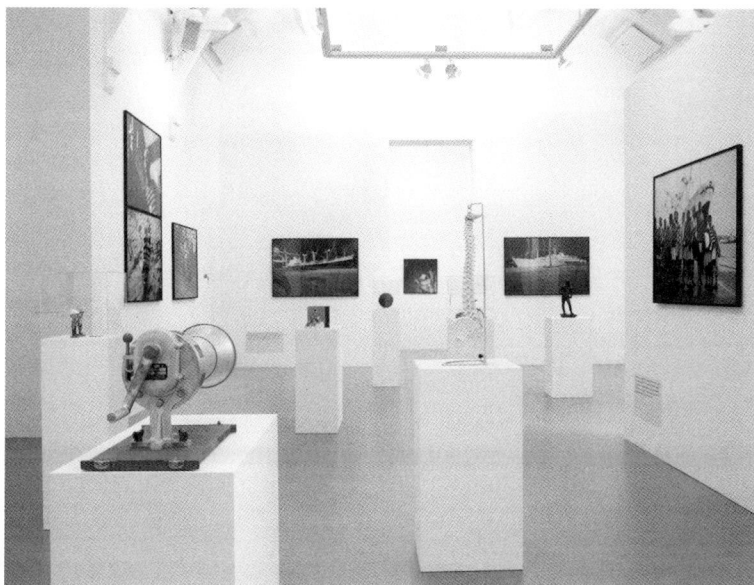

Fig. 1

Allan Sekula, *The Dockers' Museum*, installation view, Rennes, La Criée, 2012. Collection M HKA, Museum van Hedendaagse Kunst, Antwerpen / Collection Flemish Community of Belgium. © Photo: Marc Domage. Courtesy Allan Sekula Studio.

Sekula's Collections

Allan Sekula's vast collection of maritime objects and the various displays of these objects in his *Ship of Fools | The Dockers' Museum* exhibitions have embodied many of the parameters that characterize the collector's contribution to our notions of objecthood. There is diversity, idiosyncrasy, and a sense of interest and value largely determined by the focus of the respective collection, and a specific coherence that is produced by the act of collecting itself. It is also noteworthy that in Sekula's displays the objects have been treated with a near-anachronistic respect and reverence: putting them under glass or on top of a pedestal, each in its own place and each in its own right. (fig. 1)

Although their politics may have been very different, Sekula's take on objects has a lot in common with that of Neil MacGregor, former

Director of the British Museum and editor of the 2012 book *A History of the World in 100 Objects*. Both Sekula and MacGregor believe in the "eloquent object": the thing that contains a plethora of references and more than just one narrative; an object that, under the gaze of the knowing interpreter, "becomes a document not just of the world for which it was made, but of later periods which altered it." (MacGregor, 2012: xxv; xxi)

MacGregor's book of things, in which every one of the 100 objects is represented by its very own photographic "portrait" and accompanied by a close reading, is the structural equivalent of Sekula's pedestals and glass cases. In terms of attention, both displays work magic as they draw attention not just to the connections and communications that shape the material world, but also to each object's importance as a storage device of stories and histories, containing "messages about peoples and places, environments and interactions, about different moments in history and about our own time as we reflect upon it." (MacGregor, 2012: xv)

To call this reflection a luxury does not intend to diminish its merits: the insights that are to be gained from the close readings and the profound respect for the material world. However, one thing to be learned from both projects is that such an approach is time and space intensive and can therefore only ever be directed at a very limited number of things—100 in the BBC and British Museum project; a few dozen in the exhibitions set up by Sekula in galleries between 2010 and 2013, such as at La Criée in Rennes or the Johann Jacobs Museum in Zurich. Our general attitude towards the material world is less attentive and certainly less generous. We are not inclined to invest attention, time, and space but to keep time and space free of clutter, of items old and new, and not to hold on to things once they are no longer of use and value. For that very reason, the following is not a text about museum displays and the close inspection of things. Instead (and maybe in some defiance of that old-school attention to things that has been so important in the curatorial work of Sekula), this text is organized around a different question: is there a way to pay homage to objects while not holding on to them?

Land Speed Record

I would not have asked this question had I not, one afternoon in the fall of 2016, happened across Chris Larson's installation *Land Speed Record*. On that day, I was visiting the exhibitions at the Walker Art Center in Minneapolis; or, rather, I had meant to visit them but ended up spending most of my time in a darkened gallery on the fourth floor, watching two runs of the video constituting the main part of Larson's installation.[1] To say that the experience was overwhelming is not exaggerated.

To describe this experience as stressful, noisy, tiring, and slightly nerve-wracking is also true: the loudest object lesson to which I have ever been exposed. It was also a long one. For almost half an hour, Larson's installation offers little change in focus or perspective. (fig. 2 and pl. 6)

The main projection in *Land Speed Record* consists of two tracks, i.e. an audio and a video recording, with another audio track looming eerily underneath. The audio track is the percussion part of the punk rock album *Land Speed Record* by Hüsker Dü, first performed during a concert in the summer of 1981 by drummer Grant Hart, and performed again as a solo in the spring of 2016 by percussionist Yousif del Valle. Both performances were recorded live at the well-known Minneapolis music venue 7th St Entry. The video track, of exactly the same length, was filmed in 2016 by Minneapolis-based artist Larson at his studio in a warehouse in St. Paul. In the studio, Larson had set up a construction that permitted a video recording, in one long automated tracking shot, of a vast array of objects loosely arranged on the studio floor, while the camera slowly moved below the ceiling, always at the same pace and distance.

Not surprisingly, most of the reviews published after the opening of *Land Speed Record* in September 2016 have been focused on the objects in the tracking shot and on the question of how they came to be in Larson's studio: "the biography of things," as MacGregor might call it, always ready to bestow on an object a near-animistic and proto-actorial quality.[2] (MacGregor, 2012: xxi) But while MacGregor's *A History of the World in 100 Objects*, like the collections of Sekula, is an assemblage of separate biographies and highly individualized objects, the story about the stuff in Larson's studio is both collective and inclusive, i.e.

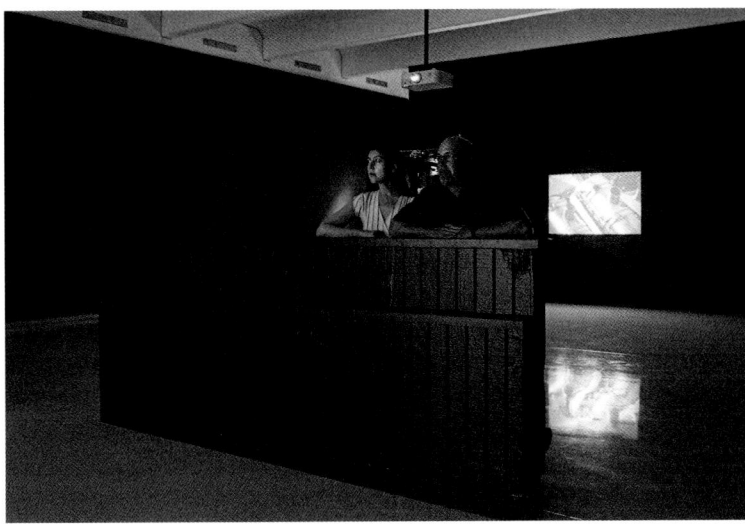

Fig. 2

Installation view of *Chris Larson: Land Speed Record, 2016*. © Walker Art Center.

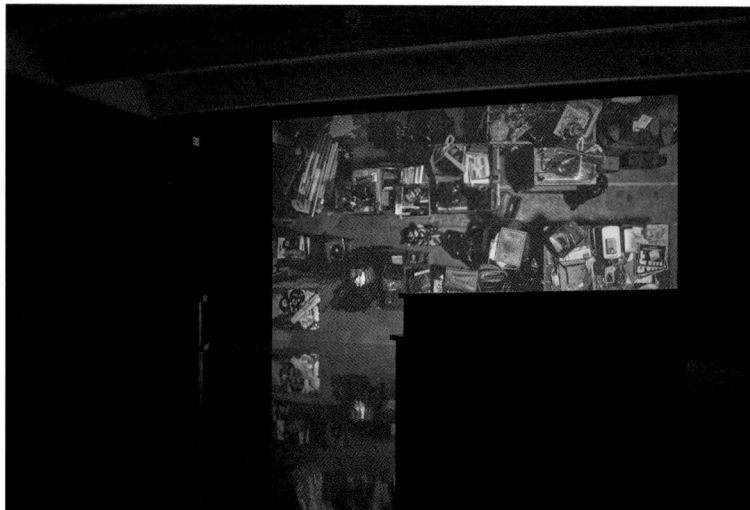

the kind of story that reduces the potentially diverse biographies of the respective objects to a single, defining event.

The Stuff in the Studio

Collective biographies: There was, or so the story goes, a fire at Hart's childhood home about twenty-five years after his former band, Hüsker Dü, had been disbanded. (Walker Art Center, 2016: n.p.) A surprisingly large number of things were salvaged from this fire; objects that Hart had kept or stored at the house. Because the house was now gone and the objects had to be taken somewhere, Larson agreed that they could be moved to his studio at the warehouse. There, in the studio, the things remained, damaged by fire and water, never reclaimed by their owner, never thrown out by their host. A collection of remnants in a specific type of limbo: beyond repair, retrieval, reuse, but still lying around, as if waiting for some change to come.

Finally, after two years, Larson constructed the scaffold and the pulley rig for the camera to record the objects for almost half an hour. He did this, or so he tells it, because after walking past the stuff in the studio for such a long time, he began "to think about how these objects would look through the lens of a camera moving slowly over the pile" and, he adds, "It is the juxtaposition of this potential speed and current stasis that interested me." (Larson, 2016: n.p.) It was decided that the duration of the recording (26' 35" to be exact) should match that of Hart's percussion track on Hüsker Dü's *Land Speed Record*; that the video and the installation should be named after the album; and that the percussion track, newly recorded as a solo, should accompany every other projection, thereby contrasting speed and stillness, noise and silence, the presence of the audio track and the slow disappearance of things that is staged in the choreography of the automated camera.

Without that story, the status of the objects in the video would remain somewhat enigmatic. They are obviously very diverse: boxes, records, photographs, tape recorders, an old-fashioned electric fan, a drainer, several neon tubes, a cable, a shovel, and some video tapes and books, to mention just a fraction of the items that appear in the first two minutes. Diverse as they are, however, the objects are not shown individually and are only vaguely sorted into groups: tapes with tapes, tubes with tubes, papers with other papers, records with more records—not entirely unlike the objects in that other illustrious British museum that goes by the name of Pitt Rivers, which has long been famous for its somewhat brutalist exhibition practices.[3] (fig. 3)

Unlike the Pitt Rivers curators, however, Larson does not make use of glass cabinets to separate one group of objects from another. Instead, everything remains on the floor, loosely arranged into one long narrow rectangle, with borders that also define those of the video image. Whatever is part of the stuff is inside the frame; whatever is not part of it is kept outside. If there is no *hors cadre* in *Land Speed Record*, it is precisely because this video depicts a material world that is both total (*everything from that fire*) and isolated, no longer in touch with the world that surrounds it, nor linked to the classificatory systems that govern the place of objects in everyday life.

"Immanence" is one word for it ("a profane source of experience"). (Rölli, 2004: 69) "Desolation" is another. As a matter of fact, the overall impression of the arrangement is both daunting and confusing. Too many things at once, but no evident coherence; too much visual information, but too little in terms of organization or systematization; no end to the tracking shot (or so it seems), but very limited insight into the former use and relevance of the stuff; and certainly no exploration of any individual object's characteristics or history. More than a little storytelling is needed to soften the overall impression of a material world reduced to the state of dead matter. And while the automated tracking shot displays this state incessantly, and with little variance, it is remarkable that most reviews insist on discussing *Land Speed Record* in terms of homage and commemoration. For example: "[*Land Speed Record*] explores how memories and objects change over time." (Dickinson, 2017: n.p.) And again: "Larson focuses…on the objects (and memories) left behind." (*Artsy*, 2016: n.p.)

Reading this installation as a videographic *vanitas* seems all too tempting, even if the word does not come up in any of the reviews. Larson's video is very much about the stillness of things but it is also about decay and decomposition, all put into a near-elegiac perspective—slow motion and prolonged contemplation included. Yet, at the same time, there is also an irony, i.e. the aesthetics of the garage sale. And the impression that beyond the garage sale arrangement there is little future for the stuff in the studio, except being moved on to the next category, which in this case would be garbage.

Display

If garbage is the future of most objects, there is a past to garbage that goes by the name of "*Zeug*."[4] Interestingly, this term has a dual history. There is its colloquial use: the word "*Zeug*" is German for "stuff;" to address an object as "*Zeug*" is one of the less respectful ways of hinting at its state and value. There is also another history, one of philosophical reflection, where the word "*Zeug*" is used as the transitional object category par excellence in Martin Heidegger's reflections upon the material world and its representation in works of art. (Heidegger, 1935/2008: 20–24)

Heidegger's "*Zeug*" (usually translated as "equipment") refers to everything that is neither *Ding* (the supposedly pure state of material that is not or cannot be put to any use) nor *Werk* (that other state, which transcends the profanity of usage and utility by reinstating the thing as an object of the gaze).[5] While both *Ding* and *Werk* are comparatively stable categories (an object may be one or the other, but there is little indication that from the state of *Ding* or *Werk* it may be transformed into something else), the category "*Zeug*," per se, is temporary because an object will be part of it only as long as it is still in use.

It has already been established that for the objects in Larson's studio, the status of "*Zeug*" is more past than present. Yes, a lot of them could be described as tools, machinery, and technical equipment and, yes, most of them can be identified as everyday objects affiliated with some context of usage and utility, i.e. Heidegger's *Dienlichkeit* (usefulness; utility). (Heidegger, 1935/2008: 21) However, in their present state, any further usage is largely out of the question. The only option to work with the stuff is that of putting it on display, i.e. in a situation which, to a certain extent, mimics that of the museum object in its glass case or on a pedestal.

In his writings, author Kryzstof Pomian has often commented upon the strange nature of the object on display in a museum or an exhibition. The very specific use that defines objecthood in the museum context demands that a thing be removed from all other contexts, especially those for which it has been designed. While it is undeniable that the museum object is still good for something (e.g. study, demonstration, or education), any employ in terms of handling or application is strictly denied. According to Pomian, having "no other purpose than that of being looked at" is precisely what defines the museum piece.[6] (Pomian, 1998: 14) In most cases, that state of "being looked at" is the final stage in the biography of the museum object, once it has been salvaged and restored.

The objects in Larson's video receive only part of this museum-like treatment, i.e. they have been placed *on display* and *out of reach*. However, none of the investigation, restoration, and explanation that may transform a given object into a museum piece has been bestowed on them. And no matter how extensive their screen time, the aspect of neglect and decay is essential to their presentation. More importantly, there are at least two modifications to the standard form of museum display. The first is the automated movement of the gaze, which is neither free to rest nor to move individually and according to specific interests. The second is the deafening noise of the percussion solo, which is clearly at odds with the idea of melancholic contemplation. (So much for the videographic *vanitas*.)

Temporality

No doubt, the oppositions in this display are striking. There is noise and silence, fastness and stillness, movement and immobility. There is also, at first glance, Gotthold Ephraim Lessing's classic opposition of time-based arts (signs and objects arranged in a sequence), usually associated with poetry and music, versus space-based arts (signs and objects arranged next to each other), usually associated with sculpture and painting. (Lessing, 1766/1987: 111–121) At the same time, the opposition between time-based and space-based art becomes obsolete with the introduction of the camera. The video track of *Land Speed Record* is actually best described as a temporary showcase, both in the sense that it constitutes a non-permanent display of the stuff on the studio floor and in the sense that it temporalizes the display itself, as the recording device progresses steadily and at a never-changing slow speed across the objects on the floor.

There is, however, a marked difference between Larson's *mise en scène* and other artistic displays of remnant and discarded objects, for example the photographic inventories by Hans-Peter Feldmann (*Alle Kleider einer Frau*), the scenographic displays of *objets trouvés* in the work of Nancy and Edward Kienholz (*The Wait, Roxys*, or *The Beanery*), or the multiplied garments in recent installations by Christian Boltanski (*Personnes* at the Grand Palais, Paris, in 2010).[7] While the photographic display always seems to call for a melancholic contemplation of the object's transience—"The contingency of photographs confirms that everything is perishable" (Sontag, 1973/1990: 80)—and the more or less static scenographic display offers various perspectives from which the ruined objects may be studied or contemplated, the filmic display and the automated speed in *Land Speed Record* constitute a form of representation that brings to mind Roland Barthes's much-quoted differentiation between photography and film:

> [I]n front of the screen, I am not free to shut my eyes; otherwise, opening them again, I would not discover the same image; I am constrained to a continuous voracity; a host of other qualities, but not *pensiveness*; whence the interest, for me, of the photogram. (Barthes, 1981: 55)

In the differentiation proposed by Barthes and other authors, such as Susan Sontag, Christian Metz, or Raymond Bellour, the photographic gaze is described as one that holds on to things (almost clings to them), whereas the mobile gaze in film and video deals with objects and people far more harshly, pushing them out of the frame as soon as they appear, proceeding from one item to the next.[8] In Sontag's words, "the viewing time is set by the filmmaker." (Sontag, 1973/1990: 81) This, of course, is also the basic operation in Larson's video: moving on, leaving things behind, refusing any extended contemplation, while still allowing for some moments to look at the discarded objects and maybe single out one or another, for a limited time, before it disappears into the space below.

Object Lesson 2

In various ways, the visual treatment in *Land Speed Record* changes the temporality that has marked the existence of the stuff in the studio before the intervention of the automated camera. Unretrieved and unreclaimed, the remnants from the fire at Hart's childhood home had remained in a state that Larson himself described as "limbo."[9] (Larson quoted in Eldredge, 2016: n.p.) On the one hand, nobody ever stopped by to pick them up, and nobody seemed to think that they should be put back in use or in circulation. On the other hand, no attempt was made to throw them away or have them recycled—two options that would have helped to categorize the stuff in the studio as either garbage or material. Into this prolonged interstage of indecision and immobility, the installation introduces a different sense of time as the recording device is actually *proceeding*, not with any particular end in sight but in such a way that the stuff on the floor vanishes from view, piece by piece, box by box, never to return for the duration of the video.

Nothing could be farther removed from this casual automated videography than the scenarios that have been imagined by the theorists of early cinema. As a matter of fact, the cinema of the 1910s, 1920s, and 1930s is known for its fascination with the staging of objects.[10] Its theorists spent a lot of time commenting upon the relations between the material world and the moving image. Traces of this fascination can be found in the writings of authors as different as Walter Benjamin, Jean Epstein, Béla Balázs, and Siegfried Kracauer, with Benjamin and Epstein discussing animation and the actorial potential of cinematographic objects: "… the prop, in its turn, not infrequently functions as actor." (Benjamin, 1935/2008: 47) Balázs comments on the physiognomic qualities of things: "No art is as well qualified to represent this 'face of things' as film." (Balázs, 1924/2010: 46) And Kracauer praises the cinematographic attention for detail and the "possibilities" and particularities of objecthood: "Only film is able to sensitize us, by way of close-ups, to the possibilities that lie dormant in a hat, a chair, a hand." (Kracauer, 1960: 45–46)

Cinematography is therefore a field of object lessons: objects as actors, actors as objects; animistic readings and renderings; the material world as a spectacle in its own right; and the face of things as a worthy subject of investigation and inspection. These are among the most recurrent themes in film theory all through the 1920s. The surprising and frightening potentials of things also have not been forgotten by the filmmakers and video artists of today. However, the attentive, sometimes obsessive interest in individual objecthood that characterizes early cinema and its theory can only serve to highlight the very different visual treatment that the stuff in the studio is given in *Land Speed Record*.

Instead of re-animating the objects or foregrounding any inherent qualities or possibilities, Larson's video underlines the sameness caused by damage, disrepair, and decay. The indifference that marks the limbo of objecthood, and the fact that no matter what their "biography" (MacGregor, 2012: xxi) has been, there is very little to be imagined for the future. From *here* (the studio) the objects *will not be going anywhere* (except to the dump). Larson's video therefore does not waste any more time on their closer inspection or on any particular relations between objects that are established by zooms or close-ups.[11] Instead, *Land Speed Record* both formalizes and radicalizes the concept of *moving on*, at a safe distance from the stuff and at a steady pace, accompanied by the percussion track that lends a certain pressure to the scenario, without ever becoming illustrative or commentarial.

Choreography

The installation's scenography is of great importance to the overall impression effected by the camera movement of *Land Speed Record*. Because the automated camera was turned downward and its slow progression below the studio ceiling and above the objects on the studio floor is not represented horizontally but vertically, the perspective changes and so does the perception of everything that has been salvaged from the house fire. In Larson's installation, the viewer's gaze is neither oriented from left to right, i.e. toward the future, nor is it oriented from right to left, i.e. toward the past. Instead, the recording device seems to be moving upward, with the corresponding effect that the objects seem to be sinking downward, below the line of vision, disappearing from view, after being granted a final spell of screen time.

Gravity is an important factor in this video. And disappearance is the central issue of its videographic display. If the stuff in the studio *is not going anywhere*, then the only option left is that of its *going under*, never to be retrieved. The longer you look, the clearer it becomes that Larson's installation is not concerned with object fetishism or with that final chapter of objecthood associated with garbage and destruction. Rather, this is a *mise en scène* that stages a very long interim (26' 35") during which all of the objects seem to be moving on toward oblivion: sliding and sinking, without ever reaching any fixed state or destination. Now you see them, now you don't. This is all that takes place for the duration of *Land Speed Record*. The story of what happened to the stuff in the studio after the video was recorded remains to be disclosed.

While looking at the projection, I began to think that Larson's video could be described as a well-ordered spectacle of refusal. Not only because the reclaiming or recycling of things has no part in this videographic object lesson (and none in the narratives that surround it), but also with respect to the extended and uniform choreography of the objects' disappearance. Their long slide toward oblivion, the downward movement, the *drop* that is so clearly opposed to all motions of picking up or lifting up a discarded object, which may then be transformed into something else: an object with a future, recycled merchandise, a museum piece, or a collector's item.

As a matter of fact, the gesture of lifting or raising may be the one operation that defines all forms of object reclamation and retrieval: be it a vintage item that is picked up and restored to be sold as an object with a history; or an object that is reclaimed to be reinstated as an object of value. (Reclaimed wood, reclaimed metal, reclaimed textiles, etc. are now all over the place and "reclaiming" has become the standard formula for a new type of object relation that also goes by the name of "upcycling.") Shoplifting is basically organized along the same principles of picking out and picking up, as is the more orderly and valued selection of the archeological or historical object that marks the beginning of its transformation into an object of research and exhibition.

The collector's gesture of picking out and picking up a particular object is not exempt from this choreographic pattern. (Walter Benjamin's famous chapter on collecting and collectors in the *Passagen-Werk* is marked by a terminology of lifting, raising, and rising, e.g. the collector's item "rising from the sea of things like an island.") (Benjamin, 1983: 271) It ranges somewhere between the institutionalized forms of reclamation bestowed on the prospective museum object, and the more unruly and affective energies that characterize the relation between objects and those who wish to get a hold on them. As Agnès Varda has shown so beautifully in her film *Les Glaneurs et la glaneuse*, the collector is herself or himself a salvager, a protagonist in the field of retrieval who picks up objects from floors, piles, boxes, back shelves, and glass cases to insert them into a larger formation of items and thereby also into a new context and framework.[12]

In contrast to all choreographies of selection, *Land Speed Record* is a work that foregrounds downward movement—the vector of the drop and the gesture of letting go. If anything seems to be lifted, it is the recording device alone (a *trompe d'œuil* caused by the angle of the camera), not the objects that are displayed and discarded in one and the same automated progression. For the time being, which in this installation is always equivalent to screen time, the objects on the floor may be classified as transient exhibits: here now, gone next; subjected to a somewhat distant inspection, which nevertheless also seems final. Instead of being looped, the video track has a defined beginning and ending (the camera being set in motion by Larson; the camera being switched off by Larson; 26' 35" in between). Although the ending is neither abrupt nor brutal, it clearly indicates that something has reached its limits because there is literally *no space* that would allow another perspective for the stuff in the studio to be established.

Percussion

The stuff does not go without some noise. However, the noise comes from somewhere else. Certainly not from the objects themselves, which are all too still and animated only insofar as the camera movement seems to translate itself to the things on the floor. Not even from the same space because in *Land Speed Record* the separation of the audio and video track also involves separate recording locations: Larson's studio for the video track and the automated camera below the ceiling. And the 7th St Entry music venue for the audio track and the solo recording of Hart's former percussion part. Playing both at the same time does not mean that the two "come together" in the installation— least of all in the all-too-obvious and often bland way that image and sound come together in narrative film or conventional videography.

This is not a soundtrack. Not a film score. And also not a music video. The audio and video track are coordinated only to the degree that they are the same length: two tracks running parallel for almost half an hour. And although there is something unstoppable about the pounding, hammering beats of the drum kit, there is also a marked sense of disconnectedness. These beats are not used to hammer anything into the objects; nor are they used to hammer anything out of them. Instead, they just go on, at their own pace and rhythm, in another space entirely, which is not that of the studio, where the stuff has been sitting, waiting for something to happen. Or just waiting to be removed.

Therefore, this combined presentation of a very slow video track and a very loud audio track is also not a drama. Not a ritual. And not an exorcism (although it may have required a certain force and determination to finally do something about the stuff, take it somewhere, get things in motion.) If anything, the visitor to *Land Speed Record* witnesses a dual act of *playing it through*: a musical performance that has been famously difficult and almost impossible to reproduce; and a visual disappearance that affects an extensive amount of things and seems to have been unimaginable before the video recording took place.

Object lessons: Getting rid of the stuff is perhaps the most important of these. *Land Speed Record* does so with elegance, without fuss, and with some insistence on the relentless, even merciless aspect that characterizes all forms of disposal. Sometimes, collecting follies call for drastic measures. In some cases, however, these measures translate into the finding of forms; and in this case, the form is a scenography that shows how to let go of things, while giving them the chance of a final appearance.

Notes

1. In the Walker Art Center's show of *Land Speed Record,* the main video projection is supplemented by two smaller videos in black-and-white, projected on the side and the rear walls. There is also a wooden structure modeled after a bar counter, conveniently placed in front of the projection to serve as support for those visitors who decide to stay through an entire run of the video, which plays for 26' 35".

2. For example, see Sheila Dickinson, "Do You Remember?: Chris Larson on 'Land Speed Record,' His Moving Tribute to Hüsker Dü and the 1980s Minneapolis Music Scene," *Art News*, January 4, 2017, http://www.artnews. com/2017/01/04/do-you-remember-chris-larson-on-land-speed-record-his-moving-tribute-to-husk-er-du-and-the-1980s-minneapolis-music-scene/ (accessed October 21, 2018). And Jay Gabler, "'Land Speed Record': Grant Hart and Chris Larson bring Hüsker Dü memories to Walker Art Center," *The Current*, June 10, 2016, https://blog.thecurrent. org/2016/06/land-speed-record-grant-hart-and-chris-larson-bring-husker-du-memories-to-walker-art-center/ (accessed October 21, 2018).

3. For a particularly interesting photographic study of the Pitt Rivers Museum's collecting and exhibition politics, see Baumgarten, 1993: n.p.

4. For example see: Rathje/Murphy, 1992: 30–52.

5. A particularly famous example of "*Zeug*" is the "*Schuhzeug*" in *Ursprung des Kunstwerks*. Far from being a *random example* ["ein beliebiges Beispiel"] (Heidegger, 1935/2008: 26), the pair of shoes, painted by no other than Vincent van Gogh, becomes a key piece in Heidegger's argument about the transformation of the "*Zeug*" once it is put on display and contemplated as an object in its own right. See Heidegger, 1935/2008: 26–30.

6. "[N]ur wenn man den Worten Gewalt antut, lässt sich der Begriff der Nützlichkeit so weit fassen, daß er sich auch auf einen dieser Gegenstände anwenden läßt, die allein für das Auge ausgestellt werden." (Pomian, 1998: 14).

7. For example, see: Hans-Peter Feldmann's *All the Clothes of a Woman* [Alle Kleider einer Frau] (1974). Photographs in Lippert, 1989: n.p. For a comprehensive survey of the Nancy and Edward Kienholz's installations, see: Hopps (ed.), 1997: n.p.

8. For example, see: Metz, 1985: 81–90. And Bellour, 2013: 119–123.

9. "I started to think about what these objects became when removed from their domestic function and relocated to the limbo of my studio." (Chris Larson, quoted in Eldredge, 2016, n.p.)

10. For a very good introduction into the 1920s and 1930s discourse on cinematographic objects, see Casetti, 2015: 25–41.

11. Any foregrounding or highlighting of the objects only takes place in two smaller black-and-white videos that form part of the installation *Land Speed Record*. These are projected on the back and sides wall of the gallery, quite literally "on the margins" of the large projection that is the centerpiece of Larson's installation.

12. *Les Glaneurs et la glaneuse* is a documentary, film essay, and self-portrait. It is essentially a film about the gestures of picking and lifting, including field-work, the search for leftovers and sellable items, along with the gestural operations of the collector and object lover who is Varda herself, acting as both observer and performer of object-related behavior.

Bibliography

Béla Balázs, "Visible Man. On the Culture of Film," in *Béla Balázs: Early Film Theory*, ed. Erica Carter (New York/Oxford: Berghahn Books, 2010).

Roland Barthes, *Camera Lucida. Reflections on Photography*, trans. Richard Howard (New York: Hill & Wang, 1981).

Lothar Baumgarten, *Unsettled Objects* (New York: Solomon R. Guggenheim Museum, 1993).

Raymond Bellour, "The Pensive Spectator," in *Between-the-Images* (Zurich, Paris: JRP Ringier, 2013), 119–123.

Walter Benjamin, "H [Der Sammler]," in *Das Passagen-Werk. Erster Band* (Frankfurt am Main: Suhrkamp, 1983), 269–280.

Walter Benjamin, "The Work of Art in the Age of Its Technological Reproducibility," in *The Work of Art in the Age of Its Technological Reproducibility and Other Writings*, eds Brigid Doherty, Michael W. Jennings and Thomas Y. Levin (Cambridge: Harvard University Press, 1935/2008), 19–55.

Francesco Casetti, "Objects on the Screen: Tools, Things, Events," in *Cinematographic Objects. Things and Operations*, ed. Volker Pantenburg (Berlin: August Verlag, 2015), 25–42.

"Chris Larson: Land Speed Record," *Walker Art Center: Calendar*, https://walkerart.org/calendar/2016/chris-larson-land-speed-record (accessed October 21, 2018).

"Chris Larson: Land Speed Record. Press Release," *Artsy Net*, June 2, https://www.artsy.net/show/walker-art-center-chris-larson-land-speed-record (accessed October 21, 2018).

Sheila Dickinson, "Do You Remember?: Chris Larson on 'Land Speed Record,' His Moving Tribute to Hüsker Dü and the 1980s Minneapolis Music Scene," *Art News*, January 4, 2017, http://www.artnews.com/2017/01/04/do-you-remember-chris-larson-on-land-speed-record-his-moving-tribute-to-husker-du-and-the-1980s-minneapolis-music-scene/(accessed October 21, 2018).

Barbara Eldredge, "Landmark Minneapolis Rock Club Featured in Punk Art Exhibit," *Curbed*, June 9, 2016, https://www.curbed.com/2016/6/9/11893424/walker-art-center-husker-du-chris-larson-land-speed-record (accessed October 21, 2018).

Jay Gabler, "'Land Speed Record': Grant Hart and Chris Larson bring Hüsker Dü memories to Walker Art Center," *The Current*, June 10, 2016, https://blog.thecurrent.org/2016/06/land-speed-record-grant-hart-and-chris-larson-bring-husker-du-memories-to-walker-art-center/ (accessed October 21, 2018).

Hans-Peter Feldmann, *All the Clothes of a Woman* [Alle Kleider einer Frau] (1974). Photographs in Werner Lippert, *Hans-Peter Feldmann: Das Museum im Kopf* (Köln: Verlag der Buchhandlung König, 1989).

Martin Heidegger, *Der Ursprung des Kunstwerks* (Stuttgart: Reclam, 1935/2008).

Walter Hopps (ed.), *Kienholz Retrospektive* (New York/Los Angeles/Berlin: Prestel Verlag, 1997).

Siegfried Kracauer, *Theory of Film. The Redemption of Physical Reality* (New York/Oxford: Oxford University Press, 1960).

Gotthold Ephraim Lessing, *Laokoon oder Über die Grenzen der Malerei und Poesie* (Stuttgart: Reclam 1766/1987).

Neil MacGregor, *A History of the World in 100 Objects* (London: Penguin Books, 2012).

Christian Metz, "Photography and Fetish," *October*, 34 (1985): 81–90.

Krzysztof Pomian, *Der Ursprung des Museums. Vom Sammeln* (Berlin: Wagenbach, 1998).

William Rathje and Cullen Murphy, "Garbage and History," in *Rubbish! The Archeology of Garbage* (New York: HarperCollins, 1992), 30–52.

Marc Rölli, "Immanence and Transcendence," in *Bulletin de la Société Américaine de Philosophie de Langue Française*, 14, 2 (2004): 50–74.

Susan Sontag, *On Photography* (New York/London/Toronto: Anchor Books, 1973/1990).

Filmography

The Gleaners and I [*Les Glaneurs et la glaneuse*].
Dir. Agnès Varda. Zeitgeist Films, 2001. DVD.

Reframing the Aesthetics of Censorship

Ronnie Close

Introduction

I have been researching visual image politics in Egypt since I moved to Cairo in 2012. Soon after my arrival, I noticed image editing of books in art spaces and in the Townhouse Gallery library, aimed at covering representations of the naked body. A few months later I requested a new photography textbook, Graham Clarke's *The Photograph*, published by Oxford University Press, for one of the courses I teach at the American University in Cairo. The department administrator told me that the book in question was banned because it was considered *haram* (immoral) and therefore unsuitable. This reaction to a revered art theory book came as a surprise to me, and when I talked to the university bookstore manager I learned about a government agency in charge of monitoring all visual materials in Egypt. I then decided to visit bookstores across the city to see which visual culture publications were available and whether their contents were modified as well. I found different types of photo books including images of the naked body that had been doctored for public sale indeed. I started to collect these books in order to archive these censored visual materials.

During this research, I also discovered a female only website, *www.3dlat.com,* which hosts information on cooking, personal advice, and lifestyle tips. Part of the website operates as a conservative Islamic women's magazine and here again photographs were modified to cover the model's body by using digital software. This time, however, the online censorship was performed by the community of female contributors and administrators, not a government agency, in order to conform to local standards of image culture.

In this contribution, I look more closely at these two forms of censorship and I question the aesthetics of such iconoclastic interventions in photographic images. Specifically, my examination focuses on two sets of photographic images: one gathered from the photographic art book publications sold in Cairo bookstores and one from the women-centered internet message board website managed by communities of female followers. The representation of women has been altered differently in each set, and this questions the ideological role of such iconoclastic interventions and the complexity of image politics for Egyptian society. Moreover, both sets pertain to the canon of the female form's photographic representation. The process of state censorship entails hand-painting each photographic image in each book edition to conceal the full erotic effect of the body. In the second set, female internet volunteer users employ digital software tools to transform the fashion image, fusing local Islamic dogma with global Western contemporary fashion lifestyle icons. My argument underlines that these doctored photographic images impose an evaluation on visual meaning in Egypt, underpinned by the assumed or potential cultural merit of iconoclastic intervention. By examining the political and aesthetic status of the image object, my approach is indebted to Allan Sekula's concept of "objects of interest," as presented in *Ship of Fools | The Dockers Museum*. The transformation of the original photograph, as an object of desire, can be situated in certain artistic traditions of montage to consider the surface tension created between the censorship act and its impact on the original photographic work. These hybrid images provide a political basis for rethinking visual culture encounters in the interconnected, increasingly globalized contemporary image world.

Photography and the Orientalist Image

Historically, the position of photography in Egypt and much of the Arab world is a troubled one, shaped by the visual formations of Orientalism created by the impact of European colonial empires in the region. The many volumes on Napoleon's expeditions to Egypt, *Description de L'Égypte* (1809–1829), inspired hosts of Orientalists to record this country's ancient heritage and frame its exotic milieu. Orientalist photography depicted its landscape as bathed in sunlight and filled with colorful subjects and picturesque archaic monuments that enticed European desires for the Other. The photograph transformed this European Oriental vision of the Middle East into "objective fact," so to speak, a political project that proved vital to colonial operations in the 19th century.

The Orientalist visions produced came about through representation and the indexical as a powerful tool, inflected through local culture and shaped by human behaviors, regardless of the power relations involved. The complex network of representational politics takes on aesthetic, cultural, and economic concerns when read through the transcultural complexity bound up in the formation of an Orientalist image history. Politics being a matter of appearances, local indigenous

Arab populations were largely written out of this visual history as actors. Reflecting this position, professor Charles Piazzi commented at the time:

> The ghost-like figures of the Arabs might as well as have been omitted, for with their black, unphotographicable faces they make very bad ghosts; and besides the modern Arabs of Egypt are such ephemeral occupiers of the soil that they have no right to any place amongst the more ancient monuments of Egypt. (Piazzi, 1879: 33)

The shadow of Orientalism points at a fundamental paradox of photography in Egypt, as indigenous forms of organic visual culture are largely missing from this historical narrative. This opens up a number of intriguing questions on the treatment of the visual in Egypt and how such photographic legacy can be restored. Was there an autonomous tradition of photography in the region free of any European influence? Despite the role of local culture in the production of images, plurality and hybridity cannot be assumed to be modes of resistance in opposition to political hegemony.[1]

In the 19th century, the photographic medium was exclusively in the control of colonial powers and local elites who applied its ideological potency to sustain hegemonic power systems. Rudolph Lehnert and Ernst Landrock ran one of the most successful photography studios in Cairo, set up in the early 20th century and specializing in highly erotic and exotic romanticized Orientalist imagery. This studio still remains open as a government run bookstore in Cairo, its archive of images being reproduced and available to the public as commercial products. However, the more erotic images were not freely accessible after the 1952 military coup, when the shop was forced to transfer ownership to the government, and more recently its business, like that of many shops in central Cairo, began to decline.

The Egyptian government never attached much cultural value to the country's photographic heritage. Lehnert & Landrock was one of many studios in Egypt with a rich history. This legacy has largely been lost due to the lack of state interest or organizational support for such archives, which are languishing in storage, or worse, abandoned in disarray. The demise of this photographic heritage is symptomatic and parallels the similar fate of local studios across Egypt, either local- or foreign-owned, which thrived from the late 19th-century colonial phase to the cultural heyday in the 1960s. The cultural regeneration triggered by the insurgency against British rule in 1952 influenced the transfer of power to local visual media producers, in particular in film cultures. Still, the photograph never received the same status or state support as the film medium. In this unidirectional paradigm, the form of photographic representation repositioned the European as the key active subject and the Oriental as passive, for a second time in visual history. In this way Orientalism and image politics are still informing knowledge and culture today in Egypt.

In the photograph as meeting space, official recognition and public appreciation has been mostly ambivalent and uneven. In her study *Imperial Eyes* (2008), Mary Louise Pratt uses the term "contact zone" to identify the image's social space as one where visual culture often converges and clashes "in highly asymmetrical relations of domination and subordination." (Pratt, 2008: 7) Despite the role of photography and image-making in the street politics of the 2011 uprising against Hosni Mubarak, the medium remains somewhat misunderstood and undervalued in visual culture terms. Here Sekula's "double system" is useful to acknowledge this image paradox, capable as it is "of functioning both honorifically and repressively." (Sekula, 1986: 345)

Within the visual formations of Orientalism, a powerful symbol is the objectified female subject, whose ambivalent nature hovered between fantasy and reality in photographic cultures. These erotic and sexualized images were made by foreign photographers and appealed to the tourist or external audience to draw on the imagination conjured up by the potency of the harem. This concealed space appeared to offer the lure of boundless pleasure and lasciviousness of desires to the European colonial traveler. In *The Colonial Harem,* Algerian poet Malek Alloula analyzed photographic postcards made in the early 20th century of local women. (Alloula, 1986) The staged erotic images depicted and imagined scenes from the hidden harem spaces and featured semi-naked women in veils. These postcards did not depict Algerian women in any real sense, but rather from the angle of the French male phantasm of the Oriental female, as posing in luxurious environments, suspended in time, playful and partially veiled but always available to the viewer's eye.

In the iconography of the harem, the veil is a crucial element, arousing and perpetuating the viewer's desire to cross into a forbidden space. This was, in photographic imagery, mostly directed toward the European imagination. However, the figure of the *odalisque*, curiously, has its origin in the Turkish harem, where these women commonly acted as servants to the concubines without being sex slaves themselves.[2] Moreover, they were never directly represented in visual form and usually hidden from the public eye. Whatever local erotic photography exists from this time was produced under conservative values for an elite class and crucially diverges from the European *odalisque* visual imagination. Under the instruction of the rulers, conservative dress codes for women were adhered to and the pleasures of the harem remained elusive to the photographic form. The *odalisque* photographic images that did circulate for Western audiences were made by European or foreign photographers who would normally stage harem scenes, often resorting to employ non-Arab female models and using the power of the caption to orientalize the image's erotic appeal.

The Muslim fantasy of the harem woman represents an alternate vision of a paradise populated with *houris*, meaning "sensuous woman."[3] This is often an androgynous being with a dark complexion speaking distinctly to an indigenous standard of female beauty. The veiled woman adds to the erotic capital of the viewer's voyeuristic desire to incite and to unveil her. This invitation to the imagination underpins visions of the objectified female form and in this way conflicts with the unambiguous European fantasy form. A key notion at play here is "namus," dignified respectability, as clashing with the more uninhibited nature of representation of Western woman. This explicitness can appear to signify moral corruption or a culture in moral decline to the conservative male Muslim viewer. This version of visual patriarchy in traditional Islam restricts female representation, as claimed by scholar Ali Behdad: "There is no space for mothers, sisters, and daughters, whose absence is a visible sign of their marginal role in a court that was marked by gendered segregation of space and strict control over the visibility of women." (Behdad, 2016: 148)

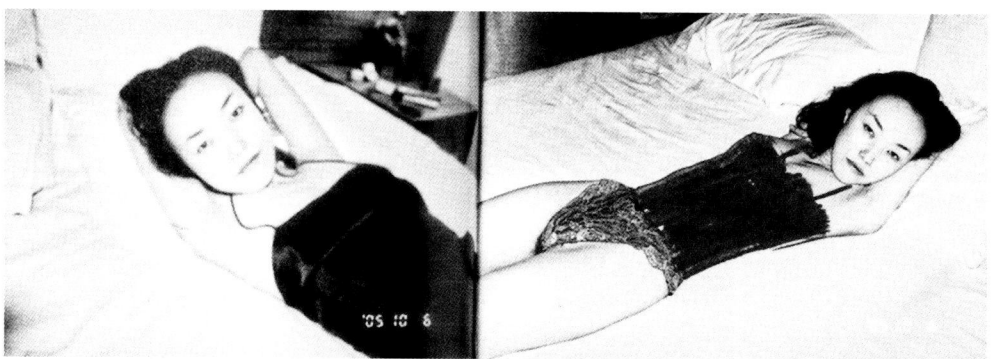

Photo Book Censorship Aesthetics

The historical aftermath of European colonial exploitation and the dominance of Orientalist cultural values continue to impact on the handling of the contemporary photographic image in the Middle East. The various censored book images I found in photography and art history anthologies sold in Cairo's bookstores between 2012 and 2014 (Badger&Parr,2004) and (Koetzle, 2011).[4] After passing through the Egyptian state-run organization *Al Riqqaba Ala El Musanafat El*

Fig. 1

From Hans-Michael Koetzle, *Photographers A-Z* (Berlin: Taschen Books, 2011), censored book sold in Cairo, original photograph Nobuyoshi Araki, *Dirty Pretty Things* (2006), p. 13

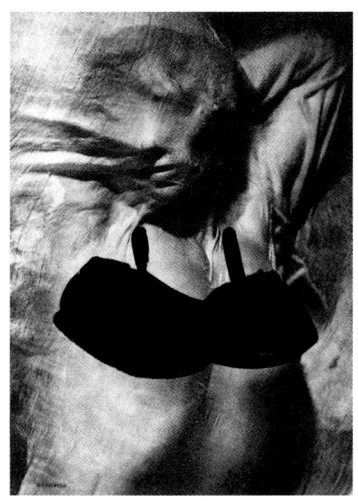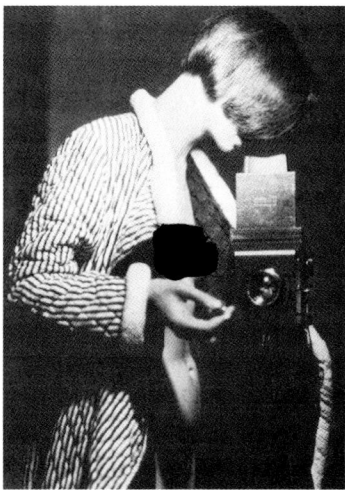

Fig. 2

From Hans-Michael Koetzle, *Photographers A-Z* (Berlin: Taschen Books, 2011), censored book sold in Cairo, original photograph Erwin Blumenfeld, *Nude Under Wet Silk* (1935), p. 42.

Fig. 3

From Hans-Michael Koetzle, *Photographers A-Z* (Berlin: Taschen Books, 2011), censored book sold in Cairo, original photograph Marianne Breslauer, *Autoportrait* (1930), p. 52.

Fanneya (Censorship of Creative Arts), a veiled filter stands between the viewer and the original photographs. The image contents of these publications constitute a representational order in the history of art, mapping out a visual culture embedded in European aesthetic traditions. The photo books are anthology productions that offer a chronological pantheon of artistic maestros that appeals to wide-ranging public audiences. These canonical collections are apt to convey misogynist tendencies commonplace in the culture of popular photographic history and this visual economy uses the human body as a site of ideological struggle, fusing the human body with the body politic.

The original book images in this "found" collection were taken from different photographic practices and aesthetic experiments. Predominately made with analog photographic technologies, the photos were made by some of the most renowned photographers and artists in the history of the medium.[5] Most of them are male and express ideas and explore themes of the self, often through the figure of the female muse. The archive collection includes work by the controversial Japanese photographer Araki (fig.1) and American transgressive diarist Nan Goldin, who embody the abject shock to disturb normative vision. More classical and erotic inflections can be read in the oeuvres of Erwin Blumenfeld, who objectifies the female form as a shadowy translucent body and covers her with a veil that emphasizes the model's breasts. (fig. 2) Other images share more Modernist turns, such as Marianne Breslauer's *Autoportrait*, (fig. 3) where the female photographer poses naked in a mirror looking at the camera in a self-conscious manner. These varied photographic practices speak to a historical constancy in the arts that is aesthetically developed to reinforce the sense of artistic autonomy, often using the naked female form as referent.

The Egyptian censorship office staff members overpainted the original image surface by hand, on each page in each book edition. Montage and collage are an integral part of the photographic history and such image interventions normally suspend the indexical. The Egyptian state censor uses a visual system to alter and transform the bias of such collections of Western-based photographic history. Michel Frizot's extensive *The New History of Photography* contains a handful of images from Western photographers based in the region, ignoring local Arab practitioners despite their historical role in influencing the medium.[6] The censor's acts indicate something is deeply amiss, both in the hierarchy of image politics and in the treatment of the autonomy embodied by the original image. The censor is an anonymous intruder who judges the representational object (naked figure) made by the photographer and gazed at by the viewer. This happens mostly through strange ink-like shapes applied to cover certain body parts or even, occasionally, the whole photograph. Different censorship hands and multiple authors have reworked the originals, covering the image book page surface with different colors in curious, unannounced, and uninvited ways. In other images, more subtle, delicate tracing, or dotting handwork is found, or roughly applied paint to an imaginary dress, undergarment, or bikini. In other images, such handiwork may give way to thick black blocks, or just arbitrary blobs to cover the naked body. Both genders are in fact covered to conceal the erotic potential of any forbidden detail. But some photographic images are deemed too excessive to be seen at all: ham-fisted blocks of industrial black tape cover them fully. Curiously, such tape rests over the image much like the blades of a closed camera shutter, and sometimes this tape can actually be peeled back to reveal the hidden, original photograph.

The intriguing variety of gestures used to mask the image could indicate the Egyptian censors' level of fatigue, as on occasion the process looks hurriedly carried out, perhaps in order to complete the daily quota of handcrafted reticence. Equally one can decipher different censors having different styles of practice or signature authorship. In others, the severity of their visual discipline relates to the perceived transgression of the photographer in the image-making. Japanese photographer Araki suffers some of the severest treatment, for his diptych works are reduced to single one-sided displays only. Such heavy-handed acts conceal not just the alleged parts of the anatomy, but the whole image by using black adhesive tape, forsaking the photograph to be locked under a dark oil-like surface, consigned to a black hole. Additional photographs are treated with more respectful, light brushstrokes to maintain the equilibrium between what is seen and unseen with delicate, responsive coloring or creative ink blobs applied on each individual image. The censors' lighter-handed intrusions are almost an embarrassed undertone or whisper—as if not overtly wanting to disturb the gaze or diminish the impact of the original. Sometimes, in the case of color photographs, matching colored inks are used, occasionally blending into the image composition to the point of opaque invisibility or camouflage, as if not overtly wanting to interrupt the viewers' voyeuristic relationship.

Despite this diversity of visual languages involved in the censorship mark making, these new surfaces reveal their own ideological logic to prevent or limit looking. This type of censorship process is a laborious one, a painstaking task to conceal volumes of images individually by hand-painting the book anthologies, often containing hundreds of photographs ahead of public sale. This interruption subverts the photographer's original intentions and what is anticipated by the viewer. And yet, through the distinctive censorship process, a visual strangeness in the images is produced bearing an uncanny resemblance to Modernist art. The Egyptian censorship process may resemble such aesthetic innovations in the arts as only skin deep, because the acts are directed toward the social sphere only, without awareness of wider debates in visual cultural or art history. Indeed, parody or irony cannot be credited to the censorship agents of the Egyptian state who have proven determined to repress freedom of expression by closing down art venues, banning books, and imprisoning photographers. This campaign of censorship determines in a patriarchal fashion what is sayable, seeable, and doable. The bureaucrats have formed images of complex meaning beyond the vision of the original image-makers, many of which can claim to speak to an autonomy of the arts and freedom of expression that liberalizes, albeit with a tinge of misogyny.

Digital Montage in the Meme

The censored photographic images hosted on the website *3dlat* originate from female fashion industries found in Western image culture, but also in more conservative Middle Eastern contexts. The diverse fashion images are circulated on message board posts and are hosted on this Egyptian female only website to offer visions on wide-ranging archetypical, gender-based subjects: cooking, relationships, housework, childcare, lifestyle, and so on. The website predates the era of global social media platforms such as Facebook and operates like an old-fashioned conservative women's magazine with large volumes of followers and internet traffic in the Arab region. Working in networks of closed groups and dedicated to "women's issues," the message boards are supervised by teams of online avatars with maternal pseudonym names. The website's homepage contains a short statement announcing the kind of content to be found on it, including information on housework, "couple relationships," and "hair, skin and everything that matters to increase your beauty, and your wedding night appearance. Plus topics on pregnancy and how to care for your child." (www.3dlat.com, 2016)

The architecture of the website is basic in design, allowing each member to upload images and post commentaries that are overlooked and managed by a community of administrators. Many of these personalities—*Om Tatu, Om Alaa, Om Seif, Shimaa*—have sizeable numbers of followers and discuss diverse issues, offering advice to online members as surrogate mother figures and agony aunts. However, the *3dlat* category of "Elegance and Beauty" comprises posts addressing contemporary and traditional female fashion trends. Often the volunteer blogger will repost content on a clothing item of particular interest and will find an online image to best illustrate it. The source images are scavenged from the internet, usually in Western stock photography image banks, but also in more Islamic styled fashions emerging from Turkey, which dominates the Middle Eastern female fashion industry. Before the contributor will upload the photograph, she will first censor it in digital software, frequently Photoshop, before reposting to the *3dlat* web forum. Each of the individual contributor members are striving to use distinct aesthetic styles of censorship in the digital manipulation of the image in order to complement the type of clothing and gather more online followers. After altering the image, the volunteer contributor will put her signature on the image, like a watermark, as if she is the author of a critical hybrid artistic image. Furthermore, the signature is also meant to identify the distinct style of the contributor as author of the fashion tip for the web community, while the followers, in turn, will often vote different merit awards to a valued post. The merit badges are wide-ranging to include "best Photoshop manipulation" or even "ideal mother."[7] Therefore, these Islamic influencers can appear to speak for and to women in Egypt and across the wider region.

The *3dlat* website attracts volumes of posts in the "Elegance and Beauty" section alone, comprising a vast array of bizarre fashion images, sourced on the Internet from various user-friendly websites and manipulated by female iconoclasts. This particular process and the conservative Islamic position appear to propose a paradoxical space for Egyptian women to express themselves as drawn to fashion, either as more sexualized or as geared to concealment of the body in public spaces, including the internet. Given the patriarchal nature of Egyptian society, and the limitations of gender relations, working-class women use these message boards to open up debate that relates to their lived lives while at the same time serving hegemonic power. Often the discussions on the message boards offer advice and support on themes considered superficially feminine in a local situation. Within these female-led communities, specialist figures have emerged offering advice on the self-image to define what is considered beautiful. In turn, the community of followers award merit badges for fashion advice and post-production photography censorship skills, among other fields. In this online space, personas such as *Om Tatu* (Mother Tatu) have considerable numbers of followers, as she defines aesthetic judgment inflected through conservative values that shapes identity and community. There is a coded visual language at work here, as Photoshop filters transform original photographic images. This social censorship restricts the visual representation of women in strange ways that can seem to lampoon Modernist avant-garde art practice. The vernacular quality of the images produced by the volunteer censors provides a window onto visual cultures of non-Enlightenment aesthetics. As commented by *Om Tatu*, who has a "Diamond Merit" badge for her Photoshop censorship work: "I received my Medal for Photoshop because of my accuracy in what I cover and what I leave out. I cover women's faces or their cleavage if the dress is revealing." (Om Tatu, 2017)

The aesthetic decisions made in covering details with digital software follows two basic censorship principles or intentions. First, naked skin is covered, so clothing can hover on top of malformed human bodies, as the digital tool often paints a strange skin, pattern, or vibrant color on the model's body. (fig. 4) Frequently, the type of pattern or color will attempt to match or harmonize with the fashion clothing itself; the fabric of a white wedding dress can extend over the exposed body as if a strange disease spreads across the body. (fig. 5) Secondly, the intention to conceal exposed parts of the body has another motivation: to hide the face and identity of the model in order to protect her from malevolent forces. This approach is more strictly applied when using Islamic models in fashion images, despite the fact that the face is usually visible. (fig. 6) In other situations the censor blanks out the face to create a strange sci-fi like image—as if to offer a portal or wormhole into another universe. (fig. 7) These two main principles regarding the protection of female modesty and identity are treated and experimented with imaginative visual ways: starbursts, metallic liquid paints, spray paints, or superimposing heads. (fig. 8) The imposed social judgment on the representation of women comes about within a strictly female community, operating within the pervasiveness of globalized image culture. These conservative matriarchy paradigms construct their own appearance of the feminine norm through hierarchical relationships, reaffirming regressive power relations and gender inequalities that condition the possible role of women in contemporary Egyptian society. The popularity of the platform reveals the disequilibrium in image politics where women are hailed: first, by the highly sexualized nature of contemporary fashion imagery and, secondly, through an Islamic version of feminine beauty that is modest and sensually conservative. Two opposing ideas of visual culture meet and compete to shape the future of the image and justify censorship in contemporary Middle Eastern societies.

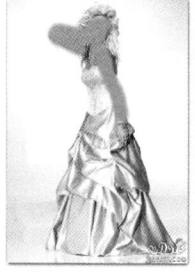 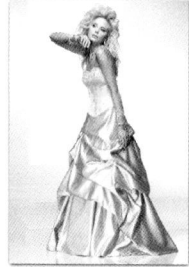

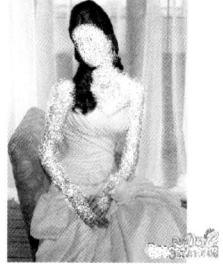 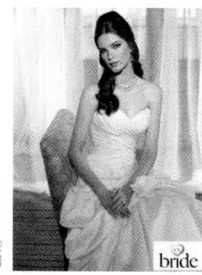

Fig. 4

Original stock photograph unknown, hosted on *World of Eve* [Iraq] (2004) http://www.iraq-angel.com/vb/show-thread.php?t=106042

Fig 5

Original stock photograph unknown, hosted on *UK Bride* [UK] (2014) https://www.ukbride.co.uk/wedding-ideas-product/mori-lee-ivory-strapless-5becee

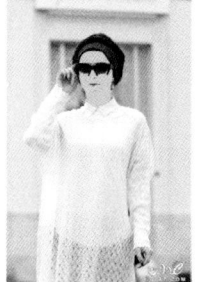 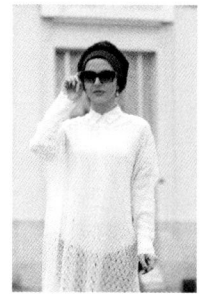

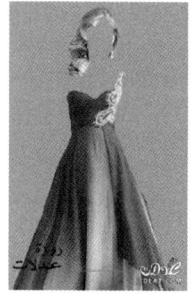 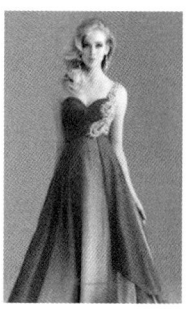

Fig. 6

Original stock photograph hosted on *Yahrenay* [Turkey] (2017) https://www.yahrenay.com/search-result?tag=Dilek%20K%C3%B6ro%C4%9Flu

Fig. 7

Original stock photograph unknown, hosted on *Stoob* (2014) http://www.stob5.com/648850.html

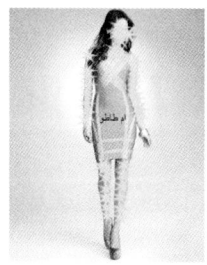 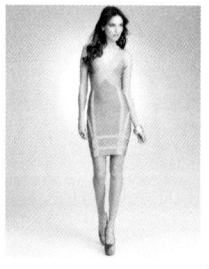

Fig. 8

Original stock photograph unknown, hosted on *El Emarat* [Untied Arab Emirates] (2014). https://women.el-emarat.com/page/21197

These images form part of a conformist internet space to maintain the visual equilibrium of censorship in the increasingly materialized memory space and spectacle of everyday life. Contemporary image culture shapes global society in a drift toward the "slow cancellation of the future." (Fisher, 2013: 189) These doctored photographs are mediated images and reactionary reminders of the values of orthodox censorship, blunt retorts and ill-informed attempts to counter the encounter with the charged consumption of the female form. The Egyptian index of visual culture is marked by an aesthetic time lag so great that censorship is not yet in place to reconcile religious beliefs and cultural sensibilities. A deeper critical framework is absent from these iconoclastic experiments in censorship, as these acts ultimately amount to bowdlerization of the photographic image culture.

Conclusion: Iconoclasm or Aesthetic Censorship

The apparent collision of image politics opens up an intriguing series of misrecognitions passed between the impulse of the original photographer, Egyptian censorship formulas, and the intended public audience. The lack of clear censorship criteria is replaced by puerile artistic motivation that undermines the authority of the original image to serve a social function, to be useful to a higher order of meaning beyond aesthetics.

In these photographic works the light-touch iconoclastic gesture produces new images and meanings to emerge strangely, invested with a kind of radical visual potency of recuperation and reiteration. As Bruno Latour points out, no matter how harsh the iconoclastic condition is, it will create an irreconcilable contradiction between the destruction of mediation and the proliferation of images. Araki's low key diptych image (fig.1) shows two photographs of reclining women looking into the camera. In the original photograph one model is topless and the other wearing a black vest, however the Egyptian censorship version paints on carefully a black vest to camouflage the model up in a mirroring gesture. The original vision is lost, the paired images neutralized, as the abusive frame is nullified from Araki's creepy gaze. The curiosity of these images as "objects of interest" is how they mediate the image culture encounter process, while remaining antagonistic to perception, thought, and act. The censorship impact on the original photograph is designed to reinforce patriarchal control over perception and discipline what is permissible in a given place and time. In the image politics of many Middle Eastern societies, such as Egypt, the human form remains contested, concealed, or obscured in public space, as an apparent natural logic of (in)visibility. Rather than diffuse the photograph, these impediments in ink, paint, or digital software tools imbue the viewer's imagination to accrue a strange visual resonance. The censored photographic images are laden with hidden and attendant meanings, to interconnect the physical world with the mental image, the conscious and the unconscious. Cultural sensibility exists in tacit forms and is understood by the general public through subtle social codes to control the visual in public space.

These coverings create a haunting presence on the original photographic images, as anonymous administrators frustrate the gaze and direct it to what you can or cannot see and through this they fuse a sensual aura around the image. Indeed, the nature of censorship itself is frustration and this denial is imbued with its own erotic capital. Despite the dominant role of the image in vernacular life in Egypt, photography remains a marginal critical tool. Islamic cultural sensibilities have toiled to align the polysemy power of the photographic medium to traditional beliefs, in particular the mimetic representation of the human form, as the medium has been associated with the colonial domination and construction of empire. Historically, the visual image played a complicated role in Arab culture, as primary focus has been awarded to the written word or non-figurative aesthetics found in Islamic architecture. In addition, religion continues to have a central role in everyday life and in apparatuses of the Egyptian state.

The altered images discussed here—the result of state control of publications and online communities doctoring fashion images—are part of an archipelago of censorship in Muslim dominated countries that divides public and private sensibilities along moral lines. Contemporary photography in the Middle East and North Africa has to navigate between two prevailing forces: deconstructing Orientalist representations and the structures of patriarchal power. Only then can photography not only speak for women but also to women in order to develop indigenous systems of visual discourse on image politics in the region. The debate about the Islamic hijab as either a marker of female oppression or a culturally specific practice of piety is generally a reductive argument. The neo-colonialist fad of "Chador Art" in contemporary Western culture continues to fetishize and embolden exotic inflections of woman, harems, concubines, and *houris*. In this sense, double censorship obstacles exist that police the public versus private layers of Egyptian society with the image playing a key role. What is needed to develop critical discourses on the forms of hidden truth is an intertwining between the operations of art and the geopolitics of image circulation and its reception. The innate polysemy of the photograph is flexible enough to morph forms and underpin social relations in diverse cultures. The aesthetics of iconoclasm censorship is not all these doctored images reveal about negative freedoms.

Notes

1. The history of photography in the non-Western world should not be read reductively through the logic of instrumentality, nor be reduced to a mere reflection of Orientalist ideology. There was hardly sufficient photography linked to an indigenous visual tradition to establish ideological autonomy of photography at the time. Iranian ruler *Nasir-Al-Din Shah* used grand photographic portraiture scenes to impose his absolute power, using the fusion of image and authority to enforce his regime. Such visual politics rested on the idea of the divine, the specialness of the religious dimension to merge representation with patriarchy.

2. An *odalisque* (Turkish: Odalık, meaning room person) was a chambermaid or a female attendant in a Turkish seraglio or harem, in particular to assist the court ladies in the household of the Sultan. Later this figure became eroticised by European travelers and depicted in romanticized paintings.

3. *Houris* are beings in Islam, described in English translations as "full-breasted companions of equal age [or well-matched]," "lovely eyed," or "modest gaze" virgins of paradise, denoting humans and jinn who enter *Jannah* (paradise) after being recreated anew in the hereafter. The word itself occurs four times in the Qur'an, always in the plural. One curious exception to this conservative dress code is the Iranian tradition of painting miniature nudes.

4. The archive of photographs was taken from a total of three publications: *Photographers A-Z* (Taschen Books), *100 Contemporary Artists* (Taschen Books), and *The Photo Book: A History* (vol. 1, Phaidon Press). Most images in the archive come from the first source, a Taschen compendium of mostly twentieth-century works arranged in biographical order. All of these books were available in limited numbers in branches of *Diwan*, a bookstore found across Cairo.

5. Many of the photographic artists in the books are well known, including *Nobuyoshi Araki, David Bailey, David LaChapelle, Helmut Newton, Robert Mapplethorpe, Cindy Sherman, Irving Penn, Bert Stern, Larry Sultan, Mario Testino, Wolfgang Tillmans, Andy Warhol, Bruce Weber, Weegee,* and *Gary Winogrand.*

6. Female Palestinian photographer *Karimeh Abbud* (1893–1940) is an example of a photo artist from the region. Other eminent photographers include Van Leo, a Cairo-based Armenian photographer who worked mainly as a studio portrait photographer. In recent years, the *Arab Image Foundation* in Beirut has saved the legacy of photography in the region and rewritten the historical narrative in this regard.

7. The merit awards consist of many categories that reflect the dynamic range of the website. Some of the most contested merit badges include: Special Themes, Best Member of the Year, Supervision, Order of Chef, Ideal Mother, Distinguished Writer, Photoshop, Special Administration, and Support of Justice.

Bibliography

Malek Alloua, *The Colonial Harem*, trans. Myrna Gozdich (Minneapolis: University of Minneapolis, 1986).

Gerry Badger and Martin Parr, *The Photobook A History*, vol. 1 (London: Phaidon. 2004).

Ali Behdad, *Camera Orientalis, Reflections on Photography of the Middle East* (Chicago: University of Chicago Press, 2016).

Mark Fisher, *Ghosts of My Life, Writings on Depression, Hauntology and Lost Futures* (London: Zero Books, 2013).

Michel Fizot, *A New History of Photography* (Berlin: Konemann, 1999).

Hans-Michael Koetzle, *Photographers A-Z* (Berlin: Taschen Books, 2011).

Bruno Latour, "A Few Steps Toward an Anthropology of the Iconoclastic Gesture," *Science in Context*, 10,1, (Spring 1997): 63–84.

Bruno Latour, "What Is Iconoclash? Or Is There a World Beyond the Image Wars?," in *Iconoclash, Beyond the Image-Wars in Science*, eds Bruno Latour and Peter Weibel (Cambridge, Mass.: MIT Press, 2002), 14–37.

Jacques Rancière, *The Emancipated Spectator* (London: Verso, 2009).

Allan Sekula, "The Body and the Archive," *October,* 39, (Winter, 1986): 3–64.

http://www.hrw.org/reports/2005/mena1105/4.htm (accessed January 10, 2016).

Om Tatu, "Elegance and Beauty," *3DLAT,* September 4, 2014, https://vb.3dlat.net/showthread.php?t=194347 (accessed December 5, 2016).

An Archive of Intensities: Vava's Video

Edwin Carels

Over the last two decades, our attention has increasingly come under the spell of electronic stimuli such as the smart phone, the tablet, television, and the Internet, often all at once. This constant urge to adopt to new technologies is also reflected in the academic world, where scholars in "media archaeology"—a quite recent strand of research— have expressed a critical attitude toward this continuous insistence on novelty and progress. One of the key characteristics of media archae- ology is that it demonstrates a concern for a non-linear and non-tele- ological approach; its vantage point is theoretical, rather than histori- cal.[1] Although media archaeology is still identified more with academic writing than with creating or curating art, most scholars also agree that media archaeology is as much a practice as it is a theoretical approach, and that it is something that should rather be executed or performed than being constructed as a narrative. Media archaeology needs to be understood as an explanation for the digital revolution, rather than a regressive reaction against it. Media archaeologists question the epis- temological break between analogue and digital culture by reverting to the multiple, sometimes shared origins of both technologies, and by mirroring the current multimedia frenzy to earlier moments in popu- lar culture marked by a similar creative confusion. This focus is not so much meant to unearth an overlooked type of logical progression, as it is to remind us that history at different stages can reflect different levels of complexity and perfection.

Informed by these ideas, the case-study presented here address- es the practice of a solitary man who collected analogue audio-visual equipment. The intention behind his collecting folly was probably to create a museum, even though this initiative never came about. After his passing, however, his granddaughter invited contemporary art- ists to visit his home and to select some items to be "recycled" into artworks. This resulted in the exhibition project entitled *Herzamelen* [Recollecting], at the occasion of which this contextualizing essay was written, based on a short documentary recording found on a VHS tape amidst the thousands of items left behind by the collector.[2] (fig. 1) This recording might offer a clue to understanding the rationale behind a seemingly anachronistic constellation of media equipment as found in situ, in combination with numerous art-historical reproductions framed and hung on the walls of the various spaces.

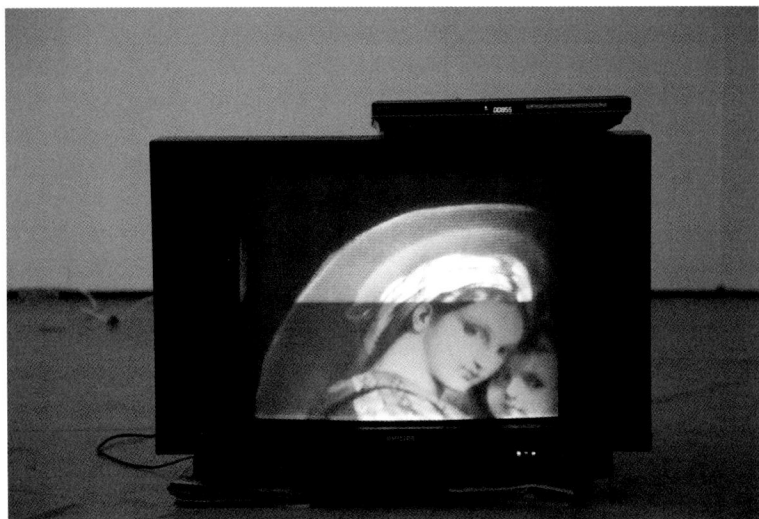

Amateur VHS tapes usually fare poorly at flea markets. You can never directly check what is on them, they take up a lot of space, and they are unattractive to handle. Also, it always takes hours to verify whether there's more on it than the label indicates. Owing to the much easier to distribute MP4 format, the fate of a man from the Belgian town of Eeklo, Samuel Verstraete (°1926 †2013), suddenly surfaced. Originally, the recording was on a VHS tape that laid dormant on a shelf for many years. Without the curiosity of his granddaughter, an art school student, the existence of this man commonly known as "Vava" and his collection would never have been shared with quite so many people. The story of Vava remains, of course, a private history, even after his death. Yet that one videotape from his legacy deserves a public life, not only as an intuitive reverie about the vulnerability of electronic home movies, but also as an artefact full of references to the history of audio-visual media—as a spontaneous piece of media art by an outsider artist.

After a short moment of white noise, the first colored images appear—initially out of focus, followed by a slight shift of the frame, after which the images become sharp. Such unstable, shaky images recur throughout the video. Vava shot the first images while he was outside, standing quite near the local church tower. The clock on the tower indicates that it is a quarter to twelve, so we know what time it is, but we do not know which day, which month, which year. Most likely it is early spring, for we hear birds sing while most trees are still bare. A few minutes into the video, we see a forsythia shrub in full bloom. It must be April. The tower is easily recognizable as that of St. Vincent's Church, in the center of Eeklo. And yet the noise of this town only faintly resonates. We find ourselves somewhere on a courtyard next to a long row of residential garages. And there are also some snippets of radio to be heard in the background. After a minute and a half, there is a sudden jump in the location, and we are inside, in a workshop full of appliances and working tools. The music is now fully present, which again gives us something to hold onto in order to reconstruct the history of this videotape.

Abruptly, we fall halfway into the ballad *Eternal Flame,* a song that has been covered several times. This is the original version by The Bangles, an American band consisting of women only. The album that this song was on appeared in October 1988, so the video recording cannot be older than that. But it was not until February 1989 that *Eternal Flame* came out as a single in Europe and enjoyed most air-time, also in Belgium, peaking in the charts in the month of April. If Vava would have begun recording a quarter of an hour later, we might have heard the radio news and the recording could have been dated much more accurately.

When Vava made his video recording, many revolutions took place, even though they remained far in the background. The spring of 1989 was certainly a momentous time in world history. In April it was exactly three years after the shockwave caused by the Chernobyl nuclear catastrophe and just three months before the protests on Tiananmen Square, Beijing, on June 4, 1989. On that same day, the Solidarność [Solidarity] movement triumphantly won the election in Poland, creating an unforeseen domino effect: the fall of Communism in one country in Eastern Europe after another. In April 1989, two decades after the Prague Spring, Europe stood on the threshold of drastic changes, both ideologically and economically.

Of course, the date of recording could also be a spring day in the 1990s or even more recent. *Eternal Flame* became an evergreen and there are plenty of radio stations that would play songs from the 1980s on a daily basis. The exact time of recording cannot be deduced from the video images either—except that there is no trace of digital technology anywhere, despite the fact that it is clear that the images were shot in part in a workshop filled with audio-visual equipment. Vava's tape also shows a tear-off calendar in his kitchen, which refers to the second day of a month, but it is impossible to read which month (due to the poor definition of the image). What's more, a tear-off calendar does not necessarily provide the correct date, for not everyone will think of removing a page each and every day. Time seems to stand still in Vava's world. The appearance of this very common type of calendar—called

De Druivelaar—also hardly changed since it first entered Flemish households in 1915, so this doesn't provide us with any better indication of the year. (In 2012, for the first time, an electronic edition was published, which immediately became popular among smartphone users with a sense of nostalgia, perhaps because this digital version remained stubbornly traditional in its outlook.)

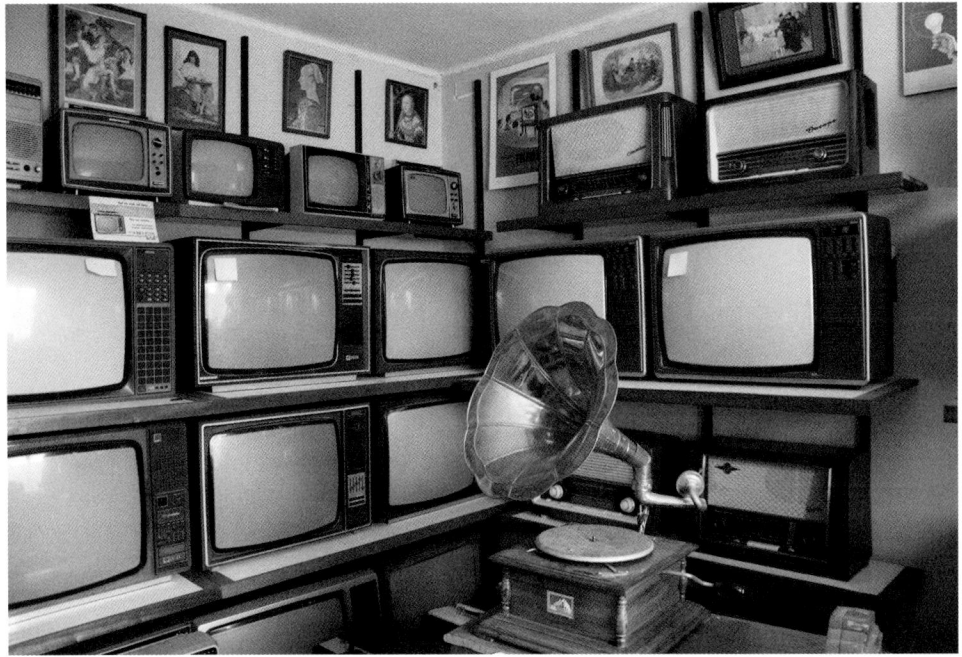

There is analogue equipment in all the rooms and storage places that Vava filmed: old radios, televisions, amplifiers, tape recorders, antennas, lamps, and electronic devices of all kinds. (fig. 2) But with his zoom lens, Vava underlines his appreciation of the many historical fine art prints that pop up everywhere between the racks full of equipment. They are all framed reproductions of classical paintings. Van Eyck's *Portrait of Margaret van Eyck* (1439), for example, hangs next to the *Portrait of a Woman with a Winged Bonnet* (1435–1440) by Rogier van der Weyden. (fig. 3) In addition to these two Renaissance works, we also see a marvelous Maria image from the early 20th century next to a reproduction of a smaller, colored wood engraving of Madonna and Child by an unknown master from the Lower Rhine region (circa 1430). (fig. 4) And on the same wall there is also a photograph of what seems to be a 17th-century canvas depicting a noble lady, her hand pointing to her heart. Next, the camera pans over a regiment of old radios stored on a shelf above the frames. The historical mix is much less eclectic in this

Fig. 2

Interior view of one of the many rooms where Vava installed his collection. Image courtesy of Emma Vanhille, 2015.

"Disassembled" Images

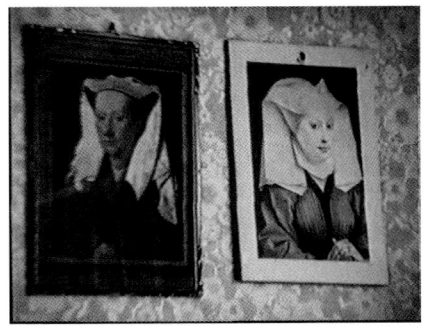

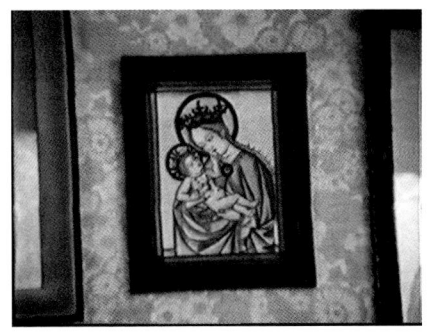

shot. They are all antique receivers with finely crafted, wooden exteriors in warm colors. The device that transmits the pop music from The Bangles into the room does not show up in the recording. Apparently, the cameraman's attention doesn't go to the working tools, but to decorative elements: the viewfinder of the camera imposes a ranking on the interior and provides clear emphasis. So there is a methodical order underlying the apparent chaos. Whole rows of similarly shaped plastic boxes with multicolored lids contain small parts; and against another wall, there are bins with numerous small compartments for the systematic ordering of even smaller components. Elsewhere in his house, in various places, Vava kept shelves with dozens and dozens of car radios. Most of them can also play audio-cassettes, a format that was produced until 2010, when in the US the last car equipped with a cassette player left the factory.

In the spring of 1989, *Eternal Flame* was issued on 7inch vinyl and CD-single, as well as on the so-called "cassingle." From a music technology angle, this year marked a moment of transition. The cassingle was launched in 1980 to promote Bow Wow Wow's only hit, *C30 C60 C90, Go!*. Riding the Walkman's wave of success, the music cassette seemed to threaten the vinyl industry for a while. But by the end of the decade, the CD took over, needing less volume for much more capacity. In 2001, when Atomic Kitten's version of *Eternal Flame* hit the charts, Napster made it difficult for music publishers by making pop music available on mp3 files for free. In the video, we can only guess which technological source is playing *Eternal Flame*. Vava prefers to focus emphatically on a reproduction of a Maria portrait before he continues filming his studio and then moves on to a next room. "I don't wanna lose this feeling" is heard again; and just as the automatic light meter darkens the image upon leaving the room and then adapts to the bright daylight, the music also ebbs away in perfect synchrony. We don't get to hear any more music or voices during the remainder of the video recording; at most we hear a bit of undefined shuffling about. No sound of breathing can be discerned.

Fig. 3

Screen grab from "Vava's video": framed reproductions of Van Eyck's *Portrait of Margaret van Eyck* (1439) and *Portrait of a Woman with a Winged Bonnet* (1435–1440) by Rogier van der Weyden. Image courtesy of Emma Vanhille, 2016.

Fig. 4

Screen grab from "Vava's video": framed reproduction of a Madonna with Child, anonymous master from Niederrhein (c. 1430). Image courtesy of Emma Vanhille, 2016.

Did Vava capture those picture frames with devout faces of women because he thought that they matched so well with the music? Did he ever think of putting his video online, like so many amateurs who combine their own moving images with their favorite music and find it worthwhile sharing on YouTube? That platform didn't start until the spring of 2005; on April 23, the first video was placed on-line. But by then, the VHS tape was no longer a commonplace medium. Due to digitization, cameras also became increasingly compact. The only glimpse we actually get of Vava is when his reflection pops up while filming a frame with an idyllic female figure, this time in the living room. His fleeting appearance is too unclear to be recognizable, as his head is largely hidden behind the viewfinder. But he clearly has a hefty video camera on his shoulder. After his death, three cameras were found in his home, including one that recorded directly on VHS cassettes: the Professional Stereo Panasonic M10 VHS Camcorder AV Recorder. Such camcorders (camera and recorder in one) entered the market in the early 1980s. We cannot know when Vava bought the camera. It is quite likely that he got it second-hand, as it seemed his mission to give a shelter or, ideally, a second life to the various electronic devices in his collection.

It is therefore most likely that his primary motivation to make the above-described video tape was simply to test the camera; it certainly wasn't to generate an explicit self-portrait. Or did Vava actually intend to document his house or his habitat? But the video doesn't provide a systematic, or exhaustive, exploration of his home. In fact, Vava had two structures at the same address at his disposal, one built behind the other: a house and a workshop/depository. (fig. 5) The upstairs rooms of the house are full of television sets of all types and generations. The

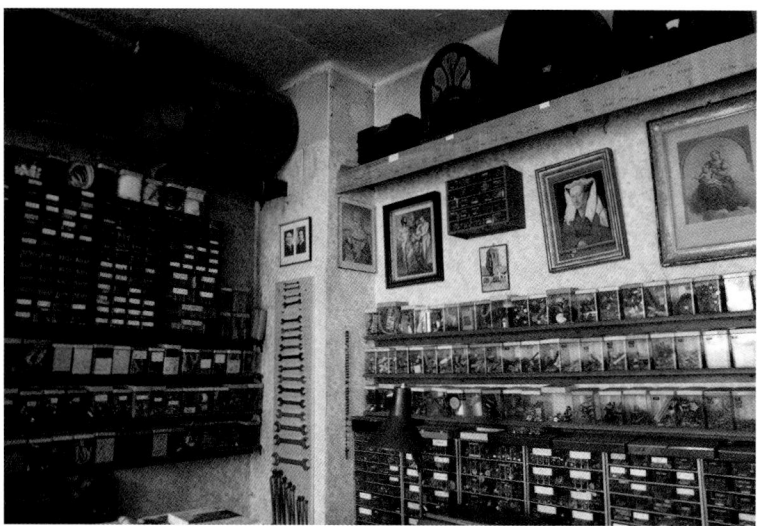

Fig. 5

Interior view of the main workshop where Vava did his repairs. Image courtesy of Emma Vanhille, 2015.

"Disassembled" Images

video recording is anything but systematic, a couple of times it spatially makes big leaps from one building to the other. Which is not really necessary for a simple camera test. What did Vava want to document—deliberately or, rather, unconsciously? What does a video hobbyist generally film? Traditionally, the repertoire of the amateur filmmaker consists of family rituals, domestic coziness, travel impressions, and other photogenic moments. This was the case indeed until video came on the market. For the same type of subjects and poses, usually a Super 8 home-movie camera was used, involving film reels with a length of three minutes only. The arrival of the camera-inserted video-cassette made it possible to record much longer for the same price. A side-effect of the introduction of VHS was that it became much more difficult for a subject to hold a pose, and thus the camera often recorded all the bored moments and less enthusiastic reactions in one go. As observed by the French film historian Roger Odin: the period of the rise of the VHS camera is also the period that divorces increased in frequency (Odin, 2014:20). The masks fell off. But also the beautiful moments were not celebrated again, because they got lost in overlong, overly banal recordings that were no longer appealing to view together.

Which spectator did Vava envisage, if indeed he had anybody in mind at all? With whom did he want to share something? There's no living soul in his house, except for his own furtive silhouette. Did no one else happen to be home at the time of his recording or was he in fact living on his own? Besides a porcelain shepherdess and a mantel clock, the video shows four empty bottles of Westmalle Trappist on the mantelpiece. Is this the household of a bachelor? The man's interests also predominate the living room. On a small, overcrowded desk, there's an old model tape recorder, alongside many magazines and other papers. It is possible to see a few rectangular cassette boxes on top of a cabinet. They have the VCR video format, which was introduced by Philips in 1972 and which by the end of that decade was already replaced by another innovative format, Video 2000.

Among the reproductions of classical paintings hanging in Vava's living room, there are also a few photographs of family members. But the camera quickly passes by them. Instead, Vava concentrates on the framed reproductions of paintings. And, each time, they are idealized representations of women, most often as a mother figure. Vava zooms in on a reproduction of a mother with a young child, hanging pontifically above the mantelpiece. This shot occurs precisely in the middle of the video's playing time, and he will return to this image once more. Between the two shots, he continues the exploration of the living room, revealing his silhouette again in an idyllic scene with two half-naked women. The strong reflection, however, makes it difficult to interpret the image better. The second time that Vava zooms in on the reproduction of Rafael's famous *Madonna della Seggiola* (1514) lasts much longer and is even more explicit. (fig. 6) In an extreme close-up of more than half a minute, the mother and baby Jesus intensely hold on to each other. At the same time, from the corner of their eyes, they focus their gaze on the viewer, as if alluding to a secret, intimate relationship. In this re-production, the painting has lost nearly all of its color, while the figure of John the Baptist got erased as well. Instead of respecting Rafael's remarkable circular composition, the reproduction was put behind an oval passe-partout in a rectangular frame. According to traditional exegesis, John the Baptist symbolizes mankind. What prevails in this version, then, is intimacy, without any notion of some outside world.

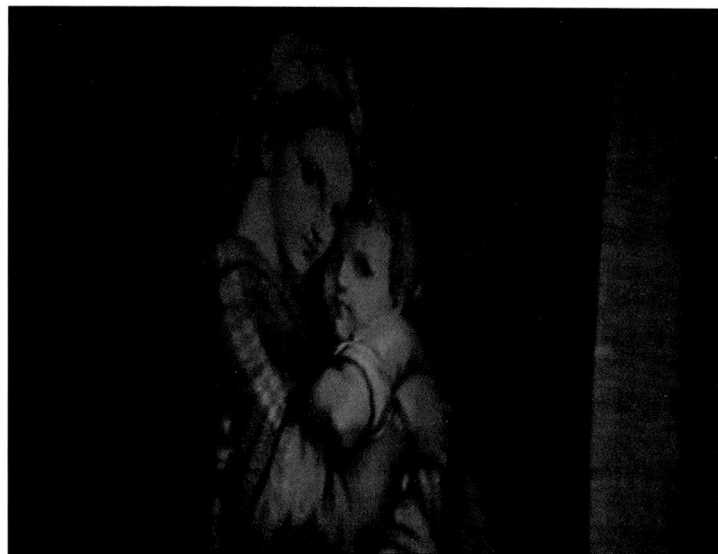

Fig. 6

Screen grab from "Vava's video": framed reproduction of Raphael's *Madonna della Seggiola* (1513–1514). Image courtesy of Emma Vanhille, 2016.

To the outside world, Vava was known as a photographer. At the front of the house he had his own photography shop. But even in his spare time, he was thus always busy producing images. Or rather, as in this video, reproducing reproductions. Vava was clearly interested in all kinds of technological aspects pertaining to the image industry. But in terms of his subjects, he was looking for them very close to home— at least for this video. The physical spaces in the video give a rather claustrophobic impression. It's not an architectural exploration, but an improvised registration of the rooms where he probably felt most at "home." Through his video, Vava evokes a mental space rather than painting a spatially coherent portrait of a house.

In several ways Vava's approach reminds one of that of the German art historian Aby Warburg, who between December 1927 and October 1929 developed an ambitious project in which the mental effort of the viewer was central. He wanted to indicate a number of motifs from art history in a purely visual way, without textual support. He called his ultimate project the *Mnemosyne Atlas*. It remained unfinished when Warburg died in 1929, but this hardly affected its meaning. After all, the *Mnemosyne Atlas* was intended as a tool that could be constantly adapted to the dynamics of new insights or associations. And it remained up to the viewer to rediscover those connections. The atlas consisted of forty wooden, individual panels covered with black cloth. Warburg pinned nearly a thousand photographic reproductions from books, magazines, newspapers, and other sources to the panels. Each panel grouped images according to a specific theme. Warburg wanted to investigate how certain visual motifs repeatedly reappear in different eras and style periods. These migrating, "surviving" image motifs he called *Pathosformeln* [pathos formulas], and thus he implied that there is a collective long-term memory (an "eternal flame"?) at work throughout art history, across all temporal and spatial boundaries.

Warburg began and ended his career studying body language in Renaissance art. According to Ernst Gombrich, the German pioneer hoped that the viewer would respond to the images with the same intensity as he himself had experienced during his research (a quite similar hope was espoused by Erwin Panofsky, Warburg's main successor). (Gombrich, 1970) More recently, the French philosopher Georges Didi-Huberman characterized Warburg's work as "an archive of intensities." (Didi-Huberman, 2001) Considering the many reproductions with which Vava surrounded himself in each room, he too clearly preferred *Pathosformeln*, or what Warburg described elsewhere as "expressive psychic poses." According to Didi-Huberman, Warburg understood that, just as it is essential for a philosopher to avoid *idées fixes*, it was important not to reduce images to a single meaning. That is why Warburg liked to use thumbnails, which allowed him to constantly move the images around. And he chose to work with black-and-white photographic art reproductions, instead of more expensive imitations of artworks. The individual panels of the *Mnemosyne Atlas* functioned for Warburg as a visual guide to a discourse that could be continually adjusted—"powerpoints," *avant la lettre*.

In exploring Vava's deserted world, we could retrace most of the objects from the video somewhere in the house, but usually in different places than at the time of the video. A visit we made to the house after his passing revealed the presence of Renaissance iconography in many more rooms. Only in the rooms found on the ground floor such reproductions were put in a frame behind glass. Elsewhere in the house, Titian's *Venus of Urbino* (1534) or Ingres's *La Grande Odalisque* (1814) hung directly against the wall, or were just lying on the floor, surrounded by boxes of electronics. Thanks to photography, Warburg was able to bring pagan artefacts together with masterpieces from Florence, antique astrological works from the Middle East with Lutheran art, and the sacred dances of the Hopi Indians with a Mary Pickford film still or an advertising photograph from a newspaper.

Over the past decade, there has been a striking revival of interest in the *Mnemosyne Atlas*, among historians, cultural philosophers, as well as curators. Perhaps the well-established use of websites and search engines has something to do with this. Nowadays, algorithms determine which collection of related images appears under a certain title or denominator on the screen, and this usually includes a number of absurd combinations as well. Warburg's associative juxtapositions of *Pathosformeln* had nothing to do with arbitrariness, however. Studying images starts with comparing images and thus collecting images. Since the breakthrough of the Internet, we can hardly imagine how expensive and time-consuming that process could be. In an era in which any type of information or visual material can be summoned at any time in a snap, images are also much less cherished while cuttings are no longer kept.

Apart from his collection of devout or at least highly idealized images of women that he displayed all over the house, Vava also cultivated a second, more discreet collection. The search term for this one was clearly "Venus" rather than "Madonna," and the emphasis was mainly on expressive *physical* poses. In the same room where Rafael's famous *Madonna della Seggiola* so emphatically demanded attention, there was also a built-in closet space in which Vava stored his video and audio tapes (not featured in the video recording). On the inside of the neutrally looking closet doors, painted in a rosy sand color, we saw a very different archive of intensities during our tour of the house: images of nude women are stuck to each door. All of the cut-out, favorite models showcase a 100% natural physique, in poses that are hardly more indiscriminate than the Venus paintings from many centuries ago. Their smile is only so much less inhibited. The pin-ups in color and black-and-white probably date from the 1970s, the heyday of sexual liberation in Flanders, as reflected in such weekly magazines as KWIK *magazine*. Because of the presence of the logo, we know with certainty that at least one woman was a clip from that magazine.

Those paper female companions cannot be regarded as merely youthful sins. Born in 1929, Vava was sixteen years old when World War II was over and American soldiers left behind their pin-up magazines on the old continent. There were, of course, many saucy stereo photos and postcards on the old continent prior to that; but it was not until the 1940s that the pin-up became more widely established, first in America and then, with some years of delay, in Europe. In Aalst in 1954, Louis Paul Boon started to work on the numerous categories of his famous *Feminatheek* [library of women], a collection of clippings from international "specialized" magazines. Vava worked much more spontaneously and therefore less structured, with no clear categories or compositional concerns. He used to adorn some furniture by sticking such pictures directly on to them, as a sort of graffiti. Not only the closet doors in the living room, but also the doors on the inside of his dark room were embellished in this way. This combination of furniture and cut-out art has existed since the Victorian era. Around 1880 the reproducibility of images increased explosively for the first time and illustrations became less expensive, and this not only stimulated literacy on a larger scale but also the collecting of images. This happened in albums and also on so-called "scrap screens," room screens decorated with a collage of clippings. In the 20th century, collage art in the hands of avant-gardists got a more critical, sometimes even subversive connotation. But at the same time, the use of this artform continued to live on as outsider art or simply folk art and family art.

The need to collect is inherently a psychological reflex. Was Vava a neurotic, a-social hoarder, like so many victims of voyeuristic TV programs that have become increasingly popular in recent years? Hoarding is symptomatic of obsessive compulsive disorder, or compulsive behavior. If the interior of Vava's domestic domain was certainly overcrowded, it also represented an organized chaos. From the basement and garage to the attic and in all of the rooms on the floors in between, he still seemed to have the situation under control, taken into consideration the many storage drawers in the workshop, the neatly arranged manuals in the room next to the photo shop, the carefully filled-out labels on all appliances, all displayed by kind and so on. It is clear that Vava loved images as well as the devices for producing and distributing them. Although his home showed all the characteristics of *horror vacui*, it also suggested an intriguing dialectic between the various audio-visual media on the one hand and a reasonably unambiguous, idealistic collection of images on the other. Over the years, this photographer by trade turned his biotope into a media archaeological ecosystem, in which hopefully he felt most at home. As a local variation on the French Facteur Cheval, who repeatedly picked up stones during his postal rounds to expand the masonry of his hand-built *Palais Idéal*, Vava focused on electronic devices which he knew he might be able to resuscitate with his own ingenuity.

As with the typical hoarder, Vava shared the vision that so many "useful" items should not be thrown away. As evidenced by the careful notes on the labels on each device, he did also repair the things that he picked up at flea markets. Vava dealt with things in the same way as propagated with increasing emphasis since the 1960s by the liberal philosopher Jaap Kruithof. This professor from Ghent spent his whole career campaigning against the disposable mentality, the globalization of the economy, and the exploitation of Third World countries. Gradually, environmental issues also received his attention. His lifelong annoyance at consumer society culminated at the end of his career in a comprehensive indictment: *Het neoliberalisme* [Neoliberalism] (2000). In the run-up to that book, Kruithof published three of his collections with columns and lectures written in a slightly lighter tone: *Omgaan met de dingen* [Dealing with things] (1991), *Ingaan op de dingen* [Getting into things] (1992) and *Doorgaan met de dingen* [Getting on with things] (1994), each time using as subtitle "On the Conduct of Modern Western Man." The latter in the series was also on Vava's bookshelf, entirely appropriate as a second-hand book, with on the back flap a price sticker from the *Kringloopwinkel* [thrift shop]. In addition to all kinds of pulp novels and books on religion, health, history, and many more varieties, Vava's numerous bookshelves also featured classics by Robert Musil, Primo Levi, Herbert Marcuse (*One-Dimensional Man*), Bill Bryson (*A Small History of Nearly Everything*), etc. In Noam Chomsky's *Power and Terror: Post-9/11 Talks and Interviews*, Vava noted on the title page: "From Peter, Dec. 2011. Worth reading."

On closer inspection, Vava cannot have been such an unworldly figure, or at least not as regressive as his interior domain would suggest. But is it possible to deduce a person's spirit from a few meters of books? We do not know if he read them, and if he did, whether or not he liked them. Maybe they were simply provided to him as gifts? Similarly, does a series of DVDs betray the cultural taste of a person, just like it is possible for media companies nowadays to distill a useful profile from a consumer's online "click behavior"? Between a few classics from Chaplin, a handful of British crime series, a Betty Boop compilation and some more widely divergent titles, we also discovered a DVD from the film *The Lives of Others* [*Das Leben der Anderen*] (2006), a reconstruction of life in East Berlin around 1984 as influenced by the Stasi (secret police). The director probably chose the year 1984 as a nod to George Orwell's novel *1984* (1949). It wasn't until 1989, with the fall of the Berlin Wall, that the large-scale and far-reaching ways in which the Stasi aimed to control and record the lives of all citizens became known. Back then, they worked with analogue equipment. In the meantime, the possibilities for monitoring and tracking have increased exponentially and have even become internalized psychologically, even in the entire "free" West. On 1 February 1989, the first commercial television channel in Flanders was launched: VTM, an instant success. Since 1999, the reality-series format *Big Brother* promoted television voyeurism to popular leisure time entertainment with worldwide imitations. Somewhere in that period, between 1989 and 1999, Vava must have withdrawn from it all. Was it just time to retire? Was it commercially no longer feasible to keep a business open for analogue photography?

Vava did not collect any more recent equipment with chips and digital circuits, which, after all, eluded his technical skills.

Did Vava address the handwritten notes on the many labels he applied to his repaired devices to himself or to an ideal visitor? Did he really hope to communicate with a wider audience through his collections, or did he simply anticipate, as with some sparse comments in his books, his future memory loss? The fairly organized way in which Vava stocked his collection suggests that he did indeed hope to "continue with things," perhaps even start a museum. Less than a year after the death of Jaap Kruithof, in 2009, the House of Alijn exhibited his entire collection of artefacts and knick-knacks, just as they were found in the philosopher's basement, on humble wooden shelves. After that, the entire inventory (or "installation") was included in the permanent collection of MAS (Museum aan de Stroom, Antwerp). Vava's collection was considerably more extensive, making it at once more vulnerable as well. But it wasn't entirely orphaned either. Individual items have now been (re)adopted by members of his family, by collectors, and by a young generation of artists.

Whatever his intentions may have been, Vava, consciously or not, managed to communicate his "archive of intensities" through his private museum (Didi-Huberman, 2001: 144). The spontaneous video exploration of his house became the ideal capsule allowing Vava posthumously to transcend his highly personal time-and-space bubble. Rather than his collection of devices and appliances, it is his recording of them that resounds strongest. It resulted in a flow of images driven by psychic automatisms, by his "optical unconsciousness,", to borrow a term from Walter Benjamin. (Benjamin, 1931/1980: 203)

With a striking jump cut from a storage room somewhere in Vava's private domain, we suddenly return to the ground floor for the last thirty seconds of the video, ending up in the front room of the house where the shop space used to be. The counter is almost empty, except for all kinds of things and papers lying on top of it. A large oval, empty frame hangs on the wall. Probably its gilded carving once held a mirror. There's a painter's easel just in front of it, on top of which there's a large grey card, as used by photographers as a standard to measure light. Positioned in front of the card, there is a portrait photo of an elderly woman, in a passe-partout but without a frame. Is she his mother? His wife? His eternal flame? A video like a devotional candle. The camera explores the space for a moment, but the movement comes to a halt just before the shop's display window comes into view, followed by the bright daylight of the outside world. And then, during the last two seconds of his video, the voice of Vava suddenly appears saying: "Yes, it is still without sound."

Notes

1. In 2013 Wanda Strauven mapped out the different strands in media archeology, categorized by generations, by intellectual hotspots, and according to more topical criteria. She sees at least four aspects that can be considered to form a shared agenda in all strands of media archeology: the relation between history and theory, the vital connection between research and art, the central role of the archive, and "lastly, and most importantly," a rethinking of temporalities. See: Strauven, 2013.

2. The first instalment of the exhibition took place in Ghent from April 29 until May 1, 2016. The second instalment (*Herzamelen 2*) took place in Eeklo from May 21 until May 29, 2017. Both exhibitions were initiated and curated by Emma Vanhille.

Bibliography

Walter Benjamin, "A Short History of Photography" (1931), in *Classic Essays on Photography*, ed. Alan Trachtenberg (New Haven: Leete's Island Books, 1980), 199–216.

Georges Didi-Huberman, "Aby Warburg et l'archive des intensités", *Études photographiques*, 10 (November 2001): 144–168.

Ernst H. Gombrich, *Aby Warburg: An Intellectual Biography* (London: Warburg Institute, 1970).

Roger Odin, "The Home Movie and Space of Communication" (2014), in *Amateur Filmmaking-The Home Movie, the Archive, the Web*, eds Laura Rascaroli, Gwenday Young, Barry Monahan (London: Bloomsbury, 2014), 15–26.

Wanda Strauven, "Media Archaeology: Where Film History, Media Art, and New Media (Can) Meet," in *Preserving and Exhibiting Media Art*, eds Julia Noordergraaf, Cosetta G. Saba, Barbara Le Maître, and Vinzen Hediger (Amsterdam: Amsterdam University Press, 2013), 59–79.

Mining Allan Sekula: Four Exercises

Barbara Baert

> My wish was to see no shape in the ocean, and not to have to come to any decision as to what it was, but that's impossible, because I, too, was a shape which others might recoil from or aim for or collide with. (Marías, 2016: 192)

This essay sprang from reflections on the space between the theoretical work of W.J.T. Mitchell and Allan Sekula (1951–2013).[1] I gradually broadened my research to the way in which an artist's oeuvre, and in particular *The Dockers' Museum* (2010–2013), invites us to interrogate the visual medium and the collection of traces from a dialog with philosophers, anthropologists, iconologists, and novelists. This led to four exercises on the status of the collector-artist and his embrace of what I would call *L'objet sélectionné*: collection from the wound (1), the artist and *Besonnenheit* (2), creativity in the *grotto* (3), and, finally, kairotic energy (4).

These interspaces are still in motion and by no means imply a stable approach of Sekula's oeuvre. Meanwhile, a strong *genius loci* is watching over them: that of the poet, collector, and activist; an artist beyond each category and his Sisyphean *The Dockers' Museum*.

Exercise #1. Collecting from the Wound

> It's true that when we get caught in the spider's web—between the first chance event and the second—we fantasize endlessly and are, at the same time, willing to make do with the tiniest crumb, with hearing him—as if he were the time itself that exists between those two chance events—smelling him, glimpsing him, sensing his presence, knowing that he is still on our horizon, from which he has not entirely vanished, and that we cannot yet see, in the distance, the dust from his fleeing feet. (Marías, 2014: 346)

"Disassembled" Images

The Dockers' Museum is an almost indescribable phenomenon; Hilde Van Gelder and her team provided it with an impressive discourse that gave a vocabulary to the *Gesamtkonzept*, while plunging into the soul of the collection: the engagement behind the jewel that gives the story greatness. (Van Gelder, 2015) This inspired me, in this first exercise, to seek parallel worlds of "collection" as an idea. Who is the collector, what underworld gives the object the status of an "object of desire"?

I will discuss two examples: one from the world of fiction and one from that of non-fiction. In her novel *The Volcano Lover: A Romance*, Susan Sontag introduces the collector's desire on the basis of the well-known Pygmalion myth narrated by Ovid:

> What does he do? How does he bring her to life? Very cautiously. He wants her to become conscious, and, holding the rather simple theory that all knowledge comes from the senses, decides to open her sensorium. Slowly, slowly. He will give her, to begin with, just one of the senses. And which does he pick? Not sight, noblest of the senses, not hearing—well, no need to run through the whole list, short as it is. Let's hasten to relate that he first awards her, perhaps ungenerously, the most primitive sense, that of smell. (Perhaps he does not want to be seen, at least not yet). [...] There are odors she does not smell, because she is in a garden—or because she is in the past. [...] She begins to dream, this consciousness-that-smells, of how she could retain the odors, by storing them up inside herself, so she would never lose them. And this is how, later, space emerges, inner space only [...] Every pleasure—and smelling, whatever she smells, is pure pleasure—becomes an experience of anticipated loss. She wants, if only she knew how, to become a collector. (Sontag, 1993: 46–47)

The lover wishes to shape his beloved, to shape her into his ideal. He instructs her, loves her, indeed, he brings her back to life. This re-awakening is described as the opening of her sensorium. The lover first gives the girl the most primal, but perhaps also the most sensuous of the senses: the sense of smell. It is scent that gives her consciousness and desire. It is scent that opens up an inner space to receive all the rest. It is scent that makes her a collector.

Susan Sontag proposes the idea that the sensorium is radically tied to love and the desire to collect, to know. Senses, love, and knowledge seem to form an archetypical node. In this passage, Sontag suggests a hierarchy that contradicts the ancient model of Plato and Aristotle, for whom epistemology begins with sight (rather than smell), and descends by way of seeing, hearing, smell, taste, and touch (*visus, auditus, olfactus, gustus,* and *tactus*). The Greeks considered truth an idea (*eidos*) having a visible form. Knowledge (*eidenai*) is a matter of seeing, as theory is related to theater. (On the hierarchy of the senses, see Nordenfalk, 1984: 135–154; Jonas, 1982: 135–156)

This creator-collector, however, is instinctive (he lets himself be guided by smell), where desire, sexuality, and impulse are at work. Instincts combined with impulses are also Allan Sekula's drives. I would like to place *The Dockers' Museum* paradigmatically at the "base of the sensorium" where energy is still linked to a primal propulsion of desire—in brief, stemming from the emotional humus of existence.

This brings me to my second example. In his essay collection *The Naive and Sentimental Novelist* (2010), Orhan Pamuk writes that he had been working on a museum in the Çukurcuma neighborhood of the city. It is housed in a townhouse built in 1897. But this is no ordinary museum; it is a museum based on an entirely new concept.

Museums as we know them today developed from humanist princely collections. Aside from the usual art objects, members of the nobility collected all sorts of other curiosities: from ostrich eggs to Siamese twins in formaldehyde. Later these princely collections, generally purged of such curiosities, came into the possession of public institutions, such as the Louvre. Pamuk identifies two types of collectors: the proud collectors who like to show off their collections and are eager to exhibit them (these predominate in Western civilizations); and the bashful collectors, who squirrel away all the things they have amassed (mostly coming from unmodern civilizations). The second group collects in response to a particular compulsion or sadness. So, in the lands of the bashful, collections are not associated with useful knowledge, but with wounds. Pamuk's museum collection belongs naturally to the second category, but it goes even further:

> My studio was gradually filling up with old medicine bottles, bags of buttons, National Lottery tickets, playing cards, clothes and kitchen utensils. Intending to use them in my novel, I was imagining situations, moments, and scenes suited to these objects, many of which (such as a quince grater) I had bought on impulse. (Pamuk, 2010: 121)

As we know, this led to the story of the great and unforgettable love affair between the girl Füsun and the young Kemal in the Istanbul of the late 1970s and early 1980s. Pamuk's Museum of Innocence involves another pact: a pact between the real object and fiction. His museum *is* the interspace. The idea of giving genuine museological stature to the pact and the interspace—the desire for restoration, the history of images as quests for the one original image—testifies to an immeasurable emotion.

Allan Sekula's objects, which unmistakably belong to the second group, must be studied in the topography of the quince grater; in the underworld of smell and in the empathic open wound for a supposedly insignificant object: anti-Narcissistic, *objet sélectionné* for the benefit of the Other. Neither the Museum of Innocence nor *The Dockers' Museum* can be understood from the paradigm of the mirror or that of high art; rather, they should be understood from the gut—based on compassion or a sense of melancholy. (Below I will return to reflections on the "gut" in "the creativity in the *grotto*," and "genius and kairotic energy.")

Exercise #2. The Artist and *Besonnenheit*

Yes, everything becomes attenuated, but it's also true to say that nothing entirely disappears, there remain faint echoes and elusive memories that can surface at any moment like the fragments of gravestones in the room in a museum that no one visits. … We never eliminate all vestiges, though, we never manage, truly, once and for all, to silence that past matter, and sometimes we hear an almost imperceptible breathing. (Marías, 2014: 310–311)

Sekula's collection can also be regarded in the context of the *bild-wisschenschaftliche Denkraum* of Aby Warburg's Mnemosyne Project. This project's phantasm of the photographic collection with captions shows similarities to Sekula's work and his well-known obsession for the medium. In my view, the idea of *primavoltità*—the paradigmatic primordial value of any *objet sélectionné*—comes quite close to how Sekula himself related to *The Dockers' Museum*.

In 1924 Aby Warburg launched the so-called Mnemosyne Project, together with Gertrude Bing. Mnemosyne is the goddess who gave all things a name, and she is also the mother of the muses. Mnemosyne was also the epigraph at the entrance of Warburg's library in Hamburg. The choice for this goddess is not without meaning, since it connects the notion of inspiration (muses) with the semantic difficulties of naming and expressing in language the meaning of images.

Warburg writes about his project in terms of a "whole range of kinetic expression of life concerning phobic and shocked humankind; 'thiasotic' border of cultural imprint transposed; primary imprintment within the expressive field of tragic emotion; Pathosformulas are 'dynamograms.'"[2] Warburg's genius consists in part of an ability to localize crucial ruptures and, moreover, to name them on the basis of hidden knowledge and sources. (Koerner, 2012: 86–105) He discovers these ruptures through historical reconstruction, but also in the disjunction of style, sense of time, and costume, where the sacral becomes the playground of the secular. "He was interested in a montage of attractions where he wished to explore correspondences between human action and aesthetic creation that kept slipping out of the picture frame, then onto the stage, then into social rituals, and then continuing to move—both forward and backward—in a non-teleological feedback loop." (Gough, 2012: 117)

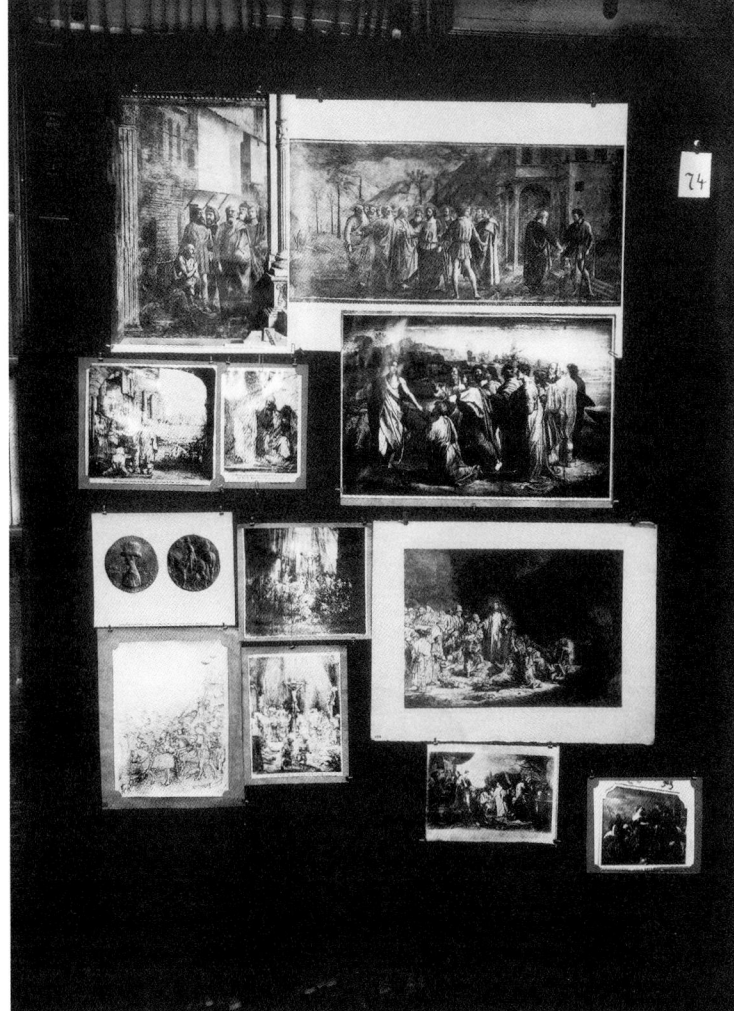

Fig. 1

Aby Warburg, *Der Bilderatlas Mnemosyne*, ed. Martin Warnke, II.1 (Berlin: Akademie Verlag, 2000), Tafel 74. © The Warburg Institute, London.

In *The Signature of all Things: On Method*, Giorgio Agamben associates Warburg's *Bilderatlas* with the definition and the origin of the paradigm as such. (Agamben, 2009: 26–32) As he writes: "In the paradigm, intelligibility does not precede the phenomenon; it stands, so to speak 'beside' it (para). According to Aristotle's definition, the paradigmatic gesture moves not from the particular to the whole and from the whole to the particular but from the singular to the singular." (Agamben, 2009: 27–28) Agamben claims that it is a misconception to read the *Bilderatlas* as the iconographic development of a repertoire on an art-historical timeline. He argues instead that Warburg's *Pathosformeln* are autonomous hybrids of archetypes. They possess an equivalent "first-timeness" (the *primavoltità*). Every photograph taken as part of the Mnemosyne Project constitutes an *archè* and, consequently, is archaic. The project defines the essence of this *primavoltità*:

> Or to be more precise, in accordance with the constitutive ambiguity of Plato's dialectic, the nymph is the paradigm of the single images, and the single images are the paradigms of the nymph. In other words, the nymph is an *Urphänomen*, an "originary phenomenon" in Goethe's sense of the term. (Agamben, 2009: 29).

In that sense, the Mnemosyne, as well as each (re)collection, each object of *primavoltità,* provides an antidote for the melancholic collector and his wound. It is in essence therapeutic as one becomes "healed" by the status of *Besonnenheit*.

Davide Stimilli digs deeper into the so-called mysterious self-healing of Aby Warburg in a recent article in *Revue Française de Psychanalyse*. Keyword for the author is the German term *Besonnenheit*. (Stimilli, 2015: 1100–1114) In fact, the term *Besonnenheit* (cf. *Sophrosyne* (Plato), level-headedness) appears at *Tafel 74* of the Atlas in the context of *Heilung ohne Berührung*. (Warburg, 2008: passim) (fig. 1) The first important introduction of the term in a therapeutic context was launched by psychiatrist Dr. Johann Christian Reil. (Reil, 1803: 98, 101) As Stimilli writes about this introduction:

> For its part, the *Besonnenheit* is "the compass [*der Compass*] [sic] that directs the action of the soul [*Thatkraft der Seele*] towards the end of its happiness [*den Zweck ihrer Glückseligkeit*]," without "relating to a single object" or wander "devoid of any guiding North Star"; more eloquently, Reil calls this the "mind's ear [*das Ohr des Geistes*], an ear that can be intentionally directed," before it is seized by an object and turned into attention [*Aufmerksamkeit*].[3] (Stimilli, 2015: 1105)

Also Hannah Arendt reflected on therapeutic *Besonnenheit*. (Arendt, 1958: 15) She considers the archetypical Aristotelian distinction between *vita activa* and *vita contemplativa* as responsible for the implication that "*Theōria*, or 'contemplation,' is the word given to the experience of the eternal," (Arendt, 1958: 20) "which can never survive the fleeting moment of the deed itself." (Arendt, 1958: 75)

Therapeutically, in fact, Aby Warburg lives in the space between active and passive: in the *Zwischenraum*. In his *illustrierte psychologische Geschichte des Zwischenraums zwischen Antrieb und Handlung* (Warburg, 1992: 156–173), he describes the need to surpass dualistic hermeneutics (*Contrasto-Spiel*) between *vita activa* and *vita contemplativa*. (Warburg, 2001: 429) Warburg's *Zwischenraum—Das Problem liegt in der Mitte*—is a place of unique cultural energy. This "middle" zone shows similarities with the chrysalis. Each montage and remontage, each depolarisation and repolarisation of the image spectrum takes place in the cocoon: in the hidden and invisible jelly of the *tertium quid*. The chrysalis is the paradigm of taking shape. It is the paradigm of oscillating itself: potential and threshold between life forms shifting in and out of existence. But this all happens hidden within, invisibly. We do not know the true operation and essence of it. The secret is held inside: the riddle, the mystery. What John Keats called "tedious agony"—that necessary time for renewal, lying fallow, gestation, in the natural cycle of creation.[4] (Olsen, 1978: 6) Perhaps it is part of the metamorphosis that the actual change—the duration and perceptibility of it—remains invisible (and silent). (Didi-Huberman, 2013: 14) The *locus* of the metamorphosis itself is not an image but "image-nary": hidden in a fold of time, in the darkest corner. This snapshot of potential and silence that comes before the scopic result critically questions, as we have seen, the dominance of the hermeneutics of mimesis within the image spectrum. Just like the chrysalis of the butterfly.

As Stimilli continues:

> The Mnemosyne invoked here is certainly not the benevolent guardian of a treasure house full of bibliophilic delicacies [*Schatzhaus für bibliophile Kostbarkeiten*], but rather "the great sphynx" of which Warburg wanted to "extract, if not the secret, at least the formulation of its riddle [*wenn auch nicht ihr Geheimnis, so doch die Formulierung ihrer Rätselfrage*]."[5] (Stimilli, 2015: 1110)

The idea that the classic collection descends into the world of the secret and the riddle, hanging there in the cocoon of empathy and *Besonnenheit*, brings me to the third exercise: mining Sekula as the chthonic place of creativity and the paradigm of the *grotto*.

Exercise #3. Creativity in the Grotto

> [A]s if nothing ever accumulated, as if no sediment built up, as if we had never covered that territory before. (Marías, 2014: 311)

The psychoanalyst Paul Verhaeghe introduced the notion of "chthonic art" in the context of a study of the oeuvre of Louise Bourgeois. "Chthonic" is derived from a classical Greek term meaning "belonging to the earth." (Verhaeghe, 2013: 85) He argues that this should not be interpreted metaphorically, but rather "phorically," i.e. as "bearing," as "carrying," as a first and necessary step in a confrontation with what is deemed "unimaginable" within the Real:

> A processing of the unimaginable makes it bearable, prepares sig-nification, so that it becomes bearable. […] It tries to shape the unutterable. […] Chthonic art differs from and contrasts with oedipal art, which in one way or another always involves a sexual genital processing of this originally undifferentiated and terrify-ing force. The oedipal development is the final phase of this pro-cess, as it channels and socializes *eros* and *thanatos*. […] Sigmund Freud calls this mourning process "*Trauerarbeit*," and equates it to analytical *Arbeit*, the work performed in psychoanalysis. [my translation] (Verhaeghe, 2013: 74)

In both cases, the identity of the person may be deconstructed by destroying the identification layers that form the ego. Either through the mourning process that removes the deceased from the identity of the person mourning, or through analysis, whereby free association pulverizes identity as such. Thus, in chthonic art, one undergoes a de-construction and subsequently a reconstruction whereby the making process serves as an aid. (Verhaeghe, 2013: 74)

According to Paul Vandenbroeck, there is a dual location of the chthonic space: corporeal art and textile, and performative expression and ritual whereby the body constitutes the pulsating underlayer (as a formal unconsciousness).[6] (Vandenbroeck, 2009: 178) The first relates to duplication: body and textile are parallels; the so-called skin-ego acts as a buffer, a membrane that functions in two directions. We rec-ognized it already in Berber weaving. The second concerns the "trans-posed" body: the energy of the body shifts to elsewhere, to a place where it can flourish unrestrictedly, as in dance, but also in a plastic sanctuary, such as camouflage. The transposed body expresses itself not so much allegorically as allodeictically: indicating in a different way, unconventional insofar as its signifiers and symbols are concerned. It occurs in a humus: "The deeper one plunges into the seething cauldron of processing the psycho-corporeal experience of existence and its par-adoxes, the further one departs from its aesthetic elaboration and the closer one gets to its source." (Vandenbroeck, 2009: 188)

This source is located between anxiety and exuberance, and be-tween oppression and expansive energy and symbolically transferred to the chthonic gate or *grotto*. Gaston Bachelard reflects on this arche-typical chthonic function of the cave as follows:

> The cave will never cease to rank as a fundamental image for Loti, who declares that: "This is the spot on earth to which, above all the very many places I have loved, I remain the most faithfully at-tached; here, more than anywhere else, I feel myself at peace, re-freshed, reinvigorated with my earliest youth and with new life."[7] (Bachelard, 2011: 138)

The cave is an escape destination where one dreams without end. (Bachelard, 1948: 208) The cave, with its mysterious hidden access, ma-terializes the threshold; it monitors the transition. The person at the entrance of the cave witnesses the passageway of the ear, the darkness of the pupil. The ear and the eye of the cave fascinate and attract, yet make one hesitate. (Oursel, 1933: 207–212) The cave remains a mystery: a cult of a forbidden love, a room harboring secrets, a birthplace, the realm of ghosts. (Bachelard, 1948: 209)

In the *Odyssey*, Homer describes how the nymphs in the cave, uti-lizing long stone looms, weave purple cloths. "The cave is mixed with stone mixing bowls and stone jars/ where the bees store their honey, and large stone looms on which/ the nymphs weave marvelous purple fabrics, and springs/ that flow on forever." (Book 13, vs. 107–110) The old looms made the textile grow from top to bottom, emulating the walls of glittering dung caves. Caves, with their glow and architectural ornamen-tation, are the principal spots of artistic inspiration and enchantment.

It is apt that the cave constitutes the place where man recognizes this *ekphrasis* and further articulates this sense visually by leaving imagery of bison and handprints as seen in caves like the one in Chauvet, Dordogne. In the 2014 documentary (Christian Tran) for Arte, *Les Génies de la Grotte Chauvet*, which examines the ambitious project which aims to copy these spaces and their murals, the Catalan painter Miguel Barceló talks about both the artistic qualities and techniques of the murals. The owl of Chauvet is a remarkable paradigm here: she was drawn in a few seconds by moving ten fingers from top to bottom. (fig. 2) The *genius loci* of this hand as well as its tender iconography may constitute the deepest and most moving *ekphrasis* of both wisdom and plastic beauty that man has ever realized. Or as Barceló says: "Tout est déjà là."

Or, as Bachelard put it:

> All caves speak. […] The voices of the earth are consonants. Vowels belong to the other elements, the air especially being the element to which belongs the breath of a happy mouth with sweetly parted lips. Words expressing energy and anger need

earth tremors, echoing rocks, and cavernous rumblings. […] A gravelly voice, a cavernous voice, and a rumbling voice are all voices of the earth. As Michelet has said, it is difficult words— hard words—that make the prophet. It is because voices from the abyss are confused that they are prophetic. Before the deep cavern, at the cave's threshold, dreamers hesitate. They look first at the black hole. The cave will then return their gaze, staring at them with its dark eye. The cavern is the eye of the Cyclops. […] We must live this transposition in the most fragile and fleeting of images, in the least descriptive images to be found. The gaze of the cave is an image of this kind. How can a mere black hole produce a good image for a deep gaze? […] The whole will to see is affirmed in the fixed stare of caves. […] In caves, blackness seems to shine.[8] (Bachelard, 2011: 141, 144, 145)

In my view, the glistening blackness of the cave is a metaphor for both Sekula's "eye" for the Other (the fisherman, the worker), but also for the "hesitation" that each would feel before entering the chthonic underbelly of *The Dockers' Museum*. There is no fitting access to Sekula's mine. There is only unconditional openness, tumbling into the cyclops' eye, radical descent into the world of the wound and contact with the prophet-artist and his *Besonnenheit*.

There is nothing but glistening blackness. *Telle est l'image du regard de la grotte.* This brings me to (a possible and provisional) end of this trail: genius and kairotic energy. Here I will defend a final provocative paradigm for Allan Sekula's *objet sélectionné* as "stumble block" or *skandalon*.

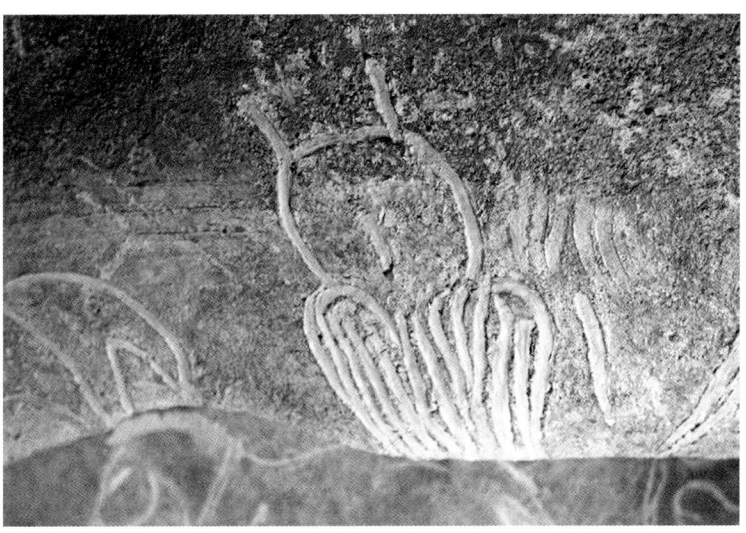

Fig. 2

The Owl in the Chauvet Cave in the Dordogne, Magdalenian, 18 000– 10 000 BC. © Caverne du Pont d'Arc, Photo: SYCPA/ Sébastien Gayet.

Exercise #4. Genius and Kairotic Energy

When you want something for a long time, it's very difficult to stop wanting it, I mean, to admit or to realize that you no longer desire it or that you would prefer something else. Waiting feeds and fosters that desire, waiting is accumulative as regards the thing awaited, it solidifies desire and turns it to stone, and then we resist acknowledging that we have wasted years expecting a signal, which, when it finally comes, no longer tempts us, or else we simply can't be bothered to answer a belated call that we no longer trust, perhaps because it doesn't now suit us to move. One grows accustomed to waiting for an opportunity that never comes, feeling deep down rather calm and safe and passive, unable quite to believe that it never will present itself. (Marías, 2014: 149)

In David Grossman's novel *Be My Knife*, Yair writes to Myriam: "[W]hat I feel when this wound of yours gapes in front of me, mercilessly, sucking me in and closing over me—ask me if I even know how to feel another person's pain." (Grossman, 2003: 195) The story is presented as a series of letters between Yair and Myriam, with a final third stage chapter, "Rain." The central idea is: Yair falls in love with Myriam just by noticing her in the distance from behind. He does not want to know her face, but he wants her to be his knife. The knife is a metaphor here for a love lived in the medium and the body of language itself. It is a love in the interstice, indeed in *the void of the almost*.[9]

The meaning of tearing and splitting as a life-, love- and wisdom-generating event (like the tearing of the temple curtain) is profoundly rooted in the visual and literary "body" of Ancient and Christian thought.[10] The primordial cosmogonic split is always sudden, sharp (like a knife), flash-like (at-once-ness and all-over) and is lived through the whole bodily sensorium (shivering, bliss, sigh, wind, breath). The split is the epiphany of the radical change, the revolution and the transition beyond.

The Greeks have a concept and deity for this radical change, for this occasion to be grasped: Kairos or the right moment. (fig. 3) Kairos says now, and in the now the abyss opens for the transition in life. Indeed, whenever there is a shift from something old into something new, whenever a diachrony is disrupted, there is an "incident": a surface that creases, water that wrinkles, paper that tears. The openings as a crease, as a wrinkle and as a tear are openings "inward" and "downward."

Fig. 3

Kairos (sculpture following the Lysippos model), 2nd century BC. © Turin, Museo di Arte Greco-Romana, Photo: Sergey Sosnovskiy.

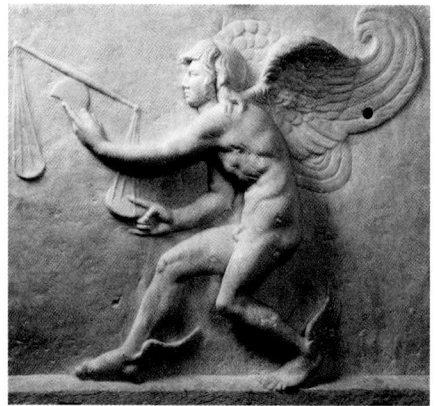

According to Sigmund Freud, Kairos, as opposed to Chronos, has access to these internal underlayers:

> Kairos has access to the unconscious, as chronological time, Chronos, the measuring of time into equivalent, quantitative components, does not. Kairotic history is the content as well as the dynamic of the unconscious. Nothing other than Kairos, and its consequences, is, properly, history and personality. […] Kairos's coming out of the past, breaks with revolutionary power against the present. (Rieff, 1951: 117, 126)

The Greeks expressed this swift and radical breakthrough of kairotic energy as the *erèmia* (ἐρημία): the "pregnant pause" between two successive moments or the epiphanic interruption. The interruption lies at the level of the gateway to the chthonic world, and hence from art as wound and *Trauerarbeit* as a crack leading to the underworld of the mine.[11] But we need to fall in the crack: the chthonic world is the Cyclops' eye: it is the necessary trap to help us surrender. This trap is the *skandalon*.

The Greek word *skandalizein* (σκανδαλίζειν) is derived from "limp," "stumble." *Skandalon* (σκάνδαλον in Greek) derives from "stumbling block." (Girard, 1984: 311–324) The meaning of "stumbling block" is highly ambivalent: it is the defect but also the opening to insight; the obstacle but also the possibility. As if, in the stumbling, everything is briefly lit up. The hope. "The void of almost." (Grossman, 2003: 195) The almost-fall before the most extreme fall: the tumble on the verge of *le noir qui brille*. The almost-disappearing into the big black hole. The almost emptying of oneself into the other.

The stumbling block says: "It's going to happen! Here I am. I am object. I am *primavoltità*, and you, visitor, falling in the cyclops' eye will 'stumble' over it."

One cannot escape the *objet sélectionné* that one literally stumbles across. It is "scandalous."

***

(For all these reasons, my four exercises in "Mining Sekula" could only be guided by the emotional state of *The Infatuations* by Javier Marías: the supposedly untranslatable *enamoramiento*.)[12]

Leuven-Bologna
June 2017

Notes

1. With thanks to Hilde Van Gelder and W.J.T. Mitchell, who gave me the opportunity to test some of my most recent hermeneutic studies against the work of Allan Sekula. Thanks also to Stephanie Heremans (assistant KU Leuven) for editing.

2. "D[ie] ganze [...] Skala kinetischer Lebens-äußerung phobisch-erschütterten Menschentums; 'Thiasotischen' Prägrand der Kultur transponiert; Urprägewerk in der Ausdruckswelt tragischer Ergriffenheit; Pathosformeln sind 'Dynamogramme'" [trans. Lars Zieke]. (Koos et al., 1994: Tafel 32/32b)

3. "Pour sa part, la *Besonnenheit* est 'le compas [*der Compass*] [*sic*] qui dirige l'action de l'âme [*Thatkraft der Seele*] vers la fin de sa félicité [*den Zweck ihrer Glückseligkeit*],' sans 'adhérer à un seul objet' ou errer 'sans Étoile polaire pour la guider;' de façon encore plus éloquente, Reil appelle cela 'l'oreille de l'esprit (*das Ohr des Geistes*), une oreille que nous pouvons intentionnellement diriger,' avant d'être saisie par un objet et transformée en attention (*Aufmerksamkeit*)" [trans. Daniel Franco].

4. Olsen speaks of "harmful silences that are not natural silences."

5. "La Mnémosyne invoquée ici n'est certainement pas le gardien bienveillant d'un 'trésor de délicatesses bibliophiles [*Schatzhaus für bibliophile Kostbarkeiten*],' mais plutôt 'le grand sphynx' dont Warburg souhaitait "soutirer, sinon le secret, au moins la formulation de son énigme [*wenn auch nicht ihr Geheimnis, so doch die Formulierung ihrer Rätselfrage*]" [trans. Daniel Franco].

6. I also discussed this in "Echoes of Liminal Spaces. Revisiting the Late Mediaeval 'Enclosed Gardens' of the Low Countries. (A Hermeneutical Contribution to Chthonic Artistic Expression)." (Baert, 2014/15: 9–45)

7. "La grotte ne quittera jamais son rang d'image fondamentale. C'est le coin du monde dit Loti, auquel je reste le plus fidèlement attaché, après en avoir aimé tant d'autres; comme nulle part ailleurs, je m'y sens en paix, je m'y sens rafraîchi, retrempé de prime jeunesse et de vie neuve." (Bachelard, 1948: 213)

8. "Toutes les grottes parlent. […] Les voix de la terre sont des consonnes. Aux autres éléments les voyelles, à l'air surtout le souffle d'une bouche heureuse, doucement entr'ouverte. La parole d'énergie et de colère a besoin du tremblement du sol, de l'écho du rocher, des roulements caverneux. […] La voix rocailleuse, la voix caverneuse, la voix grondante sont des voix de la terre. C'est la parole difficile, dit Michelet, qui fait les prophètes. C'est parce que les voix sortant de l'abîme sont confuses qu'elles sont prophétiques. Devant l'antre profond, au seuil de la caverne, le rêveur hésite. D'abord il regarde le trou noir. La caverne, à son tour, regard pour regard, fixe le rêveur avec son œil noir. L'antre est l'œil du cyclope. […] Cette transposition, on doit la vivre sur les plus fragiles images, sur les plus fugitives images, sur les images les moins descriptives qui soient. Telle est l'image du regard de la grotte. Comment ce simple trou noir peut-il donner une image valable pour un regard profond? […] Toute la volonté de voir s'affirme dans le regard fixe des cavernes. […] Dans la grotte, il semble que le noir brille." (Bachelard, 1948: 216–223)

9. On the text as body, and the body that "opens" for its reader and hence lover, see Patricia Cox Miller (Miller, 1986: 241–253); The same conceptual osmosis between novel and love, body and erotic readership, is analyzed by Roland Barthes (Barthes, 1975). See further: (Couzel, 1961). On biblical hermeneutics and *lire au-delà du verset* (Emmanuel Lévinas (1906–1995)), see: (Ouaknin, 1994: 37, 136, 283); (Nancy, 2000: 12). Jean-Luc Nancy writes: On a demandé: comment toucher au corps? […] Mais ce qu'il faut dire, c'est que cela—toucher au corps, toucher le corps, toucher enfin—arrive tout le temps dans l'ecriture.

10. I also developed this in "Notes to the Pact Between Veil and Wound." (Baert, 2015: 39–58)

11. At the Conference *Dis/Appearing* organized by the IKKM of the Bauhaus Universität Weimar in Prague, May 26, 2015, Georges Didi-Huberman developed the idea of *aperçues* on the one hand (female plural on purpose) and the idea of imagery "galloping" on the other hand. The lecture by Georges Didi-Huberman can be found online at http://www.ikkm-weimar.de/publikationen/video-audio/annual-conference-2015-dis-appearing/georges-didi-huberman-que-ce-qui-apparait-seulement-sapercoit/ (accessed September 2, 2017).

12. The infatuation, the frenzy; de verdwazing (v); the folly; the blinding; the dazzlement; infatuation, to love someone to distraction or be madly/insanely in love with someone.

Bibliography

Giorgio Agamben, *The Signature of all Things. On Method*, translated Luca D'Isanto and Kevin Attell (New York: Zone Books, 2009).

Hannah Arendt, *The Human Condition* (Chicago: University of Chicago Press, 1958).

Gaston Bachelard, *La terre et les rêveries du repos* (Paris: J. Corti, 1948).

Gaston Bachelard, *Earth and Reveries of Repose: An Essay on Images of Interiority*, trans. Mary McAllester Jones (Texas: The Dallas Institute Publications, 2011).

Barbara Baert, "Echoes of Liminal Spaces. Revisiting the Late Mediaeval 'Enclosed Gardens' of the Low Countries. (A Hermeneutical Contribution to Chthonic Artistic Expression)," in *Antwerp Royal Museum Annual*, 2012 (Brussels: Ministerie van de Vlaamse Gemeenschap, appeared in 2014/15), 9–45.

Barbara Baert, "Notes to the Pact Between Veil and Wound," in *Bild-Riss: Textile Öffnungen im ästhetischen Diskurs*, ed. Mateusz Kapustka, Textile Studies, 7 (Berlin: Mann Verlag, 2015), 39–58.

Roland Barthes, *The Pleasure of the Text*, trans. Richard Miller (New York: Hill and Wang, 1975).

Henri Couzel, *Origène et la 'Connaissance Mystique* (Paris: Desclée de Brouwer, 1961).

Georges Didi-Huberman, *Phalènes. Essais sur l'apparition*, 2 (Paris: Editions de Minuit, 2013).

George Didi-Huberman, « Que ce qui apparaît seulement s'aperçoit," http://www.ikkm-weimar.de/publikationen/video-audio/annual-conference-2015-dis-appearing/georges-didi-huberman-que-ce-qui-apparait-seulement-sapercoit/ (accessed September 2, 2017).

René Girard, "Scandal and the Dance: Salome in the Gospel of Mark," *New Literary History*, 15, 2 (1984): 311–324.

Kathleen M. Gough, "Between the Image and Anthropology. Theatrical Lessons from Aby Warburg's 'Nympha'," *The Drama Review*, 56, 3 (2012): 114–130.

David Grossman, *Be My Knife*, trans. Vered Almog and Maya Gurantz (New York: Picador, 2001/2003).

Donald E. Hill, *Ovid. Metamorphoses IX-XII* (Warminster: Aris & Phillips, 1999).

Hans Jonas, "The Nobility of Sight: A Study in the Phenomenology of the Senses," in *The Phenomenon of Life: Toward a Philosophical Biology*, ed. Hans Jonas (Chicago: University of Chicago Press, 1966/1982), 135–156.

Joseph Leo Koerner, "Writing Rituals. The Case of Aby Warburg," *Common Knowledge*, 18, 1 (2012): 86–105.

Marianne Koos, Wolfram Pichler, Werner Rappl and Gudrun Swoboda (eds), Aby Warburg, *Mnemosyne. Begleitmaterial zur Ausstellung im Hamburger Kunsthaus. 63 Bild- und Texttafeln* (Hamburg: Dölling und Galitz 1994), Tafel 32/32b.

Javier Marías, *The Infatuations*, translated Margaret Jull Costa (London: Penguin, 2014).

Javier Marías, *Thus Bad Begins*, translated Margaret Jull Costa (London: Penguin, 2016).

Patricia Cox Miller, "Pleasure of the text, Text of Pleasure. Eros and Language in Origen's 'Commentary on the Song of Songs," *Journal of the American Academy of Religion*, 54, 2 (1986): 241–253.

Jean-Luc Nancy, *Corpus* (Paris: Métailié, 2000).

Carl Nordenfalk, "The Five Senses in Flemish Art Before 1600," in *Netherlandish Mannerism: Papers Given at a Symposium in Nationalmuseum Stockholm, September 21–22, 1984*, ed. Görel Cavalli-Björkman (Stockholm: Nationalmuseum Stockholm, 1985) 135–154.

Tillie Olsen, *Silences* (New York: Delacorte Press, 1956/1978).

Marc-Alain Ouaknin, *Lire aux éclats. Éloge de la caresse* (Paris: Seuil, 1986/1994).

Paul Masson Oursel, "Le Symbolisme Eurasiatique de la Porte," *La Nouvelle Revue Française*, 239 (1933): 207–212.

Orhan Pamuk, *The Naive and Sentimental Novelist,* trans. Nazim Dikbaş (Cambridge: Harvard University Press, 2010).

Johann Chr. Reil, *Rhapsodieen über die Anwendung der psychischen Curmethode auf Geisteszerrüttungen* (Halle: Curtschen Buchhandelung, 1803).

Philip Rieff, "The Meaning of History and Religion in Freud's Thought," *The Journal of Religion,* 31, 2 (1951): 114–131.

Susan Sontag, *The Volcano Lover. A Romance* (New York: Anchor Books, 1992/1993).

Davide Stimilli, "L'énigme de Warburg," *Revue française de psychanalyse,* 79, 4 (2015): 1100–1114.

Paul Vandenbroeck, "The Energetics of an Unknowable Body. The Sacred and the Aniconic-sublime in Early Modern Religious Culture," in *Backlit Heaven. Power and Devotion in the Archdiocese of Mechelen,* exh. cat., eds Paul Vandenbroeck and Gerard Rooijakkers (Mechelen: Lamot, 2009), 174–204.

Hilde Van Gelder (ed.), *Allan Sekula. Ship of Fools/The Dockers' Museum* (Leuven: Leuven University Press, 2015).

Paul Verhaeghe, "Louise Bourgeois. Chtonische kunst of de weg naar het Reële en Terug," in *For your pleasure? Psychoanalyse over esthetisch genot,* eds Mark Kinet, Marc De Kesel and Sjef Houppermans (Antwerp: Garant, 2013), 69–90.

Aby Warburg, *Mnemosyne Atlas,* in *Die Beredsamkeit des Leibes. Zur Körpersprache in der Kunst,* eds Ilsebill Barta Fliedl and Christoph Geissmar-Brandi (Salzburg/Vienna: Rezidenz Verlag, 1992), 156–173.

Aby Warburg, *Tagebuch der Kulturwissenschaftlichen Bibliothek Warburg mit Einträgen von Gertrud Bing und Fritz Saxl,* Gesammelte Schriften, VII, eds Karen Michels and Charlotte Schoell-Glass (Berlin: Akademie Verlag, 2001).

Aby Warburg, *Der Bilderatlas: Mnemosyne,* Gesammelte Schriften, II.1, eds Martin Warnke and Claudia Brink (Berlin: Akademie Verlag, 2008).

Part 2
Maritime Failures and Imaginaries

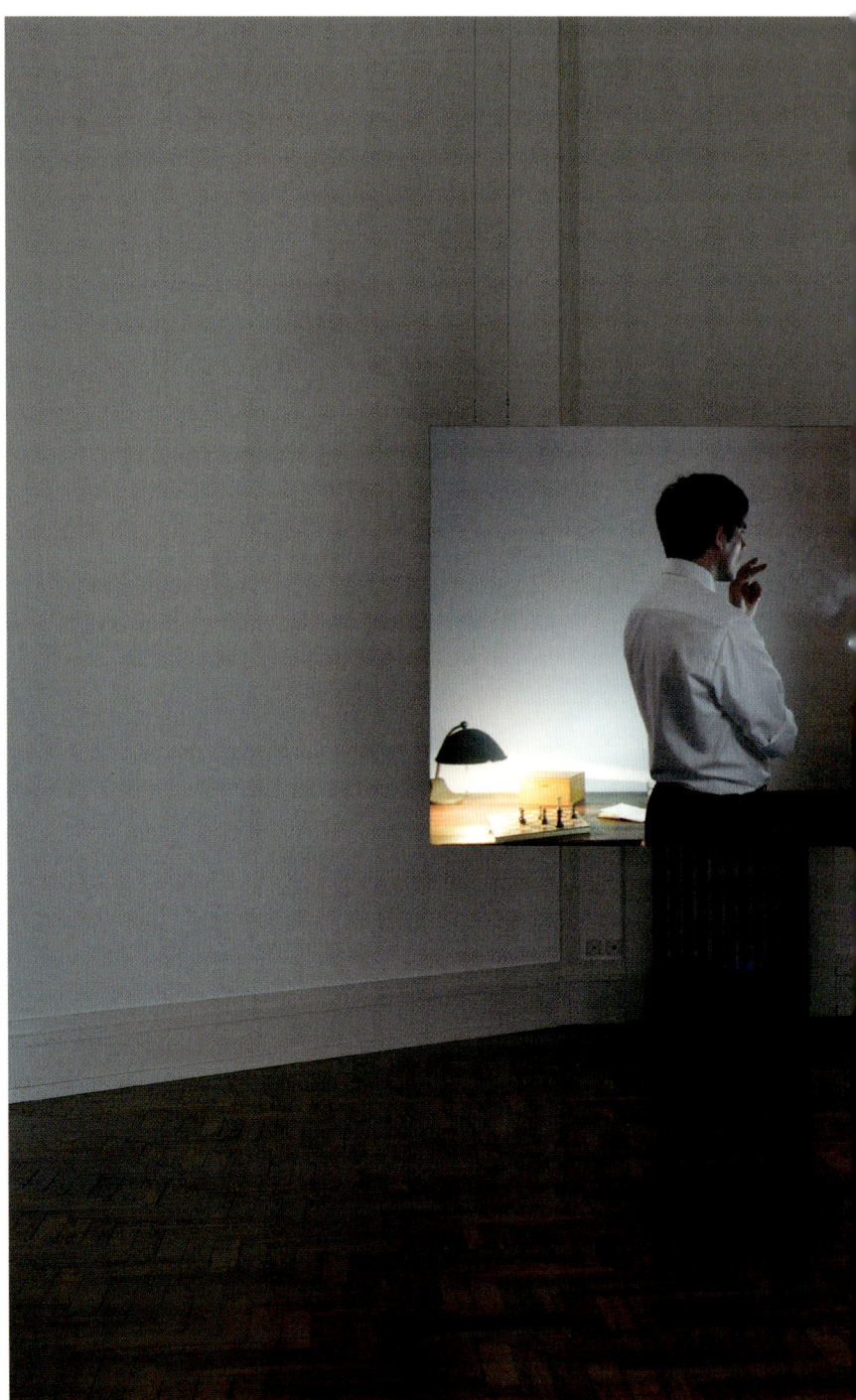

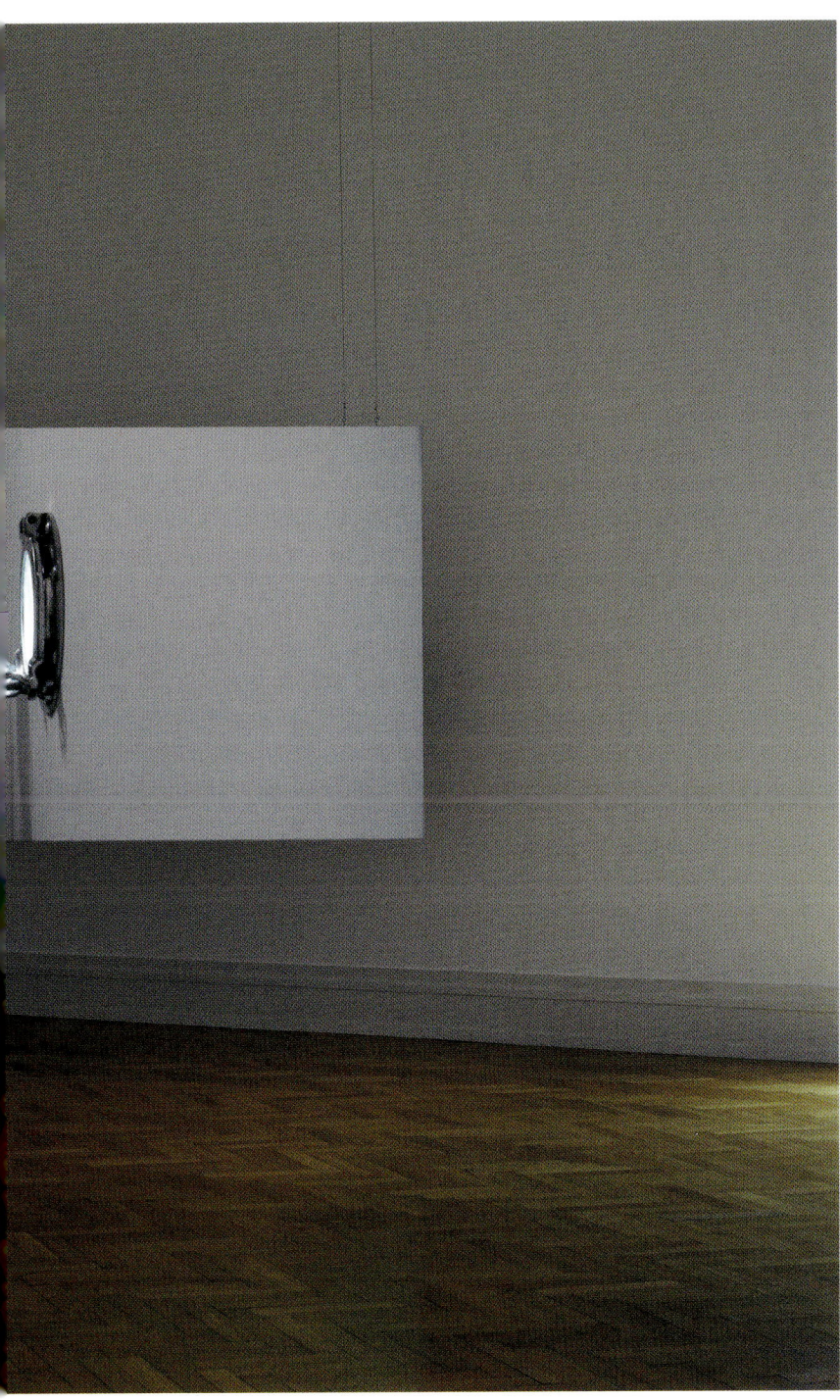

Pages 114–115

Marco Poloni, *Majorana Eigenstates*, 2008. Continuous film projection with sound, HD video, 1:2.35, colour, stereo, dimensions variable, loop of 43 min 52 sec. Film still. Courtesy of the artist and Galerie Campagne Première Berlin. Photograph Dominique Uldry.

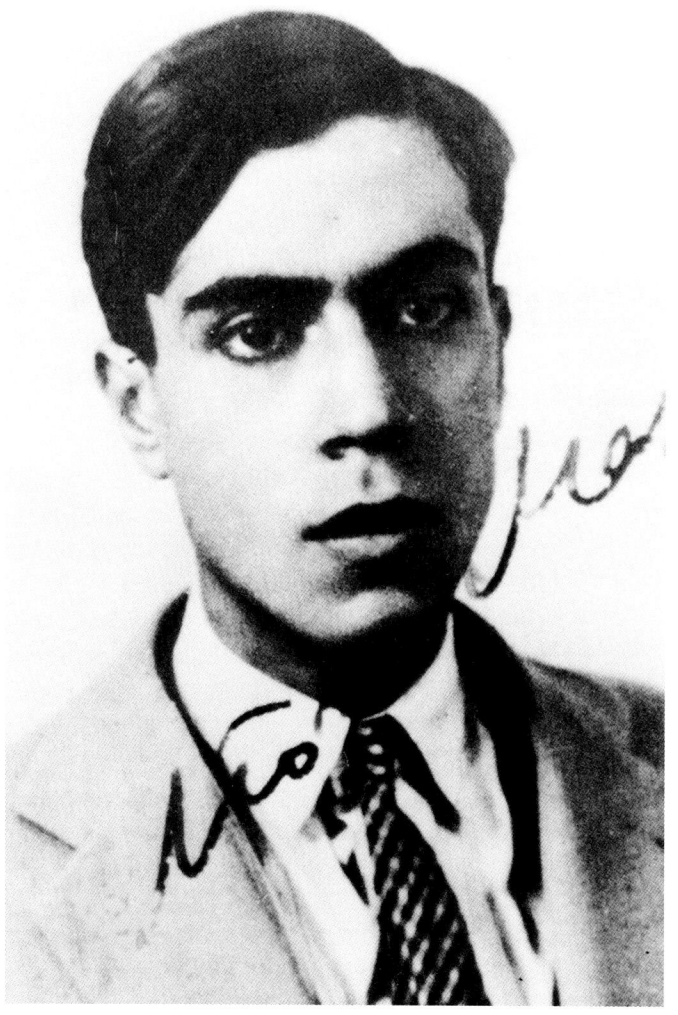

Page 116

Ettore Majorana when 23. Courtesy of Erasmo Recami and Maria Majorana.
Reproduction forbidden.

The Land Seen by the Sea

Marco Poloni

In 1938 the Italian theoretical physicist Ettore Majorana sent a note to the director of the Physics Institute at the University of Naples, where he had just been appointed professor. It included an intriguing phrase: "The Sea Rejected Me." In an earlier letter to the director, Majorana had mentioned his decision to suddenly disappear. This new, odd phrase seemed to imply that he had reversed his decision. Majorana eventually succeeded in vanishing at sea a few days later, somewhere between Naples and Palermo. This mysterious statement seemed to intimate that the sea is endowed with intentionality.

Majorana's life and sudden disappearance constitute a shadow line that traces the covert story of the development of nuclear weapons. The late 1930s saw the discovery of nuclear fission, the core process of the first atomic bombs. There is no historical evidence that Majorana contributed to this research. However, theoretical papers and experimental findings were quickly shared in an elite circle of nuclear physicists throughout Europe and the United States. Majorana could thereby not have been able to ignore the militarization of the nuclear project. In 1975 the Sicilian novelist Leonardo Sciascia published a book titled *The Disappearance of Majorana*, in which he postulated that Majorana had orchestrated his own disappearance because of his projection of the deadly outcome of nuclear fission and the immense energy it released. I personally believe there is a reasonable base for this claim. When Majorana made the decision to disappear in 1938, the idea of nuclear fission needed only experimental proof, a validation that came one year later, the same year that saw the start of World War II.

Between 2008 and 2010 I produced a large constellation of works entitled *The Majorana Experiment* comprising films, photographs, objects, and texts that took their cue from Majorana's journey and his mysterious disappearance at sea.[1] I presented this work in the first section of my contribution to "Maritime Failures and Imaginaries," at the second thematic session of the "Disassembled Images" conference in Antwerp. In a second and speculative section of my presentation, I discussed my ongoing research, which will be the subject of this essay. Although my present work is not connected to the Italian physicist,

I would like to describe two elements of "The Majorana Experiment" to introduce my research.

One work in particular marks my debt to Allan Sekula's pioneering body of work. Sekula clearly informed some lines of my practice, both in its scope—the exploration of the sea as a space intersected by geopolitical processes—and in its methodology. "Persian Gulf Incubator," a large constellation comprising photographs, wallpapers, and text panels, narrates a geopolitical plot while attempting to draw a metaphorical connection between the disappearance at sea of a scientist and that of a ship, the Italian luxury liner MS *Raffaello*.[2] Following the 1973 oil crisis, this vessel was put on sale and three years later it was purchased by the Shah of Iran, who used it as a floating palace in the Persian Gulf. It was eventually sunk by Iraki jetfighters in 1983, during the Iran-Iraq war. The wreck is located in shallow waters just a few miles off the coastal nuclear reactor of Bushehr, a strategic facility for Iran's nuclear development, suggesting a remarkable assemblage of two very large machines and a striking entanglement between two geopolitical narratives.

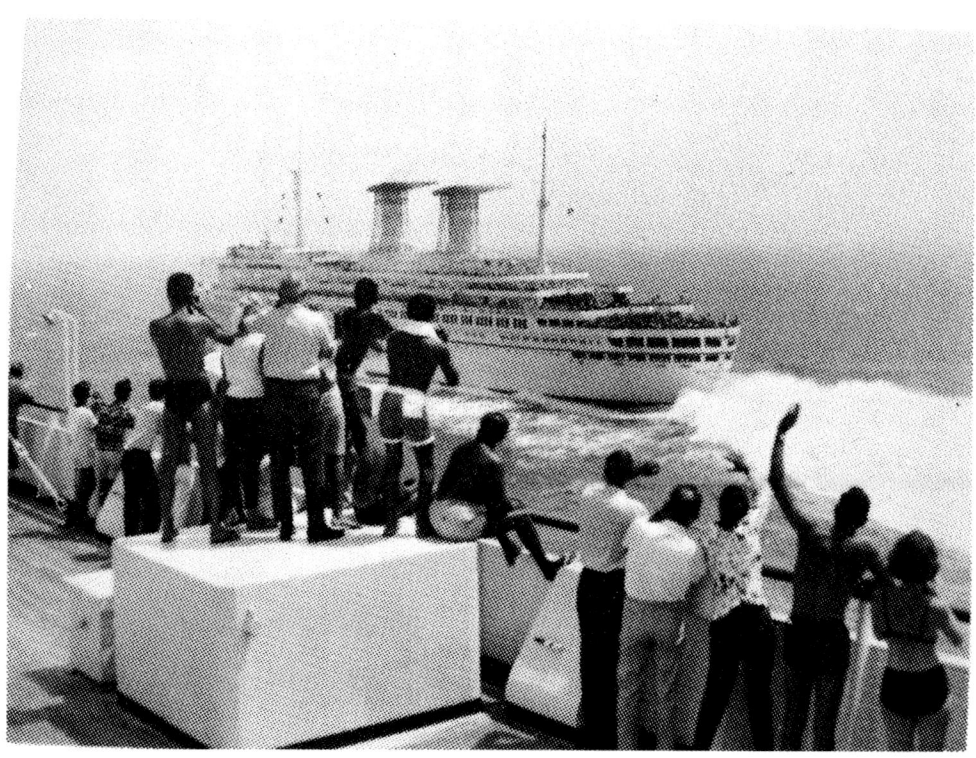

Page 119

Marco Poloni, Photograph from *Persian Gulf Incubator*, 2008. Constellation of photographs comprising 32 elements: 24 pigment prints, 3 wallpaper prints, 5 text panels, dimensions variable. Courtesy of the artist and Galerie Campagne Première Berlin.

Pages 120–121

Marco Poloni, *Persian Gulf Incubator*, 2008.
Exhibition view, Kunsthalle Bern, 2010.
Courtesy of the artist and Galerie Campagne
Première Berlin. Photograph Dominique Uldry.

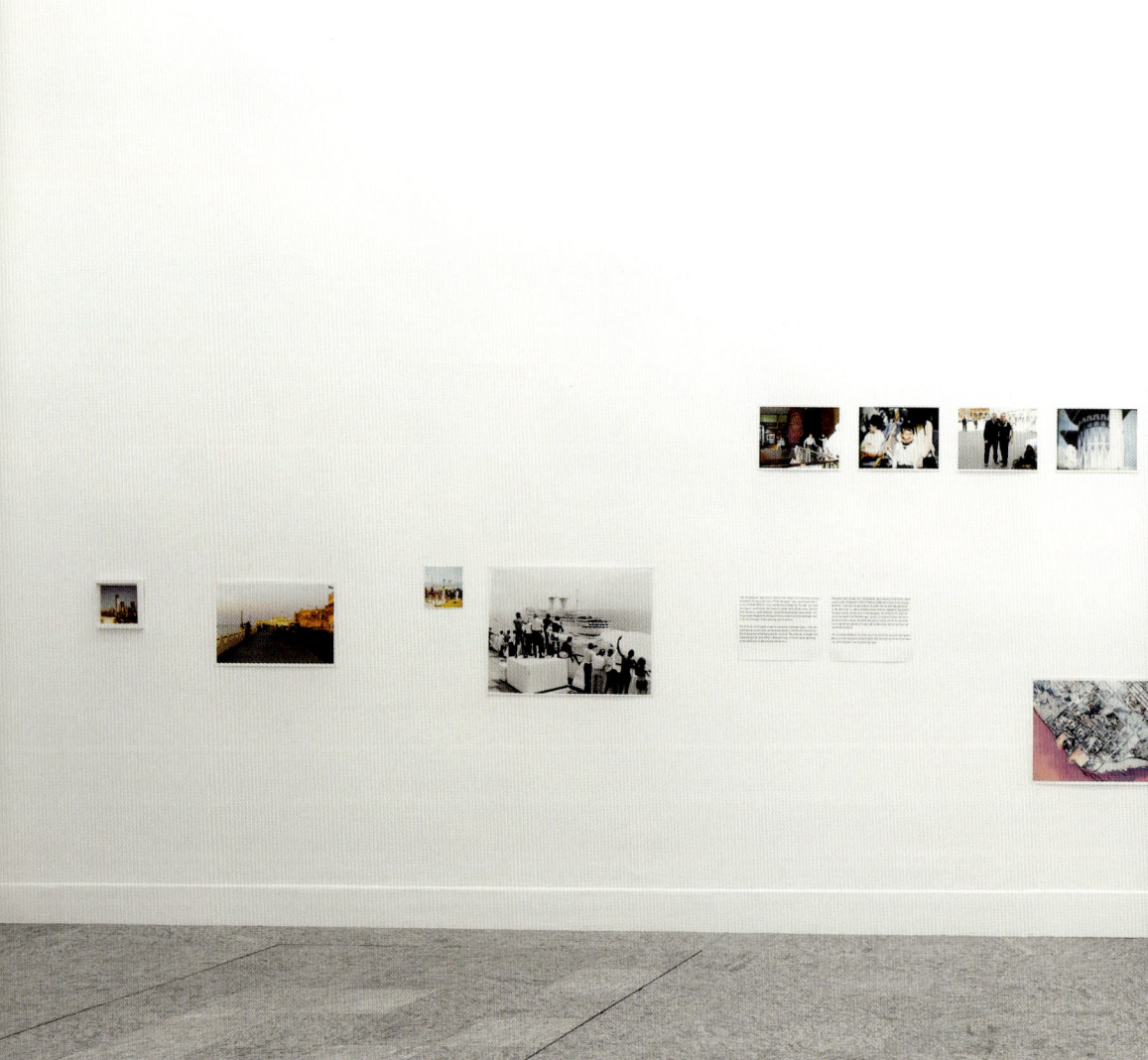

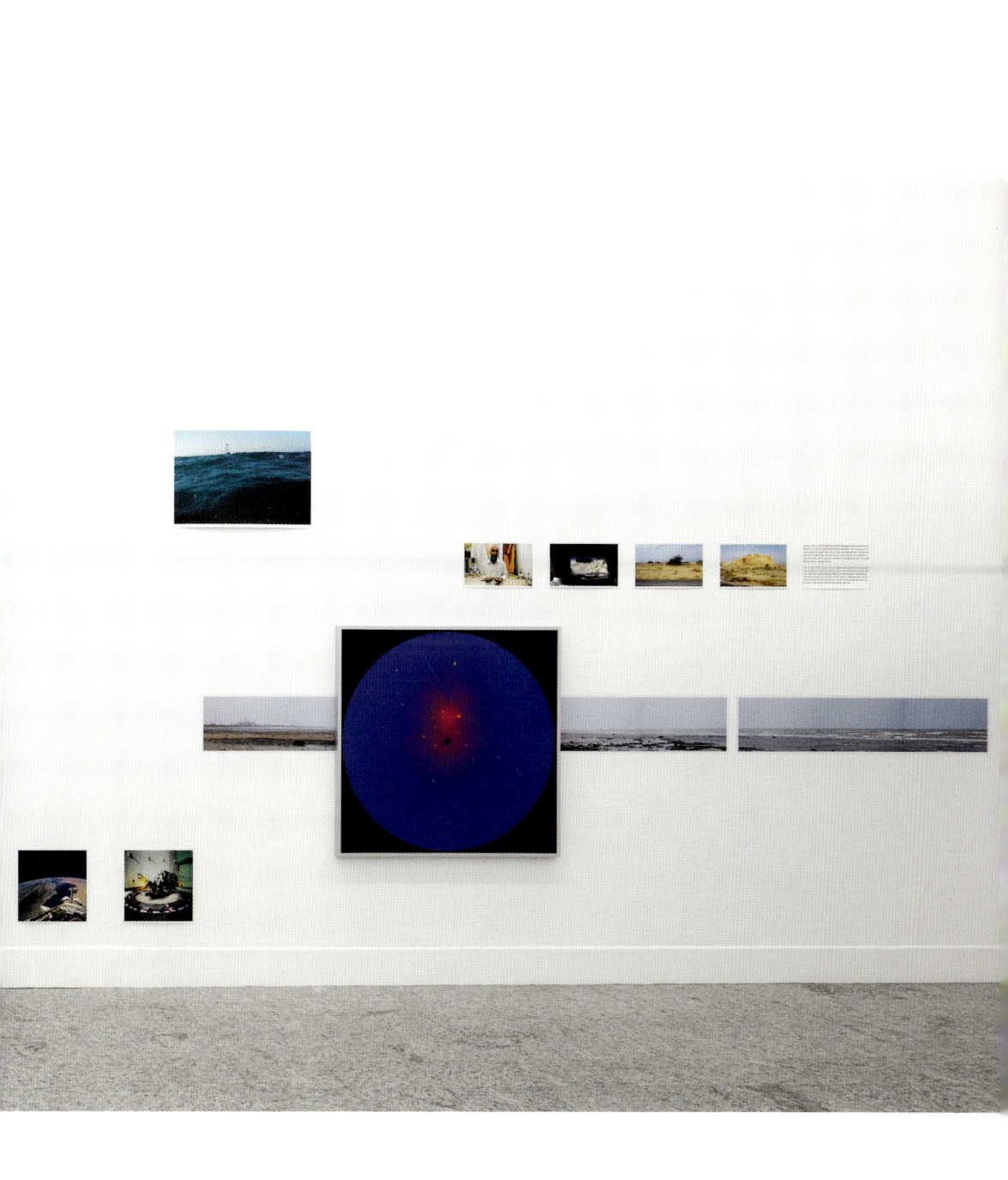

My short Super-16mm film *The Sea of Majorana* shows a post-nuclear seascape filmed between Napoli and Palermo, where Ettore Majorana disappeared in 1938. The ambient radioactivity perforates the material support of the film. A voice-over reads an excerpt from a posthumously published essay by Majorana, in which he appears to endow nuclear fission with quasi-human agency: "From a strictly scientific point of view there is nothing that prevents us from considering that a simple, invisible and unpredictable vital fact [the disintegration of an atom] could be found at the origin of human events."[3]

My work about Majorana also serves as an illustration of my research methodologies over the last decade. In my practice I generally take biographical threads as points of departure to expose broader narratives. In 2014 ago I established "The Analogue Island Bureau," an agency that brings together a body of work that started in 2008. The agency attempts to build an index of plots, problems, and tropes involving the Mediterranean Sea.[4]

I would now like to expand on the second section of my contribution to "Maritime Failures and Imaginaries." This section describes the shift I am currently attempting to articulate in my work: what if my starting-point wasn't a human subject but a non-human entity, specifically the Mediterranean Sea? In other words, could the sea be articulated not as a backdrop, i.e. a maritime expanse embedded within and subordinated to various geopolitical narratives, but as a subject in its own right?

In operational terms, this would entail exploring and producing shifts that displace the human as a privileged entity in relation to the non-human, subverting existing hierarchies inherited from modernity, those which govern, for instance, relations between subject and object or nature and culture. This process would include trying to overcome a limiting binary between the human and the non-human, allowing both terms to be entangled with equal agency. If this operation is first of all one of aesthetics, it turns into one of politics of representation.

From the perspective of my practice, which is embedded in cinema and photography, this question entails rethinking the modernist grammar inherent in both forms. Respective to photography, cinema introduces an unambiguous separation between the perspective of the apparatus and the figure of a narrator, while having the power to "make us forget the camera that is really doing the looking."[5] As a result, cinema generates both a more complex narrative space and a more intricate relationship to the viewer than photography, which is why I would like to address my issue in cinematic terms, with a specific view to realism.

Pages 123–125

Marco Poloni, Photographs from *Persian Gulf Incubator*, 2008. Constellation of photographs comprising 32 elements: 24 pigment prints, 3 wallpaper prints, 5 text panels, dimensions variable. Courtesy of the artist and Galerie Campagne Première Berlin.

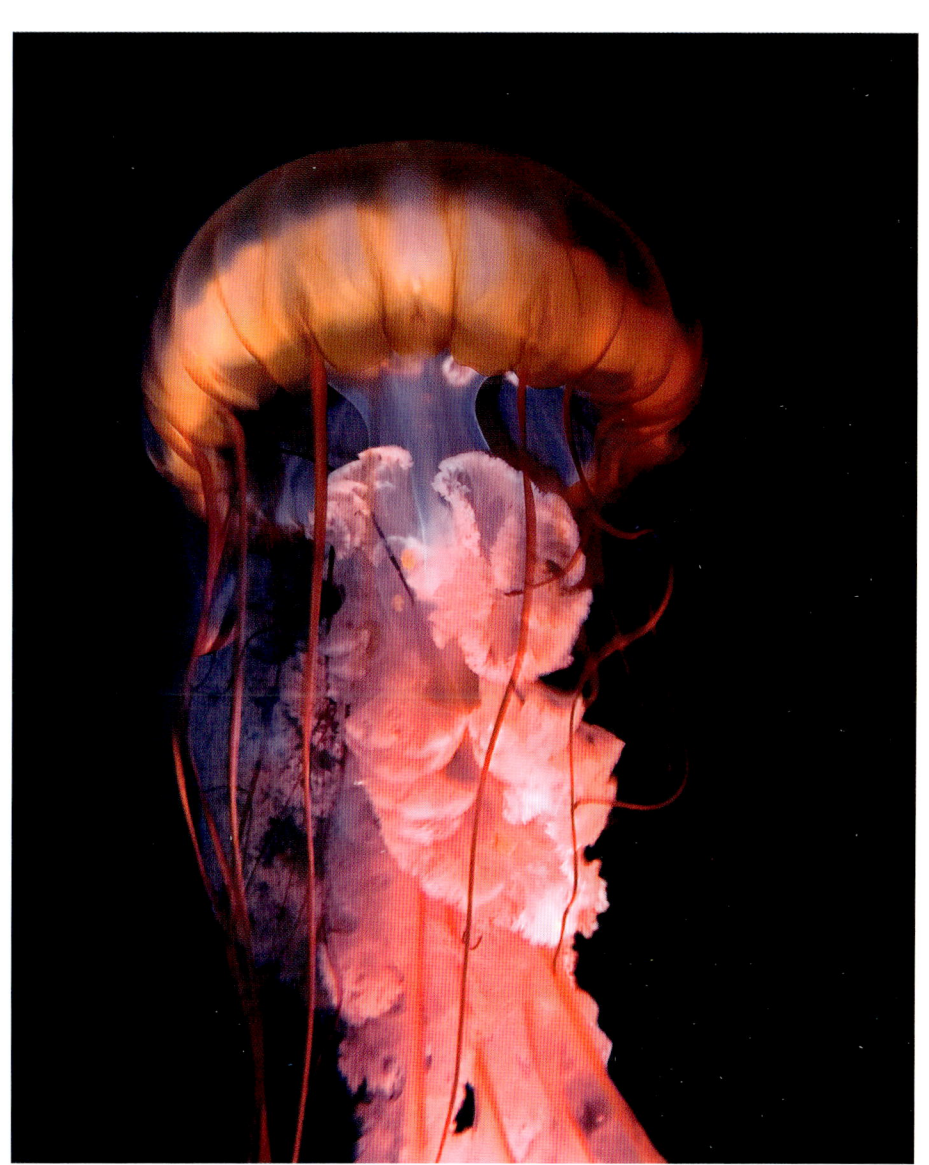

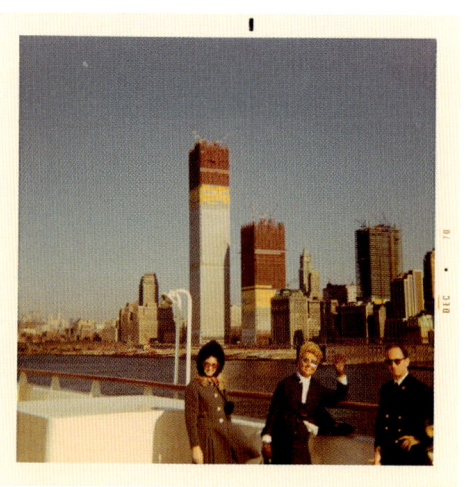

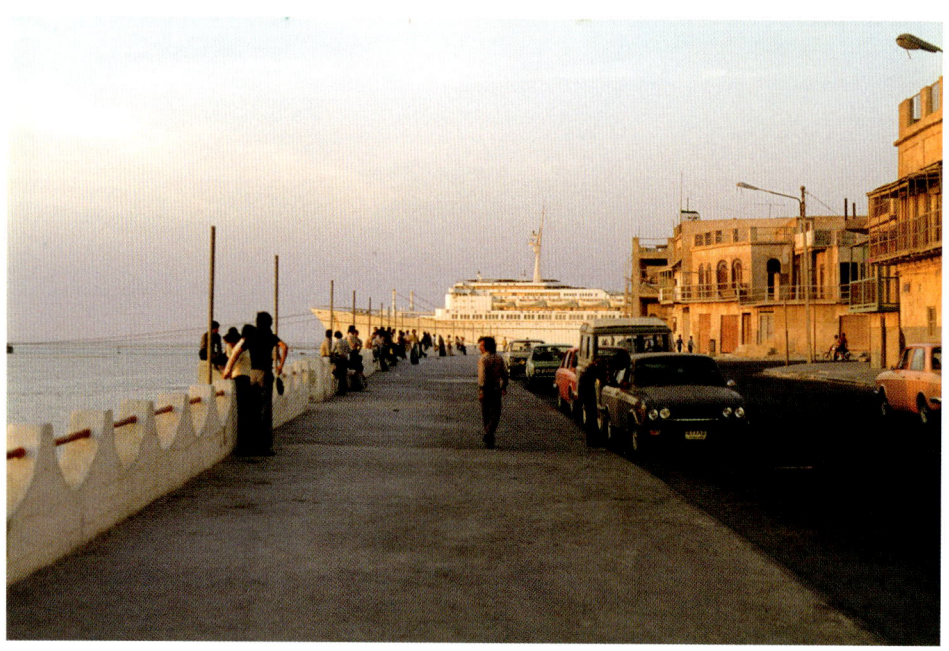

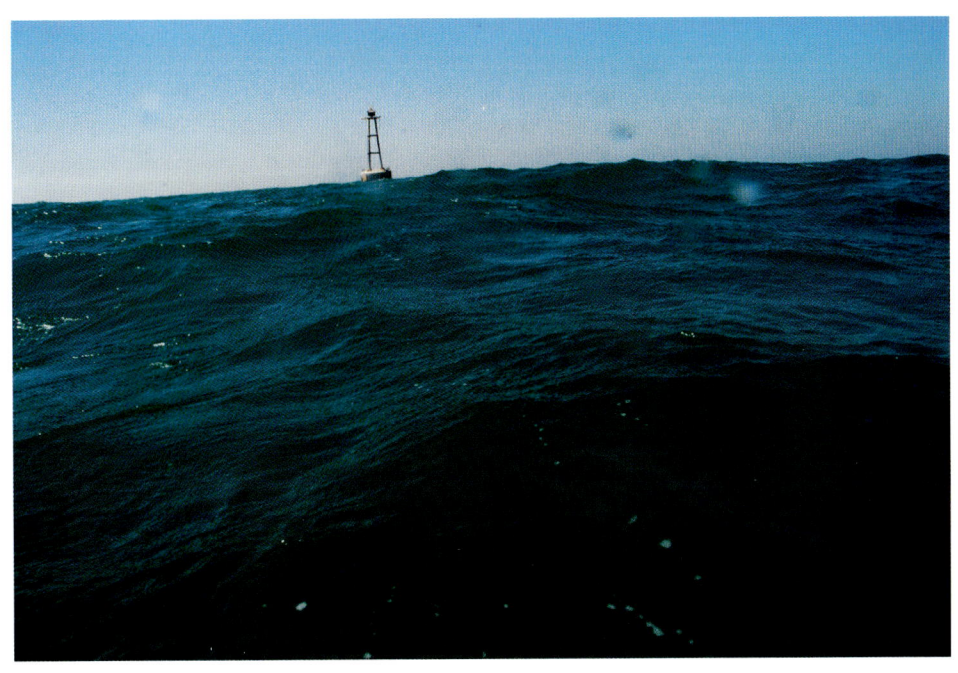

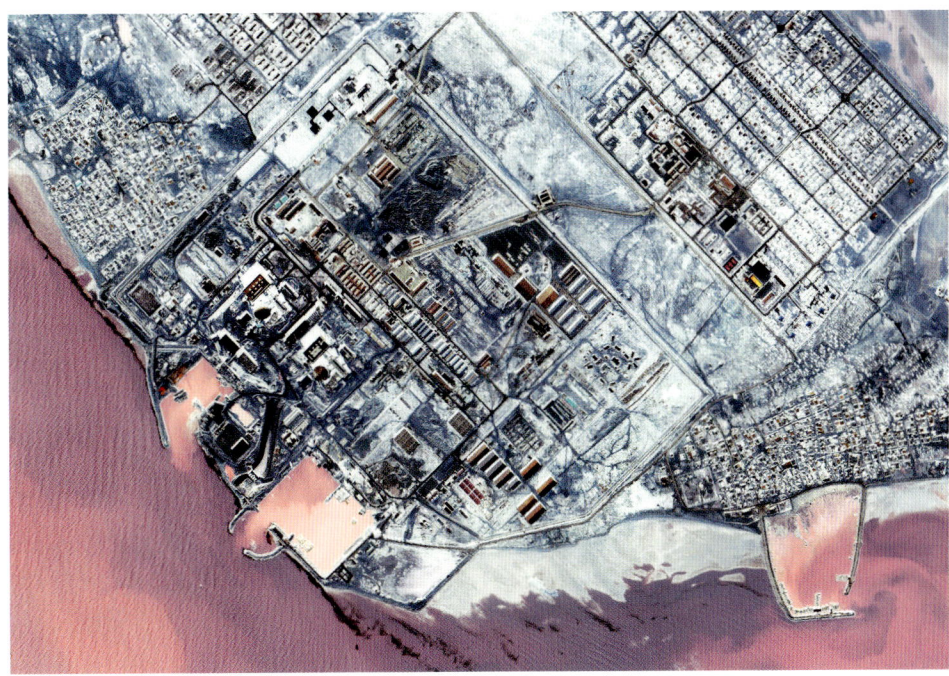

To a large extent my work about Majorana was a thought experiment. I would like to introduce a second *Gedankenexperiment* taking my cue from a poetic image by the French philosopher of science Gaston Bachelard. In 1942 Bachelard wrote that "The true eye of the earth is water." It is "a large tranquil eye."[6] Let's imagine for a moment the sea not as a screen or a projective surface, but as a large eye, maybe also as a large lens. An eye that is not necessarily laden with intentionality, as the sentient plasmic ocean that covers Solaris in Stanislaw Lem's novel. Just a large eye. How would that eye see human entities? How would it see land? How would its vision be translated, if at all possible, in cinematic terms?

This question is absurd a priori. If it is at all conceivable to imagine a non-anthropocentric perspective, it is still very challenging for humans to realize non-anthropomorphic vision for the mere reason that the tools we use to produce representations are isomorphic in relation to our human attributes. Although I am fully aware that this is speculative, I will nevertheless attempt to enumerate a few issues, conditions, and visual strategies to envision cinematic structures inspired by Bachelard's poetic image.

A first and obvious obstacle comes to mind when trying to rethink the position of the human subject vis-à-vis an entity as large as the sea and trying to imagine and represent new modes of intimacy: issues of scale, spatial or temporal. This is a well-known problem in ecology, as there is no single natural scale at which ecological phenomena should be studied. This is because systems are polyscalar and show characteristic variability on a range of spatial, temporal, and structural levels. A second obstacle in relation to scale is that every living entity is an observer of its environment, with its own perceptual limitations and biases. We know this for instance from Jakob von Uexküll's concept of "Umwelt," which is a minute part of the "Umgebung" of a living entity, its physical surroundings.[7] The "Umwelt" of a living entity is constituted only by those features of the environment that are relevant to its self-preservation and reproduction.

In this context, the concept of "hyperobjects" introduced by the American philosopher Timothy Morton is useful. Morton defines hyperobjects as "things that are massively distributed in time and space relative to humans."[8] The vastness of their scale defeats classical ideas about what a thing is in the first place. Although hyperobjects are too massive and long-lived for our minds to comprehend them, they "are not simply mental (or otherwise ideal) constructs, but are real entities whose primordial reality is withdrawn from humans." Global warming is perhaps the most apposite example of a hyperobject. Radioactivity, the overarching motif in *The Majorana Experiment*, is a hyperobject. Other such objects are ultraviolet radiation, all electromagnetic waves, the gravitational field, jellyfish blooms, oil, tsunamis, as well as the desertification and the "tropicalization" of the Mediterranean region. This latter term refers to the arrival and proliferation of tropical species as an effect of water warming.

Global warming cannot be directly seen, but it can be experienced. At my summer home in Southern Tuscany, the beach recedes year after year. This is caused in small part by sand erosion, but it most probably follows from coastal storms and the rise of the Mediterranean Sea level. This shrinking strip of sand is an index of a hyperobject.

An interesting property of hyperobjects is their non-locality. Hyperobjects are vastly distributed in time and space. Sea waves—"gravity waves" as they are scientifically named—seem to come from nowhere before they break on the shore. Very large gravity waves are almost invisible until they materialize in beach shallows. Waves transport energy, not water. This energy is born by wind power. Waves are indexes of a boundless and invisible "sea" of energy lying within the sea. As Christine Guth, the author of a marvelous book about Hokusai's *Great Wave off Kanagawa*, writes: "Waves are bodies that move freely with little regard to geographic boundaries, seemingly erasing borders and transforming the world into an interconnected whole, in the process submerging individual identity within collective identity."[9]

Because hyperobjects transcend spatio-temporal localism, they explode classical divisions of scale such as macroscopic versus microscopic. More radically, they humiliate the human by de-centering it from its place of privilege in the order of things. In other words, the concept of locality is epiphenomenal to a deeper spatio-temporal order. In that sense, non-locality extends the blow to anthropocentrism brought by Copernicus and Darwin, who removed the human from the center of meaning.

Following these introductory considerations, I would like to rethink four attributes of cinematic grammar and syntax toward possibilities for a post-anthropocentric cinema: Scale, Movement, Fragmentation and Suture, and Perspective. This inventory is of course subjective and not exhaustive. Because cinema is an assemblage of moving images and sound, I would need to engage the sonic sphere as crucial as well, but the space I have in this essay is limited.

1. First Attribute: Scale

Is it possible to imagine a scalar approach to the cinematic field, an approach that subverts the classical cinematic division in types of shots and visualizes the co-existence of different orders of magnitude?

A classical answer comes from *Cosmic Zoom*, a 1968 short film directed by Eva Szasz and produced by the National Film Board of Canada, which depicts the relative size of everything in the universe in a sequence of 8 minutes. *Cosmic Zoom* was based on the 1957 essay "Cosmic View" by the Dutch educator Kees Boeke. Szasz's film anticipates by a number of years the more known 1977 film *Powers of Ten* by Charles and Ray Eames, an animated journey into a scalar depiction of the place of the human in the universe. This trope has by now become standard fare in mainstream cinema. Szasz's progression of shots is based on a logarithmic scale, as opposed to the linear scale upon which the traditional division in types of shots is established. Interestingly, logarithmic scales are more "natural" than linear scales in that they more closely represent our perception of physical phenomena such as the change of perceived light or sound intensity as a function of the distance of the subject to the light or sound source.

The cinematic structure just described is a spatial construct. Can we now focus on the much more difficult issue of addressing cinematic time with a scalar approach? Could for instance the division of time authored by Fernand Braudel, the historian of the Mediterranean Sea, be visually representable? Braudel defines three scales of historical time: the short term, the medium term, and the long term (which he called the *longue durée*).[10] These scales correspond to three forms of movement. The long term denotes geographical time: the time of man in his relationship to the environment, which today we would call geological time. The medium term denotes social time: the history of groups and groupings. The short term denotes individual time: a history of events, brief, rapid, nervous fluctuations like "surface disturbances, crests of foam that the tides of history carry on their strong backs."[11] From the viewpoint of the human subject and from representation as we know it, this division into macro-, meso- and microscopic time scales corresponds to a history whose passage is in most cases imperceptible in the first case, slow but perceptible in the second one, and a clearly perceptible pulsation in the third one.

With this awareness of time scales in mind, can we think of strategies for representing new modes of intimacy between the human and the environment? A sound starting-point is the use of the long take in James Benning's landscape cinema. In *Measuring Change* from 2016, the digital companion to his 16mm film *Casting a Glance* from 2007, Benning filmed Robert Smithson's *Spiral Jetty* in two fixed shot takes of thirty-minutes, one in the morning and one in the afternoon. In *Casting a Glance* he had filmed the earthwork in shorter takes over sixteen trips to the site, recording its shifting ecology.

Benning's cinema does not incorporate the human presence, nor its narrative dimension. Anat Pick and Guinevere Narraway write, with reference to Canadian film scholar Martin Lefebvre, that "in filmic terms, the distinction between human and nonhuman nature can be configured as the tension between the predominance of narrative and landscape."[12] Classical cinematic storytelling generally entails subsuming non-human elements to narrative logic in order to not interrupt the flow of the story. The function of landscape is thus to provide a backdrop against which the narrative unfolds. If we recognize that landscape is itself a human construction, or, more radically, that in the new paradigm of the anthropocene it co-exists with humans in an entangled way, we can start to rethink the relationship between narrative and backdrop. In order to represent this entanglement, a clear cinematic strategy would then be to flatten out the depictive and diegetic levels, thus narrativizing the landscape and "landscaping"—so to speak—the human body. I develop this below in the fourth section, about perspective.

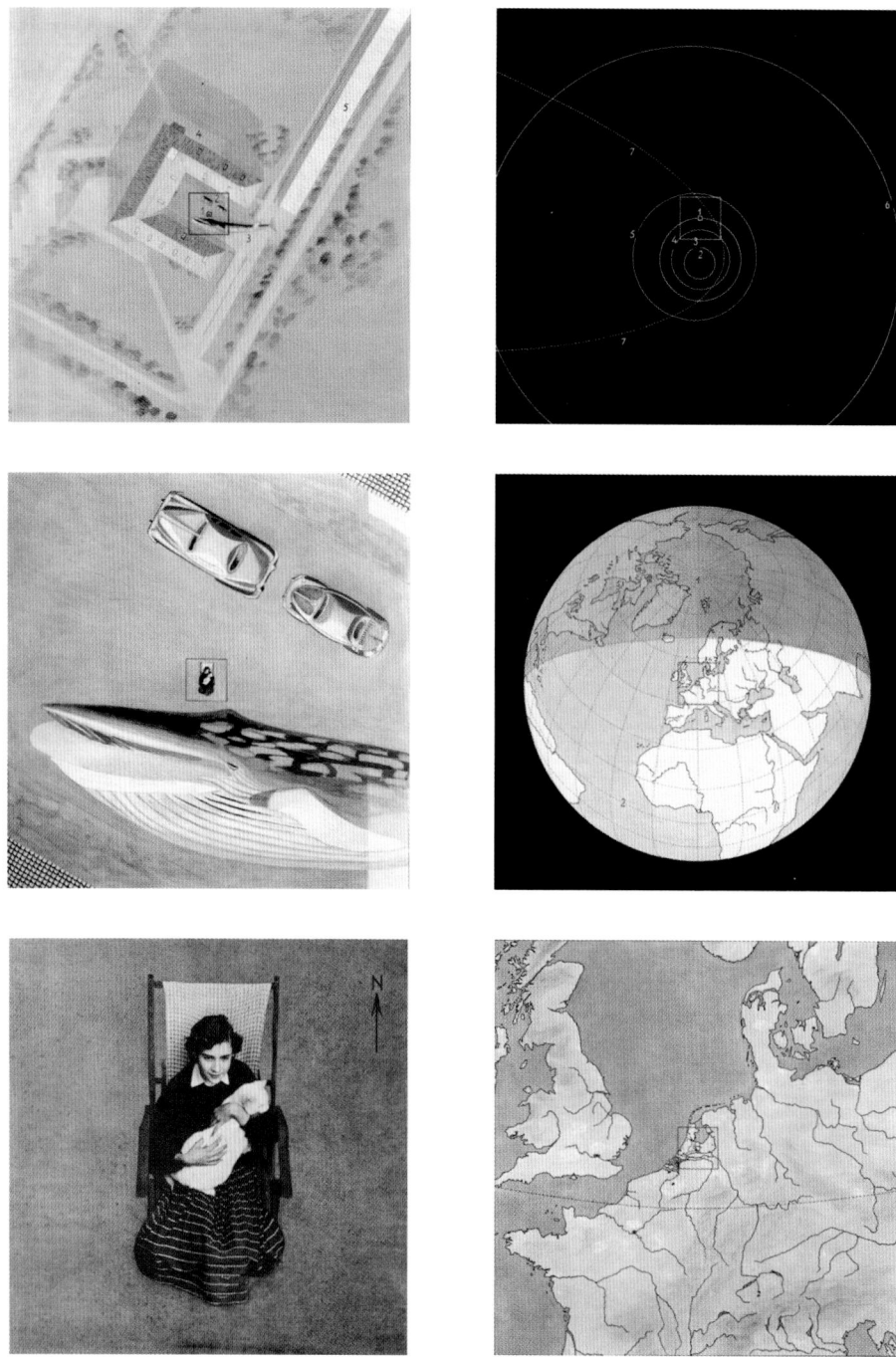

Pages 130–131

Illustrations from Kees Boeke, *Cosmic View: The Universe in 40 Jumps*, 1957.

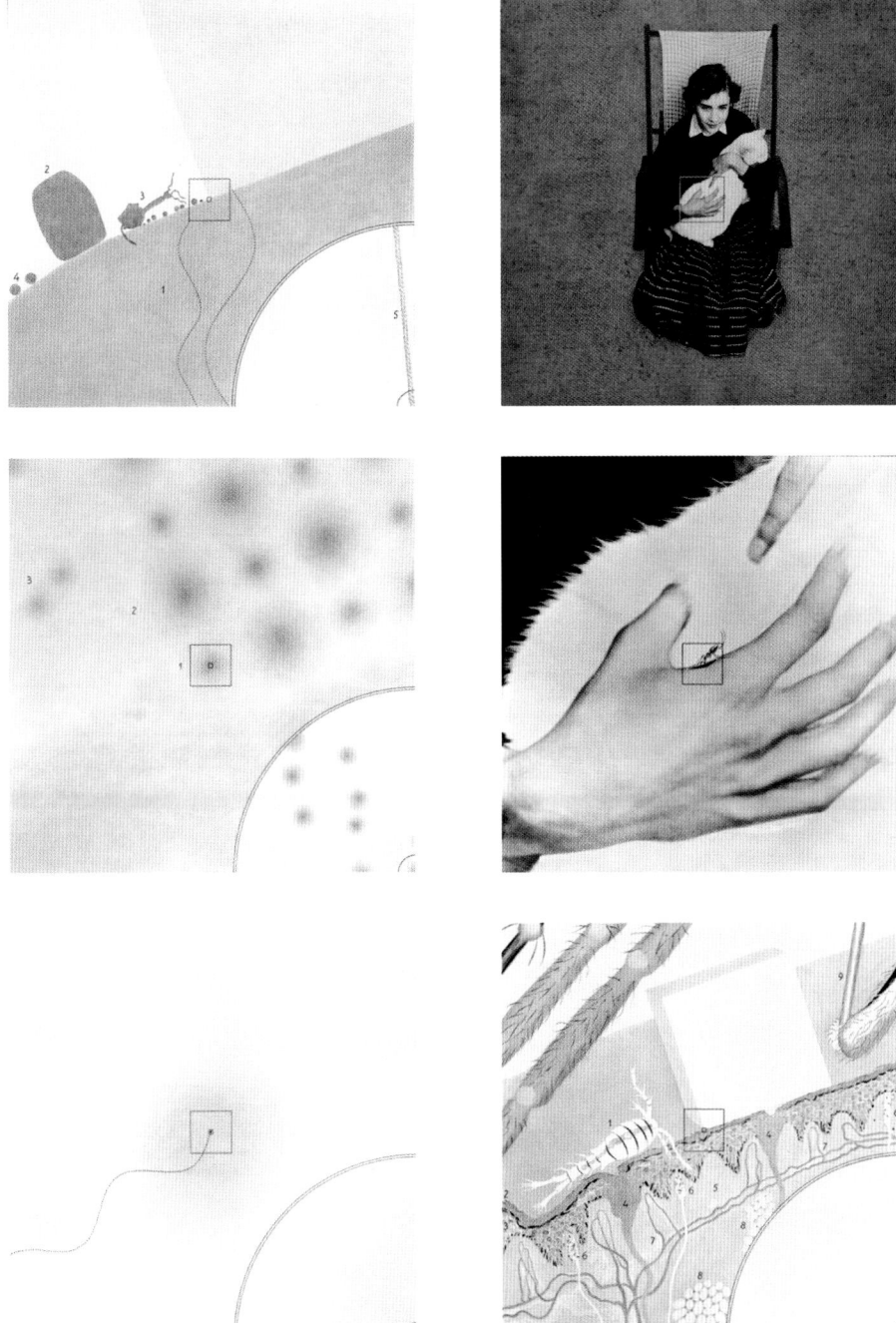

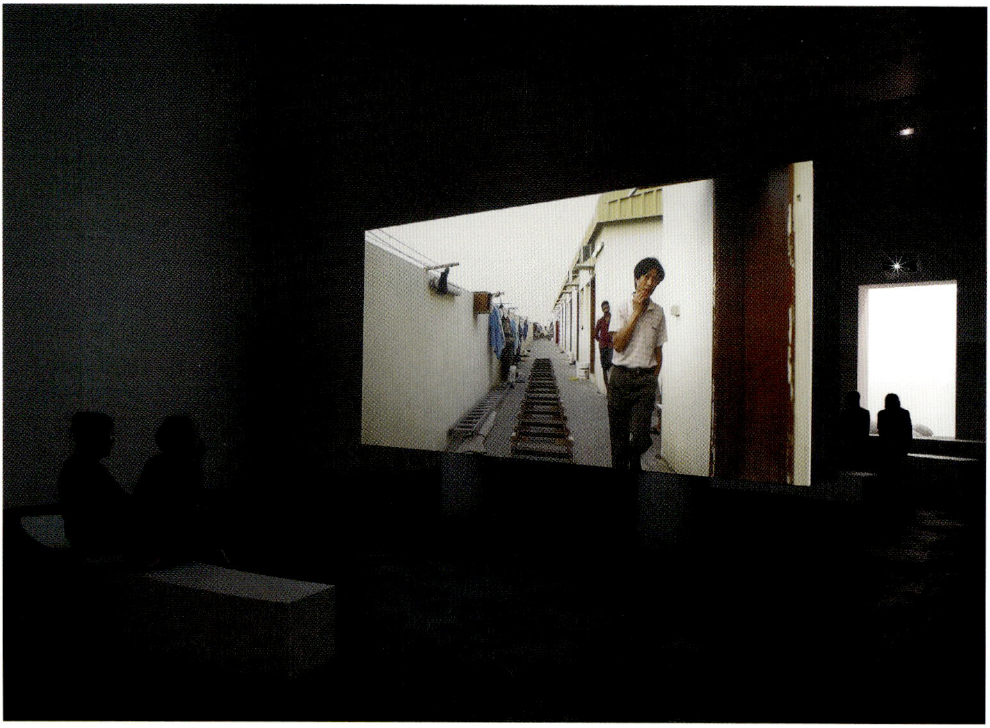

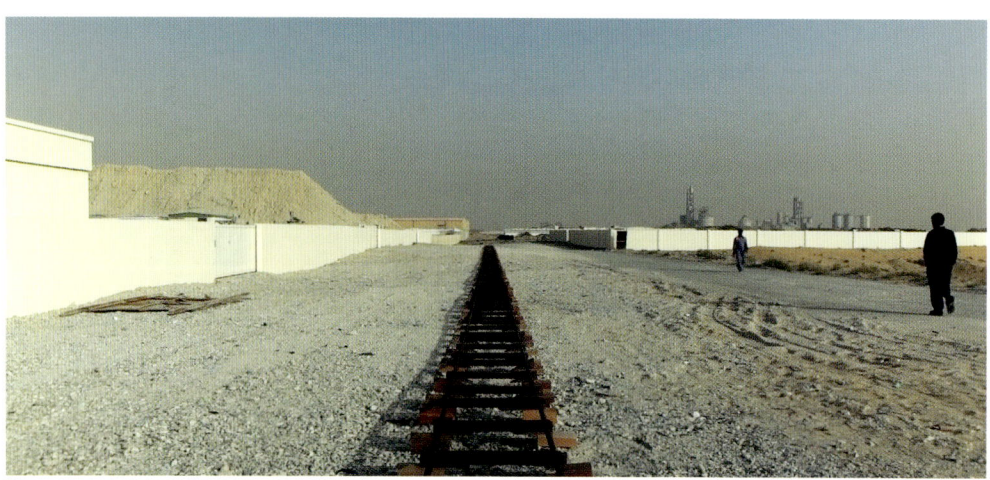

2. Second Attribute: Movement

An overt element of cinematic grammar is movement. I would like to focus on the perspectival apparatus of the tracking shot, which, arguably, can engage objects from a centerless perspective that cuts across the perspectival fixity of traditional interlocking shot formations. This opens the possibility of a displacement from an anthropocentric perspective. Jean-Christophe Royoux, a French art critic, writes that "the tracking shot involves time that stages space itself. It is at once pure time and pure space. It is an image of the duration of time." Additionally, the smooth machinic fluidity of the tracking camera endows it with a non-human, abstract quality. Royoux indicates that "the movement of tracking, which is mechanical, almost indifferent, impossible to humanize, irrecoverable, comes close to the trace of drawing. 'Ça' tourne, 'It' films"—in a Freudian sense.[13] From a non-anthropocentric frame of reference, the eye of the tracking camera would thus be able to engage different entities within their plane of existence, seamlessly shifting from one to the other, cutting across scalar attributes and conceivably bending the perception of their relative dimensions. I will expand on this in the next section, about fragmentation and suture.

As a closing remark, I would venture to say that the eerie quality of an extremely slow tracking shot, becoming, as Royoux argues, an image of time, would be able to engage the imperceptible passage of Braudel's *longue durée*. More speculatively even, a very slow tracking shot could almost make time be perceived as an emergent property of the objects it represents, in the sense of Einstein—that is, contrary to Newton's stable relation between space-time and the objects it contains. Einstein's theory of General Relativity of 1917 postulates that space and time are not an abstract grid of four coordinates independent of the objects it contains, but are a continuum produced and warped by them. The 2017 detection of gravitational waves—ripples in the *fabric* of space-time traveling through the universe—provided experimental validation of the last bit of Einstein's predictions that had yet to be proved.

Page 132 (upper)

Melik Ohanian, DAYS, I See what I Saw and what I will See, 2011. HD video with sound. Double synchronised projection on the two sides of a same screen. 2 x 42 min. Exhibition view, CRAC Sète, 2014. Courtesy of the artist and Galerie Chantal Crousel Paris. Photograph Marc Domage © Melik Ohanian / ADAGP, Paris 2018.

Page 132 (lower)

Melik Ohanian, DAYS, I See what I Saw and what I will See, 2011. HD video with sound. Double synchronised projection on the two sides of a same screen. 2 x 42 min. Video still. Courtesy of the artist and Galerie Chantal Crousel Paris. © Melik Ohanian / ADAGP, Paris 2018.

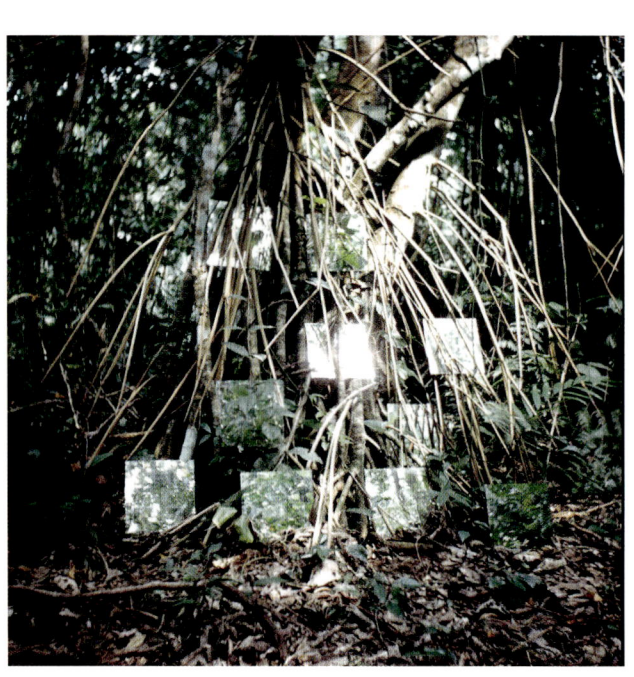

3. Third Attribute: Fragmentation and Suture

Cinema is traditionally structured as a set of coherently articulated interlocking shots. Shot relationships have the dual function of producing the syntax whereby cinematic meaning emerges and of "suturing" the spectator into filmic space, time and narrative. Conversely, in the continuum that the human subject experiences in the real world, articulation is not necessary since meaning emerges as an effect of relations of continuity and contiguity.

Robert Smithson's *Yucatan Mirror Displacements* fragmented the world around them, suggesting the impossibility of a centered, subjective vision. These temporary landmarks, produced in Southern Mexico in 1969, shattered the idea of a viewing self soundly sutured into the world. Smithson's mirrors had the effect of collapsing subjectivity into the landscape. Smithson's idea of displacement is an interesting point of departure for thinking toward post-anthropocentric cinematic structures. An example of such a structure is found in *Leviathan*, the 2012 film by Lucien Castaing-Taylor and Véréna Paravel, two artists and visual anthropologists working at the Sensory Ethnography Lab at Harvard. The film was shot on a trawler off the coast of Nantucket, in the "same waters where Herman Melville's *Pequod* gave chase to Moby Dick" with a dozen cameras "tossed and tethered, passed from fisherman to filmmaker" as the synopsis states. The cameras' eyes engage their objects—fishermen, ropes, fish, birds, water—with a gaze that is more haptic than optic. The multiplication of viewpoints coupled with their disengagement from the filmmakers' performativity, the fast-paced visual reduction of human and non-human entities (fishes, seagulls, and machines) to one single body work to break down subjective vision. The spectator is transformed into a floating entity fully immersed into this flat cosmology while paradoxically de-sutured from this universe.

Page 134

Robert Smithson, *Yucatan Mirror Displacements*
(1–9), 1969, Yucatan, Mexico. Nine original 126 format
chromogenic-development transparencies. Collection
of the Solomon R. Guggenheim Museum, New York.
Courtesy James Cohan, New York. © 2019 Holt/Smithson
Foundation / 2019, ProLitteris, Zurich for SMITHSON
ROBERT works.

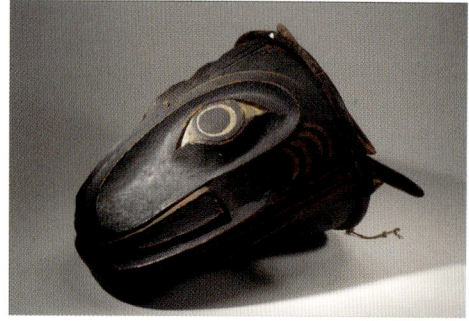

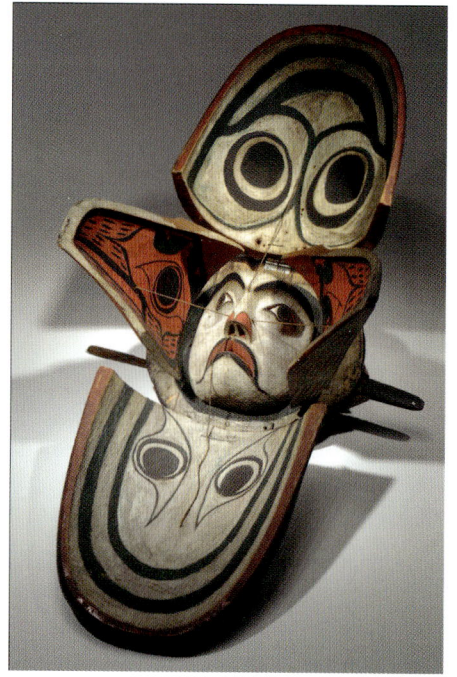

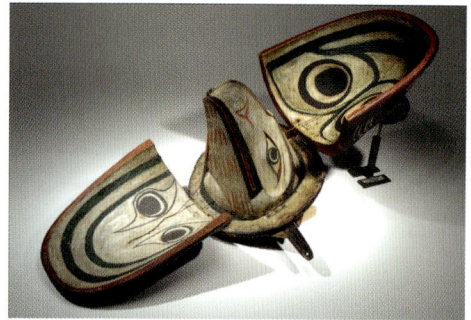

4. Fourth Attribute: Perspective

I would like to start rethinking the idea of perspective as produced by the gaze and try to imagine some qualities of a non-human gaze by calling into use some concepts from anthropology. Today we know that many non-modern societies present human and non-human entities as multiplicities that are not reducible to Western distinctions between nature and culture, a division that actually emerged quite recently in the narrative of Western history. For the French anthropologist Philippe Descola, non-modern cultures do not construct the sharp opposition between humans and non-humans of modern Western cultures. Descola establishes instead that a duality between physicality and interiority—the corporeal equipment or skin, and the spiritual dimension—is universally present. This universal can occur in a variety of modalities of connection and interaction between the corporeal and spiritual planes. Stated in Western terms, pure physicality would be a body without a mind, and pure interiority a mind without a body. In this scheme of things the Western body-mind opposition is to be considered as a special case of a general dual system. Through the principle of identity and difference, Descola establishes a second duality, that which exists between continuity and discontinuity. From these distinctions between physicality and interiority, and continuity and discontinuity, Descola defines a matrix of four cosmological categories under which each belief system falls.

I would like to briefly consider two of these categories: "animism" and what Descola calls "naturalism." Under "animism," humans and non-humans—animals, plants, the weather, the sea—possess different physicalities but similar interiorities, which can communicate by continuity. Western Modernism falls in the category of "naturalism," which inverts the premises of animism. Under naturalism, humans and non-humans possess identical physicalities—e.g. two arms and two legs or four legs for earth mammals—that is, a material continuity but different interiorities, which cannot communicate. Under this category, semiosis and the emergence of culture—language, free will, creativity, and so forth—are exceptional and specific to the human species alone.

The question of perspective is wonderfully analyzed by the Brazilian anthropologist Eduardo Viveiros de Castro, an important influence on Descola. Viveiros de Castro coined the term "Perspectivism" to describe the cosmology of the Amerindians he studied. For them, "humanity" is what binds together all beings—humans, animals, and plants. They are separated instead by their different natures, that is, their bodily assets. The perceptual apparatus specific to each body imposes upon each being a specific position and point of view in a general relational ecology. As Viveiros de Castro writes: "The visible form of each species is a simple envelope (a 'clothing') hiding an internal human form that is only accessible [...] to the gaze of members of the same species, or certain perspectival 'commutators,' like shamans."[14] In perspectivism "the way humans perceive animals and other subjectivities that inhabit the world—gods, spirits, the dead, inhabitants of other cosmic levels, meteorological phenomena, plants, occasionally even objects and artefacts—differs profoundly from the way in which these beings see humans and see themselves."[15]

If we are keen to accept the validity of native cosmologies, of alternative modes of relation between human and non-human agents, can they inspire us to imagine a cinema in which oppositional concepts such as subject and object, foreground and background, subject and narrator can be collapsed into new forms of intimacy, as entangled co-presences within one single visual universe? To achieve this, can the camera become, in the sense of Viveiros de Castro, a perspectival commutator?

Page 136

Kwakiult Mask of Transformation. Collected by G. Hunt in 1901.
Courtesy of the Division of Anthropology, American Museum of
Natural History, New York. Inventory number 16/8942.

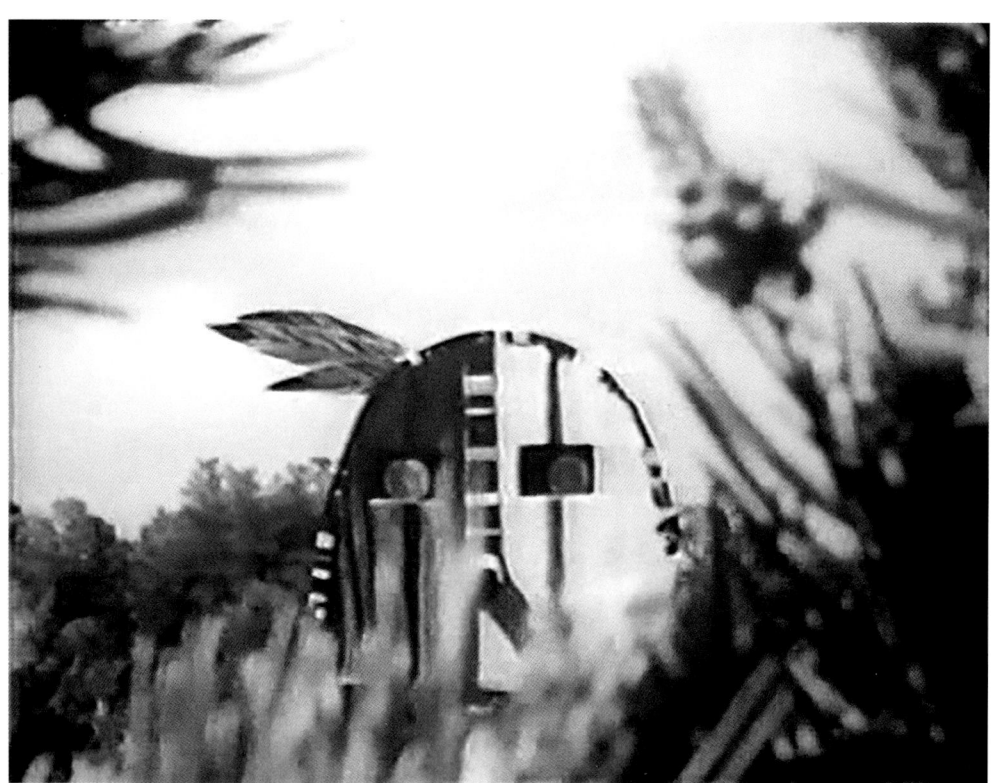

Page 138

Alfred Clah, *Intrepid Shadows*, 1966. From the film series *Navajo Film Themselves*. 16mm, b&w, 18 min. Film Still. Courtesy of the Penn Museum.

I would like to close this section with some notes about a scene in my film from 2017, *Una Cuba mediterranea*. It is a filmic essay about the failed ambitions of Italian millionaire publisher and revolutionary Giangiacomo Feltrinelli to transform the island of Sardinia into a Mediterranean Cuba in the late 1960s. The film follows filmmaker Antonia, anthropologist Eleonora, and their Sardinian friend Giuliano as they travel across the island.

We filmed one scene at Michelangelo Antonioni's summer vacation house on Sardinia's West coast. The villa is a piece of utopian architecture built by architect Dante Bini and is now a ruin. We had scouted the house in 2013 and filmed in the summer of 2015.

I believe that in *Una Cuba mediterranea* I was tentatively exploring some of the ideas contained in this essay, in particular that of the camera as a perspectival operator able to engage the universe of each entity it films, in an attempt to subvert the human versus non-human binary that I described earlier in this text.

The scene at Villa Antonioni starts with a shot of a tortoise. The camera then slowly approaches the domed house with a viewpoint that could be that of the reptile or of one of the film's characters. Next, the camera films the two female characters as they talk, moving then to frame them as if they were seen by the "eye" of the house (it's main window toward the sea). The camera then follows a lizard moving on sun-heated stones while we hear in voiceover the last part of their conversation. This is their dialog:

"I feel elementary."

"That is?"

"In front of the sea, that looks at you, indifferent. I don't have the perception that I am watched and I like this… If you think about it, how do you know that Sardinia is an island? It's the idea of an island. The only way to be certain that it is a real island would be to go around it by foot to find yourself here again."

"The characters of The Mysterious Island were wondering if they happened to be on an island or a continent…"

"You know, the cliché "an island is a continent" doesn't suffice. For me an island can be the prototype of a continent. It's a question of scale."

The energy of their voices is laid-back—"stoned," yet focused. The image of the lizard combined with the mood of the voices prompts us to feel that we might be following the thought flow of the animal. Arguably, this sequence marks a cinematic limit, in that when a human voice gives a face to a non-human agent it takes that face away, re-establishing the hierarchy of the classical human versus non-human binary. The sequence generates nevertheless a true suspension of disbelief in which the spectator is transported, if only for a brief moment, into the universe of a nonhuman subjectivity.

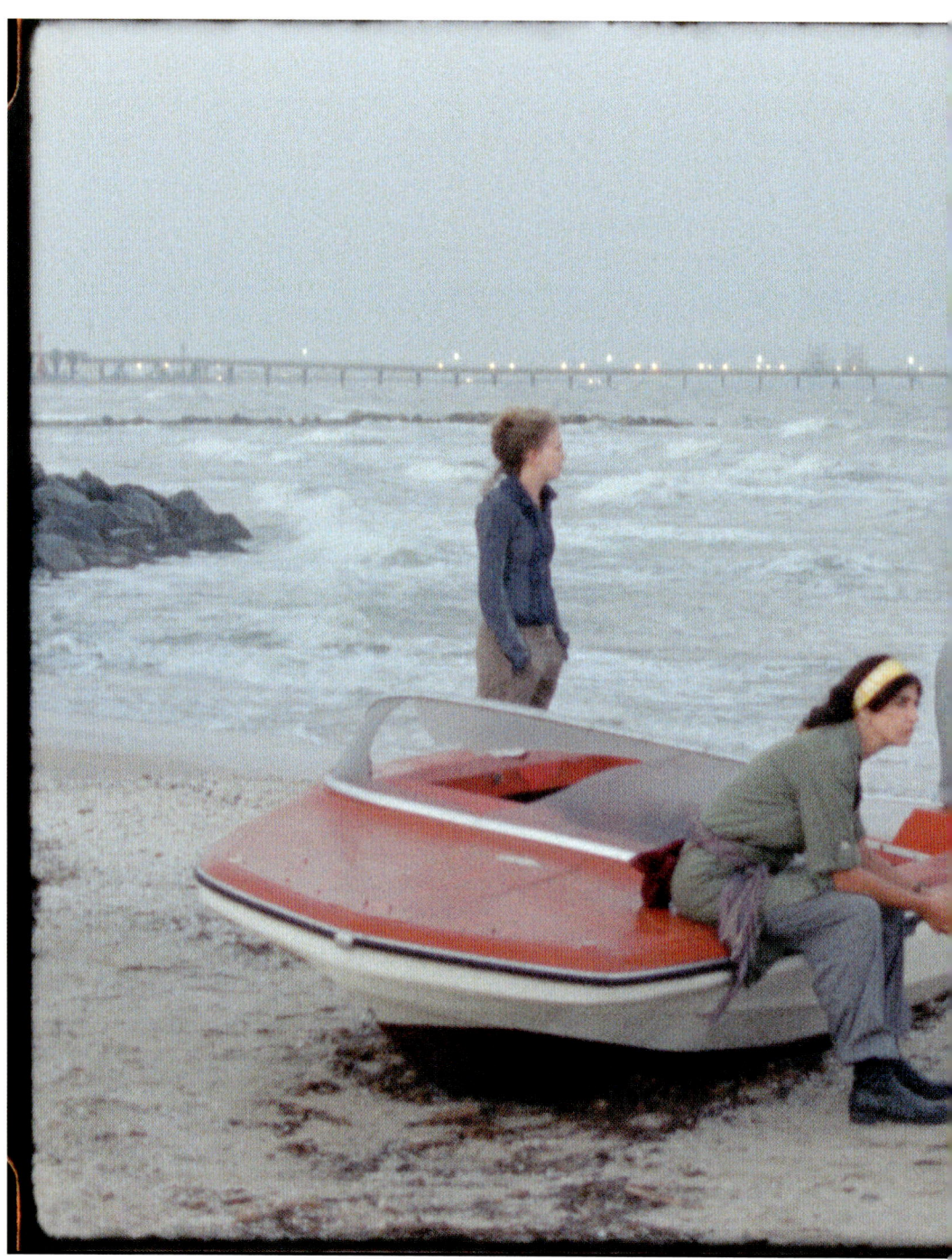

Pages 140–141

Marco Poloni, *Una Cuba mediterranea*, 2018. S-16mm, S-8mm and HD Video
on DCP 2K, colour, dolby 5:1, native 15:9 into 16:9, italian with subtitles, 56 min.
Film still. Courtesy of the artist and Galerie Campagne Première Berlin.

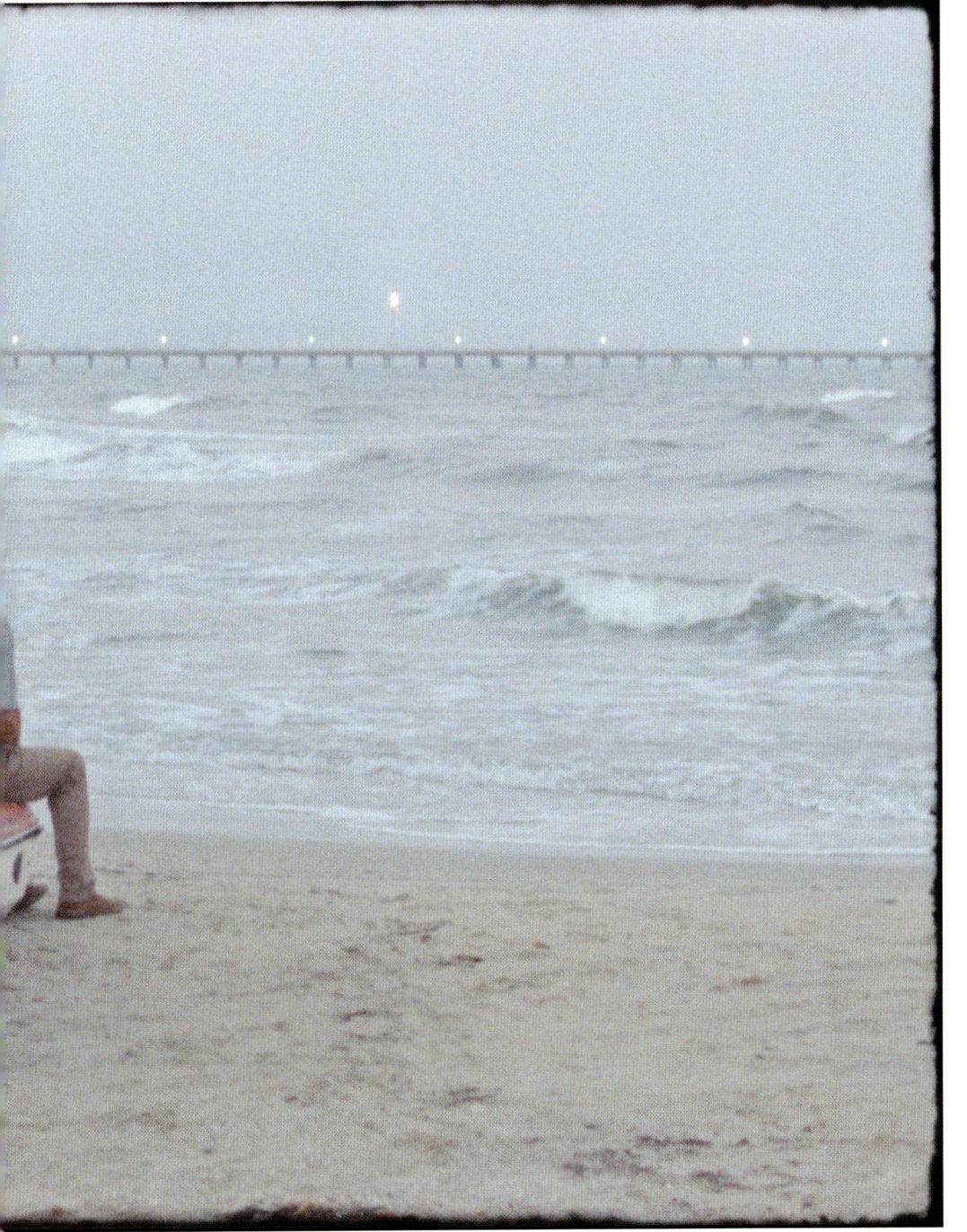

Marco Poloni, *Una Cuba mediterranea*, 2018.
Production photograph. Courtesy of the artist
and Galerie Campagne Première Berlin.

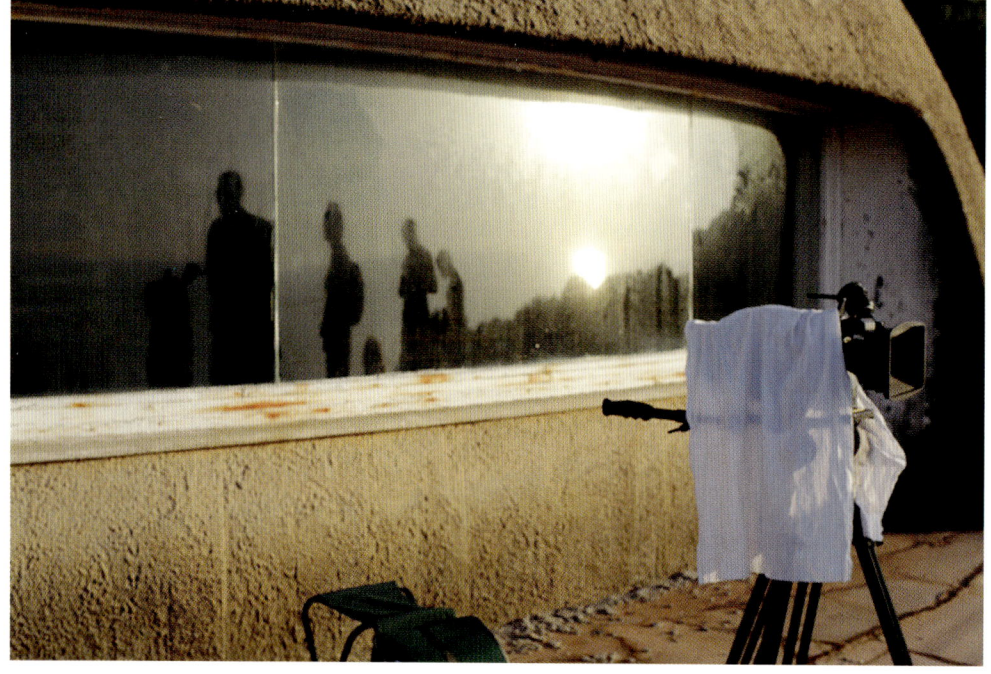

Notes

1. The Analogue Island Bureau http://www.theanalogueislandbureau.net/projects/01_the_majorana_experiment/index.html (accessed September 17, 2018).

2. The Analogue Island Bureau http://www.theanalogueislandbureau.net/projects/01_the_majorana_experiment/maj11.html (accessed September 17, 2018).

3. Mantegna, 2005: 136.

4. The Analogue Island Bureau http://www.theanalogueislandbureau.net/ (accessed September 17, 2018).

5. https://www.cla.purdue.edu/english/theory/narratology/terms/suture.html (accessed September 17, 2018).

6. The exact second phrase is "The lake is a large tranquil eye." (Bachelard, 1999: ix). It can clearly be translated to the pelagic space.

7. Von Uexküll, 1956.

8. Morton, 2013: 2, 15.

9. Guth, 2015: 128.

10. Braudel, 1995: 23.

11. Braudel, 1995: 21.

12. Pick and Narraway, 2013: 8.

13. Royoux, 2016–2017: 128–129. My translation

14. Viveiros de Castro, 2014: 66, n. 25.

15. Viveiros de Castro, 2014: 56.

Bibliography

Gaston Bachelard, *Water and Dreams: An Essay on the Imagination of Matter* (Dallas: Pegasus Foundation, Dallas Institute of Humanities and Culture, 1999).

Fernand Braudel, *The Mediterranean and the Mediterranean World in the Age of Philip II, Volume I* (Berkeley and Los Angeles: University of California Press, 1995).

Christine Guth, *Hokusai's Great Wave: Biography of a Global Icon* (Honolulu: University of Hawaii Press, 2015).

Rosario Nunzio Mantegna, "The Value of Statistical Laws in Physics and Social Sciences," *Quantitative Finance*, 2, 5, (2005): 133–140.

Timothy Morton, *Hyperobjects: Philosophy and Ecology after the End of the World* (Minneapolis: University of Minnesota Press, 2013).

Anat Pick and Guinevere Narraway (eds), *Screening Nature: Cinema Beyond the Human*, (New York and Oxford: Berghahn Books, 2013).

Jean-Christophe Royoux, "Cinéma d'exposition: l'invention d'un médium," *La Part de l'Oeil*, 30, (2016–2017): 105–141.

Jakob von Uexküll, *Streifzüge durch die Umwelten von Tieren und Menschen* (Hamburg: Rowohlt, 1956).

Eduardo Viveiros de Castro, *Cannibal Metaphysics* (Minneapolis: Univocal, 2014).

Senses at Sea:
For an Amphibian Cinema

Clara Masnatta

On October 27, 2017, at six o'clock in the evening of a storm-ridden night, the Thyssen Bornemisza Art Contemporary Academy, in collaboration with the Nationalgalerie – Staatliche Museen zu Berlin, launched the weekend-long event "Fishing for Islands" in the Hamburger Bahnhof Museum for Contemporary Art, Berlin. The program offered "a wave of oceanic activities" within "three tide cycles" (thirty-six hours) that included a series of performances, lectures, sound installations, and a video work by Armin Linke, entitled *Oceans*.

As the storm gusted through the city, each of the various parts of the initiative in the museum's historical hall was presented as "a new island emerging in the vast field of issues concerning the current state of the oceans." The phrasing of appearance and disappearance in the program resonated somewhat darkly in the aftermath of hurricane Harvey, Irma, and Maria's ongoing disaster in Puerto Rico, Dominica, and the Bahamas. Still, "tidalectics" rhymed with the poetry of the description; buzzwords here, catchy concepts there orchestrated the exploratory fête. At the exact midpoint of the sleepless initiative, the fresh MacArthur genius grant recipient Trevor Paglen addressed the audience. Around twenty people convened for his talk entitled "The Cloud under the Ocean." The lecture was to deal, specifically, with the invisibility of what is submerged under the surface of the oceans within the larger hidden world of seeing machines—the issue that established Paglen's fame.

The presentation looked back at the influence of sea powers across history, anticipated war on who controls the information running through underwater internet cables, and ended on a prophetic note. If humans traditionally had looked up at the stars for their destiny, Paglen enjoined, it was now time to look downward for the future, down at coral reefs and undersea wires. From the front row (really, a bean bag archipelago), I recalled Jorge Luis Borges' observation that no author likes to owe anything to his contemporaries.

"Disassembled" Images

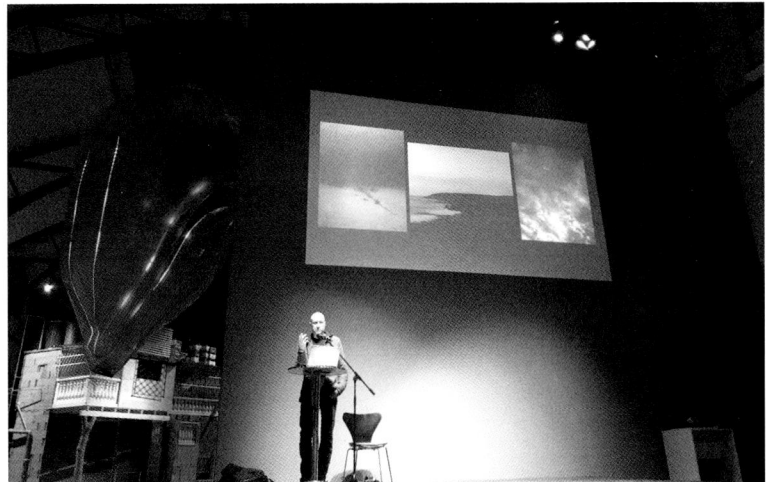

Introduced to the podium as an artist and researcher, a new species took the floor: the click-bait intellectual. Paglen offered nicely illustrated, watered-down ideas in attention-span proof packages to be easily consumed. He spoke in the old genius artist's tradition; peerless, unlike a critic with an intellectual community behind and before him. What hovered, in fact, behind Paglen was a giant balloon in the shape of a jellyfish (Tue Greenfort's sculpture *Draebergople*) that approached the speaker with its intermittent comedy of colors. (fig. 1)

Off the podium, by the food truck installed for hipster tastes, I casually asked Paglen why he did not mention the proximate work of Allan Sekula. He responded that limited time necessitated quoting quota (Paglen spoke for approximately thirty minutes of the allotted hour). A "but" immediately followed for recanting ("But, yes, we basically do the same"). To seek a consciousness of present, past, and future without paying attention to the history of one's own field is a tragic irony. Soliciting consciousness, my essay will interrogate filmmaking feats concerned with the maritime imaginary on different sides of the Atlantic after (and before) Allan Sekula.

Rather than "secularizing" hagiographies, "secular criticism" is in order—or, to be more specific, the conceptual cabinet that Edward Said (1983) drew from the literary models of filiation and affiliation. Recall how the hierarchy of genealogy that loomed large in filiation (Harold Bloom's *The Anxiety of Influence*, for example) got undone at Borges' hands. Borges' "Kafka and his precursors" presented the author's design of their own predecessors for an affiliation without haunting skeletons. Borgesian irreverence aside, transpersonal bonds make collegiality, consensus, and class possible across great distances in time and space. Horizontality of this kind lies at the core of the lineage of filiative assemblage, "disassembled images" included. Sekula's "disassembled images," as defined by Benjamin Buchloh, further present the analysis of the rhetoric of the images as well as linguistic and institutional conventions. (Buchloh, 1995: 189–200)

Foretelling, too, is done by referring. Take Sekula's piece perhaps removed furthest from the documentary, and being closest to a tonic for the imagination: *Black Tide. Fragments for an Opera* projected the prophet with his back turned to the future. This elliptic, lyrical piece on the 2002 oil-spill disaster in the Galician coast inscribed "the photographer, descendent of the augurs and haruspices" of Walter Benjamin's "Little History of Photography" in the proleptic polyphony of its script. (Sekula, 2003: 2) Sekula composed a libretto that was really not for staging, just like Apollinaire's "cinema-drama" *La Bréhatine* was not meant for filming.

This genre of fancy favored among Dadaists und Surrealists alike was defined when Benjamin Fondane published his three "scenarii intournables" [unfilmable scenarios] with the title *Ciné-poèmes* in 1928. Poetry came to Fondane in cinematographic book form; the "beauty of the fetus" returned to Sekula as opera. For Fondane, film scripts were "impossible to write," in the sense of capturing a film's complexity on the page. With the impracticable form, Sekula partook of the seemingly impossible coastal cleaning task undertaken by the locals. Sekula's variant anchored the Sisyphean task visually with *The Triptych of Fatigue*. The image clustering at once negated the single iconic image (photojournalism's holy grail) and spoke to the aesthetics of the fragment (imagination's analeptic).

Commissioned by curator Carles Guerra and the Spanish daily *La Vanguardia*, *Marea negra. Fragmentos para una ópera* materialized in the accessible and unpretentious printed form of the newspaper. The piece graphically referred back to the original publication of Benjamin's "Little History of Photography," first appearing as feuilleton in the weekly *Literarische Welt* in 1931. Benjamin's was also a work at the crossroads of writing and photography. It will be an exaggeration, however, to push the tidal precursor as far back as to Fondane's edition (which featured two Man Ray photographs) and assert that photography there appeared in triad with cinema and literature, in typical Sekulian fashion.

While the future for Benjamin appeared encapsulated in the "spark of contingency," for Sekula it was far from imminent. The endeavor in *Black Tide* remained tensed between the unrealization of the thing and its realizability. It got peppered with futurology. The coming opera, the text began, was to be performed in Galician language in 2032—a time estimated to will have marked the end of the ecological damages on the coast.

Programmatic statements and avant-garde stylistics advanced the beginning, or so it appeared. Sekula's script started with a Galician fable—flashed, but not told: a cow with a lantern suspended from the horns crossing the stage. These published fragments further included a refrain in *galego* that gave voice to "the collective Sisyphus" through a chanting gesture, making audible comparable to making visible what challenges with abstraction. Perhaps because visibility in this case seemed a temptation rather than a challenge —"You had the image of the mass deployed volunteers and other kind of workers as mass ornament which is very attractive to photojournalists," Sekula reported—*Black Tide* took an aural turn within Sekula's enduring politics of making representable. (Guerra, 2017:141)

The opera script took up the risk of spectacle, and confronted head on the possibilities of language, even its perils. The concern with language recurs in Sekula's other, equally "disassembled" slide works and photo-text pieces, as does a preoccupation with cinema and photography. Consider *Fish Story* (1995), in particular, the "Message in a bottle" section. This segment revolving around the port of Vigo in Spain took interest in the fact that Jules Verne's novel *Twenty Thousand Leagues Under the Sea* was available in Spanish, but not in Galician translation. "Proletarian cosmopolitism" of the sea notwithstanding, to dream in your mother tongue of the *Nautilus'* gallery of champions of the oppressed or of Captain Nemo as a submarine Robin Hood in the submerged treasure theater of the battle of Vigo Bay for your first, imaginary disentanglement from the tentacles of capitalism—a dream remained.

Language came to take central yet contested dimensions in the film that is the continuation of *Fish Story* by assembling means: *The Forgotten Space* (2010). This "essay film" that Sekula made with Noel Burch takes issue with the intermodal container and its rise among capitalism's modes of abstraction. Since its invention in the 1950s, the container became the primary way of transporting goods by sea and rail. The film describes the impact on landscapes and cities and on economic and labor conditions. Thanks to Sally Stein's presentation of the notebooks of Sekula, we know that language became a thorny question when assembling the film's images. Bérénice Reynaud and James Benning submitted a joint critique on discursive relevance. Against their charges of over-stating, we read Sekula's lucid grappling:

> Why is the argument that the texts [*sic*] "kills the image" that is [it] eradicates the ground for pictorial autonomy, metaphor, or ineffability; why is the argument fundamentally impoverished, and in an unwitting way logocentric [...] in the name of anti-logos? Because this argument attributes to the word a power beyond itself, a denotative certainty that is rarely if ever achieved in actual

linguistic practice. Thus the anti-logos [position] takes denotative reduction, certainty, identity, to be the Holy Grail, one that has been found, institutionalized, against which the poor image can only rebel. (Stein, 2017: 84)

And further:

Why does this stubborn refusal to accept what Barthes called the "relay function"—while absolutizing his contrary idea of the "anchorage function"—so frequently enacted and re-enacted, even by those who claim to understand the principles of deconstruction? (84)

The truth is that, however essayistic and assembled, *The Forgotten Space* was fraught with what Burch called "rambling" or digressions that successfully impeded reductive summations. *Excursus* prevented the film from becoming an artifact of easy interpretative resolution as was, for instance, Trevor Paglen's illustrated lecture.

Language will continue to be a bone of contention across two novel experimental documentaries produced on either side of the Atlantic Ocean: Lois Patiño's *Costa da Morte* [Coast of Death] (2013) and *Leviathan* (2012) by Véréna Paravel and Lucien Castaing-Taylor. Both films eschew linearity, voice-over, narrative, or a traditional point of view to chart paths to understanding the maritime or coastal world. A shared aural precedence over the black opens to starting white inscriptions. *Costa da Morte* quotes an untranslated sentence of Galician writer Alfonso Castelao: "Nun entrar do home na paisaxe e da paisaxe no home creouse a vida eterna de Galiza" ("Upon entering men in landscape and landscape in men the eternal life of Galicia was created."). *Leviathan* presents, in funny Gothic script, the English couplet in reference to the eponymous sea monster from the Bible's Book of Job. Each film will put forward a divergent take on language and articulate different tones through the literary genre marking each—poetry for Patiño, epic for *Leviathan*. The epic and the lyric, standing back to back to face reality, will place these documentaries equally far from the essayistic, which had fueled *The Forgotten Space*.[1]

The feature by the young Spanish director Lois Patiño, a first in his ongoing experiments in the poetics of landscape, is a variegated portrait of the place referred to as "coast of death" in Galician—what was considered *finis terrae* before the discovery of America. *Costa da Morte* is, in fact, at the antipodes of the film shot by Véréna Paravel and Lucien Castaing-Taylor just off the New England coast in the United States. The two films appear as polar opposites not only in geographical terms, but also concerning the driving force of each. *Mythophilia* propels

Patiño's archeology of the strata of a landscape that is both mythical and real, maritime and not. On the other hand, the dark tour de force of Paravel and Castaing-Taylor approaches commercial fishing through a pre-symbolic "sensory immersion" without distance or linguistic discourse, and thrives with *logophobia*. Or does it?

By far the most successful film produced at the Sensory Ethnography Lab at Harvard University, Paravel and Castaing-Taylor described *Leviathan* as the first of four works in the project "Canst Thou Draw Out Leviathan with a Hook?," which explores how humanity is haunted by the sea and the relationship to the oceanic world and the mythology of the Deep. In one of the many interviews that the filmmakers were invited to give, Paravel stated that "[t]he film became a physical reaction to the experience of being out at sea." (Lim, 2012: n.p.) From the critical distance that *Leviathan* ostensibly refused through the "sensuous immersion" aesthetics, the fact that Pavel and Castaing-Taylor's tetralogy did not come to fruition suggests that this film of deceivingly precarious images exhausted their representation of said universe.

However different, *Costa da Morte* and *Leviathan* integrate a cinema of senses at sea. Both examples of sensory cinema play with spectatorial expectations through a symmetrically opposite strategy. Each film brings about disorientation by operating with distance: augmenting or collapsing distance.

Disorientation is chiefly conveyed through close-ups in *Leviathan*. The goal of the film is to convey experience and represent the sensory world; this roughly translates as materiality in your face. Through the reigning haptic visuality that anchors the "sensuous immersion" we hardly get any context. Abstraction appears as mode of depicting the subject at hand. Dispositive and dizziness combine for a viscous entanglement of things without distance or much sense of place. (fig. 2)

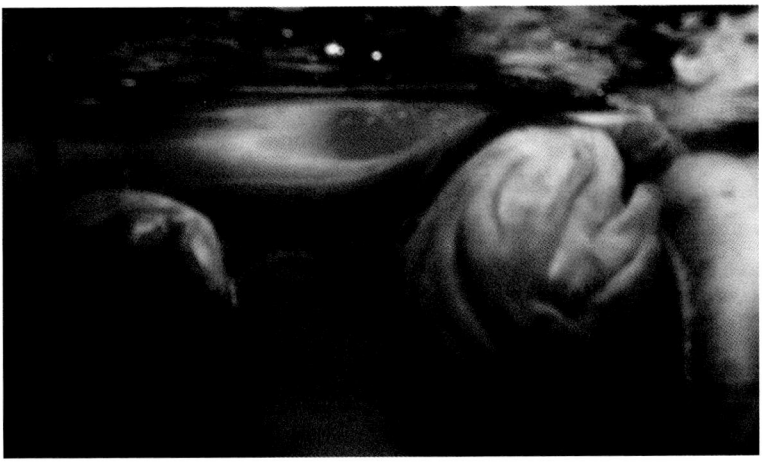

Fig. 2

Lucien Castaing-Taylor and Véréna Paravel, *Leviathan*, 2013. Courtesy of Cinema Guild.

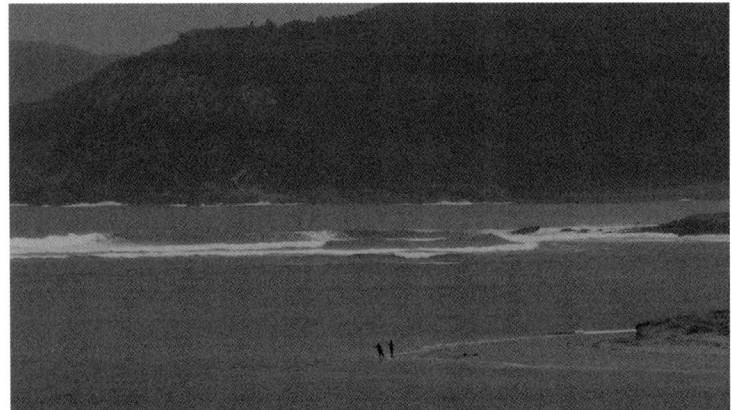

While bodily awareness is exceptional in cinema, *Leviathan* belongs to the genre that engages our bodies directly, like horror and pornography. Paradoxically, what stands behind *Leviathan*'s gripping, embodied experience is disembodied digital image-recording. The film's "sensuous immersion" was mainly achieved using twelve extreme sports GoPro cameras, which were variously attached to different things and people. As a result, we get multiple points of view that appear to be from the fish, the boat, and the sea's perspective, but not really human. There are also no intelligible voices to be heard throughout the movie's sensorial vertigo. This lack signals the attack on discursive clarity underlying Pavel and Castaing-Taylor's exercise in post-human filmmaking.

Years before their joint undertaking, in 1996, Castaing-Taylor spelled out his logophobia in a text entitled "Iconophobia." *Iconophobia* is described as distaste for propositional knowledge, narrative voice-over, the pre-researched and the pre-textualized, the false clarity of explanation, and more generally, didacticism. Against all these evils, messy sensory immersion emerged. *Leviathan*'s non-anthropocentric, animal-*cum*-machine ecology unleashed a two-fold counter-irritant: in this feature, you do not even know where you are, and you won't be told. Castaing-Taylor detailed this conjuncture as the film's quest against the dominant order of what he calls "discursive clarity," or what we sometimes refer to as phallologocentrism:

> Most documentaries' representation of the real is so attenuated and so discourse-based and language-based. We lie and mystify ourselves with words. Words can only take us so far. I think we want to get a much more embodied, a much more corporeal representation of reality that's almost a presentation of reality. Reality transcends our representation, it's not reducible to a set of statements of what commercial fishing's about. (Juzwiak, 2013: n.p.)

Costa da Morte, on the other hand, operates a double distance to construct the identity of a place. The film establishes a perceptual distance between image and sound: closeness of sound and distance of image. Long telephoto shots with a fixed camera give the first sense of distance. The second sense of distance is, strictly speaking, a prox-

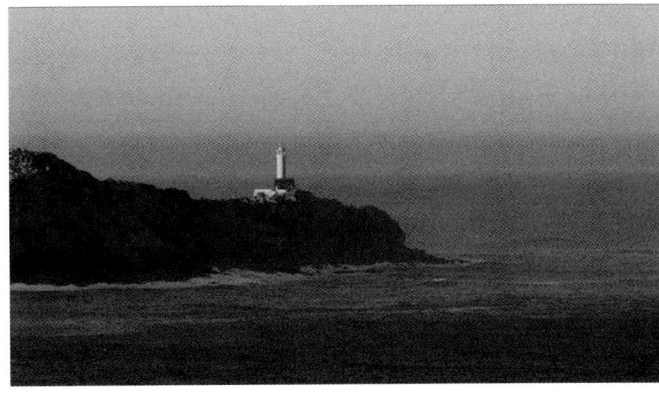

Fig. 4

Lois Patiño, *Costa da Morte*, 2013. © Lois Patiño, 2013.

imity: an aural proximity. Wide shots where the human figure is seen as distant but her voice is heard close prevail in the film. Audio was sometimes recorded through the wireless microphones, sometimes engineered onto the scene from an interview.

Sound makes distance palpable, and reveals the weaving of space and time. The film's double distance effectively conveys what Patiño pursued: "The intimacy of people in the immensity of landscape" delivers and requests a highly contemplative spectatorship.[2] Crisp, articulated voices compose the polyphony of this film *à thèse*. Yet they remain without face or name. The anonymity of the film's voices produces truly minimal characters. As if made of a subtle body, almost intangible, but characters, nevertheless, able to make vivid impressions. (fig. 3)

One of the scenes focuses on a dialogue between two (remotely viewed) occasional fishermen at the beach. They recount anecdotes and stories of vandals who attracted boats to the shore back at some point in history. We learn about the old ransack ruse of hanging lanterns from cows' horns to lure with the impression of a coastal settlement. (Sekula's *Black Tide* opening suddenly flashes under this new light.) Eventually, the two men will finish fishing, and start walking along the shore while reminiscing an incident involving a German submarine from World War II that leaked gas and killed all the fauna in the sea.

Costa da Morte's choral construction of the place it also designates inheres chronicles, memories, domestic happenings, intriguing tales. Patiño's aural prism channels the symbolic as a tectonics of place. It reveals that the orders of magnitude of history cover a broad spectrum. Shots without dialogue or trace of the voice's sonic privilege do not instead make for a non-human soundscape—the life and labor evoked by the opening shot's heavy breathing is a case in point. These "voiceless" scenes communicate sensation rather than advance a syntax of narration. The beach, the sea, the forest, the city unfold in a choreography of quasi- postcards of painterly beauty. (fig. 4)

Patiño's film interlocks a people's history unalike the history of the great narratives and events. This history of episodes and mythologies braided in conversations is a history of a minor magnitude in a decidedly minor language. The Galician language hardly enjoys scientific or literary status. (It is now, by way of Verne, that Sekula's work shines back onto Patiño's.) The politics of hearing and recording Galician voices are not identical to preserving dominant voices from the patriarchic center, to which Castaing-Taylor belongs.

Instead of following the horizon line like Patiño's panoramics, *Leviathan* capitalizes on a dynamic, up-and-down camera. Working from sea to ship to sky with vertical depth, the movie's vertiginous visuality fuses with a soundtrack combining the industrial noise of machinery with the inhalation-like sounds that the encased GoPro cameras produced when submerged. But the mono-recorded submersion of the little plastic-encased GoPro devices was supplemented with high quality professional stereo sound recording. *Leviathan* boasted a carefully designed soundtrack and surround sound that makes immersion more visceral than any of the film's images. (fig. 5)

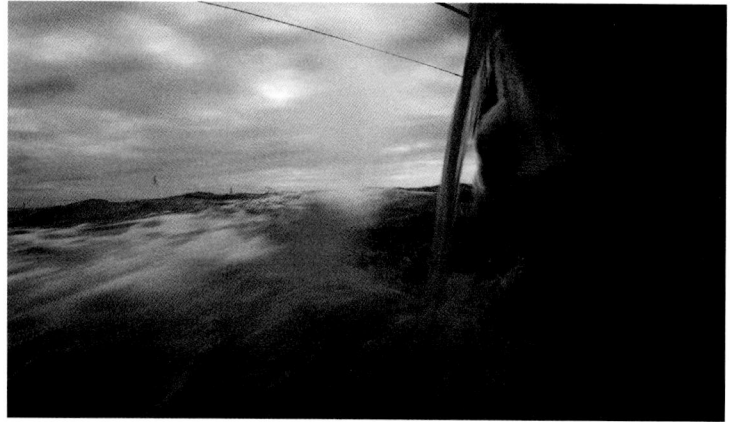

Fig. 5

Lucien Castaing-Taylor and Véréna Paravel, *Leviathan*, 2013. Courtesy of Cinema Guild.

Leviathan's orchestrated cacophony was the collaboration of renowned sound artist Ernst Karel (credited with "sound composition, edit, and mix") and Jacob Ribicoff (in charge of "sound design and re-recording mix"). A dark, opaque, noisy beginning sets the tone. The film opens with a sound storm of sea and metals, which announce the labor scene now developing, just like the natural sound of exhalation in Patiño's film heralded the men that we then viewed at work with their chainsaw.

While *Leviathan* employs sounds and shifting points of view that appear to be everything but human, *Costa da Morte*'s interplay reinscribes the human in the landscape for a disparate spectatorial experience,

"Disassembled" Images

intimate as breathing. The double distance of voices and image imparts a superimposed vision on the landscape. The proximity of voices conjures a spectral presence—a magic that harks back to the dramatics of radio and audio dramas. With the mind's eye, we come to see the face that is uttering the speech that we hear so clearly. The phantasmagorics of sound now works against the backdrop of a fixed camera. Patiño's strategy is auditory in physical terms but mighty as visual gambit in the psychological dimension—a move traceable, perhaps, to his training in psychology. It is also the polar opposite of Paravel and Castaing-Taylor's "aurally clamorous and visually ravishing, shot mainly at night and mostly in mega close-up," as *Artforum* forcefully described *Leviathan*. (Hoberman, 2013: 22) His film feels as if a patina of outdated technology, viz. radio and still photography, finished it off. Anachronisms breach through its evocative aesthetics, time and again. A complementary search for the spectral through the "atmospheric music" by Ann Deveria, a music duo from Madrid formed by Ángel Mancebo and José Tena, further inflected the faceless symphony of voices.

All in all, what Patiño shows is that language is also a materiality. Anecdotes, stories, fables, myths, *in fine*, ideology is properly material. Patiño's love for structure and superstructure—to put it in Marxist terms—sparks off a mythophilia that knows language can be poetic and altogether mythical, that is, deceiving. Like language's veil, the *nevoeiro* or mist that shrouds *Costa da Morte* appears to be confounding and revealing. The tenuous mystery condensed in this natural phenomenon is rightly placed at the film's very beginning.

How so very real language and stories are is palpable in a scene where two women are bathing at the beach. In conversation, the women retell the story of a hoax transmitted on the radio on April Fool's equivalent. Tons of TV sets, the radio announced, were suddenly available floating at sea, coming from a German shipwreck, for the rapacious few. This made-up, modern version of the riches of Vigo Bay resonated with the shipwreck record yielding the ominous "coast of death" christening. Like the layers of history submerged and afloat, glowing with silver or cathode rays, different temporalities appeared compatible. (fig. 6)

Just as lore or language is material, the converse is also true. Materiality or, really, the claim to "pure materiality," is also ideological—as a matter of fact, the ideological claim par excellence. Much like Patiño's proximal, crisp sound activated the viewer's imagination, *Leviathan*'s not so discernible images did something similar for the viewer. The low definition of GoPro cameras engaged the viewer with haptic materiality. Grotesque came hand in hand with logophobia for Castaing-Taylor: "The footage seemed to be much more opaque in a good way," he declared, "It activated the viewer's imagination much more." (Lim, 2012: n.p.)

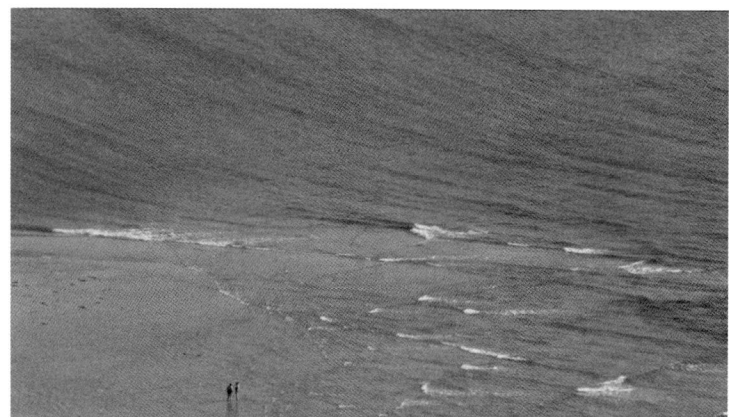

Fig. 6

A scene from Lois Patiño's *Costa da Morte*, 2013. © Lois Patiño, 2013.

The as-if-being-there intensity of *Leviathan* is in stark contrast to the spectral presence that Patiño conjured with his slow, understated film of atmospheric beauty. The difference lies in what each film demands, how they affect us, and the freedom the viewer is allowed. Sensation can be demanding, assaulting, even painful; it can also lead to sensationalism. Taking both together, Patiño's soundscape works as a caveat or critique of a certain kind of materiality, namely, the plenum of presence or, rather, "simulacral plenitude" of *Leviathan*. This is the term that Christopher Pavsek used in his critical appraisal when he examined some "basic presuppositions about the ability of film to convey experience and represent the sensory world," amidst the "uniform enthusiasm" that *Leviathan* elicited in numerous articles in scholarly journals and newspapers, as well as in the many museum exhibitions and symposia that the film also starred in. (Pavsek, 2015: 4)

In their search for presentation rather than re-presentation, Paravel and Castaing-Taylor sublated the ethnographic method of "participant observation" as *conditio humana* to make their film.[3] (Peleg, 2017: n.p.) We are far from what a particular anthropo-photographic form meant for Sekula (viz., the photographic sequencing in *Balinese Character* by Mead and Bateson) as discontinuous alternative to the series thanks to its visible inadequacy. But we are even further from Patiño's lay archeology. Because landscape is always-already human, his film streamlined scenes thick with culture. Admire the fire burning to the music of Manuel de Falla's "Ritual Fire Dance" in *rallentando*; the scene ablaze with the time-laden image theory—a covert reference to Georges Didi-Huberman's philosophy of art that appeared explicitly once excerpted into the short film *The Image Burns* (2013).

The sonic ethnography sought by the two (self-appointed) "recovering anthropologists" sets to unhear the cultural echoes resonating with Patiño. Paravel and Castaing-Taylor insist on their will to

"Disassembled" Images

express themselves with images and sounds, and abjure words. Against Derrida's "there's is no *hors-texte*," they assert that really *hors-corps* is impossible. Yet their expansion of the concept of the documentary smacks of knocking down the ladders that they climbed up on. In truth, the impulse contained in their film transpired layers of reading, and a disavowal of intertextuality that is sheer duality.

Start with the title, *Leviathan*. While the film chose to show the biblical sense of a sea monster, additional things hid in the name. The name is an allusion to the philosopher Thomas Hobbes, a champion of the sensorium's grounding the faculty of thought, in whose eponymous *magnus opus* "Leviathan" symbolized the state. Moreover, the film was shot in New England around New Bedford, former whaling capital and also the site around which Herman Melville's *Moby Dick* takes place. It is in this book that Melville referred to great whales with the term "leviathan." The filmmakers confessed in various interviews that they were reading Melville's foundational novel while shooting the film at sea. Yet *For a minor literature* by Gilles Deleuze, which thematized *Moby Dick* as example of becoming-other within Deleuze's rhizomatic musings, equally seemed to impregnate the film's eternal present of visual accumulation and de-hierarchization of nature and machine.

Next to the philosophical reflections of Julia Kristeva on the semiotic as the pre-symbolic, Gilles Deleuze on what a body can do, or Bruno Latour's affect theory, all variously informing the film, *Leviathan* is framed by parodic elements. The parody of quoting the Bible in Gothic script at the opening and ending with scientific Latin monikers for species' credits makes for an altogether ironic logophobia. To elevate seagulls with their Hitchcockian undertones as *larus marinus* or immortalize a haddock as *melanogrammus aeglefinus* requires a visit to the encyclopedia for the credited protagonists.

Leviathan sought materiality before symbolic processing, a kind of quest for tabula rasa. This negation, or, in this case, disavowal, of tradition is tantamount to the European avant-garde gesture par excellence. Vanguard gestures of this kind will less likely take place in a minor tradition such as the Galician of *Costa da Morte*. The concern over tradition differentiates, for instance, the history of Latin American Modernism from the European avant-garde. The minor, the peripheric, the semi-peripheric want a tradition. The impulse to participate or the desire for inscription in a larger, cosmopolitan universe is legitimate, and prior to any overthrowing.

A graphic illustration is to be found in each film's varying approach to Sharon Lockhardt's *Double Tide* (2009). Lockhardt's documentary film portrays the work of a female clam digger in the coastal mudflats of Maine, New England, as it is performed during the low tide at dusk and dawn. Its meditative and meticulous choreography is inverted by the

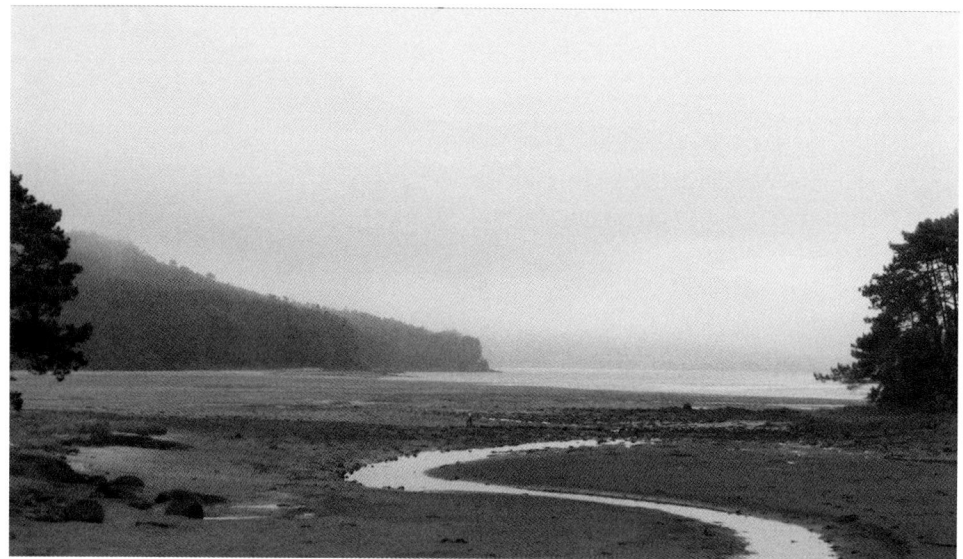

Fig. 7

Lois Patiño, *Costa da Morte*, 2013.
© Lois Patiño, 2013.

lysergic order of *Leviathan,* yet quoted by *Costa da Morte* in a homage series of ever so steadily framed shots depicting a changing landscape at three different moments in time. The long to belong is a bit more than minor as it is given away in Patiño's film structure, as well as in the frequent occasions in which he acknowledges filmmakers James Benning or Peter Hutton's trailblazing or the inspiration gathered in the pages of Gaston Bachelard, Henri Bergson, or Georges Didi-Huberman.[4] (fig. 7 and fig. 8)

So much for a cinema of senses at sea, and "contemporary art after Allan Sekula." But all art was contemporary. Following Sekula *before* Sekula, an amphibian cinema takes root to exist in a cosmopolitism that rhymes with socialism and the sea. An emphatically geopolitical, peripheric cosmopolitism will thrive in amphibian waters.

Amphibian Man (1962) [*Chelovek-Anfibiya*] is a Russian film based on the homonymous novel by Alexander Belayev, known as "the Jules Verne of Russia." Much like *Jaws* (1975) was the kitsch reversal of *Moby Dick* for Sekula, this is the romantic (in the kitsch sense) film version of socialism and the sea, however, overlooked by Sekula in the wave following Verne against the "imperialist optimism." Yet this re-version trail nicely ties in the web of films here discussed as it adds a peripheric cosmopolitism twist to the sea's proletarian internationalism. Both the 1928 novel and the 1962 film directed by Vladimir Chebotaryov and Gennadi Kazansky trace an itinerary connecting peripheries different from the colonies-to-the-metropolis recurrence. This "Global South" melodrama mixed the fairytale with the fantastic and science-fiction in beautiful *Sovietcolor.* (fig. 9)

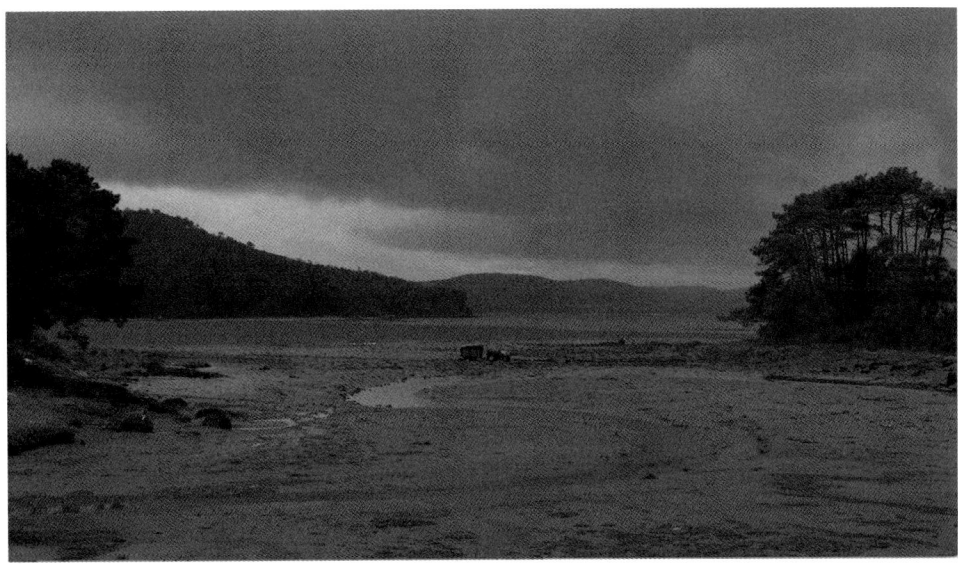

Fig. 8

Lois Patiño, *Costa da Morte*, 2013.
© Lois Patiño, 2013.

A part El Dorado, part pearldom at Del Plata Bay in silver-dubbed Argentina serves as pertinent backdrop for the communism and love story of *Amphibian Man*. Suitable as fiery Spain was to Bizet's smoking opera sensation *Carmen*, but historically less *ad rem* (even recalling that monarchs Ferdinand and Isabella of Spain charged Columbus with finding gold, silver, and pearls when their *carabelas* sailed in 1492), the feature brought us a hilarious and dramatic fantasy of communism in the ocean—a society where people should be neither poor, nor wealthy, but all happy—somewhere around Buenos Aires.

Ichtyander stars as the amphibian son of a kind-hearted, socialist-minded, mad scientist, and the first citizen of his dream underwater republic. Mistaken and feared as sea monster by the locals, Ichtyander falls in love with a ravishing earthling, Gutierre, who is the daughter of one of the exploited pearl divers under greedy Don Pedro's command. The film opens with breaking waves and paparazzi; it features pirates, a jazz song about sailors, a dance scene with maracas, and Mexican sombreros for wear in Buenos Aires. It ends with the protagonist's tragic transformation from amphibious to aquatic. Mesmerizing underwater shots and astonishing views of the city (the film's *topoi* next to the ship and the lab) of Buenos Aires' neon lights advertising brands like Cafiaspirina, Nobleza Gaucha, or Suchard in red, blue, and green make the feature unique to this day.

Now, how come the Argentine in this maritime fiction? As Sekula hypothesized, a text of Leon Trostky provided two key metaphors of Eisenstein's *Battleship Potemkin* (1925) original shooting script and his film. (Sekula: 1995, 121, n.53) Also, the historic *Potemkin* ship did wander about the Black Sea, running low on fuel, as Sekula notes, until the mutineers sought refuge in the Rumanian port of Constanza. Yet a number of seamen wandered on and disembarked in Argentina, in 1908, via Southampton. It is these *Potemkin gauchos* who probably fueled the *Amphibian Man* imaginary.

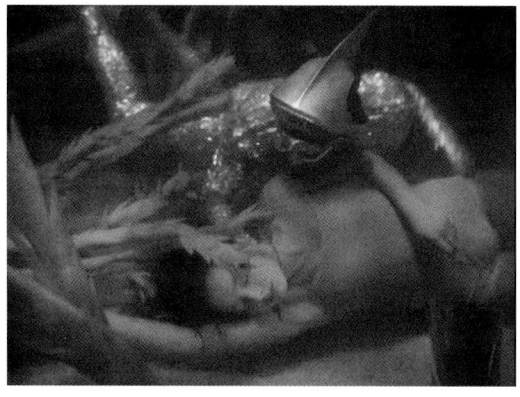

Fig. 9

Vladimir Chebotaryov and Gennadi Kazansky, *Amphibian Man* [*Chelovek-Anfibiya*], 1962.

Recently, a different ship from Russia, *Yantar,* approached the South Atlantic to take part in the search and rescue expedition for the Argentine submarine ARA *San Juan* that went missing on November 15, 2017. The submarine disappeared along with her forty-four crewmembers without leaving a trace. Another research vessel with technical equipment capable of reaching over 1000 meters deep, *Atlantis*, from the US, was also scheduled to arrive in solidarity. But the mission was, at this point, not rescue; the hope of survivors extinguished with the air reserve. The ARA *San Juan* submariners remain sunk, yet unsung. But that's a whole new kettle of fish.

Notes

1. Philip E. Steinberg compared *Leviathan* with Sekula and Burth's *The Forgotten Space* (2010) as "polar opposites in many ways." Steinberg, 2015: 86.

2. Film description available on Patiño's website http://loispatino.com/filter/landscape/Costa-da-Morte (accessed October 21, 2018).

3. Interview with Paravel and Taylor conducted by curator Hila Peleg (2017) on the occasion of the documenta 14 commission of the works *Commensal* (2017) and *Caniba* (2017).

4. This inversion of *Double Tide* is also advanced by Scott MacDonald, 2012.

Bibliography

Benjamin H. D. Buchloh, "Allan Sekula. Photography Between Discourse and Document," in Allan Sekula, *Fish Story* (Düsseldorf: Richter Verlag, 1995), 189–200.

Lucien Castaing-Taylor, "Iconophobia," *Transition*, 6, 1, 69 (Spring 1996): 64–88.

Carles Guerra, "The Last Days of December with Allan Sekula," in *Allan Sekula. Okeanos*, eds Daniela Zyman and Cory Scozzari (Berlin: Sternberg Press, 2017), 139–144.

James Lewis Hoberman, "Call Me Lucien," *Artforum International*, 51, 8 (April 2013): 32–33.

Rick Juzwiak, "Leviathan: A Documentary Made by People Who Hate Documentaries," *Gawker*, January 3, 2013. http://gawker.com/5987966/leviathan-a-documentary-made-by-people-who-hate-documentaries (accessed October 21, 2018).

Dennis Lim, "The Merger of Academia and Art House: Harvard Filmmakers' Messy World," *New York Times*, August 31, 2012. https://www.nytimes.com/2012/09/02/movies/harvard-filmmakers-messy-world.html (accessed October 21, 2018).

Scott MacDonald, "Review: Leviathan," in *Framework. The Journal of Cinema and Media*, 2012. http://www.frameworknow.com/review-leviathan (accessed October 21, 2018).

Christopher Pavsek, "Leviathan and the Experience of Sensory Ethnography," *The Visual Anthropology Review*, Vol. 31, 1 (Spring 2015): 4–11.

Hila Peleg, "Wir sind zuallererst körperliche Wesen: Hila Peleg im Gespräch mit Rosalind Nashashibi, Véréna Paravel und Lucien Castaing-Taylor sowie Ben Russell," *South Magazine*, Issue 9, *documenta 14*, 2017,

http://www.documenta14.de/de/south/25216_wir_sind_zuallererst_koerperliche_wesen_hila_peleg_im_gespraech_mit_rosalind_nashashibi_verena_paravel_und_lucien_castaing_taylor_sowie_ben_russell (accessed October 21, 2018).

Edward Said, *The World, the Text, and the Critic* (Cambridge: Harvard University Press, 1983).

Allan Sekula, *Fish Story* (Düsseldorf: Richter Verlag, 1995).

Allan Sekula, "Marea negra: fragmentos para una ópera," *Culturas*, 34, weekly magazine supplement to *La Vanguardia* (Barcelona) (February 12, 2003): 1–6.

Sally Stein, "Back to the Drawing Board: Maritime Themes and Discursive Crosscurrents in the Notebooks of Allan Sekula," in *Allan Sekula. Okeanos*, eds Daniela Zyman and Cory Scozzari (Berlin: Sternberg Press, 2017), 61–88.

Philip E. Steinberg, "Non linearity in the ocean documentary," in *Documenting World Politics*, eds Rens Van Munster and Casper Sylvest (London: Routledge, 2015), 78–95.

Daniela Zyman and Cory Scozzari eds, *Allan Sekula. Okeanos* (Berlin: Sternberg Press, 2017).

Filmography

Amphibian Man [*Chelovek-Anfibiya*], dir. Vladimir Chebotaryov and Gennadi Kazansky (1962).

Costa da Morte [*Coast of Death*] dir. Lois Patiño (2013).

Leviathan, dir. Véréna Paravel and Lucien Castaing-Taylor (2012).

The Forgotten Space, dir. Allan Sekula and Noel Burch (2010).

Breaking Open the Container: The Logistical Image and the Specter of Maritime Labor

Jonathan Stafford

> It's a nice boat this. Do you know why? It hasn't got containers.
> — Docker, *Boys from the Blackstuff*, 1982

In the 2009 horror film *Salvage*, a shipping container carrying a homicidal semi-human mutant washes up on a Merseyside beach. The monster escapes, embarking on a killing spree that terrorizes the occupants of a suburban housing estate on the outskirts of Liverpool. It is fitting that this film—one of three produced to celebrate Liverpool's status as the 2008 EU city of culture—takes as its point of origin the breaking open of a shipping container. This was of course the revelatory moment dismissed by Allan Sekula in his 1995 monograph *Fish Story* as "too easy an image of sudden disclosure, at once archaic and cinematic." (Sekula, 1995: 32) The archaic—if in the case of *Salvage* perhaps not quite fulfillingly cinematic—horror, which destroys whole communities and is the contents of the ubiquitous box, is in actuality the specter of labor, or more precisely its absence. In the context of Liverpool's history, it should come as no surprise that the container is the bearer of something horrific, given the catastrophic rise in unemployment, which accompanied the advent of containerization. The dead labor objectified in the technical apparatus of shipping is presented in *Salvage* as a modern gothic that preys upon the living.[1]

The terrific aspect of contemporary shipping manifested in *Salvage* is more explicitly articulated in the late Mark Fisher's *The Weird and the Eerie*. Fisher mobilizes the terminology of the eerie as a means to conceptualize aspects of human experience that are concerned with some enigmatic, unseen agency. Tracing the origins of this distinctive understanding of the term, he describes an encounter with Felixstowe container port, the UK's busiest port of this type:

"Disassembled" Images

There's an eerie sense of silence about the port that has nothing to do with actual noise levels. The port is full of the inorganic clangs and clanks that issue from ships as they are loaded and unloaded; what's missing, at least for the spectator watching the port from a vantage point outside, are any traces of language and sociability. Watching the container lorries and the ships do their work, or surveying the containers themselves, ... one seldom has any sense of human presence. The humans remain out of sight, in cabs, in cranes, in offices. ... The contrast between the container port, in which humans are invisible connectors between automated systems, and the clamour of the old London docks, which the port of Felixstowe effectively replaced, tells us a great deal about the shifts of capital and labour in the last forty years. The port is a sign of the triumph of finance capital; it is part of the heavy material infrastructure that facilitates the illusion of a "dematerialised" capitalism. It is the eerie underside of contemporary capital's mundane gloss. (Fisher, 2016: 76–77)

In Fisher's description, the eeriness evoked by the gargantuan container port is constituted by an absence that is doubled. The absence of the human, specifically of labor as a social activity, is complemented by a more fundamental absence: that of the grotesque agency that lies behind the port's cyclopean movement of commodities. The problematic at play in the eerie landscape of Felixstowe's container terminal is concerned with the very incomprehensibility of capital itself.

Such a concern—with the role played by the automation of containerized shipping in both the character of maritime labor and the obfuscation of capital's workings—was central to Allan Sekula's project, crystallized in the photographs and essays that comprise *Fish Story*. In emphasizing that the obfuscatory regime of containerization is not one which can be made spontaneously legible simply by revealing the box's contents, Sekula insisted that the problem of abstraction and visibility was inextricable from the specificity of maritime labor practices; if the image of the ruptured container as a moment of revelation is an unrealistic one, it is because "sailors rarely see the thrice-packaged cargo they carry nowadays." (Sekula, 1995: 32) However, given that the problem of capitalism's legibility as a global-dynamic system, the possibility of its very representation, or representability, can be traced in part to that emblematic object of logistical fluidity—the shipping container— the image of its breaking open, while in practice unrealistic, retains a certain theoretical radicality. This is a motif that might still act as a means for breaking open the outer shell of representation, for thinking through the underlying social relations that are left out of representations of the maritime.

The logic of the container, then, is one of absence, and this perhaps applies nowhere more than in modern Liverpool, a city that provides the backdrop for some of Sekula's most rewarding work on the theme of the maritime, 1999's *Freeway to China (Version 2, for Liverpool)*. As filmmaker and critic Patrick Keiller observes in his 2001 essay "Port Statistics," Liverpool is a highly significant site for understanding the visibility of modern capitalism. Witnessing the dilapidation of Liverpool's built environment, Keiller observes, he took the spectacular dereliction of the docks to be symptomatic of a past decline in their traffic, and Liverpool's impoverishment to be a result of this decline in its importance as a port. In fact, in September 1995 (when Keiller shot the footage of the city used in the film *Robinson in Space*), Liverpool's port traffic was greater than at any time in its history. (Keiller, 2013: 37)

The significant contributor to the visual decline Keiller describes was of course the revolution in maritime logistics associated with the processes of containerization. The container removed not only jobs from the city's communities, but also shipping from a position of visibility. "The dereliction of the Liverpool waterfront," Keiller writes, "is a result not of the port's disappearance, but of its new insubstantiality." (Keiller, 2014: 41) The visible dereliction of Liverpool as a city is not testament to an analogous decline in capitalism's health, but rather belies a system that owes both its continuing vigor and lack of visibility to the innovations of containerization.

This disconnect—between economic activity and its visible comprehensibility—forms a key element that concerns Keiller in *Robinson in Space*, the second of his "Robinson" films. Where the first film of this series, 1994's *London*, had attempted to come to terms with the metropolis from the perspective of the urban modernity of the 19th century, its sequel proceeds from the position, articulated in the former film, that "the true identity of London is in its absence." (Keiller, 1999: 223) This is an absence that Keiller identifies as the disappearance of any visual manifestation of the city's activity as a major global port. For Keiller, while shipping has disappeared from social experience, it has retained a certain cultural resonance, forming something of a lacuna in contemporary capitalism. The film follows this lacuna down narrow country lanes to massive automated container ports where colossal quantities of anonymous cargo are imported and exported every day, despite employing only a negligible labor force. What the peripatetic protagonists of *Robinson in Space* testify to is a disappearance: the removal from the majority of people's field of vision of the everyday experience of the concrete reality of capital, the vast movement of goods at sea.

Keiller's films could be said to bear witness to the invisibility of economic activity, its abstraction at the level of social experience. This is of course a core concern of Sekula's project, and with *Fish Story* he traces this trend, which he diagnoses as a cultural "forgetting" of the sea, from the introduction of steam-driven ships to the logistical processes of containerization that have governed the transportation of goods at sea for over half a century. (Sekula, 1995: 49) While the processes associated with the container have brought about a revolution in the global movement of commodities, facilitating the standardization and homogenization of logistical space, enabling large-scale automation of cargo distribution and integration into a total and continuous system, they have also given rise to the movement of this activity away from the sphere of everyday experience. Sekula was insightful in *Fish Story* in recognizing that these changes have led to a structure of ontology whereby the material constitution of our lived world is obfuscated, to be replaced by a mythology of immateriality and ephemerality, the apparent fiber-optic instantaneousness of a contemporary capitalism that is characterized, even by many of its critics, by an ideology of perpetual acceleration and intractable fluidity.

Despite over ninety percent of global commodity flows still taking place by sea transportation (George, 2013), there has been an ignoring of this material process, giving way to an immaterial, disembodied conception of global circulation as one of fiber-optic instantaneousness. In "Liquid Networks and the Metaphysics of Flux," Thomas Sutherland has argued that an excessive ontological emphasis upon the fluidity of capital results in the myth of what he terms "friction-free capitalism," an ideology that imagines space as topological; abstract; homogeneous, ignoring the materiality of processes of production and circulation. (Sutherland, 2013: 15) Sekula privileged the materiality of maritime logistics as a representational mode possessed of a radical veracity: an aesthetic charge antithetical to the ideology of "friction-free capitalism." In *Fish Story*, he promotes a sustained preoccupation with the materiality of shipping as a means to explode this myth. He argues "for the continued importance of maritime space in order to counter the exaggerated importance attached to that largely metaphysical construct, 'cyberspace,' and the corollary myth of 'instantaneous' contact between distant spaces." (Sekula, 1995: 50) Paying attention to the materiality of capital's abstraction foregrounds the concrete processes of circulation.

An instance of such a representational efficacy might be posited in an image of the shorelines of the Indian subcontinent, where vast tonnages of obsolete ships accumulate on the beaches awaiting salvage by low-paid, unregulated manual workers who pick apart their immense hulks with rudimentary tools. As John Urry has observed, this "gargantuan landscape" is predicated upon the globally integrated nature of the capitalist world system, the exploitation inherent in uneven development. (Urry, 2014: 126–127) Edward Burtynsky's 2000 photographic body of work *Shipbreaking*, shot in Chittagong, Bangladesh, is just one example of the attention paid to this spectacle. Such a representation highlights the extent to which the production of capital flows are rooted in the violent materiality of labor. But it also prefigures an ironic shift in contemporary artistic representation. If Sekula endorsed a focus on the mechanisms of shipping as an antidote to the ideology of "friction-free capitalism," a recent cultural turn toward the logistical image has encountered a perhaps too-enthusiastic fetish for the maritime as spectacle: the mathematical uniformity of the container; the landscape of the automated port; the vast sublimity of the modern vessel. For instance, Henrik Spohler's 2016 photographic series *In Between* seeks to document the logistical spaces through which container transport is actualized. However, such an image of logistical perfection is one which threatens to further elide the specter of labor behind the complexity of the mechanized movement of goods at the global level. In the excessive, *too* great attention to the sea and shipping we see in contemporary representations, the container takes center-stage as the overdetermined object, a synecdochic emblem for the incomprehensible totality of capital.

The container has become, then, a ubiquitous symbol of contemporary capitalism, providing the raw material for works of art, experimental architecture, and "pop-up" shopping centers. Even a 2015 performance of the *Rise and Fall of the City of Mahagonny*, Brecht's operatic satire of the excesses of capitalist society employed the container as its setting.[2] In *Cartographies of the Absolute*, a book concerned with the problem of capital's representability, Alberto Toscano and Jeff Kinkle identify in the persistent figure of the container the signifier par excellence of such a crisis of representation. The container provides, they suggest, "an allegory of sorts for the condition of disorientation and lacking knowledge." (Toscano and Kinkle, 2015: 197) The simple rationale of the container lies in the optimization of capital accumulation as flow, the minimization of time in circulation. It is this drive—for the ever greater imbrication of the various material processes of commodity circulation—which the container embodies that accounts for the simultaneous excess and void of meaning of which this object is the bearer in our contemporary world-historical situation. The real logic of the container is an aesthetic of concealment: of the commodities it is used to carry, the labor practices it is implicated in, or the total system of movement that it facilitates, it reveals very little. Discussing Roberto Saviano's 2006 book *Gomorrah*, Toscano and Kinkle observe that the book opens with the moment of the breaking apart of a container:

> The starkest contrast between the seamless opacity of containerisation and the dramas of the kind of social life it makes possible ..., is to be found in the book's opening scene, as dozens of dead

Chinese migrants are disbursed by a broken container—suppos-edly being shipped back to China for burial while their passports are acquired by a new levy of living labour. (Toscano and Kinkle, 2015: 199)

Again, this depiction of the container's rupture acts as a moment of the revelation of capital's contradictions. However, in view of Saviano's claim that this occurrence was quickly and surreptitiously glossed over by port employees, and Toscano and Kinkle's insistence upon the spu-rious veracity of the story altogether, it merely serves as a reminder of the extent to which the regime of the container is one of concealment. (Saviano, 2007: 3; Toscano and Kinkle, 2015: 199)

Given the empty homology of the container-as-object, it is perhaps unsurprising that Philip Steinberg has questioned whether the visual reproduction of maritime logistical processes is possessed of any in-trinsic radicality today, arguing that the sheer scale and complexity of circuits of capital accumulation as a total system are fundamentally unrepresentable. For Steinberg, while it is not a challenge to identify and depict material aspects of the total logistical processes, which, like the ship—or the container—are critically implicated in the functioning of capitalism, "the resulting representation of these capitalist artifacts will inevitably fail to reveal the totality of underlying processes that govern how they are produced, moved and consumed." Such a "partial representation," he writes, "can actually serve to *obscure*." (Steinberg, 2015: 35, original emphasis) If shipping as a signifier of capital is an in-complete one, this representational impasse owes its origins to the fact that today, the ship is caught up in such a series of connections that it is only one part of the totality of social relations which combine to pro-duce the conditions of mobility as process.

While Steinberg's point is a valid one—representing capital at the level of the concrete by no means ensures its spontaneous comprehen-sibility, and he is of course arguing for a critically engaged form of rep-resentation, not its abandonment—I would argue that the ship retains a distinct representational charge, even in an age characterized by the obfuscation of the material processes of capital. Where I differ from Steinberg is in suggesting that the ship is a specific type of object whose radicality lies precisely in its relation to a fractured totality. If the ship's ability to render this totality legible has been compromised to the ex-tent that the complexity of capital is similarly fractious and incompre-hensible, I would argue that it retains the capacity to represent capital specifically *as* contradiction, *as* complexity.

Steinberg's engagement with this topic is lodged in a critique of *The Forgotten Space*, Sekula and Noël Burch's essay film document-ing the various human narratives imbricated with the global maritime economy. Steinberg's evaluation of the film is rooted in an assertion that it neglects to engage with that most forgotten of spaces, the sea itself: that it fails to provide a counter-narrative to the triumph of capital, a depiction of the sea not as the space of seamless flows, but as a material space of frictions, both spatial and human in character. (Steinberg, 2015: 41–42) For Steinberg, the film thus reproduces capital's dream of the sea as a featureless medium for the movement of containerized goods, again reinforcing the persistent ideology of "friction free capital." While the image of human failure in the face of capital is ever-present, the image of capital's failure is crucially lacking. In the light of such an impasse, the figure of maritime catastrophe would appear to be possessed of a radical potentiality for undermining the power of the logistical image. One must thus ask what the kind of image hoped for by Steinberg might look like? As an alternative to the critical realism of *The Forgotten Space*, Steinberg draws attention to *Intermodal Flow*, a project proposed by the Delta Arts Collective to place artists on container ships in order to produce artworks, which would be able to engage with and draw upon the complex interconnectedness of global trade. (Steinberg, 2015: 43–44)

Intermodal Flow is just one of a number of such projects, including the *Container Artist* and *Owner's Cabin* residencies, an abundance bearing witness to the contemporary fetish for maritime logistics as art's object.[3] While as of late 2017 Delta Arts' project is still yet to bear fruit, Steinberg's consideration of such an artistic engagement was rendered strangely prescient in the light of events that have occurred since his essay's publication. Another such residency, Vancouver's Access Gallery's *Twenty-Three Days at Sea*, was recently the subject of extensive press coverage, but not for the sake of the artworks it was intended to produce. In September 2016, an absurd pantomime was played out aboard the container ship *Hanjin Geneva*, as the British artist Rebecca Moss became stranded in the middle of her *Twenty-Three Days at Sea* residency on board the vessel. The South-Korean container shipping company Hanjin—aboard whose ship, the *Hanjin Budapest*, Sekula and Burch themselves produced footage for *The Forgotten Space*—had filed for receivership, requesting that its assets be frozen, and thus the ship aboard which Moss was completing her residency was forced to a halt due to the consequent uncertainty regarding where the money would come from to unload its cargo. The maritime economy provides a key signifier for the health of capitalism, and this image of inertia, of the ship in stasis, its containers full of commodities left undelivered, provides a powerful vision of slowdown in the capitalist system of which Steinberg might perhaps approve. It is again Toscano and Kinkle who supply, in a passing remark, the mode of envisioning this resistance, pointing to a contemporary global-economic system in which "the shiftless container ships idling in the pacific" could be seen to be a very real visual rendering of the current crisis of capital. (Toscano and Kinkle, 2015: 159)

With ghost ships such as the *Hanjin Geneva*, zombie ships—a term that describes those vessels which only manage to earn enough to pay off the interest on the shipping company's loans—and the phenomenon of slow steaming, the deceleration of global shipping to save on fuel and other costs, the logistical image of the ship is perhaps a more adequate representation of capital's crisis than ever before. (Ficenec, 2016; Vidal, 2010) The collapse of Hanjin swelled what is known as the "idle fleet" of container vessels—those ships out of use due to lack of demand—to 1.7 million twenty-foot equivalent units (TEU) at the end of 2016. (Knowler, 2016) As Brett Neilson and Ned Rossiter have observed, "what is striking is the stasis, if not the slowing, of maritime transport in a time when the globalizing nexus of transport and communication is almost universally characterized by metaphors of speed or acceleration." (Neilson and Rossiter, 2013: 51) However, such a spectacle is deceptive. "That things are 'status quo' *is* the catastrophe," wrote Walter Benjamin in the notes that make up the convolute N of the *Arcades Project*. (Benjamin, 1999: 473, original emphasis) With the slowing of shipping, the true catastrophe of capital is rendered visible: it is not the periodic crises which punctuate its continuity, but rather that it endures, that it keeps on repeating these same patterns into perpetuity, developing new means of adapting to crisis. This catastrophic continuity is perhaps why Benjamin's thesis, that revolution is humanity's reaching for the "emergency brake"—not the possibility of history's realization, but rather its interruption—has proved so appealing in recent years. (Benjamin, 2003: 402) That the remedy to capital's relentlessness should be interruption would seem plausible.

The epitomic instance of such an interruption to capital's continuity in the context of maritime logistics is the shipwreck, a sudden and violent reminder of the materiality of capital flows. In *The Forgotten Space*, Sekula makes an observation that could be said to act as a riposte to Steinberg's critique of the film. "Of all the forgotten spaces," he observes, "the sea, in its ancient terribleness, is the most forgotten—even though more than nine-tenths of the world's commerce travels in this way. The sea is really remembered only when maritime disaster strikes." (*The Forgotten Space*, 2010) It is at the moment of catastrophe that the sea is really rendered visible as a material space, one replete with idiosyncratic frictions of its own. Capital is governed by its perpetuation, its continual passing back into circulation— that which Marx identifies as the "constant continuity of the process, the unobstructed and fluid transition of value from one form into the other." (Marx, 1973: 535) The wreck thus appears as the exemplary figure of catastrophe; antithetical to the logic of capital, it is the absolute interruption, a disjuncture in the process of circulation. Such a revelatory physicality can be seen in the spectacle of the wreck of the container ship the MSC Napoli, which was beached off the south coast of England in January 2007, resulting in dozens of its containers washing up on a Devon beach. The subsequent breaking open of these containers, and the attendant scramble by scavengers to claim the commodities such as BMW motorbikes held within, as Tim Cresswell and Craig Martin observe, made visible "that phase of contemporary capitalism typically hidden from the consumer gaze." (Cresswell and Martin, 2012: 516)

But while the shipwreck remains a potent figure for representing catastrophe, I would suggest that it fails in itself to register visible the contradictions of modern capitalism. This was the problematic engaged with by Sekula in *Shipwreck and Workers*, a photographic installation project exhibited in three different forms from 2005–07. The installation consisted of a photographic triptych of a wrecked ship in the port of Istanbul, juxtaposed with multiple images of "workers affected, directly or indirectly, by the growing social inequalities that neoliberal globalisation is generating." ("Shipwreck and Workers (Version 3 for Kassel)") What *Shipwreck and Workers* is testament to is the simultaneous fidelity to the radical potentiality of the maritime, with an insistence on the human element of a critical realism, rejecting the easy image of the shipwreck as spectacle. Instead, what is presented is the radical collapsing of the global and the everyday. This is a collapsing that was presented as violently catastrophic in the case of the film *Salvage*, as maritime and domestic space collide, but whose catastrophe is social and lived in Sekula's work. Such a dynamic is apparent in his photographs of those regions in the UK most affected by the changes to the maritime economy of the last half century: North-East England, Glasgow, and Liverpool.[4] The radicality of Sekula's oeuvre is in its inevitably miscarried attempt to depict totality, to grasp the interconnectedness of unemployed Liverpool dockers with Mexican fisherman, the Californian welder with the group who eat at McDonald's in the North-East English coastal town of South Shields. While this last is a fairly innocuous example of globalization's impact on the everyday, it bears witness to a shift in the lived experience of those who live in areas whose economies once relied upon maritime industry, of their social and cultural identity. The significance of labor's legibility and representation in Sekula's photographic project elides that it is not just labor he is concerned with, but also the everyday, the impact on and extension into all lives of the global-dynamic world systems of capitalism, at the level of lived experience.

It is with this theme that I want to end, returning to Liverpool, specifically to Alan Bleasedale's 1982 television drama series *Boys from the Blackstuff*. Following the fortunes of a group of unemployed work-ing-class men and their families through a series of often harrowing domestic narratives, the *Blackstuff* both mirrors and rejects Sekula's Liverpool, a city where, he observes "one thing that struck me strongly ... was this sense of generational rupture and continuity within working class families. That the sea itself was a kind of thread of escape and be-coming." (Contemporary Documentary Photographers: Allan Sekula) *Boys from the Blackstuff* depicts a Liverpool in which such a relationship with the sea has itself become subject to rupture, in which the collaps-ing of maritime and domestic space I have described is catastrophic precisely in its impact on the everyday lived experience of the charac-ters. Itself named for a logistical medium—the "black stuff" being the tarmac laid by the program's protagonists before they are laid off in the television play that preceded the series—I want to draw attention to a generally overlooked aspect of the series: to foreground the signifi-cance of maritime industry and labor as the great absence that frames and underpins its narrative.

This maritime context is most evident in the series' second episode, "Moonlighter", which depicts a strange, picaresque drama played out in the hold of a cargo ship moored in the port of Liverpool. Dixie Dean, working as a low-paid night watchman on the docks while still sign-ing on for unemployment benefits, is approached, cajoled, and brow-beaten one night by a gang of dockers-turned-thieves. A remark made by one of the gang furnishes the epigraph to this essay, the ship's lack of containers making it far easier for the dockers to illicitly access its cargo. We are then witness to the breaking apart of a shipping crate to reveal boots, which the dockers proceed to put on. "Won't nobody say nothing?" asks a perturbed Dixie. "Oh yeah, they'll go friggin' mad in South Africa," the docker replies. "But by the time this boat gets there, it'll have already been to three other ports. They'll be lucky to have any boots left." (*Boys from the Blackstuff*, 1982) The dockers understand that the complexity of global capitalism, its implication in convoluted pat-terns of trade, means that it is impossible to trace the trajectory of a cargo that travels through both licit and illicit logistical networks. This petty theft, however, is only the forerunner of a much larger job, which Dixie is bribed and bullied into overlooking.

Dixie's story is a manifestation of the "isolated, anonymous, hidden work, of [the] great loneliness, displacement, and separation from the domestic sphere" diagnosed by Sekula in the modern maritime econo-my. (Sekula and Risberg, 1999: 247) However, the history of maritime trade is characterized not just by labor, but also its inverse, unemploy-ment. *Blackstuff* depicts the catastrophe of the everyday, in the lives that intersect with and are buffeted by the complexity of capital flows, the maritime as a human, social landscape of affect and personal narrative.

Dixie weeps after he is threatened by the gang with the tool of their trade, the docker's hook, itself rendered obsolete by containerization. The issue at stake here is not a complex one; like the rest of the characters who people the Liverpool of the *Blackstuff*, Dixie's identity, formerly implicated with labor, with his role as breadwinner, has been crudely undermined and compromised.

But if the *Blackstuff* documents the limits of lived experience in a city whose intimacy with the maritime economy makes its inhabitants cruelly vulnerable to changes in the mechanics of logistical processes, it also offers a means for thinking beyond this impasse. The radicality of the series lies precisely in its assertion of modes of solidarity—rooted in the maritime—even in the midst of personal and collective failure, affirming a Liverpool in which, as Sekula observes, dockers manage to "sustain [a] solidarity, based on work, when work has been cravenly stolen away." (Sekula, 2000: 414) In the context of the history of maritime class struggle, the word solidarity has taken on what could perhaps be considered an excessive burden of meaning: the Gdańsk museum which commemorates the Polish trade union of that name (Solidarność) looks out over the now desolate landscape of the former Lenin Shipyard, the site of the union's birth. Solidarity's betrayal can already be seen in the queues at the unemployment office in Gdańsk photographed by Sekula in November 1990, soon after the fall of communism (in which the union played no small role). (pl. 7) This is not to promote an apologist revisionism for the Soviet system, but an attempt to redeem the lost opportunity of Solidarity's ethos, to reclaim the meaning of a solidarity rooted in a shared history of struggle and hope.

It is the specter of class identity and solidarity that haunts the Liverpool portrayed in the *Blackstuff*. The series' final episode, "George's Last Ride," depicts the death of the former docker and union official George Malone, who had previously been forced out of his job due to his left-wing activism, a role which mirrored the career of the actor who depicted him, Peter Kerrigan.[5] Dying from an unspecified illness, George is pushed in a wheelchair through his beloved docks by his friend Chrissie, in a sequence where the dereliction of the old dock is juxtaposed with the unpeopled automation of the container port. In one of the series' most memorable scenes, George is depicted delivering a monologue on the dilapidated Albert Dock, itself a persistent signifier of the city's poverty—and subsequent regeneration—in the postwar period.[6] Standing on the docks he recounts his personal history, one deeply intertwined with the city's maritime labor history.

"My dreams," George exclaims as he stands on the dock with his friend's help, "they still give me hope and faith in my class. I can't believe that there's no hope." (*Boys from the Blackstuff*, 1982) The vision of class identity articulated by the dying ex-docker is not an individuated, singular one but one that rests upon a shared maritime history: a history of struggle but also of solidarity. To return to the insights of Mark Fisher, such a solidarity is one now faced with changes in the organization of labor which have undermined sociability: the finding of a common language, a means of communicating. In his controversial 2013 article "Exiting the Vampire Castle," Fisher laid out a program for the renewal of left struggle around just the sort of shared identity George's monologue expresses. "We need to learn, or re-learn, how to build comradeship and solidarity," Fisher observes. (Fisher, 2013) Perhaps this is where the breaking apart of the container's false veneer of logistical perfection begins, in paying attention to the histories of struggle and solidarity which the sea holds. It is precisely this lesson which Sekula's long engagement with the maritime has taught us to hold dear.

Notes

1. As Steve Edwards observed, in Antwerp, in the discussion that followed the paper this essay is based upon, the truly grotesque absence that haunts Liverpool's maritime legacy is of course the slave trade. Although I am not able to adequately address the significance of this topic within the confines of the current piece of writing, this point is an important one to acknowledge, not least because it highlights the significance of the maritime as a means of engaging capital's complex history. Paying attention to the maritime draws our attention to the fact that there is not just one history of capitalism, but that capital is constituted through multiple overlapping histories of exploitation.

2. Intriguingly, the container has come to the fore as a representational mode for indicating the complexity of the contemporary global economic situation, with photographs of containerized landscapes featuring prominently as a means for illustrating recent news stories regarding the impact of Brexit upon the British economy.

3. See https://intermodalflow.wordpress.com; http://www.containerartistresidency01.org/exhibitions/creative-operational-solutions; http://www.theownerscabin.com; https://nac.org/exhibitions/twenty-three-days-at-sea-christopher-boyne (accessed August 28, 2017).

4. See Sekula, 1999: 191–206 for his photographs of Glasgow and North-East England, and Sekula, 2000: 415–421 for Liverpool.

5. Kerrigan's 1958 article "What next for Britain's port workers?" was itself a call for solidarity and a tribute to the forms of struggle and resilience specific to maritime workers.

6. On the verge of a Tory regeneration at the time of filming, it would of course be these same docks that would house the Tate Liverpool, an irony which was not lost on Sekula when he photographed his *Portrait of John Stanson, Museum Guard and Former Docker* in 1999.

Bibliography

Walter Benjamin, *The Arcades Project*, trans. Howard Eiland and Kevin McLaughlin (Cambridge: Harvard University Press, 1999).

Walter Benjamin, "Paralipomena to 'On the Concept of History'," trans. Edmund Jephcott and Howard Eiland, in *Selected Writings: Volume 4, 1938–1940*, eds Howard Eiland and Michael W. Jennings (Cambridge, MA: Harvard University Press, 2003), 401–411.

"Contemporary Documentary Photographers: Allan Sekula," (Interview) *Victoria and Albert Museum*. [This content was originally created to accompany the exhibition Stepping In and Out, on display at the V&A South Kensington between 5 September 2002 and 26 January 2003] http://www.vam.ac.uk/content/articles/c/contemporary-documentary-photographers (accessed October 21, 2018).

Tim Cresswell and Craig Martin, "On Turbulence: Entanglements of Disorder and Order on a Devon Beach," *Tijdschrift voor Economische en Sociale Geografie*, 103, 5 (November 2012): 516–529.

John Ficenec, "Zombie Ships Send Maritime Freight into Worst Crisis in Living Memory," *Telegraph*, January 22, 2016, http://www.telegraph.co.uk/finance/12108453/Zombie-ships-send-maritime-freight-into-worst-crisis-in-living-memory.html (accessed October 21, 2018).

Mark Fisher, *The Weird and the Eerie* (London: Repeater, 2016).

Mark Fisher, "Exiting the Vampire Castle," *The North Star*, November 22, 2013, http://www.thenorthstar.info/?p=11299 (accessed August 28, 2017).

Rose George, *Ninety Percent of Everything: Inside Shipping, the Invisible Industry That Puts Clothes on Your Back, Gas in Your Car, and Food on Your Plate* (New York: Metropolitan Books, 2013).

Peter Kerrigan, "What next for Britain's port workers?," *The Newsletter*, December 20, 1958: 338–341.

Patrick Keiller, *Robinson in Space* (London: Reaktion, 1999).

Patrick Keiller, "Port Statistics," in *The View from the Train: Cities and Other Landscapes* (London: Verso, 2013), 35–49.

Greg Knowler, "Idle Container Shipping Capacity Soars to 1.7 Million Teu," *Fairplay*, December 6, 2016, https://fairplay.ihs.com/commerce/article/4278921/idle-container-shipping-capacity-soars-to-1-7-million-teu (accessed October 21, 2018).

Karl Marx, *Grundrisse: Foundations of the Critique of Political Economy*, trans. Martin Nicolaus (London: Penguin, 1973).

Brett Neilson and Ned Rossiter, "Still Waiting, Still Moving: On Labour, Logistics and Maritime Industries," in *Stillness in a Mobile World*, eds David Bissell and Gillian Fuller (London: Routledge, 2010), 51–68.

Roberto Saviano, *Gomorrah: A Personal Journey into the Violent International Empire of Naples' Organized Crime System*, trans. Virginia Jewiss (New York: Farrar, Straus and Giroux, 2007).

Allan Sekula, *Fish Story* (Düsseldorf: Richter Verlag, 1995).

Allan Sekula, "Freeway to China (Version 2, for Liverpool)," *Public Culture*, 12, 2 (Spring 2000): 411–422.

Allan Sekula and Debra Risberg, "Imaginary Economies: An Interview with Allan Sekula," in Allan Sekula, *Dismal Science: Photo Works 1972–1996* (Illinois: Illinois State University, 1999), 235–251.

"Shipwreck and Workers (Version 3 for Kassel): Allan Sekula," *Museu d'Art Contemporani de Barcelona*, http://www.macba.cat/en/shipwreck-and-workers-version-3-for-kassel-3121 (accessed October 21, 2018).

Philip E. Steinberg, "Maritime Cargomobilities: The Impossibilities of Representation," in *Cargomobilities: Moving Materials in a Global Age*, eds Thomas Birtchnell, Satya Savitzky and John Urry (New York: Routledge, 2015), 35–47.

Thomas Sutherland, "Liquid Networks and the Metaphysics of Flux: Ontologies of Flow in an Age of Speed and Mobility," *Theory, Culture & Society*, 30, 5 (April 2013): 3–23.

Alberto Toscano and Jeff Kinkle, *Cartographies of the Absolute* (Winchester: Zero, 2015).

John Vidal, "Modern Cargo Ships Slow to the Speed of the Sailing Clippers," *Observer*, July 25, 2010, https://www.theguardian.com/environment/2010/jul/25/slow-ships-cut-greenhouse-emissions (accessed October 21, 2018).

John Urry, *Offshoring* (Cambridge: Polity Press, 2014).

Filmography

Boys from the Blackstuff, dir. by Phillip Saville (BBC, 1982).

The Forgotten Space, dir. by Allan Sekula and Noël Burch (Doc.Eye/WILDart, 2010).

"Do not Trespass."
An Interview Conversation on the Genesis of Allan Sekula's *Black Tide/* Marea negra (2002–03)

Carles Guerra and Hilde Van Gelder

Barcelona, Fundació Antoni Tàpies, 7 April 2016

Allan Sekula has a broadly established reputation today as a man who prolifically performed a wide variety of roles. One such role was being an excellent matchmaker. During a career that lasted four decades, he befriended numerous of his professional "allies." Sekula was always pleased to learn that further ties of friendly relations were established among those with whom he had bonded. Over the years, Sekula— ceaselessly sailing the seven seas—saved himself no efforts to make sure that a worldwide network of "partners in crime" saw the light of day. Thus it happened that in 2006, when the Brussels Art Fair asked Hilde Van Gelder to do a suggestion for a public speaker knowledge- able about Allan Sekula's oeuvre, the artist instantly proposed her to approach Carles Guerra. This time, too, he added the delicate phrase that he commonly used on such occasions: "I think you should like to meet him." Carles Guerra accepted the invitation.

As predicted by Sekula, we rapidly struck up a friendship and have collaborated on numerous occasions ever since. During our ample conversations extended over the years, one particular story returned frequently as a reference. It was that of Guerra's and Sekula's fieldtrip by car to Spanish Galicia. They traveled together in order to see with their own eyes how the coast was trying to cope with the disaster of the *Prestige*, an oil tanker that had "split in half about 210 kilometers off- shore" on November 19, 2002. (Guerra, 2017: 139) The ship sank. More than twenty million US gallons of heavy fuel oil was released into the ocean. The polluting impact on the surrounding seabed and beaches was overwhelming. Today the *Prestige* oil spill is considered the largest environmental disaster in the history of Spain. But at the time of the catastrophe itself, national Spanish media reporting tried to downsize the ecological damage of the oil leak.

Keen to make an unconventional reportage about the heroic and determined efforts of mostly local volunteers to clean up the beaches, Carles Guerra drove Allan Sekula to the area during the closing days of that year. Once there Carles Guerra filmed both the activities of the volunteers and Allan Sekula at work. He also extensively interviewed Sekula in the aftermath of their journey, and bundled the material in a fascinating documentary entitled *The Last Days of December with Allan Sekula* (2003). (pl. 8) Reminiscing those remarkable days, Guerra is always fond to bring in the personal recollection that at the time he and his wife had become parents of their first child only recently. As such, it really was not an opportune time for a young father to be away from home for Christmas Eve. But the lure of smeared Galician mermaids turned out to be irresistible. The artistic outcome of this productive journey to the far Southwestern corner of the European continent is the well-known and meanwhile influential photo-textual work entitled *Black Tide*/Marea negra (2002–03).[1]

Our discussion in the meeting room of the Fundació Antoni Tàpies, on an early spring day in 2016, starts with both of us going through the sequence as Sekula included it in the exhibition catalog *Performance Under Working Conditions* (2003). Our attention is drawn to the fact that there almost isn't a single image in there in which the unattractive, chemical-looking black oil sludge does not figure as a preeminent protagonist in one form or another.

Hilde Van Gelder (HVG): Carles, do you recall how Allan Sekula's intensive camera focus on the oil slicks came about?

Carles Guerra (CG): Allan and I were basically obsessed with the idea of removing the dirt—the *chapapote* as it was called there. What struck us was the fact that none of the volunteers working on the beaches seemed to wonder where all this disgusting stuff that they were loading into open body tippers was being transported to. We decided to follow by car, or actually rather chase, one of those trucks filled with an impressive load of *chapapote*. To our great surprise we ended up driving around seventy kilometers inland, away from the coast. Amidst the countryside, the ride came to a halt near a brick factory. We actually found ourselves facing a huge compound entirely surrounded by gates. These prevented everyone from entering, unless one was in possession of an authorization to access. Luckily for us it turned out not to be too difficult to sneak in.

Once inside the domain, we discovered huge ponds filled with all this black, rubberlike material. You have to realize that, as it was very cold outside, the *chapapote* was freezing. As a result, the sludge turned out to look more like rubber or at least it resembled something rather elastic. We saw cranes that were trying to remove objects from this mass, like dustbins or the barrels that had been used along the coastline as small containers for the sludge. As the cranes were trying to remove all these objects, this created a sight of enormous, gigantic chimneys— it really made a strange impression on us. The irony, so we found out soon, turned out to be that the *chapapote* was supposedly meant to be reconverted into raw material for the production of bricks. Can you imagine a young couple spending all their money, all their savings, to purchase their first apartment and then find out that this very apartment is actually made out of that abject material?

HVG: So while the *chapapote* was collected on the beaches by volunteers in dramatic and difficult circumstances, a nearby company was cynically making plans to commercialize it? Was there some form of public communication going around that this was actually happening?

CG: No, not at all. Certainly not among the volunteers and not even was there any mention of it in the press. From the perspective of media analysis, then, this disaster evolved into an early revelatory case with regard to the narrow frame by which we have become used to observe such catastrophes and events. Everyone worried about the state in which the coast and the maritime landscape were finding itself. No one wondered what happened merely a few minutes away from there.

HVG: Indeed, this exemplifies well how people tend to take in the information reaching them via mainstream news reporting rather naïvely, as is true in particular as well of how the story is presented to them via these channels. With the sludge removal from the beach, the job is considered done. About what happens afterward nobody cares anymore. But how did you then find out that story about the bricks? Was there perhaps a rumor circulating when you investigated the matter further?

CG: We had to reconstruct this puzzle piece by piece. Someone we had met near the beach had told us that all the trucks were heading for Lendo, a tiny and remote village in the countryside. Someone else informed us that in Lendo there was a brick factory and that it seemed the material was being recycled for the fabrication of bricks. Of course I wasn't sure back then if it was just a tall tale or not. Even today I have not been able to find out the true facts. Yet this scenario seemed quite plausible and even feasible from what we saw there in Lendo. There were two enormous ponds containing the sludge, one that was photographed by Allan and another one that was even bigger. Something eventually had to be done with their contents. It had to be removed and recycled in one way or another. Unfortunately I cannot possibly know

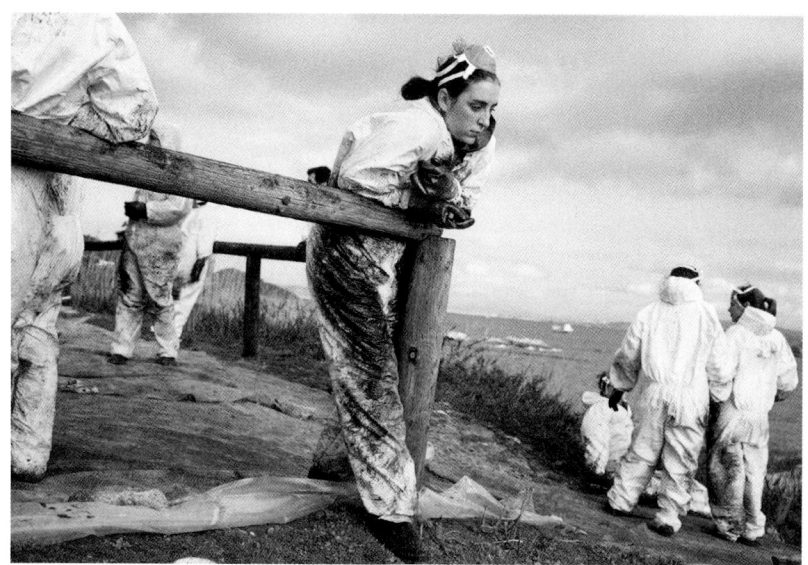

what exactly has happened, as the public has been completely misinformed. [pointing at Allan Sekula's *Disposal Pit (Lendo, 12/23/02)*, (pl. 9–10)] Look how big it was. It is huge. You have to remember it was winter: the material was freezing, as it was stored in the open air. It was easy to imagine for us how it could be turned into a more and more chewing gum-like, solid texture.

HVG: Looking back at this episode now it remains striking to observe how Allan Sekula never shied away from coming to terms with utterly catastrophic events. Sometimes it even seems as if he wanted to investigate them in order to be able better to anticipate any future disaster situations. Within the context of his ultimate project *The Dockers' Museum*, this is best articulated in his embryonic conception of the so-called "Bombing Section."[2] (pl. 11) During the public conversation he and I had in Antwerp in May 2010, on the occasion of the *Ship of Fools* project's first installment at M HKA, he called himself Nostradamus.[3]

CG: Wow. I am not sure whether we should understand his way of working entirely as starting from a sense of anticipation. In my view, documentary practice for Sekula was always related to a "presentness," to an empirical contact with the event as he saw it unfolding while he was in the process of capturing it. Inevitably, as a consequence, he always had to deal with some present situation.

HVG: Definitely. Possibly my approach and understanding of Allan Sekula's working methods is overdetermined by the overtly anticipatory nature of his last project, *Ship of Fools | The Dockers' Museum*. My horizon of thinking may also be too overdetermined by all sorts of likely

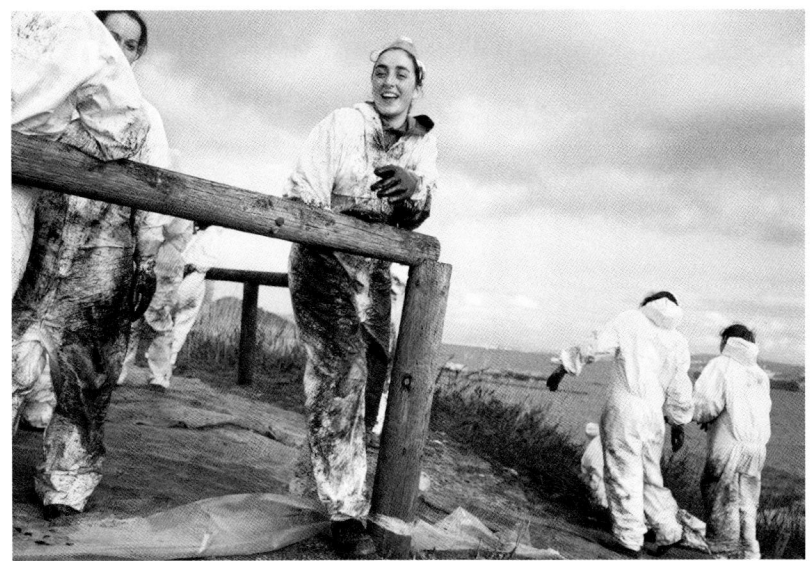

Fig. 1

Allan Sekula, *Volunteer watching, volunteer smiling (Isla de Ons, 12/19/02)*, part of *Black Tide/ Marea negra* (2002–03). Horizontal diptych, Cibachrome print, 53,3 × 159,4 cm / 67 × 171,6 cm (framed). © Allan Sekula Studio.

to happen socio-economic, political, and ecological calamities—about which he and I often speculated in private conversation. It remains a difficult exercise to find out what exactly we may conclude with regard to the earlier works when looking back at them from the open-ended perspective of *Ship of Fools | The Dockers' Museum.*

CG: What Allan beyond any doubt managed to do, at least with *Black Tide*, is to extend the limited timeframe of the documentary genre into a fictional story. For example, he destroys the idea of the photographer as a privileged witness, an approach that is very much connected to documentary practice. With double takes, such as *Volunteer watching, volunteer smiling (Isla de Ons, 12/19/02)*, he completely works against the notion of the single moment. (fig. 1) In the first image, the volunteer woman appears immersed in absorption. Yet in the other photograph she is almost facing the camera. *Black Tide* thus is a very well-orchestrated deconstruction of documentary practice. You have to bear in mind that—while we visited the area—many photographers, journalists, and reporters were simultaneously at work there.

HVG: Yes, one imagines them to have been all over the place and everyone producing a similar type of reporting about what was going on there.

CG: Indeed, and in response to that our intention was to find out what the voice of someone like Allan Sekula, himself a well-known documentary photographer, had to add to that sea of documents, interviews, and "witnesses." We sharply realized that parts of the reality of the situation remained unchanged or were deliberately kept out of sight. Sekula thereupon decided to start operating on several levels by phrasing and framing the event as a fiction—actually as an opera. By destroying the temporality of documentary as a privileged present, as a witness connected to a particular moment and a particular place he really breaks away from this prototypical working basis. *Black Tide*, as a photo-textual work, opens up to a much larger temporality. Through that process, the photographs become, so to say, a supporting base for a fictional text.

HVG: In earlier conversations between us we have often mentioned how Allan Sekula displayed a tendency to approach reality by means of a literary construction.

CG: Absolutely. He was not, as one could imagine, a radical "productivist" who observed reality as sheer raw material. For him the material of reality is always already constituted by a text. That is very typical for Sekula's generation of artists, growing into full maturity around the mid-seventies. They make a photography of language, or rather create art and language or photography and language at the same time. That approach is part of the consequences of these artists' suspicion against truism in photographic and documentary practice. Here lies the radical aspect of documentary for me.

HVG: When did you and Allan first exhibit this work?

CG: That was in 2003, in the context of an exhibition I curated entitled *After the news. Postmedia documentary practices.* The main motif of the exhibition was to present a documentary work realized, made, and produced around the events yet while the attention on those events was already declining in the media. The idea was that exactly then documentary practice such as Allan's could step in. Not with the urgency of the reporter or photojournalist, but with a different urgency and from a different position.

HVG: Can you describe the installation a bit more?

CG: It was the first time *Black Tide* was shown to the public as a piece in an exhibition space. It was also the first work visitors could actually see upon entering the exhibition, which was produced by *La Vanguardia* and the CCCB—the Barcelona Centre for Contemporary Culture. Besides *Black Tide* we presented work by Ursula Biemann, Angela Melitopoulos, and Bruno Serralongue. I also included the then only recently deceased writer W.G. Sebald, because he is also someone deceiving the generally established belief in the conclusions that may be drawn from the immediately indexical character of photography. In his books he includes photographs along with the texts, photographs that have actually nothing much to do with the text. The sheer proximity of the image to the text makes you think, without much of a reasonable basis, that one is the illustration of the other and vice versa. But in fact it is an artificial construction. Sebald was a real master in that regard. He would just buy photographs that he found in secondhand markets and then drop that image into the text without much adjusting between one and the other.

HVG: Was this exhibition accompanied by a catalog?

CG: Yes, a little publication exists that unfortunately did not circulate very broadly. I only have one personal copy. We reproduced almost the entire sequence of *Black Tide* in it.

HVG: Let us consider the text material included in *Black Tide* a bit more closely for a moment. Somehow once again, upon reading these lines, I cannot help but think that Sekula is trying to predict aspects of the future. It is true that the larger themes with which contemporary society *after* Sekula is struggling only come up in rather general terms, but nonetheless they are all there. He explicitly addresses "Europa," "the last old-time fascist," or how civil society will need to react "against the state." Of course he talks about "the necessity of oil." (Sekula, 2003b: 330 and 332) These are all issues that, obviously, were on the agenda back then already. But they haven't for a moment lost their topicality ever since—rather on the contrary, one would argue.

CG: Yes. One could say that he also engages in a reflection on the meaning of collective history. Late 2002 was the moment of the outbreak of the bird flu, the Avian influenza—the one that came from Chinese chickens and was transmitted through eating fowls. It seems that in the States this really caused concern and society as a whole was almost hysterically anxious about it. For Sekula this was an example of a very particular history that became a headline story, whereas the larger issue of this huge oil spill in the Atlantic remained more or less undiscussed. He was very alarmed by how local preoccupations tend to snow under the more global scopes. How is it possible we can get so obsessed with relatively tiny problems whereas there are larger developments that remain completely disregarded?

HVG: There is one further element I would like to point out to you. It pertains to Allan Sekula's artistic project as a whole. In "Fragments for an Opera," the textual part of *Black Tide*, his draft "Song of the Ship Inspector" ends with the following words: **"You can't send a postcard from the bottom of the sea."** (Sekula, 2003b: 332; original emphasis) In a footnote it is added that this is a sentence Bert Kanter, ship inspector for the International Transport Workers Federation, expressed to Sekula in "Rotterdam, October 1999." (333, n. 11) Sekula transformed that line into one of the "pink wall texts," meant selectively to accompany the exhibition installations of *Ship of Fools | The Dockers' Museum*.[4] When doing research for the likewise titled book, I vaguely remembered having read it somewhere in Sekula's writings at some earlier point in time. I searched and searched for it, in my impression rather endlessly, but eventually I didn't trace it back to "Fragments for an Opera."

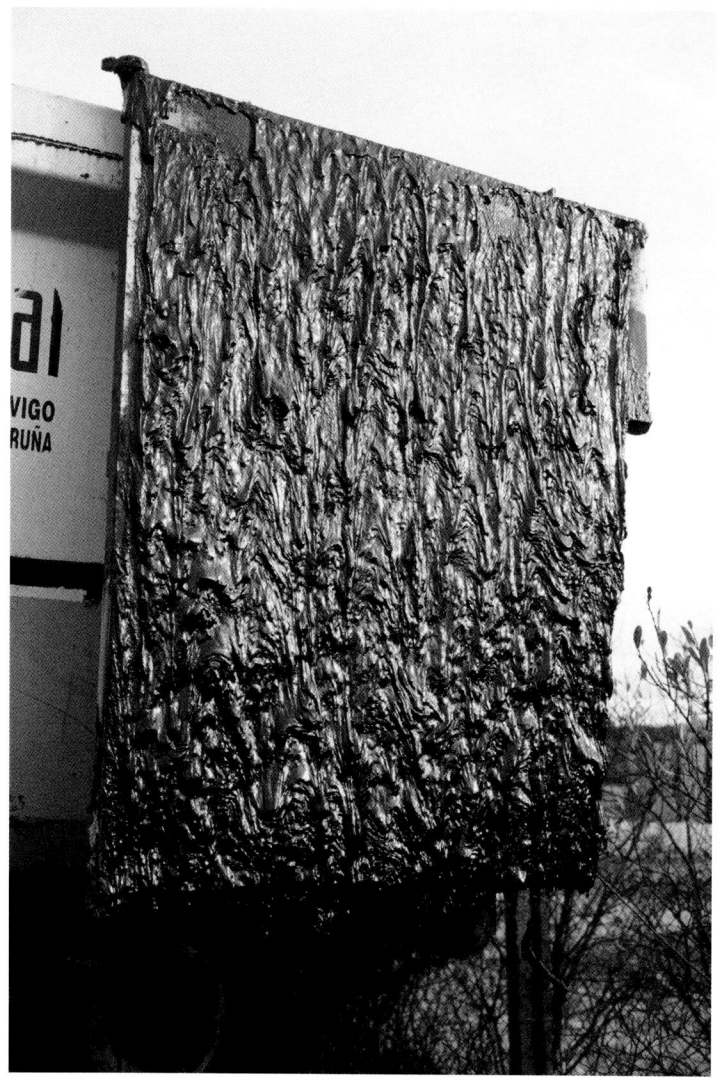

Fig. 2

Allan Sekula, *Dripping black trapezoid (Lendo, 12/22/02)*, part of *Black Tide/ Marea negra* (2002–03). Cibachrome print, 89,6 × 60,9 cm / 104,3 × 73,1 cm (framed). © Allan Sekula Studio.

I admit to have disregarded this text, because for some retrospectively unexplainable reason, there seemed to be quite a far stretch between that project and *Ship of Fools | The Dockers' Museum*. But nothing in Sekula's body of work can be considered as remote from anything else he ever produced. Here is a lesson learned once more about what he used to refer to himself as the montage principle at work in his oeuvre, larger "than that internal to any single work, or even book."

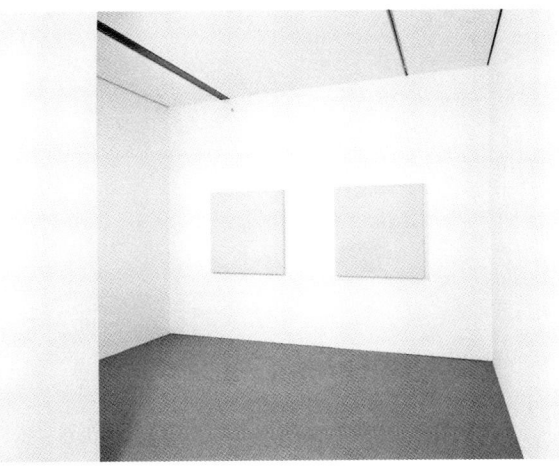

(Risberg, 1999: 238) For researchers who want to engage with that principle it takes painstaking years to find your way in the extremely rich constellation of elements that makes up Sekula's oeuvre. Gathering in the right order some pieces of the puzzle that he "disassembled" for us requires quite a strong dose of patience and calm. You constantly feel as if you're finding yourself having to solve the riddles that Allan came up with.

CG: Yes, I very much recognize this feeling. So Allan does provide this source here. That is interesting. What did you eventually mention in the book?

HVG: After careful discussion with Ina Steiner at the Allan Sekula Studio, we decided to opt for "oral history." (Van Gelder, 2015: 239) But if there ever appears a new edition of the book we will have to correct that.

CG: *Black Tide* as well still contains a lot of similarly unresolved issues. One of the pictures that most bewildered me is of course the rear door of the truck coated with the *chapapote*, the image that Allan entitled *Dripping black trapezoid (Lendo, 12/22/02).* (fig. 2) In my understanding this photograph provides a perfect analogy in the sense that, for Sekula, this is almost like a virtual representation of the surface of the sea. It reflects the water as you see it here, for example (points at *Volunteer on the edge (Islas Cíes, 12/20/02)*). (pl. 12) At the same time it also refers to the Modernist tradition of the monochrome painting. More specifically even, this photograph reminded me of Sekula's own *Gallery Voice Montage* (1970), you know, that early installation piece composed of two unprimed stretched canvases from which secretly recorded dialogs about looking at art resonate from a concealed built-in speaker. (fig. 3) This larger montage principle is clearly at play here as well.

HVG: Going back to the transcription of that text, which is included in the *Performance Under Working Conditions* book, one notices another striking parallel. At some point of the conversation, a "young woman" says how she presumes the painting they're in the process of observing was made: "It wasn't painted on. It's all dripping. He did it while it was up. Upright." A "young man" appears to reply, "It really looks like it's plastic. Sheets of black polystyrene, or polyethylene. Shiny black polyethylene. In fact that's what I thought it was at first." "Wow it does, or like oil," the "young woman" remarks. Upon which the "young man" answers, "Yeah, black, it's black. It could have been very wet, you know, very wet." Immediately after, Sekula makes a "male visitor" step into the discussion and say, "That sold for one million dollars." (Sekula, 2003a: 59) In light of the photograph of the black trapezoid from *Marea negra* that you and I are now observing, this dialog almost feels uncannily fit for it.

CG: Certainly if you also bear in mind that this raw material, oil, which is transported in vessels, has a hugely speculative market value. When oil tankers such as the *Prestige* leave the harbor filled with a good load, they begin to circulate around the globe without any fixed destination. They sail off while waiting for its cargo somewhere to be valued and then acquired at an auction. For example, say the ship departs from a reachable harbor in Northern Russia or Lithuania. It then goes out at sea, basically headed nowhere. It halts. It waits near the Northern part of Spain. Galicia has become some sort of a huge parking lot for these vessels until their merchandise is sold on the global market. When this has happened, the captain of the vessel receives a message that tells him where to sail his ship to. The value of this raw material is produced as long as it is circulating within the economic chain. At the moment circulation comes to a halt, as it turned out to be the case with the shipwreck, the worth of its cargo devalues—the value goes down exponentially. Oil is liquid, like capital. It has to circulate. The moment this circulation stops [*snaps his fingers*], it's like in photography. There you have the decisive moment.

HVG: That is a fascinating analogy you are making.

CG: This analogy between the flow of capital and photography, depending very much on endless circulation, both for its value making and for the maintenance of its value, is very productive. Sebald says the same when he states that photographs have a "nomadic existence." (Scholz, 2000: 51) Of course, in this kind of nomadic circulation you may encounter a snap from some people that basically means nothing to you because they are not part of your family. Nonetheless it is within this circulation mechanism that photography creates its meaning and its value. With the *Prestige* disaster the circulation of goods was interrupted. The accident was capital but no longer flow. The freezing moment, and we can use exactly the same word for photography, is the moment of the catastrophe, when flows are arrested. In response to that

Allan Sekula photographs himself through this veil of fuel, obscuring part of his eye and limiting his own vision. (pl. 13)

HVG: Whenever I look at this photograph, it comes to my mind that he looks like a pirate in that picture.

CG: You're right, I never thought of that. After all, in the wake of creating *Black Tide* Sekula was obsessed with the idea of publishing a book that would be entitled *Do not trespass*, meaning exactly the opposite: you have to disobey that sign, and trespass. He conceived of the book as a series of recommendations about how an activist photography slash documentary should conduct itself and behave. As for myself, I can tell you I was freaking out while we had illegally entered that compound. You have to realize that I was the one who speaks Spanish and understood everything. I knew how the guards were likely to react in case we would get caught. But Allan, focused as always, was very much disregarding my fear.

HVG: He knew he possibly had not more than five minutes left, right?

CG: Yeah. Well, he made quite a lot of work in that rather short amount of time. Besides the dripping trapezoid and the self-portrait, he took that double shot of the disposal pit. Sekula recorded video footage as well that became a prominent part of his film *The Lottery of the Sea* (2006). We held interviews with local fishermen and the material was translated, but eventually these never made it into *The Lottery of the Sea*. We were working intensively during the ten days that we spent there, always waking up at six or seven o'clock in the morning and then we went on until late. At night we would meet other journalists, actually people from Galicia that Sekula knew. He already had an established network from 1992, when he had been invited to Vigo for the biennial, which was the very first time that he ever worked in Spain. That project became the fifth chapter of *Fish Story*, "Message in a Bottle." (fig. 4)

HVG: Allan often mentioned that Spain was his favorite country in Europe by far. He gained special ties to it, especially to Galicia and Catalonia. Vigo remained a crucial reference all through his career. While working on the *Ship of Fools | The Dockers' Museum* book, Allan prioritized showing me in his studio outtakes from *Fish Story* that he had made in Vigo. As he imagined himself possibly returning to these images in the context of finding meaningful ways to display *Ship of Fools | The Dockers' Museum*, they were published in the book. (Van Gelder, 2015: 78–81) One of the images is made in 1992, but the other one two years later, in 1994. So he went back several times, and a long-term relationship with the area was clearly established.

CG: That was always the case with Sekula. The difference between him and regular photo reporters is that they go and grab their materials of an event's supreme moment only. Allan instead made a case of recurrently revisiting the same places over time.

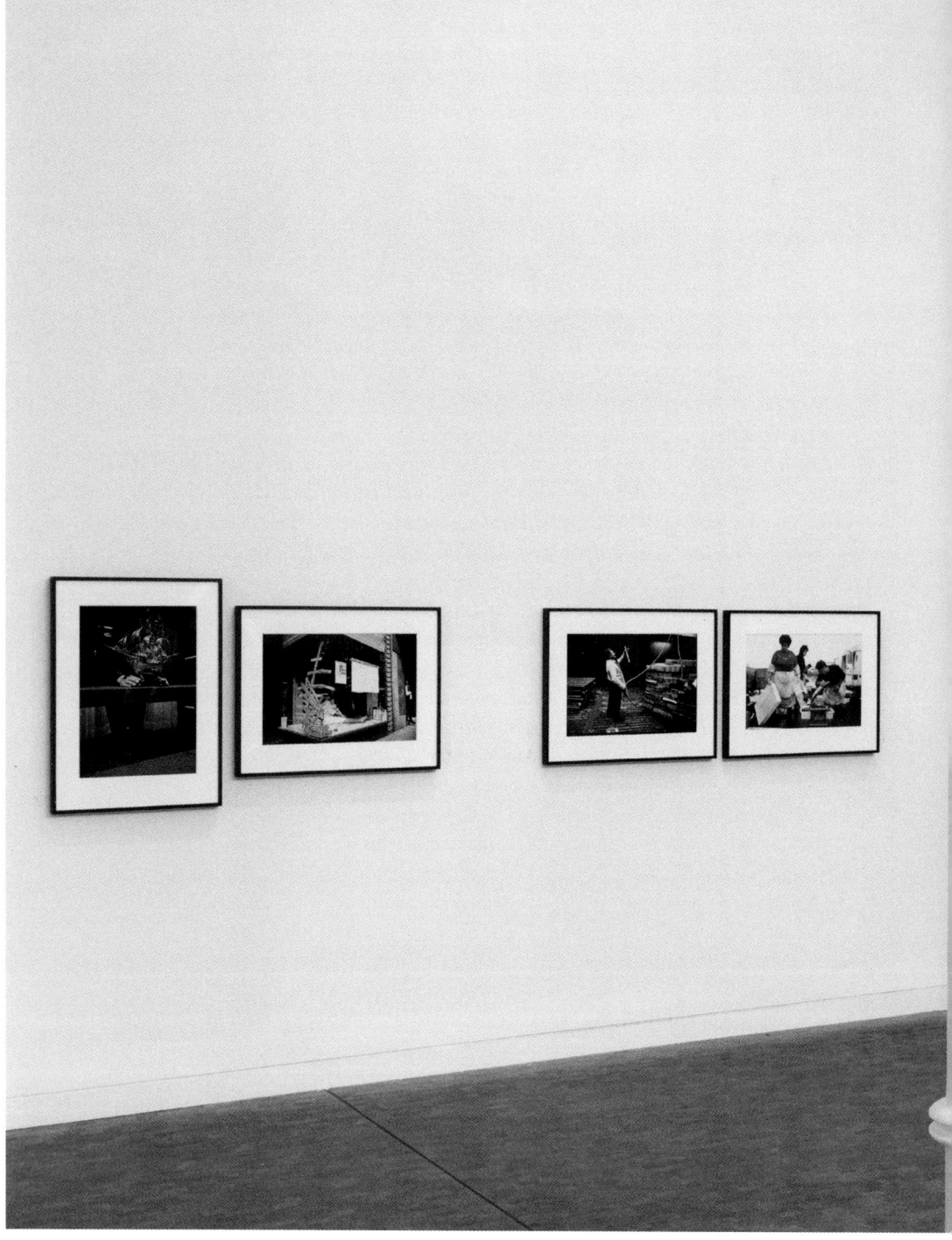

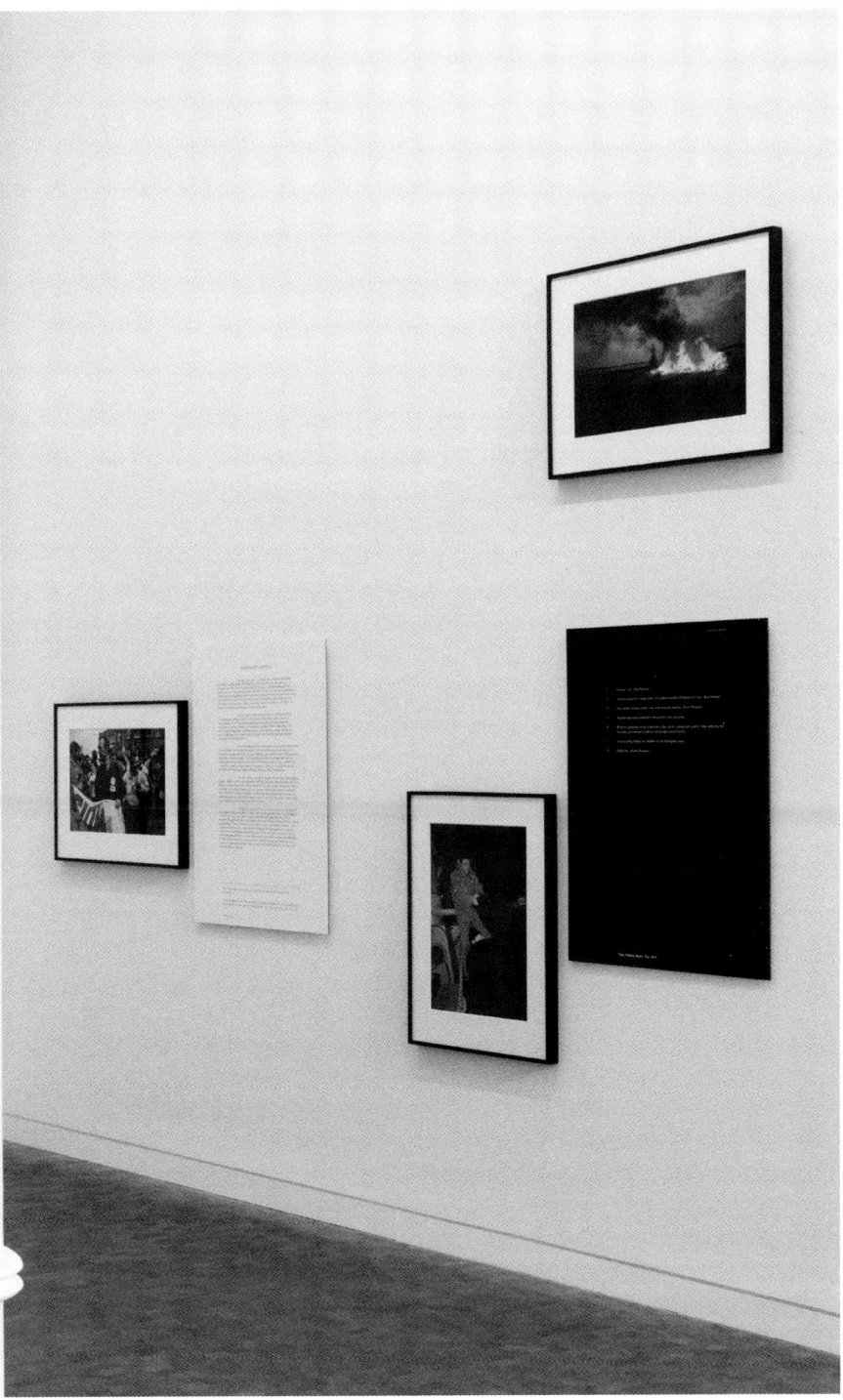

Fig. 4

Allan Sekula, "Message in a Bottle," 1992/1994. Chapter five from *Fish Story* (1989–1995). 7 Cibachrome prints and 2 text panels, various dimensions. Installation view of *Allan Sekula. Collective Sisyphus*, Fundació Antoni Tàpies, 2017. Collection Thyssen-Bornemisza Art Contemporary, Vienna. © Photo: Roberto Ruiz. Courtesy Allan Sekula Studio.

HVG: And amidst working this way he tended to insert cryptic references along with his images. Take this example from *Black Tide*: **"'Should these predictions prove wrong, we can promise without fear of error that the ship will stop leaking on the 15th of January, 2003.'"** (Sekula, 2003b: 329; original emphasis). Seemingly a neutral choice, as a quotation there is nothing specific about it until one realizes that January 15 is Allan Sekula's birthday.

CG: Ah *(smiles)*, I didn't notice.

HVG: No, but once you know, reading that sentence takes an extra, funny turn. Those who identify with Allan Sekula's sense of humor may imagine him thinking, "I wish that prediction to come true; I would consider it an ideal birthday present."

CG: Maybe these are real quotations from the prime minister José Maria Aznar.

HVG: Surely they must be.

Notes

1. The work was first published as a supplement of the Barcelona newspaper *La Vanguardia*. Composed by Sekula and Guerra, this special issue appeared on February 12, 2003. It is reproduced as a facsimile in *Allan Sekula. Okeanos*, 2017, 146–151.

2. For a summary introduction to the "Bombing Section," see Van Gelder, 2015, 88.

3. This conversation remains at present unpublished yet a recording exists.

4. This wall text is reproduced in Van Gelder, 2015: 202.

Bibliography

Carles Guerra, "Arrested Flow: Allan Sekula in Galicia," in *Allan Sekula. Okeanos*, eds Daniela Zyman and Cory Scozzari (Berlin: Sternberg Press, 2017), 138–144.

Debra Risberg, "Imaginary Economies: An Interview with Allan Sekula," in Allan Sekula, *Dismal Science: Photoworks 1972–1996* (Bloomington: University Galleries of Illinois State University, 1999), 235–251.

Christian Scholz, "'Aber das Geschriebene ist ja kein wahres Dokument.' Ein Gespräch mit dem Schriftsteller W. G. Sebald über Literatur und Photographie," *Neue Zürcher Zeitung*, 26/27, 2000: 51–52.

Allan Sekula, "Gallery Voice Montage, 1970," in *Performance Under Working Conditions*, ed. Sabine Breitwieser (Vienna: Generali Foundation, 2003a), 58–63.

Allan Sekula, "Fragments for an Opera," in *Performance Under Working Conditions*, ed. Sabine Breitwieser (Vienna: Generali Foundation, 2003b), 322–333.

Hilde Van Gelder (ed.), *Allan Sekula*. Ship of Fools / The Dockers' Museum (Leuven: Leuven University Press, 2015).

Part 3
Critical Realism in Dialogue

"Cultural Work as a *Praxis.*" The Artist as Producer in the Work of Victor Burgin, Martha Rosler, and Allan Sekula

Alexander Streitberger

The myth of "inspiration," of "the idea," reigns in the creation of advertising at the present time. In reality however the most original ideas, the most audacious advertisements, appear as transpositions of rhetorical figures which have been indexed over the course of numerous centuries. This is explained in that *rhetoric is in sum a repertory of the various ways in which we can be "original."* It is probable then that the creative process could be enriched and made easier if the creators would take account consciously of a system which they use intuitively. (Jacques Durand)[1]

Toward the end of his essay "Photographic Practice and Art Theory," Victor Burgin quotes these comments about the creative act by the French semiologist Jacques Durand. (Burgin, 1975/1982: 81) In his semiotic study on the production of meaning in the photographic image, Burgin voices his opposition to "romantic" aesthetic attitudes, which imply that an object has a unique essence that only artistic genius can reveal. The terms used by Durand in his text on advertising creation—"inspiration," "idea," and "originality"—serve in fact as key concepts of such an aesthetic attitude, and when Burgin wrote his text in 1975 these featured prominently in heated discussions at art schools and in art critique, still heavily influenced as they were by Modernist formalism and its presuppositions about the autonomy and self-reference of the work of art.

It is hardly surprising, then, that Burgin passes on the message intended for advertising creators to artist creators: as all artistic creation depends on pre-established codes and norms, naive intuition is not an adequate basis for the creative process, which must always involve

"Disassembled" Images

awareness of its conditions of production. On this basis, Burgin insists that theory and art, rather than being two clearly distinct activities, must be part of a permanent dialogue that feeds general cultural critique: "the division of labour between 'theorists' and 'practitioners' is problematical for a truly *critical* cultural initiative." (Burgin, 1986: viii) Of course, this cultural critique cannot be purely aesthetic or artistic because artistic creation depends on codes and norms that relate not only to art but also extend to other sociocultural fields and practices (which is certainly the case for the rhetorical system described by Durand), and therefore it cannot be separated from its sociocultural context. Any critical examination of creation must therefore involve reflection on society as well. Burgin shares this point of view with other artists such as Allan Sekula and Martha Rosler, and in the 1970s all three of them embarked on a dual activity of artistic practice and critical writing while adopting photography as both their means of artistic expression and their theoretical object.

In this article I propose to link the concept of creation in this artistic approach to the model of the author as producer as formulated by Walter Benjamin in a 1934 lecture at the Institute for the Study of Fascism in Paris. (Benjamin, 1966/1998) Specifically I will explore two questions: how does the author/producer become an artist/theorist? What is the fundamental creative concept of this new type of artist?

Photography as an Object and Tool of Critique

Before getting to the heart of the matter, it is relevant to discuss why the abovementioned artists use photography in both their artistic production and their theoretical work. There are in fact two reasons for this, which are simultaneously negative and positive. First, the fact that photography is used for many different purposes, making it difficult to identify and define what it actually is, supports these artists in their opposition to an essentialist aesthetic that removes art from its sociocultural context. Burgin believes that because of photography's ubiquity, found as it is just as easily in art as in everyday life, it is the perfect medium for exploring the links between art and sociopolitical realities. (Burgin, 1976: 361) Secondly, their adoption of photography should be seen as a reaction to the discovery of the medium by art critics and institutions in the late 1960s and early 1970s. On the initiative of John Szarkowski, head of the Photography Department at the Museum of Modern Art in New York since 1962, galleries and museums started to exhibit photographers such as Diane Arbus, Lee Friedlander, and Garry Winogrand, whose images are now judged on the basis of Modernist aesthetics. In her article "Lookers, Buyers, Dealers and

Makers," Martha Rosler observes this shift from documentary value to expressive value, taking as an example Dorothea Lange's photographic work for the FSA, which, after being appropriated by the art institutions, was seen to have moved beyond social documentation and was interpreted instead as the creation of an expressive, solitary genius. (Rosler 1979/2004: 36–37) Like Rosler, Burgin cautions against the formalism of Szarkowski, who by ignoring the context of production and presentation reduces the photographic image to a formal composition dependent on cardinal rules such as detail, framing, and perspective. (Szarkowski, 1966; Burgin, 1980: 73–75) In their theory and practice, then, Burgin, Rosler, and Sekula set about deconstructing the shift from documentary photography to aesthetic expression, from reporter to genius, a shift that—as they believed—serves the liberal politics of capitalism in which the image, removed from its political context, becomes a product that is appreciated for its inherent formal and material qualities: "The invention of the photograph as high art was only possible through its transformation into an abstract fetish, into 'significant form.'" (Sekula, 1975/1982: 103)

Photography can be seen to embody two myths of Western society, objective scientific truth through the documentary photo and subjective experience through the artistic photo, and as such it is a major tool of capitalist ideology, which, according to Burgin, presents itself continually, in every moment of our daily lives, in the form of ads, in newspapers and magazines; the framing of this ideology, in other words, relies on photography and text.[2] (Burgin, 1976: 364) The challenge is not to define photography as either a science or a form of art, but to understand the laws according to which it is used within everyday life in industrial societies. (Sekula 1983/1999: 191) This is why Burgin, Sekula, and Rosler speak out against the idea of the genius who delves into the subjective imagination to find his art. They dismiss intuitive and expressive creation in favor of an artistic practice that is contextual and socially engaged and that takes account of the ideological forms operating in a society at the aesthetic, social, and political level.

The Author as Producer

The guiding example for this practice is clearly inspired by the model of the author as producer, as conceived by Walter Benjamin in the wake of Bertolt Brecht's reflections on his concept of epic theater. Indeed, to define artistic practice and the artist's role in society, Burgin, Rosler, and Sekula refer explicitly to Benjamin's essay "The Author as Producer," based on a 1934 lecture at the Institute for the Study of Fascism in Paris. As their quotations from his work suggest, they single out three aspects as basis of a theoretical-practical artistic practice. When Rosler, quoting Benjamin, writes that "to supply a productive apparatus without trying … to change it is a highly disputable activity," she is highlighting the artist's responsibility toward society. (Benjamin, 1966/1998: 93–94; Rosler, 1979/2004: 44) And Sekula, quoting Brecht, highlights the need to maintain a critical distance from the production apparatus and to adopt a meta-reflexive attitude:

> The muddled thinking which overtakes musicians, writers, and critics as soon as they consider their own situation has tremendous consequences to which too little attention is paid. For by imagining that they have got hold of an apparatus which in fact has got hold of them they are supporting an apparatus which is out of their control.[3] (Sekula, 1978: 869)

The artist, in other words, is expected to develop a body of work that implies its own critical reflection within the context of the aesthetic and social discourse of which it is part. In this context, Burgin, drawing on Benjamin, suggests a "pan-discursive" attitude, whereby photography and writing, artistic and political tendencies, are intertwined to embrace technical progress: "And we shall lend greater emphasis to this demand if we, as writers, start taking photographs ourselves. Here again, therefore, technical progress is, for the author as producer, the basis of his political progress." (Benjamin, 1966/1998: 95; Burgin, 1980: 80)

Social transformation, meta-reflection, and interdisciplinarity are all vital components of a creation that is radically opposed to the romantic orientation of modernism based on concepts of intuition, autonomy, and purity. As Rolf Tiedemann states in his postface to the French edition of Benjamin's *Essais sur Brecht*, this model of the artist replaces the notion of creation in the conventional sense with the notion of production:

> For Benjamin, a producer is an author who stops treating his activity—writing—and the result of this activity as if it were something irrational, generally referred to as a "creation" or "work"—an author who considers the social conditions of both and, in doing so, feels obliged to draw conclusions from this for his writing. (Benjamin, 2003: 225; my translation)

In a dialectical movement, the creative process borrows its means from society's production process while also aiming to have an impact on the latter. Basing his theory of the artist as producer on Brecht's principles of epic theater, Benjamin puts forward a model of the creative process, which—after having been lost in the monumentalism of the

Nazi aesthetic and, subsequently, in the Modernist formalism of the 1950s and 1960s—was rediscovered and applied by this generation of artists who have an affinity with the Marxist materialism of the New Left. This does not just relate to their critical stance on capitalism, on a political level, and formalism, on an aesthetic level, but also, as we will see, to the strategies they used to create works of art.

For Benjamin, the quality of the work is found not in formal, symbolic values, but in a dialectical link between literary trends and the socio-political reality: "the rigid, isolated object (work, novel, book) is of no use whatsoever. It must be inserted into the context of living social relations." As he continues: "Before I ask: what is a work's position *vis-à-vis* the production relations of its time, I should like to ask: what is its position *within* them?" (Benjamin, 1966/1998: 87) For this reason, it is impossible for Benjamin to contemplate art apart from its social context. If artists wish to exert an influence on their era and change the society in which they are living, they must embrace the means of production of this society. They must start from the latest technologies—film and radio, according to Benjamin—in order "to apply them and to learn from them—in short, to enter into a dialogue with them." (Benjamin, 1966/1998: 99)

Brecht's epic theater served as the aesthetic model for Benjamin's theory of the author as producer. For Benjamin, the key principle of epic theater—interruption—is related to montage as the basic process involving the latest advertising tools such as film, radio, the press, and photography, because "montage interrupts the context into which it is inserted." (Benjamin, 1966/1998: 99) By interrupting the action, Brecht aims to surprise the audience, and because this "always works against creating an illusion among the audience," this strategy distances the audience from "the conditions of our life." (Benjamin, 1966/1998: 99–100) Being thus invited to take a step back from the play for a moment, the spectators are compelled to "take up a position towards the action," which refers to the position of the actors as well as to the spectators' own situation. The creative process thus requires the artist to adopt the dominant tools and processes of production, and, in transforming them, encourage the attitude of maintaining critical distance toward the conditions of production in art and society. The three works discussed below, which were created between 1973 and 1975, reflect and illustrate the critical and dialectical perspective highlighted in the writings of Brecht and Benjamin.

VI (1973) is the first work in which Burgin appropriates advertising photographs. The series consists of ten parts, each comprising three distinct elements: the photograph of a nuclear family taken from a British mail-order catalogue, a caption for that photograph, and a text similar to those of the preceding text works. Whereas the photograph remains the same throughout the whole series, the two verbal parts change, thus offering alternative ways in which the image can be interpreted. The advertising photograph represents a Western family in a cliché format: the woman in the foreground, flanked by a boy and a girl, takes care of the children while the husband stands behind his family to protect and provide for them. His gaze is directed at the mother of his children, who, in turn, looks down at the boy as the legitimate son and heir. At first glance, the large type captions dealing with questions of value pertaining to objects, actions, and goals are completely disconnected from what is happening in the image they are meant to explain. But this is precisely Burgin's intention. The difficulty in reconciling image and caption destabilizes our preconceived idea of the family cliché; it de-naturalizes it. In fact, the caption is not intended to explain the visible content of the image. Interrupting our expectation that it will have an explanatory function, the caption redirects, in a Brechtian manner, the reader's attention toward the underlying ideological structure of the family as a social convention, while at the same time denouncing advertising as a tool for legitimating and spreading such shared beliefs in the name of the dominant social order. (Burgin, 1973/2009: 36)

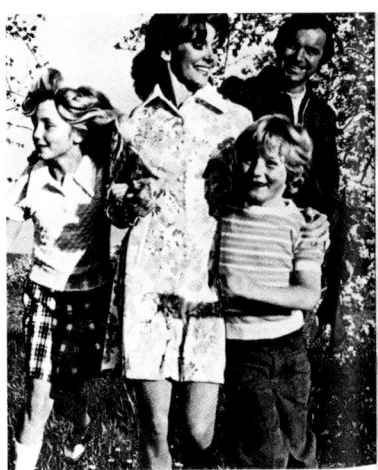

A complex of phenomena so integrated as to be seen as a unit with properties not derivable from the parts of that unit in summation; a sector of a given perceptual field identified, at a given moment, as a whole and as having attributes more extensive than the sum of the attributes of its constituent elements; a *gestalt*

Any physical object is to be positively valued only if it may be instrumental in the achievement of a goal.

Fig. 1

Victor Burgin, *VI* (Panel I), 1973. © Victor Burgin.

The first caption, then, "Any physical object is to be positively valued only if it may be instrumental in the achievement of a goal," refers to the advertising photograph as ideological object. (fig. 1) It is not what it depicts that is important, but rather the purpose for which it is used: to sell a particular product, and, on a more general level, to consolidate the social role of the family as one of the main pillars of Western capitalist consumer society. As Burgin wrote in 1975:

> The desirability, the "closeness", and the joy of family life are centrally important concepts in legitimating and supporting this unit. In an environment of billboards, popular press, television, and commercial cinema it is difficult to pass a single day without encountering some visual representation of the family. (Burgin, 1975/1982: 41)

Burgin's aim is to appropriate advertising as a contemporary means of communication in order to lay bare its rhetorical structure, which is supposed to naturalize conventional social patterns and stimulate consumption. The dichotomic divisions into personal and collective, perpetuation and perpetual revision, objective deliberation and subjective intuition, and circumspection and precipitance invite the reader to think about how the roles of the family members are distributed in society and confirmed through images in the media. In this case, the words "objective," "circumspection," and "goal" might be attributed to the man, while "intuition," "precipitance," and "subjective" are qualities conventionally associated with the woman and the children.

The text juxtaposed with the photograph, in contrast, begins with a statement on the perception of a *gestalt*, similar to those of earlier text works, such as *Any Instantaneous Appearance* (1970). Already in the second panel, however, the parallel text introduces basic semiotic concepts such as "signifier," "unmotivated," and "motivated" signs, "code," and "message" that can be used as tools of interpretation. Panel VI is of particular interest because here Burgin describes the two possible functions of an image's caption, anchorage, and relay. (fig. 2) Introduced by Roland Barthes in his classic essay "The Rhetoric of the Image" (1964) in order to analyze advertising images, "anchorage" occurs when the linguistic message directs the reader toward a preferred meaning, whereas "relay" signifies a complementary relationship between text and image, in which "the unity of the message is realized at a higher level."[4] (Barthes, 1964/1977: 41) Apparently, Burgin invites the reader to apply Barthes' terminology to the image-text combination on the left-hand side. As the caption provides no clues to the specific meaning of the image, the reader tends to understand the caption as a relay function. Yet, the overt contradiction between the image's emphasis on the

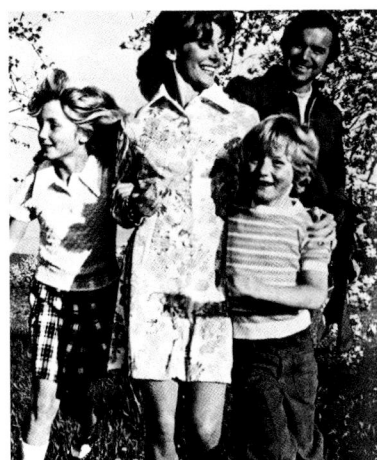

VI

1
The juxtaposition of a visual image and a supplementary linguistic message, this latter indicating prefered meanings from amongst the connoted meanings of the former; anchorage

2
The juxtaposition of a visual image and a complementary linguistic message indicating a meaning not signified by either of the component messages; relay

The perpetual revision of all extant goals and their means of achievement is to be positively valued.

Fig. 2

Victor Burgin, *VI* (Panel VI), 1973. © Victor Burgin.

family as a stable unit, as well as the caption's suggestion that we positively value the perpetual revision of all extant goals and their means, makes it nearly impossible to find a "higher level" of meaning other than the notion of revising values commonly associated with the family. Consequently, the texts of the subsequent panels refer to the way individual actions are pre-determined by the ideological framework of values commonly accepted by a given society (VII-IX). The final panel reveals the three possibilities of congruence between the sub-codes of sender and receiver: complete congruence signifies "full *concordance* of ideologies," for partial congruence the interpretation of a message would be successful only to some extent, and, finally, complete incongruence leads to "*discordance* of ideologies."

Ultimately, it becomes clear that Burgin does not set out to describe or explain the image by means of verbal language. The work is rather a critical comment on the complex ways ideologies are established through visual and verbal forms of representation. The repetition of one and the same photograph through all ten panels reflects the standardized nature of advertising, while the unrelated, changing, and sometimes contradictory value statements of the captions destabilize the reader's expectations and prevent easy interpretation. The text on the right-hand side provides a theoretical meta-text that "anchors" the family photograph within the general context of ideology. The final aim of the work might be to encourage readers to consider the extent to which they agree or disagree *with* the dominating ideology and the values it carries.

In a public debate in 1977, Burgin actually outlined an aesthetic program aimed at highlighting the contradictions of our life in society by fragmenting the integrity of the texts that make up a given society or community. He suggested:

> And one way of doing that is to make texts out of components which won't marry happily together, so that there are cracks in the structure, and this text then becomes a sort of critique of the other texts. So I think it is possible to avoid the trap of straightforward realism, straightforward representationalism, which is already ideologically loaded. (Burgin, 1978: 137)

This is exactly how Burgin proceeds in *VI*, thereby announcing a new critical aesthetics—an aesthetics of cracks and fragments. Drawing on the concept of false consciousness, defined by Georg Lukács as a problem of perception and knowledge that could be countered by new theoretical orientations (Eyerman, 1981: 49), Burgin aims, first, to dismantle photography and advertising as a manipulative instrument of the dominant ideology, and, second, to establish a counter-rhetoric that invites the viewer/reader to distrust and question the existing social order. In reference to Benjamin, he does so through a "pan-discursive" gesture, testing the advertising image against theoretical ideas from different areas (*gestalt* theory, semiotics, Marxist-inspired critique of ideology).

Frame the Crime: Allan Sekula's *Aerospace Folktales*

A 1973 work by Allan Sekula, *Aerospace Folktales,* tells the story of the artist's family after his father was made redundant from his job as an aeronautical engineer at Lockheed. (pl. 14) The work is made up of three separate narrative elements, each showing a different perspective: a series of black-and-white photos with captions presents this social drama in the form of a photo-reportage; on the soundtrack we hear the voice of his parents, who are interviewed by the artist about their difficult situation; and, finally, there is a written commentary by the artist, which is a critical reflection on the ideology of American liberalism and its impact on art and social life. Image, text, sound—all the elements of a film are there, if in a disjointed fashion because they are presented separately: the written commentary is juxtaposed with the series of images, while the soundtrack is playing in the adjoining room. Sekula calls this method a "disassembled movie," which, by disassembling the elements, leads to the possibility of negation and meta-commentary in his view. (Sekula, 2003: 92) The aim is therefore not to document the life of one particular family, but to conduct a critical deconstruction of the ideological and economic conditions underlying the situation in which the family finds itself: "A truly critical social documentary will frame the crime, the trial, and the system of justice and its official myths." (Sekula, 1978: 864)

To denounce these myths, Sekula uses exactly the means and strategies that Benjamin borrowed from the theory of epic theater to define the author as a producer: interruption and montage. Aside from the fact that the whole work is made up of a montage of heterogeneous elements, these principles are primarily applied to the series of photographic images to confront us with the fundamental myths of the family as a microcosm of society. The series begins with the reproduction of advertising copy used by the American aeronautical manufacturer Lockheed, and two news images portraying progress and prosperity based on military power and national identity. Next, the first interruption follows rather abruptly, as this success story is juxtaposed with the humdrum, gloomy story of a family suffering the effects of unemployment. The caption for the photo of his father and a friend in a vast deserted parking lot reads: "The engineer and his old friend stood in the empty Lockheed parking lot while I photographed them. Unable to fathom my motives, they were uneasy." (fig. 3)

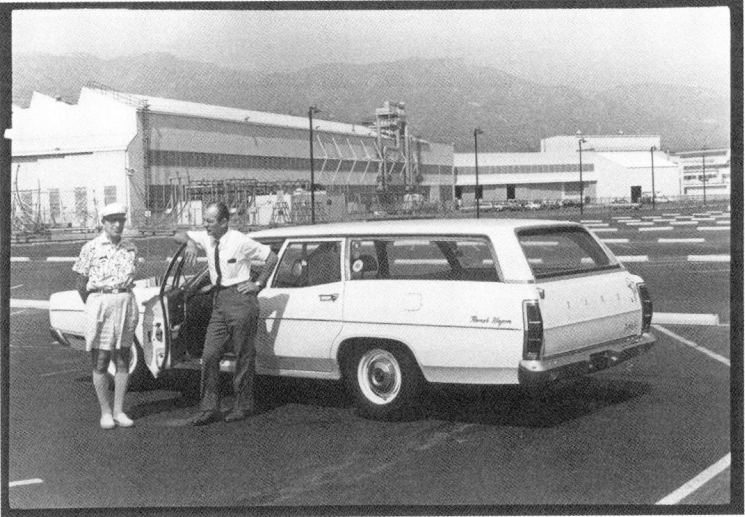

Fig. 3

From Allan Sekula, *Aerospace Folktales*, 1973. 51 b&w photographs in 23 frames. Three red canvases director's chairs, six potted fan palms, three CD players, three speakers, three simultaneous, unsynchronized CD recordings. Each frame 55,9 × 71,5 cm. CD total play time 17 min, 21 min, and 23 min. © Allan Sekula Studio.

The laconic caption is in marked contrast to the American dream represented in the previous panels, while it also encourages critical reflection on the technique used, photography, or, more specifically documentary photography. In mentioning the discomfort of the people in front of the camera, Sekula directs our attention to their rather unnatural poses, thus anticipating Barthes' description of the portrait-photograph as a "closed field of forces" marked by inauthenticity, or even imposture. (Barthes 1981: 30) In denouncing the objectivity and neutrality of photography, Sekula argues that it is not enough to present a social and engaged photo-reportage; after all, a true deconstruction of a society's ideology does not stop at its systems and techniques of representation, including documentary photography and its folk myths of realism.[5] In the written commentary that is part of the work, Sekula explains:

> i am writing because of the limited representational range of the camera   one cannot photograph ideology   but one can make a photograph step back and say look in that photograph there is ideology   between those two photographs there is ideology (Sekula, 2003: 161; original typesetting)

Consequently, the photographic panels are not a documentary photo-essay, but rather recount a meta-narrative in which the spectator-reader faces many interruptions that contrast elements from different realities: a sequence showing the redundant engineer with his family is followed by a photo of their house. This is juxtaposed with the real estate holding company's contract, listing all the rules with which the tenants must comply. Following the interruption created by the mundane rules of bureaucracy, everyday life is depicted in a cinematographic sequence in which the family members go into the house; we see details of the interior, signs of a typically bourgeois life: family photos, a statue of the Virgin Mary, etc. Next, we see the father in the process of writing application letters or fitting a lamp—typical pastimes of the

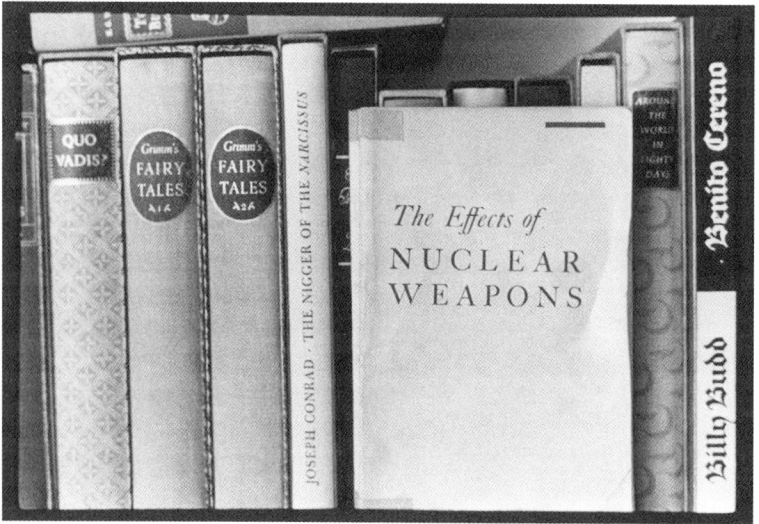

Fig. 4

From Allan Sekula, *Aerospace Folktales*, 1973. 51 b&w photographs in 23 frames. Three red canvases director's chairs, six potted fan palms, three CD players, three speakers, three simultaneous, unsynchronized CD recordings. Each frame 55,9 × 71,5 cm. CD total play time 17 min, 21 min, and 23 min. © Allan Sekula Studio.

"Disassembled" Images

unemployed—while the mother, in her role as housewife, works in the kitchen. These images are contrasted with close-ups of American political and cultural symbols: brought together in the children's room, the US Army helicopter is a symbol of military power and the crucifix above the door symbolizes Christian religion. Naturally, the classics of Western literature—which Sekula calls "totems of high culture"—are forcefully present in this accumulation of bourgeois values—among them the Grimm Brothers, Jonathan Swift, Joseph Conrad, and Jules Verne. (fig. 4) We learn that the engineer gave his children one dollar for each book they read, before reading on the following panel that, at one point in his career, the engineer himself had studied the effects of nuclear weapons. This abrupt shift from the cultural ambitions of his private life to his professional preoccupation with a deadly military technology—from the Grimm Brothers to the atomic bomb—is expressed in the contrast between photos of several pages of the work in question and, in the following images, the mother carefully arranging flowers in a vase. The last panel once again plays on the contrast between professional and private life by showing the father's CV alongside several photos from the family album. As the commentary reads:

> that's how he has to represent himself if he's going to get a job   we might call that resume the most minimal form of white collar art   we might call it the most minimal form of capitalist art   we might call it a map of my father's potential value as a commodity (Sekula, 2003: 159; original typesetting)

By subjecting modern photography and film techniques to meta-criticism with a simultaneous focus on the "family folktale" and the "folk myth of photography," Sekula strives to deconstruct the ideological and economic discourse of capitalist liberalism. As we have seen, he uses interruption to create breaks in the fabric of the documentary narrative, which encourages the spectator to adopt a position on the content and the technical apparatuses of representation.[6]

Martha Rosler's *The Bowery* as a Possibility of Negation and Meta-commentary

Martha Rosler's definition of art as a "practice of critical photography and text," and her "quotational ('appropriational') and ironic" approach aiming at a "critical engagement with the images of mass culture, visual and verbal, and with those of photography (and art) as a practice" are perfectly in line with Sekula's and Burgin's position around 1975. (Rosler, 1982/2004: 139) *Bringing the War Home* (1967–1972) is an antiwar series comprising twenty photomontages in which news photographs of the war in Vietnam are combined with images of domestic interiors from architectural and design magazines.[7] (pl. 15) These photomontages are clearly a nod to the tradition of avant-garde collage in the 1920s and 1930s. Rosler explicitly refers to Max Ernst's Surrealist collages, based on the "hallucinating succession of contradictory images," (Ernst, 1937/1970: 128) as well as to Heartfield's political photomontages for their critical deconstruction of photographic truth. (Rosler, 1998: 25; Rosler, 1988–1994: 279) Another major influence seems to have come from Soviet films, most notably Serge Eisenstein and his theory of montage. (Rosler, 1998: 31) Asking himself in his 1929 essay "The Cinematographic Principle and the Ideogram" by what montage is characterized, Eisenstein replies: "By collision. By the conflict of two pieces in opposition to each other. By conflict. By collision." (Eisenstein, 1949/1977: 37)

Pursuing a double critique of American involvement in the Vietnam war and feminist concerns about the classical distribution of roles between men at war and women at home, Rosler in fact juxtaposes separate categories of representation, whereby men appear in the political public sphere of the daily press while women's domain is the private space of the perfect home as promoted by lifestyle magazines:

> The antiwar series *Bringing the War Home* carried forward some of the feminist concerns in the other photomontages. […] All of them invoked the domestic interior, specifically, *representations* of the domestic interior, and the construction of separate categories and thus separate spaces. (Rosler, 1998: 47; original emphasis)

And a little further she adds: "I see much of *Bringing the War Home* as trying to solve the riddle of segregated representations of clean spaces and dirty spaces of human habitation." (Rosler, 1998: 50) In fact, most of the works in the series clearly suggest that *Bringing the War Home* is less about realities and more about the way we are confronted with realities through images. When the large glass fronts of modern homes, designed for connecting the interior with the landscape outside, reveal photographs from the war in Vietnam, it becomes clear that the media are not only providing us with images from distant lands, but that they are also blocking our view of the outside world: transparent windows become opaque surfaces of projection. The staging of these images as a kind of home-cinema setting further emphasizes the constructed, fictional nature of photojournalism.

Rosler denounces both kinds of representations, those naturalizing common gender stereotypes as well as those fictionalizing the war, by

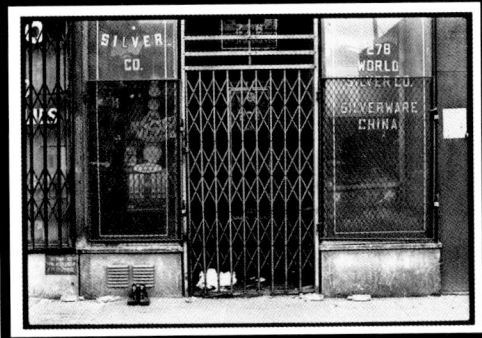
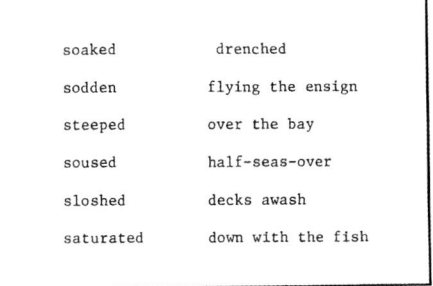

soaked	drenched
sodden	flying the ensign
steeped	over the bay
soused	half-seas-over
sloshed	decks awash
saturated	down with the fish

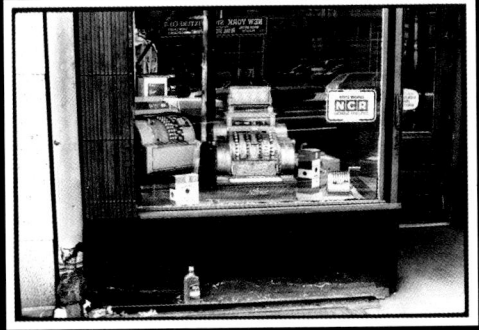

stewed
boiled
potted
corned
pickled
preserved
canned
fried to the hat

means of the so-called "realistic" media of photography and film. In this respect, her claim about John Heartfield's work as "unsurpassed example of political photomontage" equally applies to her own work: "In every photomontage was the implicit message that photography alone cannot 'tell the truth' and also the reminder that fact itself is a social construction." (Rosler 1988–1994/2004: 279)

The principles underpinning this deconstruction are, of course, interruption and alienation (*Verfremdung*), as introduced by Brecht in his epic theater and later claimed by Benjamin for "The Author as Producer." Drawing on John Heartfield's use of the book jacket as "a political instrument," Benjamin highlights, as mentioned, "the technique of montage, for montage interrupts the context into which it is inserted." (Benjamin, 1966/1998: 99) Several years later, in 1974/1975, Martha Rosler applied the principles of interruption and appropriation to her photo-text series *The Bowery in two inadequate descriptive systems*. Described by the artist as "a work of refusal" and "an act of criticism," *The Bowery* is an installation of twenty-one black-and-white photographs, representing a walk down the Bowery in New York, and twenty-four text panels, all put together as a grid. (Rosler, 1981/2004: 191) (fig. 5)

Fig. 5

Martha Rosler, selections from *The Bowery in two inadequate descriptive systems*, 1974–75, gelatin silver prints.
© Martha Rosler.

The title reminds us, as Rosler remarks, that all "descriptive systems are inadequate to experience." (Rosler, 1998: 44) This general inadequacy of representational systems is further confirmed by the gap that, in this particular case, separates image and text. Whereas the photographs show deadpan frontal views of storefronts, bank façades, and debris in the Bowery area, the words, chosen from a dictionary for their connection with "the culture of drunkenness," (Rosler, 1981/2004: 194) constitute what Sekula called "an immense slang lexicon of alcoholism." (Sekula, 1978: 867) There is, of course, continuity and overlap between text and image: both refer to poverty and social desolation; the words are grouped in semantic clusters; the sequence of photographs suggests a walk downtown; and, finally, some of the photo-text juxtapositions refer to the same objects, for example when the photographed empty bottles lying in the street are juxtaposed with their slang terms "dead soldiers" and "dead marines."

But what is really at stake here are the underlying contradictions in the representation of social misery as they can be observed in the photographic history of social documentary. Actually, the photographs of *The Bowery* deliberately quote the tradition of American documentary photography, from Jacob Riis to the photographers of the Farm Security Administration (FSA).[8] At a moment when "concerned" photography became fashionable in museums and in the art market for its newly discovered aesthetic originality and expressive value, Rosler adopted a quotational approach in which she referred to Walker Evans' "documentary style," now purged of any humanist aspiration, by presenting strictly depopulated expressionless views of urban bleakness.

Avoiding the traps of "meliorism" (the use of social documentary to improve living conditions without changing the underlying ideological conditions of capitalism) and "sensationalism" (the transformation of misery into psychologically charged expressive images of urban alienation), *The Bowery* constitutes, in Allan Sekula's words, a "*metacritical* relation to the documentary genre." (Sekula, 1978: 867) "The object of the work, its referent," Sekula suggests, "is not the Bowery per se, but the 'Bowery' as a socially mediated, ideological construction." (Sekula, 1978: 867) Which brings me back to Benjamin and Brecht's concept of epic theater. In contrast to a theater that competes with other means of entertainment to win over the audience with the most sophisticated stage effects, Benjamin propounds Brecht's epic theater as a dialogical platform that "must not develop actions but represent conditions." (Benjamin, 1966/1998: 98) The use of familiar techniques of modern communication (documentary and press photography, ordinary language, cinema), while interrupting the very process of communication, creates "the opportunity to expose the present"—to expose, in other words, *what* is represented and *how* it is represented within contemporary society. (Benjamin, 1966/1998: 100) This can only be achieved if the spectator can be persuaded to step back, to look, and to think. Offering "decoys" (familiar imagery, common language and interrelations between both) and "disruptions" (fences, shutters, locked doors as literal barriers in the photographs, disconnected text-image combinations), *The Bowery* invites the inattentive beholder to become an active, conscious spectator. As Rosler notes: "The first time around you are straining, the second time around you are already standing back in your world and you think, 'Now I can *think* about this!'" (Rosler, 1998: 55)

In her work, Rosler suggests, the spectator is confronted with questions—questions about social difference and about how social difference is constructed through representation. The answer has to be provided by every single spectator (Rosler, 1998: 55). It is perhaps in this sense that, as Benjamin puts it, "the reader is always prepared to become a writer." (Benjamin, 1966/1998: 90) Rosler summarizes her position as follows:

> As viewers of Godard, we wanted to parasitize all forms—and foreground the apparatus. As readers of Brecht, we wanted to use obviously theatrical or dramatized sequences or performance elements together with more traditional documentary strategies, to use text, irony, absurdity, mixed forms of all types. (Rosler, 1998: 33)

As readers of Benjamin, one might now add, Rosler and her peers situate their work within the production relationship in order to challenge the productive apparatus by effecting "a break with preceding practice in a strong and meaningful way."[9] (Rosler, 1979/2004: 44)

Conclusions

As my argument reveals, the works of Burgin, Sekula, and Rosler concur with all the decisive points of the model of the author as producer. First, the hybrid character of their works, oscillating between text and image, film and photo, image and sound, contrasts with the formalist tendency in photography already criticized by Benjamin, such as New Objectivity, which in his view "has turned the struggle against misery into an object of consumption." (Benjamin, 1966/1998: 96) Like Benjamin, these artists stress that a work should incorporate a critical reflection of the context in which it was produced. Thus, they insist the photographer should frame the images with language to anchor, contradict, reinforce, subvert, supplement, specify, or extend the meanings depicted by the images themselves. (Sekula, 1978: 866)

Such a meta-criticism of the representation is aimed both at the social and political system of capitalism and at the technology used to produce the images that are likely to propagate the ideological and aesthetic issues of said system. Burgin's "aesthetics of fragments and cracks," Sekula's "disassembled movie," and Rosler's "possibility of negation and metacommentary" all constitute an analytical device that allows the creative process involved to comprise its own process of reflection, so to speak. Montage and interruption are the key components of this approach, which is diametrically opposed to the Modernist aesthetic model. While Modernism champions the autonomy and self-reflexivity of the artistic medium, which, removed from the social context, references only its own formal qualities, Burgin, Sekula, and Rosler advocate another reflexivity model. By juxtaposing the advertising image with a theoretical metatext (Burgin), documentary photography with two narratives—one biographical, the other critical—(Sekula), and socially engaged photography with a poetry of drunkenness (Rosler), they suggest that a medium is defined, on the one hand, according to the social and economic context in which it is used and, on the other hand, by the interactions, rivalries, and reciprocal influences between it and another medium. This is completely in line with Benjamin's theory that the author as producer embraces the production apparatuses of his time, using its tools (here, photo and film), and referencing the production context in which, and for which, these tools are used.

Finally, this contextual approach must include the spectator. As in Brecht's epic theater, interruption (medium, genre, style) invites the spectators, who are constantly pulled out of the narrative, to distance themselves from what they see. The impact created by the brusque juxtaposition of photography and film, family photographs and bureaucratic documents, advertising copy and laconic commentary, encourages the spectator to become a politically-aware "pensive spectator."

(Bellour, 1984/1997) If the question of creation essentially serves as a domain for art to reflect on itself, on its own operations and practices, the works discussed here are that very domain, not in the sense of the closed aesthetic domain of Modernist self-referentiality, but a domain of social and aesthetic struggle in which reflection on art is inextricably linked to reflection on society because aesthetic, social, and political discourses are bound by the same ideological conditions.

The aim is not to create something *ex novo*, but to transform the production apparatuses drawing on a pan-discursive activity in which the artist's intervention incorporates theoretical reflection. It can therefore be concluded that we can look at the artist/theorist of the 1970s as an updated take on the Benjaminian artist/producer. Certainly, the historical context is quite different—the fascism of the 1930s is not to be confused with the capitalist liberalism of the 1970s, and the artists are aware of this—but ultimately the aim is quite similar: the artist as theorist, in the words of Benjamin, addresses "to the intellectuals the far-reaching demand that they should not supply the production apparatus without, at the same time, within the limits of the possible, changing that apparatus in the direction of Socialism." (Benjamin, 1966/1998: 93) To this, Sekula conclusively adds:

> I'm arguing [...] for an art that recalls Benjamin's remark in the *Theses on the Philosophy of History* that "there is no document of civilization that is not at the same time a document of barbarism." Against violence directed at the human body, at the environment, at working people's ability to control their own lives, we need to counterpose an active resistance, simultaneously political and symbolic, to monopoly capitalism's increasing power and arrogance, a resistance aimed ultimately at socialist transformation. A naive faith in both the privileged subjectivity of the artist, at the one extreme, and the fundamental "objectivity" of photographic realism, at the other, can only be overcome in a recognition of cultural work as a *praxis*. (Sekula, 1978: 883; original emphasis)

Notes

1. Translation and emphasis by Victor Burgin ((Burgin, 1975/1982: 81). Jacques Durand's article, "Rhétorique et image publicitaire" (Rhetoric and the Advertising Image), was published in *Communications*, 1970: 91: "Dans la création publicitaire règne actuellement le mythe de 'l'inspiration', de 'l'idée'. En fait les idées les plus originales, les annonces les plus audacieuses apparaissent comme la transposition de figures de rhétorique répertoriées depuis de nombreux siècles. Cela s'explique puisque la rhétorique est en somme le répertoire des différentes manières par lesquelles on peut être 'original'. Il est donc probable que le processus créatif pourrait être facilité et enrichi si les créateurs prenaient une pleine conscience d'un système qu'ils utilisent intuitivement."

2. Sekula, 1981: 15: "Photography is haunted by two chattering ghosts: That of bourgeois science and that of bourgeois art. The first goes on about the truth of appearances, about the world reduced to a positive ensemble of facts, to a constellation of knowable and possessable *objects*. The second specter has the historical mission of apologizing for and redeeming the atrocities committed by the subservient – and more than spectral – hand of science. This second specter offers us a reconstructed *subject* in the luminous person of the artist."

3. In his essay, Sekula does not give any reference to where he found this passage. Most probably, he took it from the essay collection *Brecht on Theatre: The Development of an Aesthetic* (Brecht, 1964: 34). It is worth noting that Benjamin quotes exactly the same passage in his essays "What is Epic Theatre?" (1931) and "The Author as Producer" (1934), both contained in *Understanding Brecht* (Benjamin, 1998: 1–2 and 98–99).

4. Burgin's slightly different rendering reads: "The juxtaposition of a visual image and a complementary linguistic message indicating a meaning not signified by either of the component messages, *relay*."

5. In an interview with Benjamin Buchloh, Sekula remarked: "I was looking for the founding myths and antinomies of institutional photographic discourse, much as I had sought to reveal conflicting patterns of legitimation and self-justification in family life: the realist and symbolist 'folk-myths' of photography and the 'folktales' of the family." Sekula, 2003: 25.

6. In the final passage of his commentary, Sekula insists on the individual view of the spectator according to his education and profession (2003, 161): "i cannot provide you with an experience   because you will relate to this differently depending on who you are if you are the president of lockheed you will relate to this in a different manner from the manner of an engineer   if you are an important professor you will relate to this in a different manner from the manner of a student   if you are a pizza cook you will relate in a different manner from the manner of a sociologist   if you are a man you will relate in a different manner from the manner of a woman   and so on." (original typesetting)

7. Originally disseminated in underground newspapers and on flyers, the series was divided into two categories: *Bringing the War Home: House Beautiful* included fifteen photomontages, while *Bringing the War Home: In Vietnam* contained five photomontages (Rosler, 1998: 295).

8. For a more detailed account of the relationship between the documentary photography tradition and the Bowery as a favorite subject of photographers, see Edwards, 2012: 11–15.

9. Rosler ends her 1979 essay "Lookers, Buyers, Dealers, and Makers: Thoughts on Audience" with an extensive quotation from Benjamin's *The Author as Producer,* in which he warns of the assimilating capabilities of the bourgeois apparatus of production and calls for changing the productive apparatus instead of supplying it (Benjamin, 1966/1988: 93–94).

Bibliography

Roland Barthes, "Rhetoric of the Image," in *Image, Music, Text*, ed. and trans. Stephen Heath (New York: Hill and Wang, 1964/1977).

Roland Barthes, *Camera Lucida. Reflections on Photography* (New York: Hill and Wang, 1981).

Raymond Bellour, "The Pensive Spectator," (1984) in *The Cinematic*, ed. David Campany (London: Whitechapel, 2007), 119–123.

Walter Benjamin, "The Author as Producer," (1966) in *Understanding Brecht*, ed. Stanley Mitchell (London and New York: Verso, 1998), 85–105.

Walter Benjamin, *Understanding Brecht*, ed. Stanley Mitchell (London and New York: Verso, 1998).

Walter Benjamin, *Essais sur Brecht*, ed. Rolf Tiedemann (Paris: La fabrique, 2003).

Bertolt Brecht, *Brecht on Theatre: The Development of an Aesthetic*, ed. John Willett (New York: Hill and Wang; London: Eyre Methuen, 1964).

Victor Burgin, "Work and Commentary," (1973) in *Situational Aesthetics. Selected Writings by Victor Burgin*, ed. Alexander Streitberger (Leuven: Leuven University Press, 2009): 15–41.

Victor Burgin, "Why Photography," in *Arte Inglese Oggi 1960–76*, exh. cat., Palazzo Reale Milan (Milan: Electra Editrice, 1976), 360–367.

Victor Burgin, "Photographic Practice and Art Theory," (1975) in *Thinking Photography*, ed. Victor Burgin (Hampshire, London: Macmillan Press, 1982), 39–83.

Victor Burgin, "Images of People," *Studio International*, 194, 989 (2/1978): 132–138.

Victor Burgin, "Photography, Fantasy, Fiction," *Screen*, 21, 1 (Spring 1980): 43–80.

Victor Burgin, *The End of Art Theory. Criticism and Postmodernity* (Atlantic Highlands: Humanities Press International, 1986).

Jacques Durand, "Rhétorique et image publicitaire", *Communications*, 15 (1970): 70–95.

Steve Edwards, *Martha Rosler: The Bowery in two inadequate descriptive systems* (London: Afterall Books, 2012).

Serge Eisenstein, *Film Form. Essays in Film Theory*, ed. Jay Leyda (New York and London: Harvest/HBJ Book, 1949/1977).

Max Ernst, "Beyond Painting," (1937) in *Surrealists on Art*, ed. Lucy R. Lippard (Englewood Cliffs, N. J.: Prentice-Hall, 1970), 118–140.

Ron Eyerman, "False Consciousness and Ideology in Marxist Theory," *Acta Sociologica*, 24, 1–2 (1981): 43–56.

Martha Rosler, "Lookers, Buyers, Dealers, and Makers: Thoughts on Audience," (1979) in *Decoys and Disruptions. Selected Writings, 1975–2001* (Cambridge, Massachusetts and London: MIT Press, 2004), 9–52.

Martha Rosler, "In, Around, and Afterthoughts (on Documentary Photography)," (1981) in *Decoys and Disruptions. Selected Writings, 1975–2001* (Cambridge, Massachusetts and London: MIT Press, 2004), 151–206.

Martha Rosler, "Notes on Quotes," (1982) in *Decoys and Disruptions. Selected Writings, 1975–2001* (Cambridge, Massachusetts and London: MIT Press, 2004), 133–148.

Martha Rosler, "Image Simulations, Computer Manipulations: Some Considerations," (1988–1994) in *Decoys and Disruptions. Selected Writings, 1975–2001* (Cambridge, Massachusetts and London: MIT Press, 2004), 259–317.

Martha Rosler, *Positions in the Life World*, ed. Catherine de Zegher (Cambridge, Massachusetts and London: MIT Press, 1998).

Allan Sekula, "Dismantling Modernism, Reinventing Documentary (Notes on the Politics of Representation)," *The Massachusetts Review*, 19, 4, Photography (Winter 1978): 859–883.

Allan Sekula, "The Traffic in Photographs," *Art Journal*, 41, 1 (Spring 1981): 15–25.

Allan Sekula, "On the Invention of Photographic Meaning," (1975) in *Thinking Photography*, ed. Victor Burgin (Hampshire, London: Macmillan Press, 1982), 84–109.

Allan Sekula, "Reading and archive: photography between labor and capital," (1983) in *Visual Culture: The Reader*, eds Jessica Evans and Stuart Hall (London: SAGE Publications, 1999).

Allan Sekula, *Performance under Working Conditions*, cat., ed. Sabine Breitwieser, Generali Foundation Vienna (Ostfildern-Ruit: Hatje Cantz, 2003).

John Szarkowski, *The Photographer's Eye* (New York: The Museum of Modern Art, New York, 1966).

The Face of Protest

Stephanie Schwartz

> To insist on the social is to practice purposeful immersion.
> — Allan Sekula (2003: 14)

This is the face of protest. (fig.1) It is "the face of protest" all the more so for not providing us with a face—a descriptive physiognomy. Made up of multiple faces—blocked and hooded—this face is familiar. We have seen it before. By now, we have seen it hundreds of times. It fills our film and computer screens. It makes up our newsfeed. Accordingly, this face needs no caption. It is both or necessarily incomplete and replete. We are given a time and place: in darkness, bodies dressed in blacks and greys and browns stand before a spray of neon lights and neo-classical architecture. The hallowed institution frames—and diminishes—those standing before, and beyond, it. It is framed by their vernacular. Red paint on a cardboard sign sets off a command: "Out of Berkeley Nazi Scum." The megaphone—much like the photograph—signals a relay.

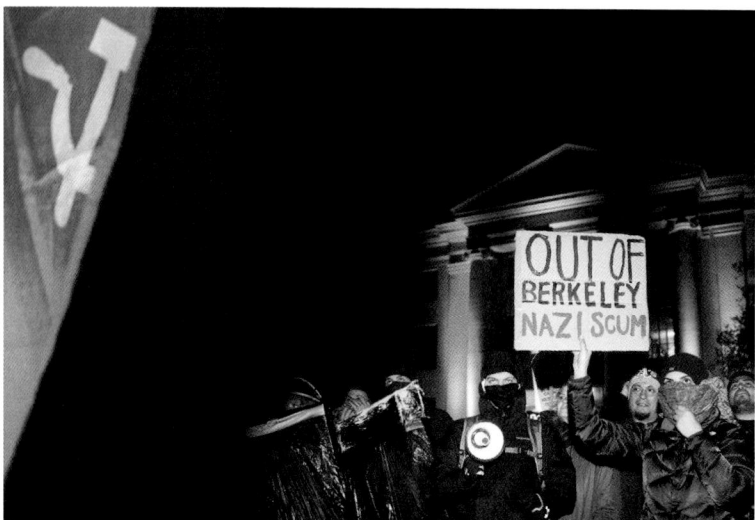

Fig. 1

Violent Protests Erupt at uc Berkeley Against Speech by Breitbart Writer, 2017. © Elijah Nouvelage / Getty Images.

"Disassembled" Images

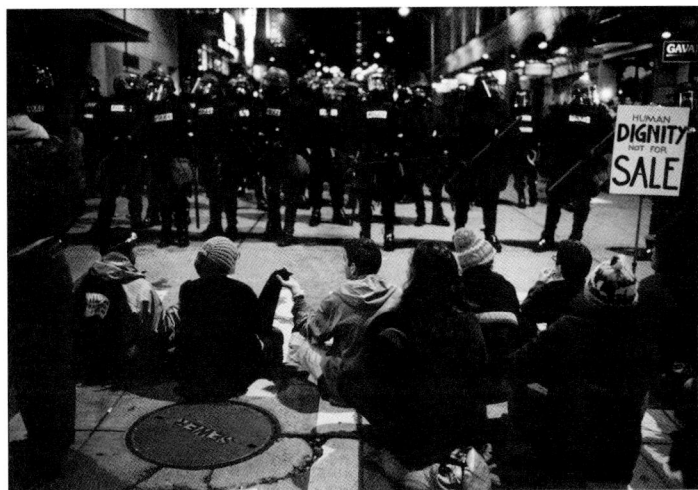

Fig. 2

From Allan Sekula,
*Waiting for Tear Gas
[white globe to black]*,
1999/2000. 81 slides, 35
mm, color, and wall text,
13–16 minutes (depending
on the selected interval
within the allowed
range of 10–12 seconds),
looped. Sequence
coeditor: Sally Stein
© Allan Sekula Studio.

We know this face and the story it tells—has told. It is not a story about the protest pictured here, against Milo Yiannopoulos or his invitation to speak at the University of California, Berkeley in February 2017. It is a story about photography and its uses. If bodies are now or once again beginning to gather in the streets, to take up physical space, to clog up traffic, to don hoods and masks, it is the space they make up in the media that precedes their presence and makes them recognizable. Replete and incomplete, "the face of protest" is always—must be—looped. It always comes again.

I take the phrase "the face of protest" from Allan Sekula. It appeared in the text he penned to preface *Waiting for Tear Gas [white globe to black]* (1999–2000), the slide sequence of eighty-one color photographs he made following his decision to join and record the anti-World Trade Organization (WTO) protestors who filled the streets of Seattle, Washington on November 30, 1999. (fig. 2 and pl. 16) Describing his working process—the move from recording protestors in the street to editing photographs of them in his studio—Sekula wrote:

> working at a light table, and reading the increasingly stereotypical descriptions of the new face of protest, I realized all the more that a simple descriptive physiognomy was warranted. The alliance on the streets was indeed stranger, more varied and inspired than could be conveyed by cute alliterative play with "teamsters" and "turtles." (Cockburn and St. Clair, 2000: n.p.)

With these lines, Sekula plainly announced the logic of his work: to counter iconic—stereotypical—shots of violence or revelry circulating in the press as representations of protest. Instead of isolating and monumentalizing "the face of protest," Sekula sought to reproduce, over and over again, the multiple faces of the protestors. As one slide slips into the next, the media stereotypes filling the daily news literally dissolve into and remerge out of the motley crew of teamsters and environmentalists, teachers and students, preachers and longshoremen taking up space in the streets and waiting for the tear gas in Seattle. *Waiting for Tear Gas*, in short, refuses the principles of iconicity and equivalence. By organizing a representation of protest and the protestor "from below," both from the street and through the series, Sekula allows identities and differences to proliferate. (Sekula, 1983: 202; Sekula, 1984: 67) "The anti-capitalist crowd," as Steve Edwards put it in his examination of the anti-dictatorial perspective of the sequence of shots making up the work's loop, "emerges in this body of images as a horizontal social form united, rather than separated, in difference." (Edwards, 2009: 455) Sekula called his practice "anti-photojournalism." The above-noted description of his working process begins as follows:

> In photographing the Seattle demonstrations my working idea was to move with the flow of the protest, from dawn to 3 AM if need be, taking in the lulls, the waiting and the margins of events. The rule of thumb for this sort of anti-photojournalism: no flash, no telephoto zoom lens, no gas mask, no auto-focus, no press pass and no pressure to grab at all costs the one defining image of dramatic violence. (Cockburn and St. Clair, 2000: n.p.)

Again, the logic of the work's critique—of its work—is made plain. It is on the surface and made public. It also, I want to argue in what follows, makes a public. This is not—or not simply—because, with *Waiting for Tear Gas*, Sekula took his work to the streets, immersed himself in the protest, as my epilogue suggests, in order to insist on the existence of the social. It is because Sekula's anti-photojournalism keeps us attentive to the machinations of the screen. It is because it asks us to recognize photography's necessarily doubled—public and private—"face." As Walter Benjamin taught us (and Sekula) with "the tremendous physiognomic galleries" of the Soviet filmmakers in mind, the face only took on "immeasurable significance" when people were drawn out of their private spaces, drawn out—for prosperity—through the screen. (Benjamin, 1931/1979: 251–252) This immersion, Benjamin explained, was the significance of photography. *Waiting for Tear Gas* is a work about the relationship between publicity and privatization; it is a work about what happens when we are no longer able to participate publicly—immerse ourselves in—the relay of sounds and words and images on and through the screen. When the loop stops, it warns, the "Nazi Scum," fascism, ensues.

Sekula coined several neologisms to characterize his work and its method. "Anti-photojournalism," for example, is joined by "counter-forensic," "counter-site," "counter-image" and the rather particular "anti-*Titanic*." (Keenan, 2014: 68) The latter term was developed in the context of Sekula's thoughtful and extended response to Hollywood's romantic rendition of the perils of seafaring and industrial hubris, James Cameron's 1997 blockbuster film *Titanic*. Sekula visited the movie set in early 1997 and recorded what he would later refer to as the studio's "lugubrious arrogance." (Sekula, 2003: 41) Seeking profits from lower Mexican wages, Twentieth Century Fox built the film set, which featured the largest freshwater filming tank ever built, adjacent to a fishing village on the Baja California coast that had no running water. Efflux from the tank lowered the salinity of the village's coastal tidal pools, devastating the mussel-gathering livelihood of the villagers.

A diptych of photographs taken on the set, which opens Sekula's photo essay *Dead Letter Office* (1997), is "anti-*Titanic*." Its promise of a panoramic view, the view in the film associated with the line "I'm the King of the World," is blocked. Instead of the possibility or promise of the possession of space along the horizon, a claustrophobic maritime space is issued. The sinking set seems to slip out of sight behind a crane, mounds of dried, cracked earth, and a now all-too-brilliant polychrome landscape. As Sekula explained:

> We peer morbidly into the vortex of industrialism's early nose-dive into the abyss. The film absolves us of any obligation to remember the disasters that followed. Quick as a wink, cartoon-like, the angel of history is flattened between a wall of steel and a wall of ice. It's an easy, premature way to mourn a bloody century. (Sekula, 2003: 41)

On the set and the screen, Hollywood remixed industrial hubris in accordance with the buoyancy of the 1990s' dot-com bubble. Speculation, Sekula charged, submerged—at least for a moment anyway—the lessons and tragedies of modernization.

The claustrophobic diptych was one part of an exhibition program and book project Sekula eventually called TITANIC's wake (2001/2003). The pun on the damage and destruction left in the film's mechanized wake framed a tripartite meditation on the damage and destruction wrought by neoliberalism and globalization, of which the WTO was one major development. In addition to *Waiting for Tear Gas*, the TITANIC's wake project featured *Dear Bill Gates*, a triptych of photographs, including one depicting the media mogul's colossal home, accompanied by a type-written letter from Sekula to Gates querying his purchase of Winslow Homer's painting of two fishermen, *Lost on the Grand Banks*

(1885). What, Sekula asks, could Homer's painting of the brutality of work at sea mean to Mr. Bill Gates of Microsoft? What could it mean "for the faceless virtual power that he extols?" (Sekula, 2003: 17) Sekula dated this letter November 30, 1999, the day he protested in Seattle and waited for the tear gas. *Waiting for Tear Gas* and *Dear Bill Gates* joined the title project's twenty-three-photograph documentary diary of the antimonies of globalized production: two overhead shots of the gleaming and undulating surfaces of Frank Gehry's Guggenheim Museum for Bilbao confront, for example, a detail of another watery grave, a shipwreck in Istanbul.

In the book and exhibition, top-down nostalgia for the sea in Gates's taste for nineteenth-century shipwrecks, Cameron's spectacularization of a mass grave, and Gehry's imported maritime mausoleum confront a movement from below querying the promises of the new economy. Or, as Sekula put it in one of the texts he penned for the 2003 publication, the slick liquidity of the markets (as well as the internet and post-modernism's rhizomatic architectural forms) confront the forced and controlled liquidity of the police state's chemical production of tears. "The resort to tear gas," Sekula explained, "serves not only to "control the crowd," that is, to prevent the radical redefinition of the use-value of the city streets but also to produce through chemical means the exaggerated liquid symptoms of human empathy and grief." (Sekula, 2003: 14) This is also, of course, the work of much photojournalism. As Sekula explored on numerous occasions, Lewis Hine's photographs of child laborers, for example, were designed to elicit grief, outrage, compassion, and contempt. (Sekula, 2003: 20; Sekula, 1984: 17–21) Turned into "human junk" in the factory and on page, the small bodies Hine recorded eventually produced tears. (Dimock, 1993: 50)

To draw out this comparison is not to confirm photography's work as one of the tools that the state uses "to control the crowd." This fact needs little confirmation. Rather, it is to historicize the relationship between that work and the work of photojournalism. As Sekula taught us, the elicitations of work like Hine's necessarily ebbs and flows. The photographer's model of "liberal-utilitarian realism," that is, was useful—found a public—when Homer painted those fishermen lost at sea *and* when being lost at sea was a way of representing, at least for Mr. Bill Gates, the risks of the new liquid economy. (Sekula, 1984: xii) Forced liquidity, of all kinds, needs a history, as does the work of photography.

The photo-essay or a choreographed sequence of photographs that emerged as the means of reportage on the pages of the newly illustrated press in the 1920s and 1930s was deemed outmoded the very year Sekula began to work in its form. It was in 1972, when Sekula completed *Untitled Slide Sequence*, his physiognomic study of labor and the laborer, that *Life* stopped printing. After thirty-six years selling the news in photo essay form, the editors saw the television screen finally eclipse the page as a means of both its generation and distribution. The page had expired and photojournalism seemed to be withering along with it. If we account for this history—that is, if we account for histories of media—then new questions necessarily emerge about Sekula's "counter-move." With *Waiting for Tear Gas*, was Sekula, to borrow another of his key concepts or terms, "reinventing" photojournalism in the wake of the rise of another new means for circulating and generating news, namely the internet? (Sekula, 1984: 53)

To pose this question is not to suggest that Sekula's work is nostalgic, that with his essays and slide sequences he sought to return to an old or outmoded form. He was, after all, highly suspicious of the popular press and what he characterized in 1978 as its "corporate form." Writing of the "reinvention" of documentary in his seminal essay about the ways in which our canonical histories of modernism have purposely repressed histories of documentary, Sekula spoke with disgust about the photo-essay, referring to it as a "cliché-ridden form that is the noncommercial counterpart to the photographic advertisement." "Photo essays," he continued, "are an outcome of a mass-circulation picture-magazine aesthetic, the aesthetic of the merchandisable column-inch and rapid, excited reading, reading made subservient to visual titillation." (Sekula, 1984: 60) This is quite damning prose. With *Waiting for Tear Gas*, Sekula did not return to this form. He "reinvented" it. He offered a "meta-critical" analysis of its production as photojournalism. (Sekula, 1984: 60)

Recording the protest in Seattle through an investigation of the protest's mediation, Sekula took stock of the ways in which photojournalism had been co-opted and historicized. As Sekula acknowledged in the pages of the very same essay in which he condemned the mass-circulation picture magazine, the photo essay was also—or once—a radical platform for disseminating information and the news. Sekula offered readers the productions of the Workers Film and Photo League as one important example. (fig. 3) Before they were appropriated to form "the merchandisable column-inch," choreographed sequences worked to dismantle the photographs by-then conventional morphology: a cut in time. In the League's productions, a multiplicity of views were organized and projected. More to the point: representation was always multiple. The League's filmmakers and photographers, as Russell Campbell has explained, made footage, not films or photographs. (Campbell, 1985: 126–127) One photograph was never enough but the point of the photo essay or film sequence was to historicize iconicity and its claims for autonomy. It was to confront the relationship between pictorial isolation and the organization of a public.

Taking a cue from the "physiognomic galleries" of the Soviet filmmakers and their photographic avant-garde, the League's footage refused commemoration or individualization. Through it, these journalists announced that dictatorial representations from above could any longer comprise the language of subjectivity. (Buchloh, 2015: 481–482)

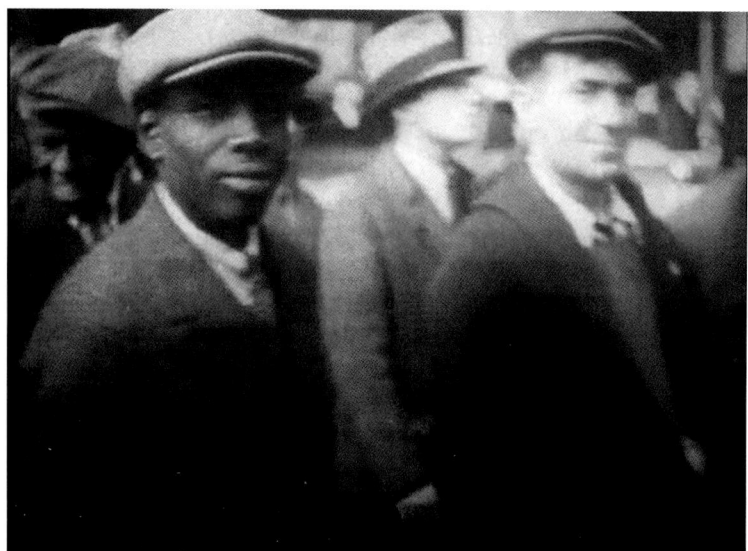

The death of photojournalism, however, may just be one of those myths, much like the end of work and the promises of free trade, the subject of Sekula's *Fish Story*, a study in words and photographs of the material realities of sea trade, which he also sought to counter (Sekula, 1995/2002). In fact, its codification coincides with the production of *Waiting for Tear Gas*. It was in the late 1990s that photographers, both new and seasoned, were forced to confront the fact that the page was no longer the means for circulating their work. This was not, as we have come to believe or have been told, simply because the screen replaced the page as the site for the circulation of news. It was because mainstream magazine editors radically reshaped the organization of the news on the page and in print. Instead of publishing lengthy photo-essays offering extended, in-depth and multiple perspectives on war and famine, the subjects of much of the 1990s news cycle, they circumscribed editorials around one or two iconic shots. (Squiers, 1996; Ritchin, 1991) Even (or especially) old wars, including the last war to be narrated in essay form, the Vietnam War, were recast around a few "singular" photographs. The Vietnam War came to be represented through, for example, Eddie Adams's harrowing photograph from 1968 of police chief General Nguyen Ngoc Loan executing a Viet Cong suspect and Nick Ut's shot of Kim Phuc Phan Thi running naked down a road following a napalm attack on her village in 1972. Photo-essays by Akihiko Okamura, such as the fourteen-page, seventeen-photograph essay accompanying "A Little War, Far Away—and Very Ugly" which ran in the June, 12 1964 issue of *Life*, disappear in the face of Larry Burrows's cover shot of the single, stalwart solider.

Photojournalism did not die in the 1990s, nor was it necessarily outmoded by new technologies, be they television or the internet. Rather, it was revamped or reshaped into a form more conducive to the myths of neoliberalism. As art historian Julian Stallabrass argued in his study of the emergence of the "fine art of photojournalism," also a 1990s phenomenon, extended essays narrating war and famine did not suit the neoliberal narrative that history was over and capitalism was triumphant. (Stallabrass, 1997) In turn, photojournalists, many consciously, left the page behind, turning instead to the walls of the museum or the pages of books to circulate their production. Sebastião Salgado's *Workers: Archaeology of the Industrial Age* (1993), Gilles Peress's *Farewell to Bosnia* (1994) and Susan Meiselas's *Kurdistan: In the Shadow of History* (1997) are just a few varied and significant examples of such publications. In short, in the 1990s photojournalism actually bloomed or boomed only to be rebranded, especially by those on the left and in academia, as synonymous with spectacle culture and a retrogressive modernism. Few, in other words, have historicized the form. Much like documentary, photojournalism it is simply characterized disparagingly as humanist. There were too many bodies; too much pain. Bodies could be recorded and publicized but that was bad press— bad art. The faces of war and famine made people cry.

The death of photojournalism may be a myth, but it still buoyed the definition of photojournalism as synonymous with the iconic shot. Notably, we see this nowhere more clearly than in the media response to the protests in Seattle. This is not simply because the same iconic shots of violence saturated the mainstream news, shots of either police or fringe anarchist (Black Bloc) violent actions. It is because the protestors' response to the mainstream news explicitly countered this one-dimensional coverage. A case in point was the organization of the Independent Media Center, a grassroots media network established in 1999 for the purpose of providing coverage of the Seattle protests. As noted on the Center's website, "The Independent Media Center is a network of collectively run media outlets for the creation of radical, accurate, and passionate tellings of the truth." (Indy Media, 2004) The site, which also produced a newspaper and hundreds of hours of audio segments distributed on the web, acted as a clearinghouse for a wealth of information about the protest. In short, it operated in direct opposition to the top-down, hierarchical structure of mainstream media outlets.

The myth of the death of photojournalism and its simultaneous spectacularization, in other words, has been incredibly generative. It fostered
the birth of citizens' journalism, the explosion of new democratic forms
of recording and telling the news. Not despite but because of the neoliberal revamping of the media, individuals can now make, record and
circulate the news. They can become the "face" of protest. More to the
point: it is becoming more and more evident in the news—or what we
in the US and Europe now take as journalism—that neoliberalism does
not need a public press. It needs twitter accounts or individually customized media platforms. (Joselit, 2017: 16) "Market ideology demands
that everyone sails alone" was how Sekula once put it with regard to Mr.
Bill Gates's megalomaniacal enterprise. (Sekula, 2003: 20)

Waiting for Tear Gas offered a wholly different response to the mainstream mythologies. Sekula worked alone, in his studio, at a light-table
and with analog technologies. He also circulated his work, for the most
part, in books and museums or galleries. The work's institutionaliza-
tion in no way mitigates its charge. Still working with the essay form,
Sekula did not embrace, in order to reject, the new, old history of photojournalism as iconic. He produced a different history of media. This
history, like his work, begins in the 1970s and not the 1990s. It begins
when the pages of magazines, even those magazines wholly associated
with corporate culture and cultural imperialism such as Life, could be
read counter-culturally and critically. As numerous historians of journalism have argued, the television did not replace the page in the 1970s,
such that the collapse of Life cannot be accounted for through histories
of technological innovation. The magazine's end was inseparable from
corporate capital and the state's response to the fact that the news coming out of Vietnam—on the page and through the screen—had a remarkable and negative impact on public support for the war. (Kennedy,
2011) As the journalist Robert Elegant famously stated, "For the first
time in modern history, the outcome of a war was determined not on
the battlefield, but on the printed page and, above all, on the television
screen." (Elegant, 1981: 73)

Although there has been much debate about whether or not the
circulation of photographs and footage from the war zone instigated
the change in public support for the war effort or simply confirmed
it, the photographic representation of violence in the mainstream
media certainly altered the future of photojournalism. Iconic images
ruled, but that was not all: with the first Gulf War (1990–91), US policy was to keep photographers as far as possible from the battlefields.
This "screen war," to borrow the term used by media theorists Paul
Virilio and Jean Baudrillard, in turn, "never happened." (Baudrillard,
1995, Virilio, 2002) By the second Gulf War (2003–11), photographers
were embedded with troops and signed contracts stipulating what

"Disassembled" Images

photographs could be published. (Ritchin, 2013: 15–22) Television was merely the scapegoat, not the means to a so-called end of photojournalism. It mythologized the coming of a private press. Notably, the same year Baudrillard and Virilio published their theses, Sekula exhibited his "counter-image" of war's dematerialization: *War without Bodies*. The 1991 photo-essay juxtaposes photographs of the war's protestors with those of visitors to a military parade fingering the mouths of machine guns. (Risberg, 1999: 208–234) The war takes place "without bodies"— or forced liquidity. It is now materialized as fun-fair entertainment.

Unlike many on the left and working in new media, Sekula did not negate the myths about photojournalism or protest. With *Waiting for Tear Gas*, he did not seek to provide new truths, to set the record straight about what actually happened in the streets of Seattle. That is, with his sequences of eighty-one slides, he does not tell *another* story or *other* stories. He tells the same story, the myth, differently. He loops the media. Evocative here is another photo-essay Sekula finished the year *Life* stopped printing: *Two, three, many…(terrorism)* (1972). Made up of six photographs of an Asian-looking man dressed in then stereotypical Vietnamese garb—he is wearing a conical hat and toting a toy machine gun—this essay is Sekula's response to the war's mediation. (figs. 4 and 5) Its title is derived from the famous line in Ernesto 'Che' Guevara's 1967 "Message to the Tricontinental," in which the Argentine Marxist and key figure in the Cuban Revolution calls for "more" Vietnams. Instead of calling for an end to the violence, he called for more fighting and more collective action. More revolution was necessary, Che argued; more struggle against imperialism needed to be enacted, supported, and recorded. (Guevara, 1967) If in *Waiting For Tear Gas* Sekula simultaneously gave us the stereotype of protest and dissolved that stereotype in a sea of bodies, in *Two, three, many…(terrorism)* he comically exaggerated the stereotype of the guerrilla fighter in order to remind us vis-à-vis Che that the war in Vietnam, though in the news, still went on unseen. The young man dressed up enacting war maneuvers in La Jolla, California, around suburban golf courses and swimming pools, is "hidden in plain sight." (Feldman, 2014: 167) He disrupts nothing, and no one in Sekula's photographs seems to notice him. The private exteriors camouflage the public. Sekula did not disrupt or correct the blindness; he re-enacted and reproduced it. As in *Waiting for Tear Gas*, and in much of his work, Sekula examined, meta-critically, the way media works. This is a form of photojournalism.

Waiting for Tear Gas reminds us that not thinking and working historically may just account for the triumph of photojournalism's sensationalism. And, it is this history we need to keep in mind when we stare into the "face of protest," especially when we are staring into or back at

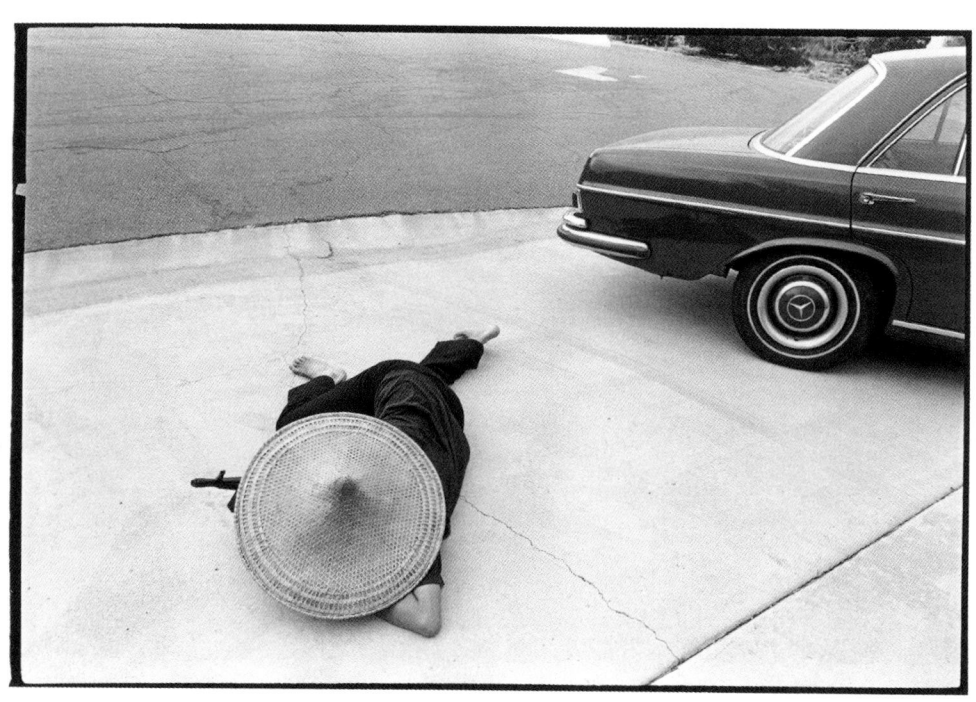

Fig. 4

From Allan Sekula, *Two, three, many...(terrorism)*, 1972.
Six b&w photographs in single frame. Each 15,4 × 22,7
cm / 80,4 × 130,2 cm (framed). © Allan Sekula Studio.

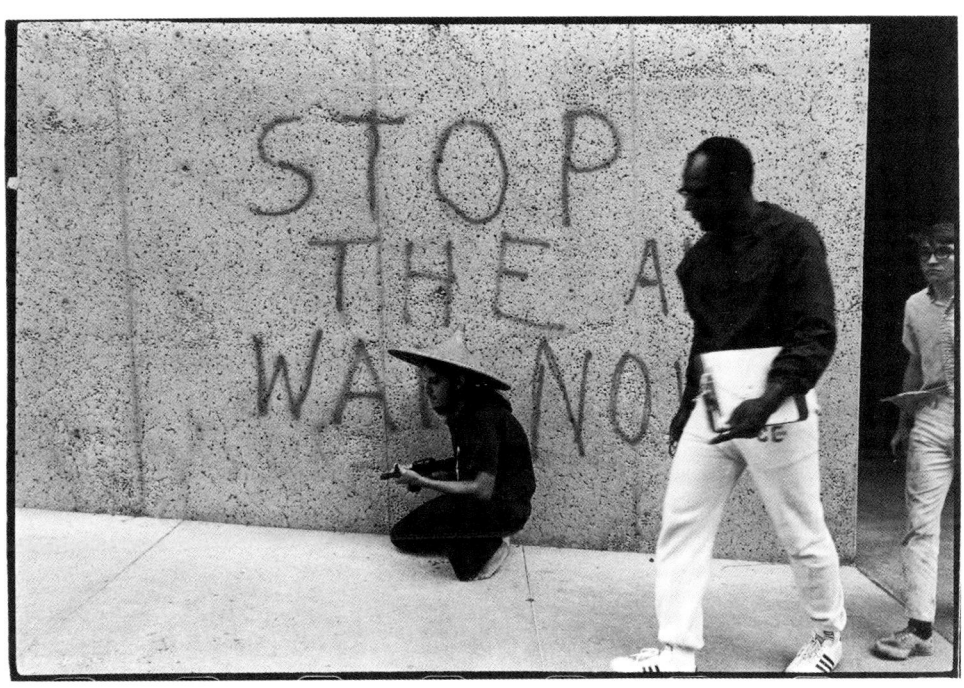

Fig. 5

From Allan Sekula, *Two, three, many...(terrorism)*, 1972.
Six b&w photographs in single frame. Each 15,4 × 22,7
cm / 80,4 × 130,2 cm (framed). © Allan Sekula Studio.

our own face. (fig. 6) This is the view of and from the new face of protest. Like the old face, the new face needs no caption. This face photographs itself. It takes control of the camera. It also complies with the media pressure—pressure from the state—to count itself, mark itself and recognize itself as present, as accounted for in the space of protest. We could wax nostalgic about the face that appeared on the screen the first time, before that face, as Benjamin put it, had a "use" for its photograph. (Benjamin, 1931/1979: 251) Or, following Sekula, we could recognize that making yourself present is always an act of mediation—and always a protest. Mapping the emergence of the photographic face along its socio-economic terrain, Sekula put it thus:

> To the extent that bourgeois order depends upon the systematic defense of social relations based on private property, to the extent that the legal basis of the self lies in the model of property rights, in what has been termed "possessive individualism," every portrait has its lurking, objectifying inverse in the files of the police. (Sekula, 1986: 7)

The process of democratization sold to the public as photography's promise was, Sekula taught us, inseparable from the need to discipline those seated—voluntarily and not—before the camera. Given our current desire to be photographed, to photograph ourselves doing absolutely everything and absolutely nothing, including protest, it goes without saying that these lines were prescient. Contemporary fears about our loss of privacy need not be measured against the ways in which we voluntarily and gleefully expose ourselves—give up our privacy as if it was something we owned and could "give up." This is also a myth. Rather, *pace* Sekula, such fears need to be measured against the relationship between the rights of individual and logic of privatization. To step into the street, to appear on the screen, is also to recognize that the rights of the individual necessarily discipline and occlude. This was exactly what was being protested in Seattle and Berkeley, as well as in Ferguson and Charlottesville (Schwartz, 2018). And, it is hardly hidden from or buried in the news. It was—is—writ large across "the face of protest."

An earlier version of this essay was published as Stephanie Schwartz, "Anti-Photojournalism: Working Against the Grain," in *In Focus: Waiting for Tear Gas 1999–2000 by Allan Sekula*, ed. Stephanie Schwartz, Tate Research Publication, 2016, http://www.tate.org.uk/research/publications/in-focus/waiting-for-tear-gas-allan-sekula/loops-in-time.

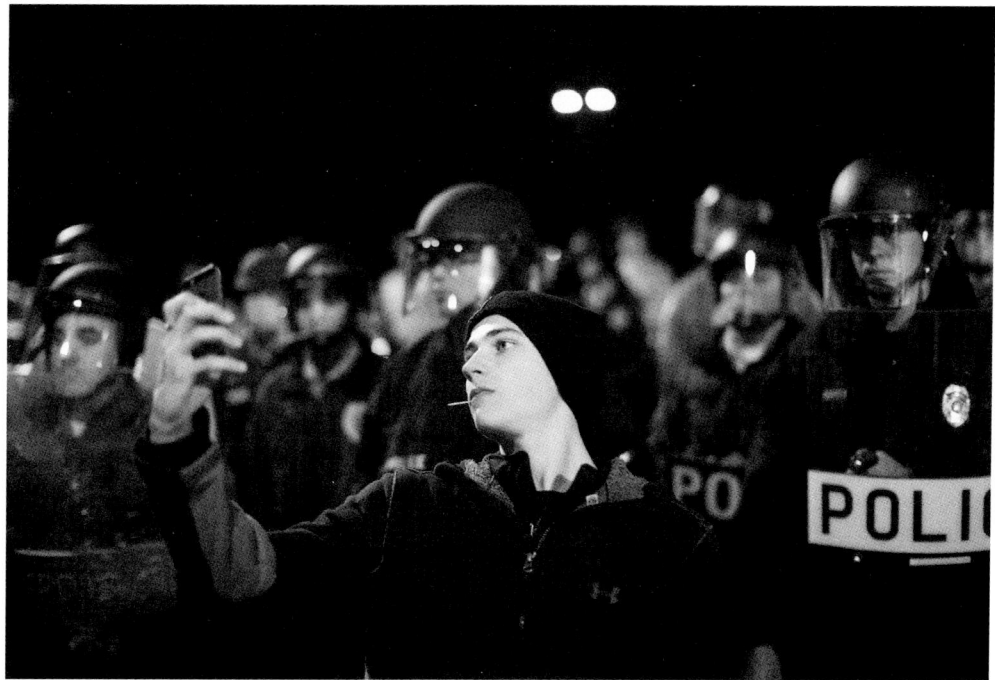

Fig. 6

Ferguson Protests Continue Two Months After
Police Shooting of Michael Brown, October 10, 2014.
© Scott Olson / Getty Images.

Bibliography

Jean Baudrillard, *The Gulf War Did Not Take Place*, trans. Paul Patton (1991; Bloomington: University of Indiana Press, 1995).

Walter Benjamin, "A Small History of Photography," in *One Way Street and Other Writings*, trans. Edmund Jephcott and Kingsley Shorter (London: Verso, 1931/1979), 240–257. This essay was originally published in *Literarische Welt* in 1931.

Benjamin H. D. Buchloh, *Formalism and Historicity: Models and Methods in Twentieth Century Art* (Cambridge, Mass.: The MIT Press, 2015).

Russell Campbell, "Radical Cinema in the 1930s: The Film and Photo League," in *Jump Cut: Hollywood, Politics and Counter-Cinema*, ed. Peter Stevens (Toronto: Between the Lines, 1985), 123–133.

Alexander Cockburn and Jeffrey St Clair, *5 Days That Shook the World* (London: Verso, 2000).

George Dimock, "Children of the Mills: Re-Reading Lewis Hine's Child Labour Photographs," *Oxford Art Journal* 16, 2 (January 1993): 37–54.

Steve Edwards, "Commons and Crowds: Figuring Photography from Above and Below," *Third Text* 23, 4 (Jul 2009): 447–464.

Robert Elegant, "How to Lose a War: Reflections of a Foreign Correspondent," *Encounters* 57, 2 (Aug 1981): 73–90.

Hannah Feldman, *From a Nation Torn: Decolonizing Art and Representation in France, 1945–1962* (Durham: Duke University Press, 2014).

Ernesto Guevara, "Message to the Tricontinental," 1967, reproduced at https://www.marxists.org/archive/guevara/1967/04/16.htm (accessed April 20, 2016).

https://www.indymedia.org/en/static/about.shtml (accessed April 20, 2016).

David Joselit, "Fake News, Art, and Cognitive Justice," *October*, 159 (Fall 2017): 14–18.

Thomas Keenan, "Counter Forensics and Photography," *Grey Room*, 55 (Spring 2014): 58–77.

Liam Kennedy, "Photojournalism and the Vietnam War," Photography and International Conflict research project, University College Dublin, Dublin 2011, http://www.ucd.ie/photoconflict/histories/vietnamwarphoto-journalism (accessed April 20, 2016).

Debra Risberg, *Allan Sekula: Dismal Science: Photoworks, 1972–1997* (Illinois: University Galleries, Illinois State University, 1999).

Fred Ritchin, "The End of Photography as We Know It," in *Photovideo*, ed. Paul Wombell (London: Rivers Oram Press, 1991), 7–14.

Fred Ritchin, *Bending the Frame: Photojournalism, Documentary, and the Citizen* (New York: Aperture Foundation, 2013).

Stephanie Schwartz, "Monumental Failure: The Face of Bigotry," *Art Monthly* 417 (June 2018): 38–39.

Allan Sekula, *Photography Against the Grain: Essays and Photo Works, 1973–1983* (Halifax: Nova Scotia College of Art and Design, 1984).

Allan Sekula, "The Body and the Archive," *October*, 39 (Winter 1986): 3–64.

Allan Sekula, *Fish Story* (Düsseldorf: Richter Verlag, 1995/2002).

Allan Sekula, *Allan Sekula: TITANIC's wake* (Cherbourg: Point du jour, 2003).

Carol Squiers, "The Truth of Our Time," *American Photo* 7, 5 (September–October 1996): 54–57.

Julian Stallabrass, "Sebastião Salgado and the Fine Art of Photojournalism," *New Left Review*, 223 (May–June 1997): 131–162.

Paul Virilio, *Desert Screen: War at the Speed of Light*, trans. Michael Degener (1991; New York: Continuum, 2002).

Terri Weissman, "This is What Democracy Looks Like," in *In Focus: Waiting for Tear Gas 1999–2000 by Allan Sekula*, ed. Stephanie Schwartz, Tate Research Publication, 2016, http://www.tate.org.uk/research/publications/in-focus/waiting-for-tear-gas-allan-sekula/this-is-what-democracy-looks-like (accessed September 11, 2017).

Benjamin J. Young, "On Strike: Allan Sekula's *Waiting for Tear Gas*," in *Sensible Politics: The Visual Culture of Nongovernmental Activism*, eds Meg McLagan and Yates McKee (New York: Zone Books, 2012), 148–181.

Reading Against the Grain: Allan Sekula and the Rhetoric of Exemplarity

Anthony Abiragi

Exemplarity

As one considers the title, but also the profusion of topics in Benjamin's "Little History of Photography," one might wonder what precise aspects of photography invite historical reflection and, more to the point, what aspects when thus delineated enable him to defend the present political importance of the medium. On the one hand, Benjamin constructs his essay as a history of major photographers (Hill, Atget, Sander), but equally of photography's dominant class subjects (the reticent bourgeoisie of its earliest phase, the imperial bourgeoisie of the late 19th century, and members of a post-imperial generation that lent both their personal anonymity and "social physiognomy" to photographic documentation). He assesses the historical debates surrounding the ontology of photography (is it art, magic, technology?) even as, in a strategy of critique, he introduces his own, now-canonical concepts (aura, reproducibility, the optical unconscious). Lastly, Benjamin reviews the major functions of photography (aesthetic, commercial, ideological, as well as the progressive functions that, with Sander in mind, he summarizes as "physiognomic, political, scientific"). Yet for all of its advances, photography is not immune to a regressive, fetishistic promotion of "the creative." Even in a time of political crisis, twice alluded to in his essay, photography can still obscure a society's relation to the real, substituting "beauty" and "arty, interesting juxtapositions" in the place of an emancipatory realism. In this, its regressive, "creative" function, Benjamin writes, "is unmasked the posture of a photography that can endow any soup can with cosmic significance but cannot grasp a single one of the human connections in which it exists." (Benjamin, 2008 [1931]: 293)

"Disassembled" Images

The answer to photography's regression, and especially to the reification of reality under the spell of advertising, is the Brechtian *construction*. Benjamin cites the crucial passage from the *Threepenny Trial* at length and its lesson was not lost on Allan Sekula. Reflecting on his own methodology in a colloquium devoted to *Fish Story*, Sekula laments a contemporary misreading of the Brechtian construction, an aesthetic ideal now largely remembered through its partial citation in Benjamin's "Little History." A photograph, Brecht writes, "tells us nothing... something must be 'constructed'." (Sekula, 1997: 49) In postmodern aesthetic theory, this phrase is misunderstood "as an argument in favor of montage, and perhaps even more so for the theatrical staging of photographs, and as a brief against photographic realism of any sort." (Sekula, 1997: 49) Yet that is not, according to Sekula, what Brecht had in mind, which we will better understand in Esther Leslie's extended translation:

> For the situation is complicated by the fact that less than at any time does a simple reproduction of reality tell us anything about reality. A photograph of the Krupp works or GEC yields almost nothing about these institutions. Reality proper has slipped into the functional. The reification of human relationships, signaled by the factory, can no longer be revealed by the photograph. Therefore something has actually to be constructed, something artificial, something set up. For this reason, art is indeed necessary. But the old concept of art, the one that rests on experience, is superseded. For whoever represents that which is experienced in reality also fails to capture it. Reality is no longer experienceable in its totality. (Leslie, 2015: 25)

This lengthy citation, though hardly broached in "On 'Fish Story'," is of utmost importance to Sekula who turns to Marx as means of addressing its central themes. Commenting upon the methodological remarks in the introduction to the *Grundrisse*, Sekula writes:

> Reified social relations are in a sense invisible to ordinary empiricism, and can only be understood through recourse to abstraction, or as Marx put it in the introduction to the *Grundrisse*, through the movement upwards from the concrete to the abstract, and back down to the concrete. Thus the need for "construction," a need in the end consistent for Brecht with the "clumsy" motto: "truth is concrete." (Sekula, 1997: 49)

In this paper, I am interested in Sekula's consistent recourse to abstraction; more precisely, in abstraction as a method of intervention into reified social relations, a particular alibi for which is what Benjamin just named "the creative" in photography. The inspiration here is eminently Brechtian: abstraction in art is a form of pedagogy or, quite simply, *pedagogical*. For as I will insist, Sekula is less a didactic teacher than a fabricator of abstractions whose purchase on reality depends on their creative appropriation by Sekula's very audience, to whom I will refer consistently as readers. In the compound summary of Brecht-Marx, we learn that reality has become unreadable for mere empiricism, and photography—for its part—seems only to ratify modernity's slide into "functionality." The totality of human relations escapes us so long as our concrete relations remain unmediated: we stare upon cosmic images of soup cans instead of grasping the human relations that created them. Hence, the need for abstraction, according to Marx, Brecht, and Sekula. For the concrete will accede to its own intelligibility only through a confrontation with theory, abstraction, and—so we will see—a host of aesthetic forms and practices. What role can art play in the mediation of seemingly unrelated elements of reality? How might it bring about a unity or synthesis of diverse elements through its own power of abstraction? How might art, following the methodological guidelines of Marx, mediate among disparate facts and thus render concrete a vision of totality? These are the central questions that I take Sekula to be asking.

Contested Allegory

In what seems a deliberate echo, Brecht's mention of the factory soon merges into Sekula's reading of Robert Frank's extraordinary "Assembly Line, Detroit" (1955), wherein we are invited to see something more than a factory. "Imagine the façade, or the layout of the assembly line, or the repetitive gestures of work as fragments of something that is both an instrumentalized totality and already to a sensitive observer a contested allegory of its own existence." (Sekula, 1997: 50) The etymology of allegory is instructive: *allos* = other + *agoreuei* = to speak. By definition, allegory interrupts the naïve empiricism of third-person denotation, for in *speaking of…*, it simultaneously *speaks other*. This is especially remarkable in photography, the indexicality of which guarantees referentiality. In Frank's photograph, the referent is unmistakably the claustrophobia of an "instrumentalized totality," a reified social order from which human beings seem indistinguishable. But what is the sensitive observer looking at when she registers in the photograph "a contested allegory of [the referent's] own existence"?

A photograph is an invitation to behold a certain referent. But an allegorically-charged photograph acquires a theoretical valence that surpasses its denotative, indexical claim. As a moment of the real transposed into an abstraction, an allegorized image exceeds the lighted referent from which it emerged, soliciting us no longer in its claim to referentiality, but in its potential applicability to adjacent contexts. Hence, the shared concern between Marx, Brecht, and Sekula to break with the reifying effects of mere denotation through recourse to abstraction. An allegory—the contested allegory of Frank's *Detroit*—becomes properly readable only when transposed into new contexts; indeed, its descent from abstraction and into unforeseen contexts *is* its readability, and she who applies it thus achieves a theoretical insight (let us call it as well a political experience) that allows her "to speak other" than according to the rules dictated by context. A contested allegory is an invitation to read the world otherwise—such that a fulfilled reading of that allegory is an appraisal of reality from the standpoint of what, from within the original photograph, exceeds its mere referentiality. To learn to speak (or see) otherwise all while remaining within one's confines, to import the abstract back into the concrete, is to experience a freedom from one's situation, but equally a sense of greater comprehension. With these initial thoughts in mind, we can turn to Sekula's own works and experiences to make better sense of his uses of abstraction.

In the late 1990s, The International Transport Workers Federation (ITF) recovered the nearly defunct *Global Mariner* in its effort to stage an agitprop campaign against maritime labor abuses—specifically, their perpetration under the cover of the "flags of convenience" shipping system wherein wealthier, first-world shipping companies can register their ships under the flags of poorer nations, themselves often bereft of robust worker protections. (pl. 2) The ITF sought to regulate the standards of pay and safety protocols for maritime workers and the recovery of the *Global Mariner* was thus something of a theatrical *coup*: a campaign of consciousness-raising with a specific focus on, again, abuses in maritime labor practice. In Sekula's description, the *Global Mariner* was "an 18,000-deadweight-ton general cargo vessel carrying in its converted holds a remarkable exhibition about working conditions at sea, and—in a broader sense—about the hidden social costs and probable consequences of corporate globalization." (Sekula, 2002a: 28) He was aboard the ship for a fair portion of its twenty-month journey to eighty-three cities. The theoretical result, published in "Between the Net and the Deep Blue Sea," is perhaps Sekula's most concise account of abstraction in art—here specifically under the auspices of an ancient rhetorical form: exemplarity.

Although the internal exhibit was certainly an important draw for visitors, Sekula highlights "the *ship and the voyage* in and of themselves." Crucially, the vessel and its journey bear the hallmarks of the readymade as an artform: they are, he writes, "readymade-like in the subtlety of their ambiguous status as *already existing but transformed* object and context." (Sekula, 2002a: 29; original emphasis) The importance of this "ambiguity," namely, the real in itself and in its (capacity for) metamorphosis, is what allows Sekula to pursue an emancipatory form of abstraction while equally sustaining a commitment to materialism. Lightened of its work burden and for this reason disparaged as a "toy ship," the *Global Mariner* can transform itself into an idea or appearance, a moment of the real that transcends the compulsions of reality and, as befits a "toy," shuttle us its readers into play and performativity, ideality and fictionality. Instead of disappearing into the functionality of maritime transport, of disappearing, equally, beneath a series of flags of convenience, the ship becomes a prospective memory of global maritime labor—a "contested allegory" challenging the regimes of a "flexible" neoliberalism, on the one hand, and an "amnesiac" culture industry, on the other, forces that today conspire to negate the very existence of the sea, according to Sekula. "The great strength of the *Global Mariner* experiment was to raise the question of society from the very space that is imagined to be beyond society." (Sekula, 2002a: 32)

In a further elaboration of the ship's "ambiguity" (its status as already existing but also transformed), Sekula writes: "This was a *meta-ship*, representing and figuring within itself, within the exhibition that was its only cargo, all the other invisible, ignored, and silent ships of the world. The *Global Mariner* had to be a real ship functioning in an exemplary way." (Sekula, 2002a: 31; original emphasis) One can isolate at least six aspects of exemplarity as they are embodied in the *Global Mariner*, but before turning to what we can call the rhetoric or poetics of exemplarity in Sekula, we might pause to better understand the historical meaning of the term.

Alexander Gelley distinguishes in Ancient Greece two different logics of exemplarity. First, with Plato, the exemplar is a paradigm or archetype (from the Greek *paradeigma* and, later, the Latin *exemplar*). Plato's theory of forms is archetypal in that it stages a mode of knowing based on deduction: a transcendent idea delimits in advance our cognitive and aesthetic investigations of empirical reality. The second logic of exemplarity is to be found in Aristotle's *Rhetoric* where he sets forth a more lateral or horizontal understanding of the exemplar: "neither from part to whole nor from whole to part but from part to part, like to like, when two things fall under the same genus but one is better known than the other." (cited in Gelley, 1995: 1) This is what a photograph and, more widely, what a pedagogical artifact like the *Global Mariner* can hope for: to overcome its singularity in becoming "better known" than other sectors of reality, and, on the basis of this notoriety, orienting our searches inductively through lesser known particulars. It follows that meaning is not intrinsic to the exemplar, but lies rather in its applicability to related, but nonetheless external others. This is the aim, I am arguing, of Sekula's traffic with abstraction: the elevation of a concrete singular item into a modest beacon of normativity by virtue of which it can serve as cause for judgment, thus enabling us to assess as yet unknown or invisible or under-represented sectors of reality in the moral or cognitive light that it casts forth. Gelley speaks intriguingly of the exemplar as a "nexus of converging articulations," indicating that, in itself, it remains insufficiently meaningful, but can—when pressed into relation with adjoining particulars—become constitutive of a more-or-less unified chain or network of meaning. Aristotle spoke of moving from part to part, but this very movement from part to part can eventuate in the construction of a previously inexistent context or whole. And this is what an exemplar like the *Global Mariner* might have meant most significantly for the later Sekula: orienting his travels not merely from port to port, but in the direction of some invisible whole without which one could not sustain the movement of part to part, of hidden maritime labor here to hidden maritime labor there.

Heterotopia

What aspects then of the *Global Mariner's* history and mission allow us to construct a rhetoric or poetics of exemplarity?

First, the ship is *heterotopic* in Foucault's sense. Sekula is brief in his definition (heterotopias are "real spaces that call other spaces into question"), and so it is worth quoting Foucault at greater length. Unlike utopias, which equally call real spaces into question but are not themselves real, heterotopias are real places, localizable within society, but which yet function as "counter-emplacements" or counter-sites (*contre-emplacements*): elements of exteriority that interrupt, offer relief from, and/or contest the space of ordinary human commerce. A heterotopia, writes Foucault, exhibits "the curious property of being in relation with all the other sites, but in such a way as to suspect, neutralize, or invert the set of relations that they happen to designate, mirror, or reflect." (Foucault, 1986: 24) Heterotopias include churches, cemeteries, specific architectural conventions, even colonies. Yet it is Foucault's theoretical example of the mirror that is particularly intriguing. While mirrors are both utopic and heterotopic, according to Foucault, the following passage concentrates on the latter:

> [The mirror] is also a heterotopia in so far as the mirror does exist in reality, where it exerts a sort of counteraction on the position that I occupy. From the standpoint of the mirror I discover my absence from the place where I am since I see myself

over there. Starting from this gaze that is, as it were, directed toward me, from the ground of this virtual space that is on the other side of the glass, I come back toward myself; I begin again to direct my eyes toward myself and to reconstitute myself there where I am. The mirror functions as a heterotopia in this respect: it makes this place that I occupy at the moment when I look at myself in the glass absolutely real, connected with all the space that surrounds it, and absolutely unreal, since in order to be perceived it has to pass through this virtual point which is over there. (Foucault, 1986: 24)

This mirror function, as it were, provokes a doubling in its beholder who feels herself at once present and absent, actual and virtual, real and fictional. For the mirror itself is as real a place or object as any other and as such confirms one's own real-world spatiality. Yet the mirror equally interpellates a fictive version of myself, a fiction or virtuality that I see from the position of my absence in the real world and which, crucially, I can smuggle back therein in order to "reconstitute" myself. Without doubt, the crucial phrase here is "in order to be perceived." One can traffic easily and unthinkingly with reality, but in order to obtain an outlook on one's situation, one must behold oneself via the detour of a de-realizing fiction—which is to say, via an abstraction. The philosophical, but also political, implications are important. A heterotopic space alerts us to a structural gap in our being which, when opened, reveals that we are not so definitively territorialized in and among real spaces, in and among the instrumentalized totalities that keep us in place. A sense of freedom haunts our beings, a feeling for the virtual that can, in a movement of return or descent, recalibrate our outlook on reality.

The *Global Mariner* is heterotopic not merely in its "maritime" contestation of our landlocked everyday lives. It is heterotopic in the outlook it provides to dockers, seafarers, and those (but who in our global economy is exempt from this category?) who rely on their labor. As with the "contested allegory" of Frank's *Detroit*, it yields an abstract layer of meaning whose readability can be enacted within the real world. No wonder, then, that the *Global Mariner* was occasionally refused entry in various ports. Second, as an exemplar the ship is no mere fiction. It is material or "already existing," in Sekula's words. It is of a given social order, thus fulfilling Sekula's long standing concerns to work "from within" the parameters of a social order, but equally with a view to identifying what is "typical" (Sekula, 2016 [1984]: 70) or "emblematic" (Van Gelder, 2015: 79) of that social order. Third, following its status as heterotopic and material, it is inoperative in a strictly functional sense—bereft of real cargo and thus relieved of customary labor obligations. The ship was empty, and this is a significant clue as to the non-sovereign nature of the exemplar (a point to which I will presently return). Fourth, it was asystematic—demonstrating, by virtue of its age, an incompatibility with respect to the protocols of standardized global shipping. It thus lent itself naturally to an aesthetics of obsolescence and recuperation. Fifth, in its "ironic counterenactment" of previous maritime voyages, it self-consciously enacts an element of theatricality, of parody or semblance. Finally, the ship is mobile—a point that Foucault makes and that is especially important to Sekula's concept of exemplarity. No matter the name of this figure (exemplar, allegory, construction, enigma, and even theory), it yields a portable meaning that emerges from its material being and, as portable, carries its readability into other, adjacent spaces. To enact that readability, I am claiming, is to enact a critical consciousness of one's place within the economy.

Performativity

The exhibition aboard the ship was of course informative; one can learn about abusive labor practices from a viewing of the exhibit itself. Yet the true content of an exemplar, I have been arguing, lies not in its proper symbolic content, but rather in its meaning for another entity, in its infiltration of sealed, alien, or simply adjacent spaces and its creative appropriation therein. This is the anti-modernist and metonymic quality of the exemplar: as a sign it is empty and yet constitutive, non-sovereign and yet orientational. The exemplar must be "taken up" and, for this to happen according to Judith Butler, a fortuitous set of conditions must prevail.

In "Performative Agency," Butler revisits the Austian distinction between illocutionary and perlocutionary performatives, wondering in particular about an unsubstantiated preference for the former among economic theorists such as Michel Callon and Donald MacKenzie. Illocutionary performatives, in the instant of their declaration, bring about the reality that they declare. The authority underwriting their enactment resides sovereignly in the speaker and, more specifically, in the speaker's institutional position or discursive situation. The very act of declaration brings about a change in reality—for example, a change in one's legal status. Butler wonders whether we are unfairly overlooking the very different, and possibly more emancipatory, operations of perlocutionary performatives:

> Why is there no consideration of the "perlocutionary" model from these discussions? After all, Austin made clear that certain kinds of performative speech acts could only have "effects" if certain kinds of conditions were first met. So a certain utterance

can only bring about a state of affairs in time (and not immediately) if certain intervening conditions are met. The success of a perlocutionary performative depends on good circumstances, even luck, that is, on an external reality that does not immediately or necessarily yield to the efficiency of sovereign authority. If illocutions produce realities, perlocutions depend upon them to be successful. Whereas illocutionary performatives produce ontological effects (bring something into "being"), perlocutionary performatives alter an ongoing situation. In this sense, the illocution appears more clearly to rely on a certain sovereign power of speech to bring into being what it declares, but a perlocution depends on an external reality and, hence, operates on the condition of non-sovereign power. (Butler, 2010: 151)

Butler's insistence on luck (on risk and wager) is crucial: the power of the performative will be revealed only in time, in the creative adoption of its codes. This moment of "uptake" sits at heart of exemplarity and its epistemological consequences are important. In the moment of uptake, which is never guaranteed and can possibly occur much later in time, we can appreciate the difference between the mere imparting of knowledge, on the one hand, and the production of political consciousness or experience, on the other. The former need not entail any subjective commitment; the latter, by contrast, entails the existential constitution of knowledge insofar as one's life, held up to oneself in the mirror-effects of the exemplar, is self-consciously grasped as a testimony to the imbrication of subjectivity in objective social orders. The exemplar is not in itself a piece of knowledge; it is a vector of "epistemologisation" in which the receiving other—the addressee—becomes an agent of knowledge and, more pertinently as we will see, freshly knowable to herself. What we are glimpsing in the performative uptake of an exemplar is less the display of codified knowledge, than the realization that knowledge might be lived at the eventful intersection of subjective and objective orders of reality.

Working Object

W. J. T. Mitchell has relayed the story behind the *Welder's Booth* photo from Sekula's *Fish Story*. (Sekula, 2002b [1995]: 16) (pl. 4) It was Sekula himself who flipped the wrench, thereby doubling the abandoned tool with its mirror-like trace. (Mitchell, 2010: 26) The photo seems a tale of two aesthetics: the first, an aesthetics of indexicality; the second, in its combination of two forms (the indexical trace and the instrument responsible therefor), an aesthetics of exemplarity.

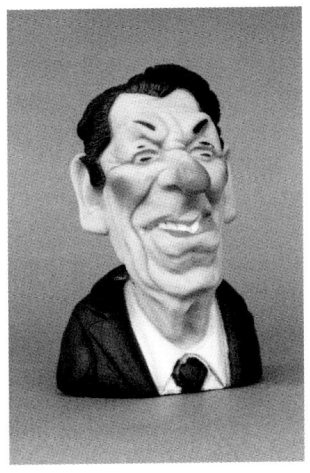

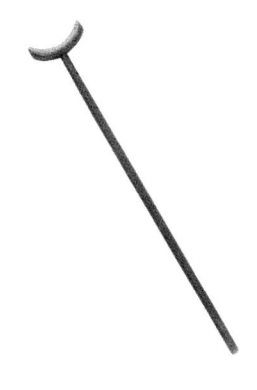

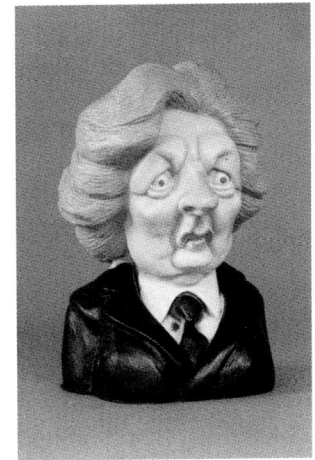

Fig. 1

*Ronald Reagan Official Spitting Image
Squeaky Head* [title given by Allan
Sekula], unknown manufacturer, rubber
toy, 1984, 14,6 × 9 × 6 cm. Purchased
by Allan Sekula through eBay on 21
June 2010. Part of Allan Sekula, *Ship
of Fools / The Dockers' Museum*
(2010–2013) [TDM 52]. Collection M HKA
/ Collection Flemish Community of
Belgium. © Photo: Ina Steiner. Courtesy
Allan Sekula Studio.

Fig. 2

Antique Child's Crutch [title given by
Allan Sekula], unknown manufacturer,
wood, nineteenth century, 92,7 × 15
× 3,7 cm. Purchased by Allan Sekula
through eBay on 30 July 2010. Part
of Allan Sekula, *Ship of Fools / The
Dockers' Museum* (2010–2013) [TDM
51]. Collection M HKA / Collection
Flemish Community of Belgium.
© Photo: Ina Steiner. Courtesy Allan
Sekula Studio.

Fig. 3

*Margaret Thatcher Spitting Image
Squeaky Toy* [title given by Allan
Sekula], unknown manufacturer, rub-
ber, 1984, 14,2 × 9 × 10 cm. Purchased
by Allan Sekula through eBay on 26
June 2010. Part of Allan Sekula, *Ship
of Fools / The Dockers' Museum*
(2010–2013) [TDM 53]. Collection M HKA
/ Collection Flemish Community of
Belgium. © Photo: Ina Steiner. Courtesy
Allan Sekula Studio.

I have been arguing that Sekula's ideal spectator is a reader less of an
aesthetic artifact in itself (a photograph, an object) than of the world
perceived in the light of exemplarity or allegory. The *Welder's Booth*
photograph is typical of a distinctive strain in Sekula's aesthetic in that
it pictures the real and its doubling, but which of two wrenches counts
as the real? Where, more precisely, resides the power of abstraction?
On the one hand, we behold the indexical mark as if *Welder's Booth*
were an instance of photographic self-reflexivity. Given Sekula's long-
standing critiques of modernism, this seems unlikely. We might, however, locate the photograph's self-reflexivity in the abstract portability
of the wrench into other industrial settings—its capacity to do work
or to be applicable elsewhere. If we are attuned to Sekula's persistent
search for abstraction (for the capacity of an image or object to do work
elsewhere, beyond its immediate, physical boundaries), then clearly the
real wrench fits the bill. Indeed, it figures Sekula's penchant for typical-
ity over and above the singular print. For the wrench does not exhaust
itself in any single task; it retains an abstract potential for future interventions. It is in this expanded sense of portability that we behold here

a methodological reflection on photography: indexical and contiguous, certainly, but yet capable of a certain abstraction or portability that permits further interventions into the real. Thus, in this one frame, we see the concrete and the abstract, the past and the future, the indexical and the conceptual—the very characteristics of the exemplar.

I just spoke of a work's immediate physical boundaries—the thinghood of the thing, as it were. Plainly, this is reductive insofar as the photograph also testifies to, indeed, exchanges itself against an external referent. My central claim is that this referential purchase, this one-to-one exchangeability between the photograph and the dated instant, is both an indispensable form of knowledge, but equally for Sekula a limited aesthetic ambition. If social documentary is to prove emancipatory, then the making of objects with singular stories (what in photography we might call *merely indexical*) will have to be complemented by a power of abstraction that extends the demand of readability out beyond an object's physical boundaries, beyond as well its depicted referent. The emancipatory force of social documentary resides less in the construction of singular objects or singular testimonies—merely local truths, we might say, though of course this is important. The point is to make works of art that are both singular and abstract, real instances that acquire a mediating capacity within a greater social order. But why so? What is the greater purpose of Sekula's interest in abstraction, portability, exemplarity, allegory, and so on?

The venerable ends that animate social documentary—justice and equality, truth and knowledge—are all in play here, but so too are our very modes of perception which, more than we might acknowledge or even understand, are freighted with the epistemological prejudices that ratify the capitalist social order. Sekula long understood that contemporary social documentary must work within "an exhausted liberalism" (Sekula, 2002a: 3), a context in which cultural production has submitted by and large to "the disembraining machine of the market." (Sekula, 1997: 50) Corporate culture in age of digital infrastructures is a list of disavowals, but none more pressing for Sekula than the disavowal of labor and labor protections under the protocols of neoliberalism: "reduced social security, casualization of work in the name of 'flexibility,' union-busting, and privatization of public infrastructure." (Sekula, 2002a: 28) The drumbeat of the cudgel with which Reagan and Thatcher beat back the demands of labor rings in time with the consistent refrain: "The social is unknowable. The social doesn't exist." (Sekula, 1997: 49) (figs. 1–3) It is against this context of the disavowal of the social that a pedagogical strategy for reading against the grain finds traction. Implicating our modes of perception in the construction of truth (making us readers do the work, so to speak) is a manner of overcoming a specific antinomy of bourgeois-capitalist experience:

depicting the world in its implacable objectivity, on the one hand, and compensating for this loss of freedom with individualistic aesthetic experience, on the other.

To raise the question of the social is above all, then, to implicate the subjectivity of others in their own education. Performativity is the precise lever through which reader and artifact merge into a politicized perception of the world. It bears repeating that the exemplar is less a one-way, monolithic message than an instigation to engage the real under the guidance of an allegorical abstraction. Such is the strength, but also the risk of a perlocutionary performative: it is a non-sovereign sign that is underwritten not by a preceding source of authority (for example, a discursively-freighted archive or a set of institutional protocols), but by a reader's act of judgment in which an allegorical abstraction has found purchase in a new, adjacent context. The authority of the exemplar is retrospectively confirmed as, and only as, its readability operates creatively but also productively. All of which is to suggest that a reader for Sekula is not a passive assimilator of knowledge. The act of judgment facilitates the production of a knowing subject who leverages the portability of the exemplar in order to cognitively assess greater social contexts. The reader emerges performatively through her creative adoption of the exemplar.

Three conclusions follow from this insight. First, the act of judgment can assist in the self-knowledge of the (emerging, performative) subject—in the very act of judgment, she knows herself to be a knower, to have the capacity and authority for knowledge claims. Given the pernicious split in capitalist society between intellectual and manual labor, this is no small accomplishment for those "destined" to labor with their hands. Second, in her claim to knowledge, she is possibly making public for herself and for others a hidden aspect of the world. There is, in brief, a political dimension to the mutual constitution of knower and knowledge as, on the borrowed strength of the exemplar, she is now reading reality against the grain. Third, and as a synthesis, the social application of allegorical abstraction overcomes another pernicious antinomy of bourgeois thought, namely, the sense of a reified order of class relations that yet permits, for some, the experience of freedom through aesthetic contemplation. The application of an allegorically charged construction (what I am gathering here under a broadened conception of exemplarity) reconciles subject and object in the moment of their mutual production. In brief, performativity in Sekula is non-foundational; the exemplary image is not authoritative until it is "taken up" and made legible in and against contexts other than those of its immediate referent. The very taking up of the non-sovereign exemplar testifies to the experience of freedom on the part of the reader, who presses forth experimentally into the real, testing the abstraction of the exemplar against coded (and often conservative) modes of perception and thereby hoping, on the strength of the exemplar, to behold reality otherwise than is customarily allowed. The entire operation testifies to a reconciliation of subjective freedom with emancipatory knowledge, a co-construction of the subjective and objective that overcomes a long-ingrained and pernicious antinomy of bourgeois thought.

These three points speak to Sekula's central interest in the conjunction between labor (subjectivity) and labor practices (institutions). Workers, of course, have suffered from conditions of economic exploitation. Perhaps more damagingly, workers have also suffered from what epistemologists call a credibility deficit as a result of the divide in capitalist culture between intellectual and manual labor. (Fricker, 2007: 17–22) To create a work of art that engages (that demands the performance of) the capacity of knowledge is to strike, as I've just indicated, at one of the most pernicious conditions of capitalism: the relegation of a clear majority to the mere use of their hands. In a side-by-side reading of two distant works, *The Dockers' Museum* first and then the early *Untitled Slide Sequence*, I'd like to demonstrate how Sekula conceived of labor as a multitude whose energies, while often woven into the oblivion of dead labor, nonetheless retained a margin of freedom for alternative uses of their subjectivity—not least, in their capacity for thought, critique, and aesthetic judgment.

In the "Spine Section" of *The Dockers' Museum*, Sekula includes—no doubt as its centerpiece—a medical model of a human spine. (fig. 4) An idealized abstraction of the vertebral column, it is a working object that guides the physician's examination of a patient. When repositioned in an artist's museum, however, it surely exceeds its precise medical purpose; it sheds its sovereign function as an instrument of medical diagnosis. In Sekula's hands, its refashioned meaning is that of a methodological imperative, namely, that one use the spine as a vector for epistemological inquiry in an adjacent field. Two possible fields of inquiry beckon: the wider world of maritime labor, but also the proximate objects in Sekula's museum. The reader of Sekula's spine is in search of a corresponding artifact that would allow her to "materialize" to the allegorical charge of what is otherwise a merely medical model.

As Gail Day has noted, the legibility of the spine can be read productively in relation to a remarkable photograph from the *Ship of Fools* series. (Day, 2015: 67) In the latter, we see a docker guiding a bundled stack of sugar bags upward for loading. (pl. 17) His spine is clearly visible, bearing the burden of his task, but it also "extends" vertically

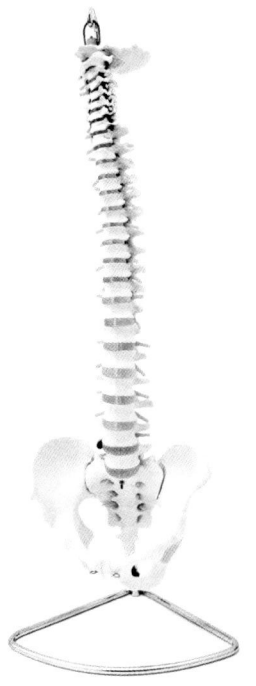

Fig. 4

Chiropractor's Life-Size Model of a Human Vertebrae [title given by Allan Sekula], plastic, 82,5 × 32,5 × 25 cm. Producer and production date unknown (most probably shortly before or in 2012). Purchased by Allan Sekula through eBay on 6 March 2012. Part of Allan Sekula, *Ship of Fools / The Dockers' Museum* (2010–2013) [TDM 41]. Collection M HKA / Collection Flemish Community of Belgium. © Photo: M HKA, Christine Clinckx. Courtesy Allan Sekula Studio.

and, as it were, virtually through the sugar bags themselves. The natural order of the human body is here exteriorized into an ordering of dead matter. What would have been a merely medical appraisal of the spine yields to an appraisal of the intensive labor conditions of dockers and, more intuitively, to a vision of labor weaving itself (but also disappearing) into the contents and infrastructures of maritime shipping. Methodologically, I have argued, the exemplar allows one to appraise empirical particulars not explicitly depicted within its own frame of reference. It is thus that it opens a relation to the future, to adjacent regions of application. But where, then, in this series of spines (the medical model, the docker's tense musculature, the bundled sugar bags), are we to spot the future? We might note Sekula's saturation of the picture plane with unbundled sacks of sugar. To the degree that they press against the frame, we can intuit that they extend well beyond the immediate vicinity of the docker's body. It is these as-yet unbundled bags that open a "beyond," a dismal future for the docker who confronts an infinity designed to preoccupy him for the rest of his days. We fear, of course, this infinite task will be misread ideologically to suggest that this is all a worker is good for: working with his body alone, weaving his energies eternally into the organization of dead matter. The infinity of bags also provokes questions regarding the conceptual possibilities of totalization and mediation—the methodological concerns we encountered in Marx. If one must bring one's body to the site where an exemplar confronts empirical diversity, how does it not become discouraged in the face of seemingly infinite tasks?

I want to offer three suggestions about how *The Dockers' Museum* was designed to confront this question. First, any single exemplar, even as powerful as the *Global Mariner*, will cast but a finite light into very complex social and economic realities. One might suspect that Sekula began designing a massive, variably installable artist's museum in order to match the complexity of global maritime trade. A work of art that is renewable and thus not so hampered by the limits of a single light source will continue to generate new and unforeseen relations to the sea. More bluntly, *The Dockers' Museum* is designed for posthumous installation and this is in perfect resonance with a rhetoric of exemplarity insofar an exemplar—by virtue of its mobility, performativity, and abstract meaning—casts forth a light whose precise point of applicability depends upon a subsequent reader's intervention. We simply know not when, where, and how a reader will thus intervene. This separation between artist and reader indicates that a rhetoric of exemplarity is structurally posthumous, as the artist has always already removed himself from the possible applications of his own work.

Secondly, we are in a position to interpret one of Sekula's specific ambitions for *The Dockers' Museum*: "what I am trying to construct is a kind of imaginary life world of a phantasmatic collective. And that collective could be all those who labor on the sea, or who engage in the cargo from sea to shore and shore to sea." (cited in Van Gelder, 2015: 76) On the one hand, the utopian dimension of a phantasmatic collective seems clear. On the other, it is also a matrix for epistemological inquiry. With its assemblage of humble materials, *The Dockers' Museum* generates a self-renewing hermeneutical context necessary for further investigations into the complex space of maritime trade. This imaginary whole or "imaginary community," as Sekula says (cited in Van Gelder, 2015: 83) is, I am claiming, a knowledge condition necessary for the possible visualization or perception of its future members.

Finally, as large and perhaps as unwieldy as *The Dockers' Museum* collection is, the idea of introducing local artifacts or of working with the local setting at each of its future installations mirrors the ungrounded, "risky" spirit of the work. Newly introduced artifacts will likely act as exemplars themselves, recalibrating the central artifact of any particular section, or assist in polarizing the exemplarity of his already assembled artifacts. Thus, the perpetual and ineluctably fragile aim of the work: to exhibit and distribute a disparate set of artifacts through a throw of the dice and see not only if we've hit upon a right number or combination, but also how far that number casts a light into the future.

Methodologically, the *Untitled Slide Sequence* shares a similar concern with futurity. (fig. 5) In nearly every frame, the camera captures both a handful of proximate workers, but also their collective oncoming progression which begins, crucially, beyond the vanishing point of each image. A privileged theme reappears here: the worker, yes, but really the inoperative worker relieved of her on-the-clock relation to the institution and its means of production. From the perspective of capital, the horizon and its vanishing point indicate an industrial reserve army of labor—all the better, then, to greet them with infinite bags of sugar. But from the standpoint of labor, one intuits the free movement of uncolonized human energy and, with it, the conscious apprehension that life exceeds the reifying conditions of work. But what do to with this mass of energy? And how? The very articulation of this question situates the worker beyond her "destined" place in the ranks of manual labor. The question itself expresses her freedom to reflect on her lot in life.

Yet despite this coming to consciousness, one must acknowledge the divergence of this photo sequence from other, indisputable uses of exemplarity in Sekula's work. In *Untitled Slide Sequence*, there is no mirror-like vehicle, no allegorical abstraction to mediate the free flow of labor. This is no ship, no wrench, no calculatedly crude mechanism like a plastic school-funnel to mediate labor's class consciousness. (Sekula, 2016 [1984]: 199) What, then, are we to perceive in the sequence? The mass of free energy, in its spatial regression beyond the image's vanishing point, exceeds the plane of visibility, but this itself is crucial. For this mass of free energy is, I contend, figured less in its post-work, off-the-clock commute than in its virtual dimension, as a ghostly underlayer of unemployed negativity that shadows all productive labor. To insist on an earlier claim, workers enact their freedom in the recognition that life exceeds the parameters of work—and that the laborer, therefore, never wholly coincides with the objective orders of capitalism (and this, as a challenge to the archival, pseudo-scientific inscription of workers within a social order that prohibits economic mobility and intellectual freedom). With this thought, we can cast a bridge between Sekula's phantasmatic collective from *The Dockers' Museum* and the reserve of uncolonized energy from the *Untitled Slide Sequence*. For one can create a work that envisions or figures a phantasmatic collective only because, ontologically speaking, this heterotopic (exemplary, allegorical) vision will "touch" upon—indeed will provoke and make contact with—a mirror-like, ghostly dimension of worker inoperativity. And to that inoperativity, the vision of a phantasmatic collective imparts a knowledge condition for reengaging the real and thus mediating one's class consciousness in a manner that is otherwise proscribed by capitalism's dominant hermeneutical resources.

One might say that Sekula's work, from beginning to end, is in dialogue with invisible partners, with the unseen streams of the global work force who, oncoming but still beyond the vanishing point, will enter into visibility only upon having appropriated the right hermeneutical resources for appraising their lot in the capitalist social order. I am also suggesting that this dialogue will carry on posthumously.

Fig. 5

From Allan Sekula, *Untitled Slide Sequence*, 1972. 75 b&w, 35 mm transparencies (three duplicate sets of 25) projected at 13-second intervals. Duration 17 min 20 sec, looped. Projection size 200 × 300 cm. Caption: dye-cut transfer text applied to external wall of projection room. © Allan Sekula Studio.

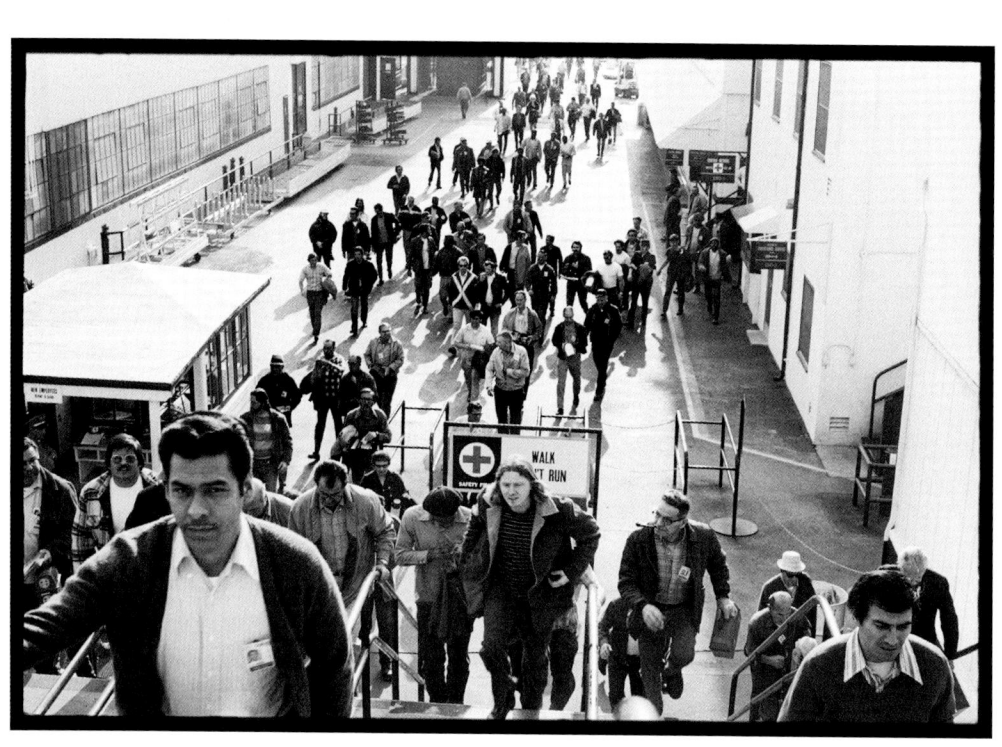

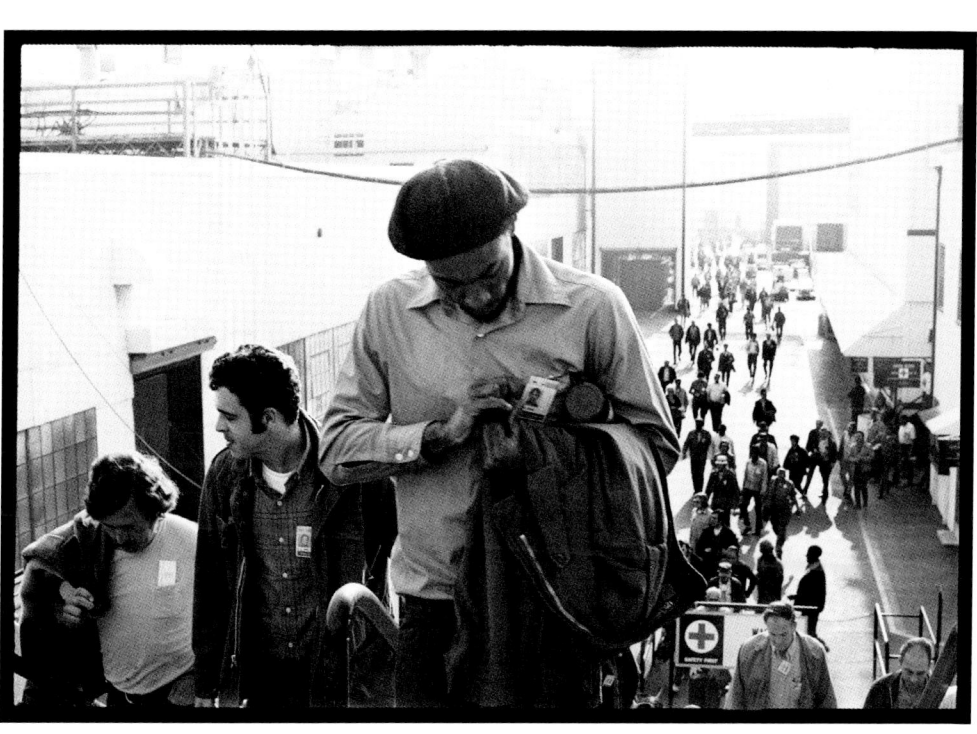

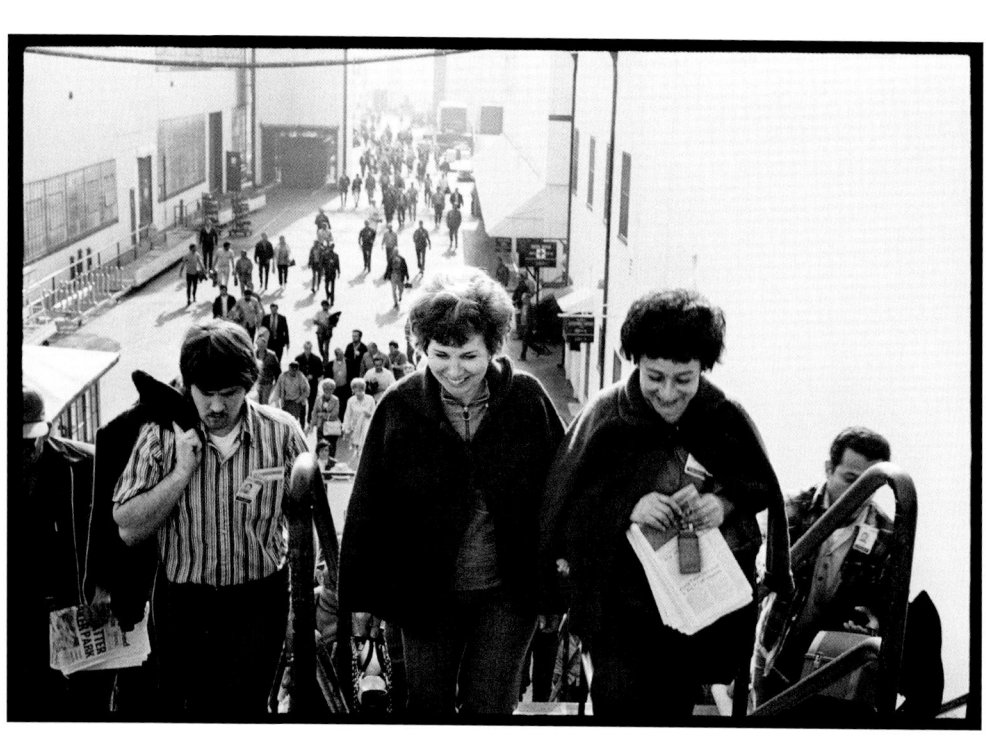

Conclusion

With Lukács and Habermas in mind, Sekula often speaks of capitalism's multifaceted "legitimation crisis," the central aspect of which (for Sekula) involves the class character of human denigration and exploitation. The working class stands in and against a world in which it cannot see its own reflection and, therefore, possibly, cannot learn to formulate and act upon its own interests. Sekula is especially concerned with the mechanisms by which the demands for social justice are distorted and depoliticized, camouflaged beneath the veneer of spectacle in which the antinomies of bourgeois culture oscillate ceaselessly—appearing now as an implacable social order underwritten by advances in science and technology, and now as a realm of Romantic, compensatory individualism that shelters the psyche from administered reality. In this light, photography is both a mediator and a symptom of capitalist order.

> As a mechanical medium which radically transformed and displaced earlier artisanal and manual modes of visual representation, photography is implicated in a sustained crisis at the very center of bourgeois culture, a crisis rooted in the emergence of science and technology as seemingly autonomous productive forces. At the heart of this crisis lies the question of the survival and deformation of human creative energies under the impact of mechanization. (Sekula 1983: 201)

To the degree that it functions scientifically as a vector of "objective truth," photography ratifies the empiricist, positivist leanings of modern science. To the degree that it is appropriated as a fine art, it promotes a Romantic *auteurism* in which creativity is not technologically stifled, but instead "reconciled" with and even liberated through the machine. For the worker, however, both sides spell silence—the first, through its inscription of the worker's body within the realm of necessity; the second, through its exclusion of the worker's cognitive and aesthetic faculties from the realm of freedom. When the worker does find her place within photography, it is typically through the latter's function as a universal mediator, "conscripting" all workers within the "globalized pictorial archive." (Sekula, 2002a: 3)

The very distinction between intellectual and manual labor is a form of testimonial injustice—a claim that knowledge comes only from above and that those who work with their hands do not have the credibility necessary to create, record, and/or impart knowledge. Further, from within the hermeneutical resources of the capitalist social order, a worker's only "capacity" for signification emanates from the body—a body that testifies to, that expresses (because it has thus been coded) its own impossibility to speak. Thus, cognitive incapacity, on the one hand, and a body coded in such a way as to signify "from itself" this very cognitive incapacity. The hermeneutical resources of the capitalist social order produce the collective perception of a laboring body that testifies to its own inability to testify for itself. Sekula's work, by contrast, lives on the fine line between offering the laborer the hermeneutical resources for self-knowledge, all while refraining to speak directly on behalf of the worker. To do so, however well-intentioned the aim, would replicate the divide between those who speak and those spoken for.

In a rhetoric of exemplarity, with its use of non-sovereign signs dependent upon a reader for their "uptake," signs do not so much speak the truth as confess to their own indeterminacy, pleading with the spectator to do something with their applicability. Hence, the ethics but also extreme fragility of the exemplar: it is mute until read experimentally in new and adjacent contexts. It is in those new contexts that the exemplar uncovers memories and experiences, affects and communal bonds, that the exemplar itself does not exhibit within its own immediate frame of reference. Such is its power to brush history against the grain. When, with Walter Benjamin's philosophy of history in mind, Sekula sought to recover aspects of reality occluded beneath reified structures of consciousness, he had in mind the "forgotten" conditions of workers' lives "that never broke the surface of human consciousness because they were never truly, that is politically, experienced." (cited in Sekula, 2016 [1984]: xvi) In this paper, I have argued that two, perhaps three criteria delineate properly political experience: first, the self-apprehension of oneself as a knower, especially in the context of hermeneutic paradigms that would deny the legitimacy of such self-apprehension; second, the willingness to make one's knowledge claims public and thus a matter of contention in contexts that otherwise suppress the very idea of social conflict; finally, and however fragilely, a reconciliation with the real in which freedom and knowledge coexist because they have co-emerged.

Bibliography

Walter Benjamin, "Little History of Photography," trans. Edmund Jephcott and Kingsley Shorter, in Walter Benjamin, *The Work of Art in the Age of Its Technological Reproducibility and Other Writings on Media,* ed. Michael W. Jennings, Brigid Doherty, and Thomas Y. Levin (Cambridge: Harvard University Press, 2008), 274–298.

Judith Butler. "Performative Agency," *Journal of Cultural Economy,* 3, 2 (September 2010): 147–161.

Gail Day, "Allan Sekula's Transitive Poetics: Metonymy and Metaphor in *Lottery of the Sea, Ship of Fools,* and *The Dockers' Museum,*" in *Allan Sekula.* Ship of Fools / The Dockers' Museum, ed. Hilde Van Gelder (Leuven: Leuven University Press, 2015), 57–70.

Miranda Fricker, *Epistemic Injustice: Power and the Ethics of Knowing* (Oxford: Oxford University Press, 2007).

Esther Leslie, "Introduction: Walter Benjamin and the Birth of Photography," in Walter Benjamin, *On Photography,* ed. Esther Leslie (London: Reaktion Books, 2015), 17–51.

Michel Foucault, "Of Other Spaces," translated Jay Miskowiec, *Diacritics,* 16, 1 (Spring, 1986): 22–27.

Alexander Gelley, "Introduction," in *Unruly Examples: On the Rhetoric of Exemplarity,* ed. Alexander Gelley (Stanford: Stanford University Press, 1995). 1–24.

W. J. T. Mitchell, "Realism and the Digital Image," in *Critical Realism in Contemporary Art: Around Allan Sekula's Photography,* eds Jan Baetens and Hilde Van Gelder (Leuven: Leuven University Press, 2006/2010), 12–27.

Allan Sekula, "Photography between Labor and Capital," in *Mining Photographs and Other Pictures: A Selection from the Negative Archives of Shedden Studio, Glace Bay, Cape Breton, 1948–1968,* eds Benjamin H. D. Buchloh and Robert Wilkie (Halifax: Press of Nova Scotia College of Art and Design, 1983), 193–286.

Allan Sekula, "On 'Fish Story': The Coffin Learns to Dance," *Camera Austria International,* 59/60 (1997): 49–59.

Allan Sekula, "Between the Net and the Deep Blue Sea (Rethinking the Traffic in Photographs)," *October,* 102 (Autumn 2002a): 3–34.

Allan Sekula, *Fish Story* (Düsseldorf: Richter Verlag, 2002b [1995]).

Allan Sekula, *Photography Against the Grain: Essays and Photoworks, 1973–1983* (London: Mack, 2016 [1984]).

Hilde Van Gelder, "Allan Sekula's Labor of Giants," in *Allan Sekula.* Ship of Fools / The Dockers' Museum, ed. Hilde Van Gelder (Leuven: Leuven University Press, 2015), 73–94.

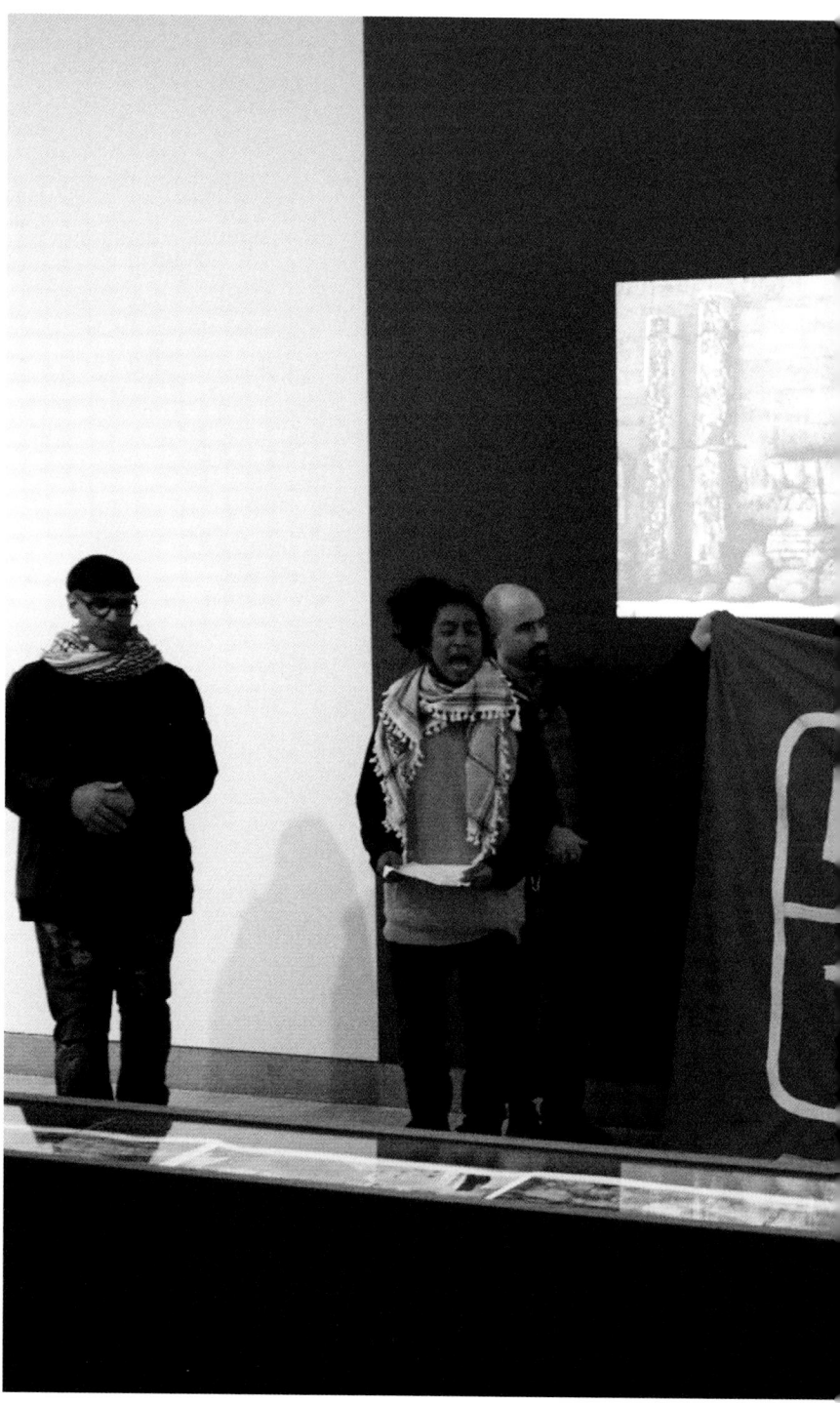

Fig. 1

Decolonial Cultural Front, Demonstration in *This Place* Exhibition, Brooklyn Museum, 2016. Courtesy Benjamin Young.

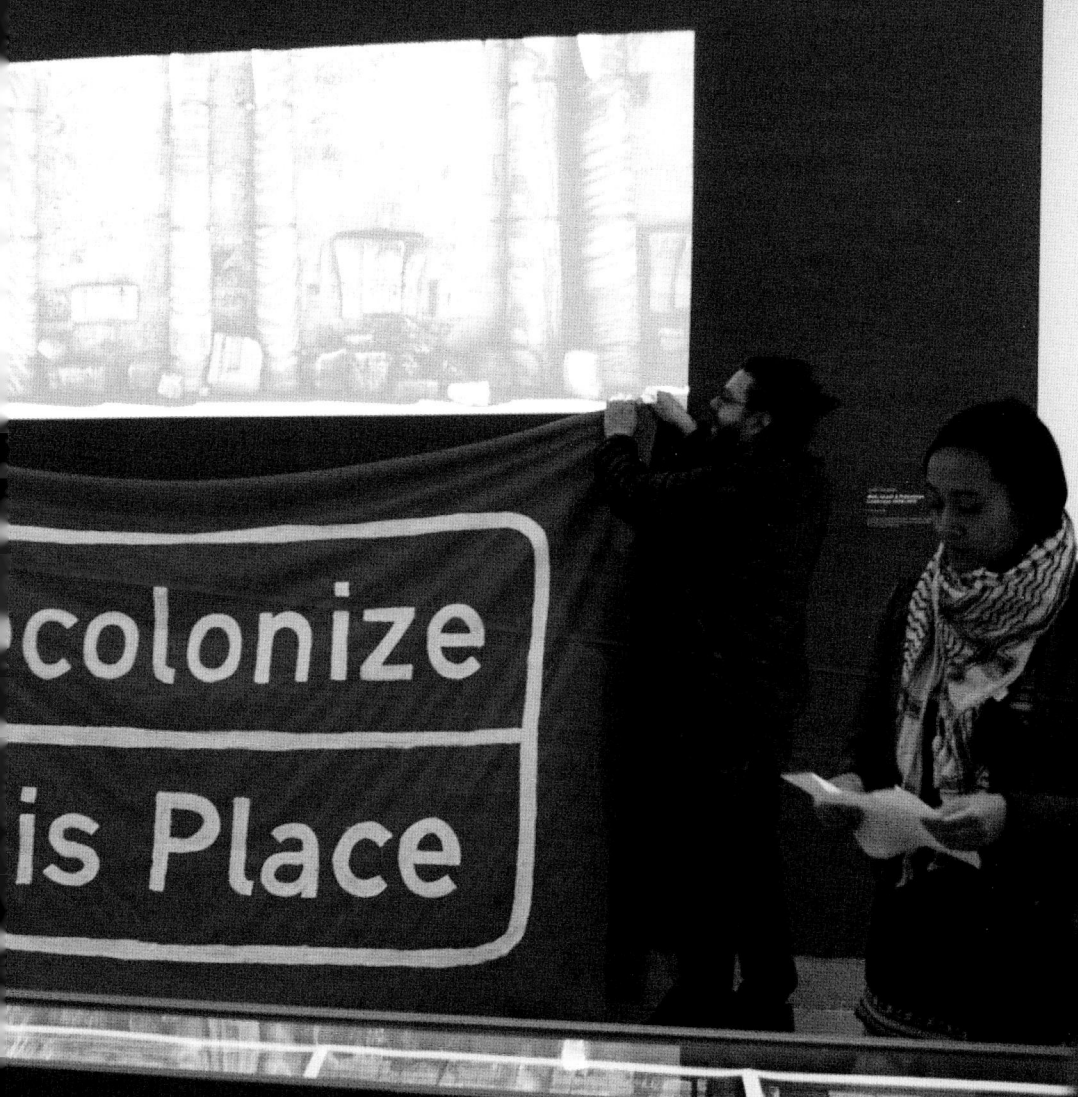

"Decolonize This Place": Realism and Humanism in Photography of Israel-Palestine

Benjamin J. Young

On May 7 2016, activists, who eventually numbered about one hundred people, filled the galleries of the Brooklyn Museum with the call to "Decolonize This Place." Their first stop was the exhibition called *This Place*, which displayed photographs taken in Israel and Palestine by twelve prominent photographers. The exhibition was commissioned and organized by French photographer Frédéric Brenner and curated by Charlotte Cotton. It had previously been shown in museums in Prague, Tel Aviv, and West Palm Beach, and would later travel to a number of university art museums in the US.[1] Amplified by the people's microphone, small groups of activists read from the flyer they also handed out to museumgoers, denouncing the exhibition as one that "aestheticizes apartheid and settler-colonialism." "By hosting *This Place*," the flyer explained, "the Brooklyn Museum lends its cultural legitimacy to a sanitized version of the region. It normalizes and aestheticizes illegal Jewish-only colonies in the West Bank. It renders invisible the daily violence experience by Palestinians living under occupation, and the ongoing dehumanization of Palestinians who live in Israel." Thus, they concluded, "*This Place* is the agit-prop of the oppressor."[2] (Decolonial Cultural Front, 2016) (fig. 1)

This would have been a surprising claim to those familiar only with the discourse surrounding the exhibition, specifically the wall text, the exhibition catalogue, and Brenner's comments in the press. In an extended profile in the *New York Times*, he explained the exhibition is really "an exploration of the human condition." The *Times* elaborated: "the universality that underlies the fractures in Israeli and Palestinian society is precisely what Mr. Brenner hopes art can display." (Lubow, 2016) Similar appeals to humanism pepper Cotton's introduction to the exhibition catalogue as well as the wall text and press material for

"Disassembled" Images

the show, including one summary text which concludes that the show "emphasize[s] the essential humanity underling this thorny conflict."[3] In their handout, the demonstrators quote the introductory wall text, which described the exhibition as "a deeply humanistic and nuanced examination that reminds us of the place of art, not as an illustration of conflict, but as a platform for raising questions and engaging viewers in a conversation." (Decolonial Cultural Front, 2016) Who could have a problem with a formulation as anodyne as that? What civilized person would choose conflict over conversation? It seems only barbarians could object—as the snarky headline to an anonymous article in the *Jewish Press* put it: "Anti-Zionist Mob Invades Brooklyn Museum to Protest Nuance and Humanism."[4] (JNi.Media, 2016)

Of course, the headline is a canard: the demonstrators were objecting not to nuance or humanism per se, but to what the ideology of humanism overwrites or occludes in this case. As the demonstrators succinctly put it: "This is a humanistic conversation in which Palestinian humanity is effaced." (Decolonial Cultural Front, 2016) How, then, could an ostensibly humanist and humanizing exhibition like *This Place* have such a dehumanizing effect?

* * *

The debate recalls that over another photographic exhibition staged sixty years before: the response by critics such as Roland Barthes and, later, Allan Sekula to Edward Steichen's *The Family of Man*, likely the most widely viewed photographic exhibition ever, shown at the Museum of Modern Art in 1955 and sent on multiple overseas tours afterward.[5] For Barthes, *The Family of Man* functioned as myth because it presumed a "human essence" prior to social difference, thereby "placing Nature at the bottom of History. Any classic humanism postulates that in scratching the history of men a little, the relativity of their institutions or the superficial diversity of their skins ... one very quickly reaches the solid rock of a universal human nature." (Barthes, 1956: 100–101) According to Barthes, this rhetoric of humanism serves to reify social difference, historical alienation, and injustice as natural and given—a reification abetted by the frozen stasis of the photographic image. For Sekula, *The Family of Man*, "the epitome of Cold War liberalism," not only "universalizes the bourgeois nuclear family" but also advances the paternalistic hegemony of the US government and American multinational corporations. Sekula is keen to show how the ostensibly universal humanism of *The Family of Man* was instrumentalized for particular ends: the exhibition traveled to "third-world hot spots" thanks to the sponsorship not only of the Modern, but also of the US Information Agency and businesses like Coca-Cola, whose largesse also served to advertise the benefits of American capitalism in places like Jakarta, Guatemala City, and Johannesburg, all in the service of neocolonialism and in implicit competition with internationalist socialism and the Soviet Union.[6] (Sekula, 1981: 84–89)

Although without *The Family of Man*'s ambition to survey the globe, *This Place*'s rhetoric of humanism and universality nonetheless presents similar problems. With over five hundred photographs, the multiplicity of views contained in *The Family of Man* was stitched together into a thematic narrative by the curatorial vision of Steichen, who is often treated as the auteur of the exhibition. Brenner plays a similar role as impresario in *This Place*, and his discourse of humanism recalls the spatial metaphysics of an essential human nature underlying history to which Barthes objected. In the rhetoric of Brenner, Cotton, and reporters such as Lubow, universal, essential humanity "underlies" politics and conflict. So too does art: as Brenner told the *Times*, "I believe art has a power to address questions that an ideological perspective cannot"; and as the wall text for his section of the exhibition declares, "Ideologies are the betrayal of the humane in the human." (Lubow, 2016) The equations are clear: art, the humane, and the human are portrayed as deeper, more fundamental—because essential and natural to human beings—than ideologies, politics, or conflict, which are secondary, superficial, dangerous illusions of history. This also means that art must be carefully separated not only from its entanglement with politics, but also from journalism, which is too fatally caught up with history. As Lubow reports, Brenner "and his colleagues are disappointed when critics perceive the pictures as news reports rather than as art." (Lubow, 2016)

In contrast with "classic humanism" that naturalizes history, Barthes insists that "progressive humanism, on the contrary, must always remember to reverse the terms of this very old imposture, constantly to scour nature, its 'laws' and 'limits' in order to discover History there, and at last to establish Nature as historical." (Barthes, 1956: 101) In turn, Sekula holds that photographs are necessarily partial selections from a world structured by power and political antagonism: the power to freeze or to frame a view not only requires power over the place and means of cultural production, but also depends on a whole history of pictorial conventions and operative conditions for making, representing, and seeing. And the claim to represent a universal humanity does not float free, underneath or above, politics or conflict, but is advanced only from a particular position within the field of the social. As opposed to conceiving ideology as a set of consciously held political views that can be freely donned and doffed like a hat, these authors argue that ideology forms the unconscious matrix of beliefs and institutions through which vision, discernment, making photographs, and depicting the human occur. The demonstrators, then, were taking issue with a particular set of views of Israel and Palestine presented *as if* they were natural and universal. And the potential objections to the show are many.

The demonstrators raised a number of concerns at the level of what could be called institutional critique. First, the selection criteria: despite Brenner's praise in the exhibition catalogue of "paradoxical and contradictory perspectives," of a project that would be "multi-voiced" and "dissonant," he revealed in the newspaper profile that "one thing would disqualify a photographer—anger."[7] (Brenner, 2014: 189; and Brenner quoted in Lubow, 2016) Anyone angry about injustice—say, the Israeli occupation—would be automatically disqualified, thereby considerably narrowing the range of what could be called dissonant voices. While Brenner invited thirty photographers to tour Israel, he ultimately invited fewer to participate in the exhibition, settling on eleven final participants, to which he added himself as well. And although he investigated adding Israeli and Palestinian artists partway through the project, no Palestinian photographer would participate.[8] Seeing the imbalance that would result by including only Jewish Israeli artists from the region, Brenner limited the final selection to what he called "outsiders." (Brenner, 2014: 189) While there are no Palestinian or Arab artists represented, at least a quarter of the artists belong to the Jewish diaspora. As long as one thinks of diaspora in the etymological sense of scattering, without any necessary return to a real or mythic homeland, this does not inherently make them any less outsiders than the other, non-Jewish photographers from Europe, America, or Korea.[9] Yet I point this out to make explicit the claims on the diaspora made by political Zionism, which considers immigration to Israel a cultural, political, or religious obligation and grants diasporic Jews a right of "return" denied to Palestinians made refugees by the founding of the Israeli state. The *Times* profile also revealed that Brenner himself lives in an apartment in Jerusalem part of the year, thus significantly qualifying his claim that all of the artists in the show are outsiders.

Second, although the show was on view in Tel Aviv, it did not travel to the Palestinian territories—suggesting it was directed at only a particular audience in the region. Third, the funding: although Brenner likes to compare the project to photographic missions such as la DATAR— the 1980s survey of the French landscape commissioned the French Ministry of Territorial Development, Housing, and Tourism—or the Farm Security Administration in the U.S., as well as the nineteenth-century *Missions héliographiques* in France, the exhibition is not a state-based program and received no direct government funding. Thus, the project does not violate guidelines set forth by the Boycott, Divestment, and Sanctions (or BDS) movement advocating nonviolent resistance to Israeli occupation through international boycotts of, divestment from, and sanction of the Israeli state and settlements in the occupied territories. Yet as the demonstrators point out, although the many funders—who contributed a considerable six million dollars to invite potential participants to tour the area, commission the works, assemble and tour the exhibition, and help to publish the monographic books that resulted—also sponsor "projects that support 'coexistence' between Jewish and Arab Israelis, they acknowledge neither Palestinians nor the illegal occupation. A few donors have directly funded Jewish-only settlements in the West Bank, and even the Israeli Defense Forces."[10] (Decolonial Cultural Front, 2016b) Although the political outlook of the funders does not necessarily determine the output of the artists, it seems Brenner made the project acceptable to the liberal Zionism of the majority of its funders at the least.[11] Although Brenner implicitly criticizes the religious fundamentalism of Jewish settlers in his texts (while ignoring the secular, nationalist wing of the movement), he simultaneously minimizes references to Palestine in the discursive apparatus of the exhibition. As one critic put it later, the commissions were rather like Birthright trips for art photographers, pointing out that it was some of the same funders paying for both expeditions.[12] (Olin 2016) Although the exhibition has the important difference of not relying on state funding, it nonetheless can be seen against the backdrop of a larger effort of *hasbara*—literally "explaining," a euphemism for propaganda undertaken by both the Israeli state as well as its citizens and supporters, including private organizations, to generate positive narratives of Israel in international media in order to counter ongoing criticisms of the state. With the slogan "BDS is the floor, not the ceiling," the demonstrators called on the museum not only to respect the tenets of BDS in refusing to collaborate with Israeli state institutions, but also to resist the ideological "agit-prop" being advanced by private funders and nongovernmental organizations.

The exhibition was reportedly first called *Israel: Portrait of a Work in Progress*, and Brenner's afterword to the exhibition catalogue also makes it clear that he was originally interested only in Israel, as both an existing, sovereign state and "metaphor" of humanity. (Weinrich, 2014; Brenner, 2014: 189) Palestine was an afterthought pushed on him by his collaborators.[13] "Israel and the West Bank," the toponym used for the region throughout the exhibition and the catalogue, implicitly but accurately acknowledges that none of the photographers went to the Gaza Strip. Yet each term in the pair belongs to a different category: Israel is recognized as a political entity, but Palestine is not, replaced only with an apparently nonpolitical, geographic placeholder. Continually using "West Bank" to refer to the Occupied Palestinian Territory—the name used in international law and the United Nations—frees the exhibition organizers from having to use the word "Palestine," to acknowledge the existence of the Palestinian national project, or to mention the half-century-long Israeli occupation of East Jerusalem, the West Bank, the Gaza Strip, and the Golan Heights.[14]

The occupation is unmentioned in the wall text, which gestures only indirectly, in one of the very few uses of the P-word, toward "Israeli-Palestinian conflict," and the exhibition catalogue nods only to Israel's "unresolved borders." (Brenner, 2014: 189) The supposed neutrality of the preferred geographic descriptor "West Bank" allows the exhibition to appeal to those who oppose even the idea of Palestine and see the West Bank of the Jordan river as land that belongs to Jewish settlers and that will soon be incorporated into the Israeli state. (The Zionist right wing abjures the word "Palestine" and consistently refers to Palestinians only as "Arabs.") It is to the credit of some of the photographers involved and Israelis who worked as Brenner's fixers and guides that the original geographic focus exclusively on Israel's pre-1967 borders was expanded to include the West Bank at all. Yet clearly to the protesters, this supplementary addition did not go far enough in acknowledging the constitutive role of the Palestinian Nakba, subsequent diasporic exile, and Israeli occupation of Palestinian territory and ongoing Jewish settlement there, as foundational to the contemporary state of Israel. Geography, mapping, and architecture are key to the exercise of political Zionism and the Israeli occupation, reaching back to the early, primary directives of the newly independent state to draw up new maps of the conquered land, erasing Arabic place names and replacing them with Hebraicized ones. Seeing this effacement repeated in the exhibition, the demonstrators reinserted Arabic place names by reading aloud and then taping to the wall their own Arabic captions beneath the mostly Hebrew names in the captions to Stephen Shore's landscape photographs.[15] Together with the banners carried through the gallery ("Decolonize This Place" and "Displacement Destroys Culture") and the call and response between speakers, the demonstrators responded with activist curating that reconfigured the narrative proposed by the exhibition and the meaning of the artworks inside it.

The demonstrators further appropriated the ambiguous grammar of the phrase "this place." The demonstrative adjective "this" can be described as a linguistic shifter, and functions semiotically like an index: by pointing at things, just as photography does.[16] The organizers used the indexical phrase "this place" to try to *avoid* politics, to avoid naming the conflict. While the organizers claim to have the laudatory goal of avoiding the thoughtless political polarization that can reflexively occur by invoking these place names, the demonstrators sought to show how this allegedly neutral overview remains embedded in a set of political choices. Pointing is always selective, and decisions had to be made about what to show and what not to show. In response, the demonstrators took up and redeployed the volatile and uncertain reference of the phrase "this place" to repoliticize allegedly impartial spaces such as the art gallery, instead using the phrase not just to cite the exhibition title, but also to point to the place in which they were standing that day: the Brooklyn Museum, the neighborhood, city, and nation-state surrounding it. That is, the call to "decolonize this place" was aimed not just at Brenner's exhibition, but also at the museum and its surroundings for other reasons: the museum was also seen as a node in the gentrification of, and displacement of poor folks from, the surrounding, primarily black and brown, neighborhoods. Thus the activists moved on to a second exhibition in the museum titled *Agit-Prop!*, where, along with the artists of Occupy Museums, Chinatown Art Brigade, and Artists of Color Bloc included in the exhibition, they called on the museum to put the principles of social justice and engagement with politics it celebrated in so-called agit-prop art to work by breaking contact with the real-estate developers on its governing board and those it had hosted at a recent symposium. Later demonstrations would also call for a "decolonization commission" to examine the museum's collection and programming. Going further to call attention to the settler-colonial history of Manhattan island as well as the US as a whole, "Decolonize This Place" became a heading under which the artist-activists who spearheaded the demonstration, a group known as MTL+, organized a three-month residency on decolonization at Artists Space, a nonprofit alternative art space in Manhattan, dedicated to five issues: indigenous struggle, black liberation, Free Palestine, global wage workers, and de-gentrification.[17]

These are all important issues, but for now I want to remain with the question of how Brenner's exhibition, under the guise of a universal humanism and allegedly neutral geographic focus, might have aestheticized apartheid and settler colonialism or effaced Palestinian humanity, as the demonstrators alleged. Interestingly, only a few of the photographers in the exhibition work in a style that might plausibly be called humanist. Most prominent is Rosalind Fox Solomon's *Them* (2011), which consists of black-and-white portraits of misfits, outcasts, or strangers she met on the street and riding the bus, recalling the anomie and alienation that settled over 1960s-era street photography after the optimism and sentimental humanism of Steichen's show had waned. In *Them* (whose title, like "this place," is also a shifter), it seems only an empty thing called humanity might connect Ghanaian religious pilgrims with a man feeding pigeons covered in their excrement in Tel Aviv with teenage soldiers in uniform in the desert. In a different vein, Josef Koudelka's *Wall* (2008–2012) embarks on a survey of the separation barrier, presented both as a slideshow of individual, gritty, black-and-white panoramic photographs and as a meters-long accordion-fold book titled *Zone: Israel/Palestine* that cuts through the exhibition space.

Clearly, calling attention to the very fact of the wall's existence, and emphasizing its monstrous monumentality, seems a kind of protest against the conditions that led to its construction. Yet one can also imagine a generic humanist denunciation of the sort that goes "there should be no walls between people," without addressing the necessary politics of any specific border. This sentiment was reinforced by the explanatory text that cites Koudelka calling the wall a "crime against the landscape," rather than a certain group of people, and his admiration for a graffito that reads "one wall, two prisons," which provides an admirable grasp of the myth of separation but fails to register how these two prisoners are treated very differently. One can equally imagine, on the other side of the fence, admiration for aesthetically striking images of a "big, beautiful wall" (as the forty-fifth American president might put it, with explicit reference to Israel as a model)—a wall with which, for example, many Israelis are quite happy. (Kershner, 2017) And by focusing on the monumental aesthetics of the watchtowers and eight-to-nine-meter-high concrete sections, the photographs risk reinforcing the ideology of separation that justifies the still partially incomplete barrier, missing the *differential* character of its control over movement. While images of the wall provide an imaginary separation of Israelis from Palestinians— fulfilling its pretext as a security barrier—they in fact obscure the fluid and mobile access Israeli settlers have to the West Bank, who zoom back and forth across, around, and through the barrier, as well as the deeply separate-but-unequal control over life in the occupied territories exercised by the Israeli state, military, and vigilante settlers. Thus the captions describing the specific locations pictured (East Jerusalem, Palestinian villages, refugee camps, Israeli settlements, roadblocks, checkpoints) and details of the barrier (that eighty-five percent runs though the occupied territory, functioning as a de facto annexation of key settlements, agricultural land, and water resources while cutting off or impeding access of Palestinians to their families, neighboring communities, farmland, workplaces, healthcare, and so on) are crucial to understanding Koudelka's depiction of the wall. They are helpfully accompanied by a timeline and political lexicon in the book version of the project, but completely absent from the exhibition catalogue and easily overlooked in the exhibition, where the symbolism of the outstretched book blocking movement through the gallery space dominates the installation.[18]

I will leave aside two outliers in the show, which seem to have little to do with the particulars of the region but fall on opposite sides of the humanist artistic coin. On one hand are Jungjin Lee's hazy, melancholic, often bathetic monochrome archeopictorialist prints of empty desert landscapes on handmade mulberry paper, whose crafted surfaces overwhelm the significance of that which they depict ("timeless human mark-making," according to Cotton [2014: 8]). On the other are Martin Kollar's deadpan views of stage-set-like scenarios—of industrial testing facilities, police or military training zones, medical contraptions—largely empty of people, which aggressively pursue a decontextualized, idiosyncratic strangeness that renders each scene as an isolate, an incomparable quiddity. Wendy Ewald's social-practice project involves a more complicated relation to humanism, and liberalism, to which I'll return later.

Instead of what might be described as a "humanist" aesthetic, the exhibition was dominated by large-format art photography dedicated to allover sharpness and infinite depth of field, printed at such large scale to almost overwhelm the viewer with a field of tiny details, whether of the built environment, natural landscapes, or people. Yet this approach is not necessarily immune to depoliticizing humanist platitudes either: Jeff Wall disclaims any particular relation to place in his composite tableau *Daybreak* (2011), which depicts Bedouin olive pickers lying on the ground, huddled under blankets in an orchard at dawn, with a brightly-lit, fenced-in prison complex lining the horizon in the background. Rather, he says, "I decided I was going to treat Israel like any other place ... Some men sleep outside under the stars, and some men sleep underground in a prison. It's like a haiku. That's true everywhere." (Lubow, 2016) Yet the contrast in Wall's picture between the small, faceless, wrapped bodies in the open air and the enclosed, warehouse-like architecture in the background is crucially qualified by its historical place and time. Although Bedouin are traditionally nomadic herders, in this scene they are sleeping outside because they are engaged in wage labor. As an interview in the catalogue makes clear, the laborers had work permits, meaning they traveled to the orchard near Mitzpe Ramon in the Negev/Naqab desert from the occupied West Bank, which also may explain why they prefer to sleep in the orchard during the harvest rather than make the return trip across the separation barrier, which they might be arbitrarily prevented from crossing. (Wall, 2014: 170–171) Thus sleeping outside may also index their lack of freedom to travel, and possibly even their displacement from their own land by the very farmers for whom they work: between 1948 and 1953, roughly ninety percent of the 100,000 Bedouin inhabiting the Negev/Naqab had been expelled by the Israeli military to Gaza, the West Bank, Jordan, and Egypt; these could be their children or grandchildren.[19] (Khalidi quoted in Weizman, 2015: 37) The prison also almost certainly houses at least some Palestinian prisoners, whether held for criminal, security, or political reasons—in contravention of international law, which prohibits removing prisoners from occupied territory.[20] Despite the contrast between openness and enclosure, and freedom and containment, that Wall attempts to sketch in the picture, it turns out the olive-pickers and prisoners may be more alike than different, at least in their subjection to the architecture of occupation.

* * *

Despite the claims to universal, human truths, much of the large-format photography featured in the show operates according to an implicitly *anti*-humanist indifference to the subjectivity of the sitter or the photographer, instead promoting a kind of neutral observation or affirmation of the wealth of surface detail recorded by the camera as well as the formal autonomy of the picture. Most of the wide-angle views of desert landscapes or low-slung urban architecture by Brenner, Struth, Shore, and Waplington are devoid of human figures. Such is the case in Thomas Struth's *City Hall* (2011), which positions the rectangular, gridded architecture of Tel Aviv's modernist city hall perfectly parallel to the picture plane, negating the perspectival distortion that would normally result from a passerby looking up at the building from the ground. By employing the view camera's mechanical movements to position the four corners of the building as equidistant from the picture plane, Struth creates a static, geometric, apparently objective regularity that seems to override any particular, embodied viewpoint. The site is historically fraught: designed in 1957 by Menachem Cohen, the Brutalist building sits on the plaza now named Rabin Square, the site of the 1995 assassination of prime minister Yitzhak Rabin for his role in the Oslo peace accords.[21] Yet looking beyond the shallow depth of the plaza in the foreground, the image turns on the tension between the minute details it contains and the allover, gridded composition that echoes the photographic frame, a grid primarily and reflexively oriented to the *surface* of the picture and ultimately to the museum wall. Struth brings the same equanimous gaze to a housing development labeled *Har Homa* (2009). Rows of new houses line the left edge of the picture, floating on a bed of bright tan, freshly bulldozed soil that rolls like a wave over the low hill in the center of the picture. Any sense of depth created by the receding rows of houses at left is destroyed by the undifferentiated tide of flattened soil on which they are carried, which also flattens out the horizon of gray-rock-and-green-scrub-covered hills in the center-right, and a scattering of hilltop homes in the distance. No indication in the picture or caption is given that Har Homa is an illegal Jewish Israeli settlement built to choke off Bethlehem, in the West Bank, from the Palestinian majority in Israeli-occupied East Jerusalem, consolidating a ring of Jewish settlements around Jerusalem in preparation for its annexation, presumably because that fact is considered immaterial to the aesthetic success of the picture in the viewer's eyes. Only those familiar with the architectural politics of the region will notice the few telltale red roofs that identify the buildings as Jewish settlements.

A similar aesthetic approach dominates Brenner's wide-angle view of the empty architectural shell of the Palace Hotel (originally built by the Grand Mufti of Jerusalem, subsequently occupied by British and Israeli governments, and in the process of becoming a hotel again), as well as the ten large landscapes by Shore.[22] Shore's views of the desert landscape—whether *Large Crater, Negev Desert* (2009), which shows the shell of a rusted-out automobile dwarfed by the surrounding, bare rocky hills, or *St. Sabas Monastery, Judean Desert* (2009), showing the 1500-year-old monastery built into the stone cliffside of a steep valley— repeat the formal tension in 19th-century religious travel photography of the Holy Land, in which barren, empty, desolate, or ruined sites seem strangely devoid of narrative or human incident, their lack calling out to be filled with spiritual meaning by the viewer. Only now, the spirituality is updated in the present from religious feeling to a kind of vague secular wonder at the historical significance or aesthetic beauty of the place.

To Shore's and Struth's credit, they also made photographs that contain traces of the occupation. Struth's *Off Al-Shuhada Street 1, Al-Khalil/ Hebron* (2009), printed smaller than his other large pictures in the show, looks down a street to the metal gate and military watchtower blocking it off, turning it into a dead end. (Shore made virtually the same photograph, only shot slightly closer to the checkpoint. Struth's version was included in the exhibition but not the catalogue; Shore's was included in the catalogue and his monograph, but not the exhibition.) The tan walls of the military installation blend in with the stone of the surrounding buildings, and the architecture of the occupation is quietly insinuated into the fabric of the city. Again, the façades of the wall and buildings are oriented flatly toward the picture plane, their formal stasis communicating little of the active force of colonization, displacement, and destruction at work in this place. Shore's *Hebron* (2011), which was included in the exhibition, depicts the regular, rectangular architecture of the city, seen from a high oblique angle, creating a diagonal grid equally in focus and distributed evenly across the frame. Only those looking closely will notice how empty is the largest street cutting across the bottom of the image, or the small Israeli flag in the corner of the picture, helping to highlight the wall and guard tower that closes off the intersecting street. In both cases, the checkpoint is perhaps mildly disconcerting. But it only becomes truly alarming when viewers consider that Hebron, known as al-Khalil in Arabic, is the largest city in the West Bank, and although the hundreds of Israeli settlers in the old quarter make up only about .003 percent of the population, the Israeli military occupies 20 percent of the city in order to protect them, with military installations that have partitioned off neighborhoods, killing the businesses and social lives of adjacent streets, including the former main commercial street seen in the pictures. The exhibition provides no such indication of this reality, neither the persistence of Palestinian life in the city nor the violence of the settlers and the army who seek to destroy it.[23]

Nick Waplington's *Settlement* (2011), a project devoted exclusively to documenting Jewish settler families and the landscapes they inhabit in the West Bank, portrays them largely as normal suburban families in normal suburban homes. Although the wall text admits the settlements depicted by Waplington are "controversial" because supported by successive Israeli governments but illegal under international law, it more prominently features his quote that "this work says these are the people, this is the landscape. But of course, the meaning of the work will depend on the interpretation of the viewer."[24] Again reverting to the apparently neutral rhetoric of "this," Waplington and the curators thereby default on any idea that the meaning of the work may also be partly determined by the politics of space, sovereignty, and nationalism that structures the place where the image was made, while simultaneously withholding further information viewers not expert in the region might need to interpret these mostly beautifying images.[25] Here the indexical "this" performs a static reification that identifies the sitters with the land, with little indication of the historical acts of violence their colonization entails.

As evidenced by Waplington's project, many of these photographers bring the same allover aesthetic of their landscapes to the other major genre of the show: monumental group portraits. In them, people are treated like landscape. Pictures of families by Struth, Brenner, and Waplington usually show what appear to be a mother and father and their children—sometimes a few, in Brenner's view of a small family in bathing suits at the beach; sometimes many, in his view of a Haredi, or ultraorthodox, family with nine children seated at their long dining table—occasionally with extended family members. Take both Struth's *The Faez Family, Rehovot* (2009), showing a large Mizrahi family on a patio, and Brenner's view of the Haredi Ashkenazi family at home, *The Weinfeld Family* (2009). With the sitters resolutely posed frontally toward the camera and therefore oriented toward the picture plane, each typically large-scale picture's composition is united and contained within a single, enclosed frame by a balance of similarity and difference in bodily resemblances among family members. This is how Michael Fried describes Struth's earliest family portraits, as structured by "two complementary axes": "the first," which "lies wholly within the picture and is essentially lateral," is "the axis of family relationships"; the second, "orthogonal to the first ... thrusts directly out from the picture toward the viewer," and forms "the axis of a frontal gaze." (Fried, 2008: 202–203; original emphasis) However much they are in tension, Fried privileges the first axis, where the unintended resemblances between family members create an "axis of absorption" within the picture, which cancels the inherent theatricality of the portrait situation and the sitters' acknowledgment of the photographer and viewer. (Fried, 2008: 203) When Fried is troubled by one particular family portrait of Struth's that Fried at first doesn't feel is artistically as successful as the others, Struth explains that Fried has correctly detected that the sitters are a mixed family including only one child of both parents and two stepchildren (each related to only one parent, with no biological relation to the other parent). Although Fried claims he's slowly becoming interested in the picture, such mixing fails his modernist criterion for aesthetic success, which is predicated on a disturbingly essentialist "family genotype" that unites the picture and secures its aesthetic autonomy: "the absolute structural unintendedness of biological resemblances" serves as "an internal ideal." (Fried, 2008: 199, 203) In addition to defaulting on more capacious, nonbiological notions of family and relatedness, Fried ignores the way that individual physical characteristics become visible *only as phenotype* in ways that are shaped by history and the environment. Thus Fried brushes aside historical differences in order to discover an underlying nature—not universally human, but specifically *familial* and *genotypical*—one protected and secured within the frame of photographic formalism. In Fried's view of Struth's family portraits, exogenetic mixing amounts to aesthetic failure.

All of the monumental group portraits in *This Place* are, with one important exception, exclusively of Jewish Israeli families. By presenting a survey of only Jewish families from a nation with a sizable non-Jewish minority, not to mention those Palestinians living under Israeli occupation, the exhibition thus seems to privilege their relatedness over other kinds of families and other kinds of social relations. While Brenner is presumably keen to highlight the visual differences between the staid Haredi family in their formal, black garb, and the colorful, casual clothes of the apparently secular family at the beach, viewers are explicitly asked to look beyond such historical details to discern the invisible human nature that they share in common. Yet Fried's insistence that "genetic" similarity between family members is key to the aesthetic success of such family portraits further discomfortingly raises the possibility of an essentialist connection *between* the family groups, as if Jews shared a genetic or racial nature more fundamental than history or religion. When Waplington pairs family portraits of Jewish settlers, who pose for pictures like normal, middle-class families everywhere, with the allegedly empty landscapes they are in the process of colonizing—but no signs of the people they are displacing—he seems to concede to their essentialist claims to the land or, at the least, offers few to no clues to the historically contested status of those claims. Thus the demonstrator's charge that the exhibition's depiction of an allegedly universal human nature aestheticizes apartheid and settler colonialism and renders Palestinian humanity invisible.

One of Brenner's photographs at first seems to provide an exception to the rule of exclusively Jewish group portraits: it shows a group of men posing with assault rifles, prayer beads, and hookahs, their heads and faces wrapped in kaffiyehs that leave only their eyes gazing menacingly ahead, with woven rugs depicting Islamic holy sites in Mecca and Jerusalem hung on the wall behind them. Their militant appearance seems to confirm all the clichés about Palestinians as either freedom fighters or terrorists. Remarkably, the picture manages both to invoke such fears and immediately to assuage them, sparing the viewer any direct confrontation with actual Palestinian resistance to Israeli rule: the title *Border Police Unit* (2010) indicates they are just a group of undercover police—Israelis *playing* Palestinians. On one hand, the initial ambiguity of the identity of these masked men provides a powerful aesthetic shock to the viewer's expectations about the meaning and trappings of identity, to the ability to visibly grasp ethnicity, citizenship, or cultural belonging with any certitude. Yet, on the other hand, Palestinians are only present in the work as a doubled specter: as an orientalist fiction and as absent targets of military and police repression.

* * *

However, aside from the monumental group portraits, it is not the case that only Jewish Israelis are pictured in *This Place*. An important counterpoint to the stultified, even reified, monuments to family are street photographs by Gilles Peress, which provide some of the only movement and life in the entire show. Shot mostly in East Jerusalem, at sites of friction between Jewish Israeli and Palestinian neighborhoods, they are also—along with some images in Ewald's broad survey—the only photographs in the show that both capture the texture of everyday life in these places *and* explicitly address the political conflict that structures those lives. Brenner and Cotton consistently present journalism as the bad object of fixed political identities and narratives, which art must transcend through the poetic celebration of land and humanity. Thus they are anxious to distance Peress's photographs from the prosaic context of photojournalism in which he often works, insisting in the wall text that Peress "uses photography as a means of understanding reality, beyond the media's calculated presentation of social and political situations." Despite the fact that Peress has been photographing in Israel and Palestine since the 1990s while reporting for newspapers and magazines, the photographs must be purged of their sociopolitical reference in order to be raised to the level of art. Peress, in contrast,

does not shy from realities of conflict that can be solved only politically, shooting in occupied Hebron/al-Khalil, on both sides of the checkpoint in Bethlehem, in Palestinian East Jerusalem, showing both daily
life there and the settlers who seek to transform it. Peress, too, depicts
someone, face obscured, sleeping outside on the ground underneath
an olive tree, a rug for a blanket, a stone for a pillow. But because the image is captioned *Bethlehem Checkpoint, Israeli Side* (2011), and presented
in a sequence of images that shows life on both sides of the checkpoint,
including waiting in line, clashing with soldiers, celebrating the release
of prisoners, playing in the street, and hanging out in the park, viewers
can begin to understand the historical significance of the figure.

One also gets some small glimpses of the diversity of Muslim,
Christian, Druze, and Jewish life in Ewald's *This Is Where I Live*, in
which she conducted photography workshops in fourteen communities, teaching mostly children but also some groups of adults the basics
of photography and how to use digital cameras, compiling the thousands of photos they took, and editing those down to about 350 five-
by-seven-inch prints. Yet the postcard-sized photos present a mostly
fragmentary sampling of close-ups of objects, occasionally with people or landscapes that become difficult to parse—an almost periscopic
look into lives without a broader sense of their context or the person
behind the camera. The uniform display of the photos on small shelves
advances a kind of normative claim about the egalitarian relationship
between each of these different views—photographers from each
group are accorded the same format and space for presentation and all
the small, identically sized photographs are simply lined up on shelves,
forming a grid. Yet this egalitarian presentation also obscures the real
differences in power between the subjects behind the camera: like
those between cadets at a Jewish military academy and those at a school
for Palestinian students affected by the occupation of Hebron, both of
whom she worked with. Brenner reportedly had refused Ewald's original proposal to work only with a group in Silwan, in Palestinian East
Jerusalem, where Peress shot his project, as "too narrow and tenden-
tious"; it was only when she included many other groups that he agreed.
(Lubow, 2016) In other words, the image of egalitarian diversity was
to be celebrated, especially among allegedly pre-political children, even
though, or perhaps because, it does not accord with the reality of unequal access to citizenship, civil and political rights, and education in
Israel and occupied Palestine.

Of course, artworks may also manage to articulate other meanings
apart from those engineered by the discursive apparatus that supports
and presents them. The glimpses of life under occupation provided by
Peress and Ewald provide the starting-point for narratives quite different from the one provided by the exhibition. One could begin to ask

what is historical, and not simply natural, about family resemblances. One could begin to scour the many landscapes for traces of history, as Eyal Weizman does in an exemplary re-reading of some of Shore's landscapes (included in his monograph but not in the exhibition). (Weizman, 2014: 77–80) Weizman examines a series of Shore's aerial landscapes that were shot while on a guided helicopter tour provided by The Israel Project, a nongovernmental *hasbara* and Israel-advocacy organization that, in addition to social-media campaigns, lobbying, and polling and focus groups, provides free narrated propaganda tours to journalists, giving them both talking points and usable footage for reporting about the country. Yet Weizman goes on to analyze the way in which a few of Shore's pictures from the trip also managed to capture the ruined remains of a Palestinian village destroyed in 1948, and seeks to reconstruct, after the fact and against the grain of the sponsoring organization's narrative, the counter-history of displacement and colonization they record.

There is one work in the exhibition, however, that does explicitly attempt to make visible the specific, violent workings of Israeli settler colonialism. In *Desert Bloom*, Fazal Sheikh presents forty-eight aerial photographs of sites in the Negev/Naqab desert. Although many of the loops, squares, and nested lines seem at first abstract, close attention to the surfaces might pick out a road or a radio tower, a wrecked airplane, a building, or the remains of a foundation. As the wall text explains, the locations featured are sites of former or existing Bedouin villages that have been displaced or destroyed, replaced by afforestation projects, industrial mines, military installations, and settlements, both since the foundation of the state in 1948 and in an ongoing struggle up to the present. An accompanying brochure provides the exact longitude and latitude of each site as well as analysis by geographers and aerial photography experts. Sheikh also conducted site visits with other experts where they gathered testimony, corroborated landmarks, and documented ongoing struggles over the land. Although the vast majority of the Bedouin inhabitants of the Negev/Naqab were expelled in 1948, those who remain struggle to gain recognition for their villages and ownership of land, which the Israeli state continually appropriates for its own purposes and to give to settlers.

On one hand, I want to argue that the forensic aesthetics of the kind practiced by Sheikh and Weizman is one of the most important inheritors of Sekula's critique of photographic humanism and his related practical engagement with realist and documentary photography. On the other hand, I also want to understand why Sheikh's project largely failed to communicate to the demonstrators any sign of resistance to colonial violence. One might argue that the demonstrators were just lazy or insufficiently savvy readers of conceptually-inflected contemporary art: failing to read the brochure that scrupulously documents the photo-graphs, they did not apprehend how Sheikh was *ironically* redeploying the phrase of his title, *Desert Bloom*. David Ben-Gurion's Zionist slogan about "making the desert bloom" is a founding myth of Israel, justifying the colonization of places like the Negev/Naqab and perpetuating the false idea that Palestine was unsettled and unproductive prior to Jewish immigration fueled by political Zionism. By depicting the traces of the forcible destruction of Palestinian villages and appropriation of their land in the Negev/Naqab since 1948, not only for the purposes of plant-ing forests but also for military bomb testing and industrial production, this "desert bloom" is recoded not as healthy, vital growth but as uncon-trolled, destructive aftermath, the way chemicals bloom in the environ-ment or a bruise blooms on flesh. (Like Koudelka and Lee, Sheikh also tends to personify the landscape.) But I am not convinced the demon-strators simply missed Sheikh's subtle point. Rather, as Sekula warned about the forensic aesthetic in works such as Fred Lonidier's *Health and Safety Game* (1976):

> The danger exists, here as in other works of socially conscious art, of being overcome by the very oppressive forms and condi-tions one is critiquing, of being devoured by the enormous ma-chinery of material and symbolic objectification. Political iro-ny walks a thin line between resistance and surrender. (Sekula, 1976/1978: 131)

By graphically depicting the objectification or violence done by oppres-sive forces, even ironic citations of those authoritative discourses risk reinstating that violence on a doubly victimized subject. Palestinians are erased from the picture a second time.

But something else is at work here: there are aesthetic reasons view-ers didn't go running to the captions to decipher the evidential clues of colonial violence to be found in *Desert Bloom*. In short, Sheikh's aerial photographs, beautiful monochromes, flat and parallel to the picture plane, verging on abstraction like any good Modernist picture, also fit the aesthetics of the other landscapes in the exhibition, especially when hung, as they were in Brooklyn, directly across from Shore's large-scale prints. They share a formalism of the photographic surface that discouraged viewing them as referential traces.

* * *

Sheikh's work in Israel-Palestine, however, also extends beyond the *This Place* exhibition. Weizman, a key practitioner and theorist of contemporary forensic aesthetics, took the *Desert Bloom* photos as the basis for a follow-up book, *The Conflict Shoreline*, which tracks in precise detail the political, technical, and ecological means by which the Israeli state controls the Negev/Naqab, weaving Sheikh's photos together with colonial-era aerial photographs, evidence produced by human rights researchers, as well as archival documents from Bedouin themselves, such as tax receipts, ledgers, deeds, and family photographs, that help to prove their long inhabitation and stewardship of the land. (Weizman and Sheikh, 2015) This is precisely the kind of practice in defense of individual human rights and against the forces of an oppressor state that Sekula imagined when he coined the term "counter-forensics."[26] (Sekula, 1996/2003) After many of the Bedouin's legal claims to the land had been thrown out of Israeli courts, the accumulated evidence was made public in a report by the NGO Zochrot, in a commission staged by Israelis and Palestinians that became a forum of last resort. And Sheikh has subsequently expanded this forensic forum to art and museum galleries by presenting the evidence of and accounts of resistance by the Bedouin in the Negev village of al-Araqib, which has been destroyed by the IDF close to one hundred times. These and other projects documenting the ongoing destruction of Palestinian settlements partly answer Sekula's appeal for "a truly critical social documentary that will frame the crime, the trial, and the system of justice and its official myths." (Sekula, 1976/1978: 122)

In one video shot by the villagers documenting their struggles, viewers see them sleeping out in the open desert after their homes have been destroyed.[27] Unlike Wall's account of the olive pickers in his picture, the geopolitical situation that forces them to sleep under the stars is essential to the meaning of the scene. Such activist media that explicitly takes the side of the oppressed is precisely the kind of work that Brenner would dismiss as merely journalism, which lacks the sufficiently universal and transcendental qualities to be included in an art exhibition such as his. Yet a single frame from this noisy, low-quality video provides just as powerful an aesthetico-political depiction of vulnerability, violence, and the exercise of freedom as Wall's meticulously shot and stitched-together image.

Desert Bloom is also only one part of the larger *Erasure Trilogy* that Sheikh used his time in Israel-Palestine to make. *Memory Trace*, another part of the trilogy, has been shown at other venues concurrently with *This Place*, and unlike the latter also traveled to exhibition spaces in Palestine. Similarly to *Desert Bloom*, *Memory Trace* seeks out and documents the ruins of Palestinian villages destroyed during the Nakba and often erased from Israeli maps. The photographs sometimes discover standing buildings, or ruins, or just an empty clearing in a forest, and are paired with captions describing the village that include: the population and number of houses in 1948; date of military occupation, with the name of occupying military or paramilitary forces and the name of the military operation; the history of the site after 1948 and its contemporary status; and a note on whether the village has an official Israeli name and what that is, and whether it appears on contemporary maps of Israel. Yet *Memory Trace* also combines this forensic photography with portraits of elderly Palestinian refugees who, prohibited from returning to their villages, provide testimony of their flight and exile, detailed in an accompanying caption. One of the most poignant, *Anisa Aḥmad Jāber Maḥamīd, Umm el-Fahem, Born in 1908* (2011), shows a seated elderly woman wearing a headscarf, positioned toward the camera with her eyes pinched closed. The portrait turns on the contrast between her frontal address toward the camera and the pictorial resonance that plays across the surface of the picture between her deeply lined face and the folds of her scarf. Not simply a picture of absorption or the natural aging of a face-as-landscape, the picture turns on her outwardness and directedness toward the viewer, which are evident in her pose for the camera as well as the accompanying text that carries her spoken testimony, and which are not canceled but further accentuated by her blindness. Breaking from the horizontal view from above of the aerial photograph and from the lateral axis of absorption in the family photographs, these testimonial portraits introduce an axis of ethical address distinct from the accumulation of tabular evidence or the internal ideal of inward relatedness.

* * *

In the case of the official framing discourse of *This Place*, its abstract humanism ultimately rests not on a recognizably "humanist" style of photography, but paradoxically on an authoritative, impersonal discourse of aesthetic formalism, which, in the case of photography, privileges the large-format tableau. Even as the photographs are presented as only neutrally pointing at things without judging or even naming them—merely indexing "this place"—the internal formal cohesion of the apparently autonomous, enframed artistic works elevates them to a transcendent aesthetic level "above" or more fundamentally "below" the contingencies of history and politics. In contrast with this abstract humanism and its naturalization of the political present, it turns out that work like Sheikh's forensic realism ultimately finds recourse to another humanism, in testimony of those excluded from the full visibility or rights as humans, without a place of their own. As Sekula maintained: "If we are to listen to, and act in solidarity with, the polyphonic testimony of the oppressed and exploited, we should recognize that some of this testimony … will take the ambiguous form of visual documents, documents of the 'microphysics' of barbarism." Our problem, he continued, "as artists and intellectuals living near but not at the center of a global system of power, will be to help prevent the cancellation of that testimony by more authoritative and official texts." (Sekula, 1986: 64) Through these documents, a claim to universal humanity reemerges, a claim made precisely from the place of dehumanization.

Notes

1. Exhibitions venues to date include: DOX Center for Contemporary Art, Prague, October 24, 2014–March 2, 2015; Tel Aviv Museum of Art, May 14–September 6, 2015; Norton Museum of Art, West Palm Beach, Florida, October 15, 2015–January 17, 2016; Brooklyn Museum, February 22–June 5, 2016; and smaller versions of the exhibition have been shown at University Art Museum, Albany, State University of New York, February 1–April 7, 2018; Picker Art Gallery, Colgate University, February 1–May 20, 2018; Tang Teaching Museum, Skidmore College, February 3–April 22, 2018; Wellin Museum of Art, Hamilton College, February 10–June 10, 2018. See the exhibition website, http://this-place.org.

2. The Decolonial Cultural Front was an umbrella for various activist groups including MTL, G.U.L.F. (Gulf Ultra Luxury Faction), We Will Not Be Silent, Direct Action Front for Palestine, Jews for Palestinian Right of Return, Rename and Reclaim, Rude Mechanical Orchestra, and the Brooklyn AntiGentrification Network. In the interest of full disclosure, I attended and documented the demonstration but was not involved in its organization or execution.

3. The phrase is repeated in press material for the show; see, for example, "This Place," The Frances Young Tang Teaching Museum and Art Gallery at Skidmore College, https://tang.skidmore.edu/exhibitions/216-this-place. A similar rhetoric is repeated in the review by Smith (2016).

4. Aside from some factual errors, the article seems to be a second- or third-hand account based on McCarthy (2016).

5. The critical literature on *Family of Man* is vast. In addition to the essays by Barthes and Sekula discussed here, key texts include Sandeen (1995), Hirsch (1997), Back and Schmidt-Linsenhoff (2005), Turner (2012), Azoulay (2013), Garb (2014), Hurm, Reitz, and Zamir (2018).

6. Sekula emphasizes the connection between American military and economic power through the example of Guatemala, where an American-backed coup had recently installed a military dictatorship in 1954, overthrowing the democratically elected president in order to halt his labor reforms and nationalization and redistribution of uncultivated land, the vast majority of which was still owned by the American United Fruit Company and the comprador class.

7. The latter statement is commented upon in Decolonial Cultural Front (2016).

8. According to Lubow (2016). Those familiar with the show indicated to me that at least one Palestinian with Israeli citizenship was invited to and then disinvited from the project, at the insistence of a foreign photographer, and a collaborating curator quit in response.

9. On thinking diaspora beyond the horizon of return, see Hall (1994); with regard to political Zionism in particular, also see Boyarin and Boyarin (1993).

10. A complete list of sponsors, including Bank Hapoalim, a major commercial bank in Israel that also finances and provides bank services to illegal settlements, can be found at http://www.this-place.org/about/supporters/. The figure of $6 million is from Lubow. The BDS movement holds that projects promoting "coexistence" between Israelis and Palestinians serve to normalize the status quo of the occupation and should be boycotted; they call instead for "coresistance." See Palestinian Campaign for the Academic and Cultural Boycott of Israel (2014).

11. By liberal Zionism I mean the justification of the current state of Israel as both a Jewish and democratic state, and that the Palestinian Nakba and subsequent occupation are unfortunate but secondary epiphenomena to its existence. The

viewpoint is clearly articulated by Gaviszon (2015). Gaviszon's interview is one of a series of interviews with eleven Jewish Israeli intellectuals, plus one Palestinian peace activist, conducted by Brenner to accompany the exhibition; see http://www. this-place.org/photographers/frederic-brenner/. The Basic Law titled Israel as the Nation-State of the Jewish People, adopted in 2018, declares that the right of self-determination in Israel is unique to the Jewish people and that complete and united Jerusalem is its capital (meaning the illegal, unilateral annexation of East Jerusalem); demotes Arabic from its status as an official language; and declares the national value of promoting Jewish settlement. For the claim that the nationality law, on the one hand, makes explicit the unequal contradiction between Jewishness and democracy present since Israel's founding and, on the other, further accelerates the expropriation of the rights of non-Jews, see Boehm (2018).

12. Taglit-Birthright Israel is an organization that offers free ten-day trips to Israel for young Jewish adults from across the world (mostly from the U.S. and Canada), funded by the government of Israel, the Jewish Federation system and Keren Hayesod, the Jewish Agency, and many private organizations and individual funders, including cofounder Charles Bronfman, whose philanthropy also contributed to *This Place*. Tour participants are introduced to young Israelis serving in the military to further their identification with the state, but prevented from traveling to the Occupied Palestinian Territory and, beginning in late 2017, from meeting with Palestinians, including those with Israeli citizenship. In Summer 2018, a number of Birthright participants walked off their tours after they had been given maps that showed all of the West Bank as part of Israel, and their questions about the occupation, the separation wall, and Palestine were ignored or downplayed. See Maltz (2017) and Hasson (2018).

13. Miki Kratsman, an experienced Israeli photographer and fixer for the show, agreed to facilitate only on the condition invitees also had the opportunity to visit the West Bank; Miki Kratsman, interview with author, July 26, 2018.

14. The UN and international law refer to the West Bank and Gaza Strip, occupied by Israel after the 1967 Six-Day War, as Occupied Palestinian Territory. The state of Palestine was declared in 1988 and applied to join the United Nations as a member state in 2011, when its application was denied by a veto from the United States, a permanent member of the Security Council. Palestine was accepted to the UN as a non-member observer state by a vote in the General Assembly in 2012 (resolution 67/19).

15. Both the logotype for the exhibition and the chapter titles for Shore's monograph *From the Galilee to the Negev* include text in English, Hebrew, and Arabic, like Israeli road signs. However, Shore's book, which also includes a helpful map indicating the sites where his photographs were taken, notes that the names of geographic features, presumably including those used in his photograph titles, are drawn from the *Times Atlas of the World*, supplemented by conventional English place names. Thus Shore did not directly adopt Hebraicized place names from Israeli maps, but did inherit them from other more authoritative sources, including those marked by an earlier, British colonial history.

16. This point is also made in MTL Collective (2018), which was published after my essay was completed.

17. See Decolonize This Place, http://www.decolonizethisplace.org; and, on subsequent organizing and actions, MTL Collective (2018).

18. The captions, chronology, and lexicon are by Ray Dolphin and Gilad Baram, in Koudelka (2013).

19. See also Sheikh's *Desert Bloom*, included in *This Place* and discussed below. This point is also articulated in relation to Wall's photograph by Felshin (2016).

20. Based on the prison's proximity to Mitzpe Ramon and the description in Wall's interview how the orchard owner recycles wastewater from the prison, it is most likely Nafha Prison, a high-security prison that also houses Palestinian "security" detainees from the West Bank and Gaza. Virtually all criminal and security cases against Palestinians without Israeli citizenship are tried in military

courts that have a 99.74 percent conviction rate, and also allow for administrative detention without charge; the conviction rate for Israelis indicted for crimes against Palestinians in the West Bank, which are tried in civilian courts, is 43.3 percent, but only roughly 10 percent of investigations lead to an indictment. See Wall (2014: 170–171); Levinson (2011); and Yesh Din (2017).

21. On the important role of artistic modernism in legitimating the post-independence Zionist state as part of a universal, secular, nominally socialist, and cosmopolitan political order, see the forthcoming dissertation by Chelsea Haines, "Staging the Modern, Building the Nation: Exhibiting Israeli Art, 1939–1965" (CUNY Graduate Center). I thank her for generously sharing her insights on art, architecture, and politics in Israel with me.

22. Shore's landscapes in the exhibition are only part of a larger project of more diverse views that include street photographs and scenes of everyday life as well as surveys of archeological sites; see Shore (2014).

23. Remarkably, the essayist in Struth's monograph argues that although the "ideological agenda" of Brenner's project is clear—"to curb and deflect criticism directed at the politics of the Jewish state"—Struth's photographs do not participate in it because, with reference to the simulationist theories of Jean Baudrillard, they are ultimately about the impossibility of accessing or photographically representing reality. (Loock, 2014)

24. The wall text is drawn from an interview published in the catalogue, where Waplington elaborates that he thinks the work "succeeds in depicting Jewish life in the West Bank outside of the distraction of the narrative of war and political conflict presented in the media," thus rehearsing the exhibition's larger claim to separate a more fundamental form of life from the superficial "distraction" of politics and its representation in journalism. (Waplington, 2014: 9).

25. Waplington told an interviewer, "I believe emphatically … that everybody should be allowed to go where they want on this planet. It's a Utopian position, but in that context, I agree that the settlers can be there—though what I don't agree with is that they can forcibly remove everyone else." (Waplington quoted in Hodges, 2014). Such a "utopian" position requires ignoring that Israeli state and military facilitation of settlement in occupied territory is a war crime. The settlers are not simply "being" there, but expropriating conquered land, which is by definition forcible.

26. See also the discussion of the term in Keenan (2014). I am also indebted to Keenan's ongoing reading of Barthes and humanism in various public talks and conversations.

27. Available in the compilation video *Demolitions* (ca. 2016), online at *Erasures*, Slought Foundation, https://slought.org/resources/erasures.

Bibliography

Ariella Azoulay, "'The Family of Man': A Visual Universal Declarations of Human Rights," in *The Human Snapshot*, eds Thomas Keenan and Tirdad Zolghadr (Meilen, Switzerland: Luma Foundation; Annandale-on-Hudson, NY: Center for Curatorial Studies, Bard College; Berlin: Sternberg Press, 2013), 19–48.

Jean Back and Viktoria Schmidt-Linsenhoff (eds), *The Family of Man 1955–2001: Humanism and Postmodernism: A Reappraisal of the Photo Exhibition by Edward Steichen* (Marburg: Jonas Verlag, 2005).

Roland Barthes, "The Great Family of Man" (1956), in *Mythologies*, trans. Annette Lavers (New York: Hill and Wang, 1972).

Omri Boehm, "Did Israel Just Stop Trying to Be a Democracy?" *New York Times*, July 26, 2018, https://www.nytimes.com/2018/07/26/opinion/israel-law-jewish-democracy-apartheid-palestinian.html. Accessed July 26, 2018.

Daniel Boyarin and Jonathan Boyarin, "Diaspora: Generation and the Ground of Jewish Identity," *Critical Inquiry* 19, no. 4 (Summer 1993): 693–725.

Frédéric Brenner, afterward, *This Place*, exh. cat. (London: Mack, 2014).

Charlotte Cotton, introduction to *This Place*, exh. cat. (London: Mack, 2014).

Decolonial Cultural Front, *Decolonize This Place*, flyer, 2016, https://decolonizethisplace.files.wordpress.com/2016/05/decolonizethisplace.pdf. Accessed February 26, 2017.

Decolonial Cultural Front, "Unprecedented Funding for *This Place*," 2016, https://decolonizethisplace.files.wordpress.com/2016/05/fundingthisplace.pdf. Accessed February 26, 2017.

Nina Felshin, "A Photo Exhibition About Israel and the West Bank that Chooses Sides," *Hyperallergic*, May 13, 2016, https://hyperallergic.com/298529/a-photo-exhibition-about-israel-and-the-west-bank-that-chooses-sides/. Accessed May 13, 2016.

Michael Fried, *Why Photography Matters as Art as Never Before* (New Haven: Yale University Press, 2008).

Tamar Garb, "Rethinking Sekula from the Global South: Humanist Photography Revisited," *Grey Room*, no. 55 (Spring 2014): 34–57.

Ruth Gaviszon, "Israel as a Jewish and Democratic State," 2015, *This Place: Thinker Series*, https://vimeo.com/119585337. Accessed July 14, 2017.

Nir Hasson, "For Second Time in Two Weeks: U.S. Jews Walk Off Birthright Trip to Join Anti-occupation Activity," *Haaretz*, July 15, 2018, https://www.haaretz.com/israel-news/.premium-young-jews-walk-off-birthright-trip-to-join-anti-occupation-activity-1.6271943. Accessed July 15, 2018.

Isabel Kershner, "Trump Cites Israel's 'Wall' as Model. The Analogy Is Iffy," *New York Times*, January 27, 2017, https://www.nytimes.com/2017/01/27/world/middleeast/trump-mexico-wall-israel-west-bank.html. Accessed July 17, 2018.

JNi.Media, "Anti-Zionist Mob Invades Brooklyn Museum to Protest Nuance and Humanism," *Jewish Press*, http://www.jewishpress.com/news/breaking-news/anti-zionist-mob-invades-brooklyn-museum-to-protest-nuance-and-humanism/2016/05/10/0/. Accessed September 13, 2016.

Stuart Hall, "Cultural Identity and Diaspora," in *Colonial Discourse and Post-colonial Theory: A Reader*, eds Patrick Williams and Laura Chrisman (New York: Columbia University Press, 1994), 392–403.

Marianne Hirsch, *Family Frames: Photography, Narrative and Postmemory* (Cambridge, MA: Harvard University Press, 1997).

Nick Hodges, "British Photographer Nick Waplington Captures the Lives of Jewish Settlers in the Occupied Territories," *Independent*, October 26, 2014, https://www.independent.co.uk/news/world/middle-east/british-photographer-nick-waplington-captures-the-lives-of-jewish-settlers-in-the-occupied-9815174.html. Accessed July 27, 2018.

Gerd Hurm, Anke Reitz, and Shamoon Zamir (eds) *The Family of Man Revisited: Photography in a Global Age* (London: I.B. Tauris, 2018).

Walid Khalidi, *All That Remains: The Palestinian Villages Occupied and Depopulated by Israel in 1948* (Washington, DC: Institute for Palestine Studies, 1992).

Thomas Keenan, "Counter-Forensics and Photography," *Grey Room*, no. 55 (Spring 2014): 58–77.

Josef Koudelka, *Wall* (New York: Aperture Foundation and Éditions Xavier Barral, 2013).

Chaim Levinson, "Nearly 100% of All Military Court Cases in West Bank End in Conviction, Haaretz Learns," *Haaretz*, November 29, 2011, https://www.haaretz.com/1.5214377. Accessed July 26, 2018.

Ulrich Loock, "Thomas Struth's Photographs from Israel/Palestine," in *Thomas Struth* ([London]: Mack, 2014), i–xi.

Arthur Lubow, "For 12 Photographers, an Anxious Gaze on Israel and the West Bank," *New York Times*, February 11, 2016, https://www.nytimes.com/2016/02/14/arts/design/for-12-photographers-an-anxious-gaze-on-israel-and-the-west-bank.html. Accessed May 6, 2018.

Judy Maltz, "Birthright Orders Trip Providers to End Meet-ups With Israeli Arabs," *Haaretz*, November 2, 2017, https://www.haaretz.com/israel-news/.premium-birthright-orders-trip-providers-to-end-meet-ups-with-israeli-arabs-1.5462267. Accessed July 27, 2018.

Rebecca McCarthy, "Faced with Brooklyn Museum Inaction, Protesters Target Two Exhibitions," *Hyperallergic*, May 8, 2016, https://hyperallergic.com/297401/faced-with-brooklyn-museum-inaction-protesters-target-two-exhibitions/. Accessed September 13, 2016.

MTL Collective, "From Institutional Critique to Institutional Liberation? A Decolonial Perspective on the Crises of Contemporary Art," *October*, no. 165 (Summer 2018): 192–227.

Margaret Olin, "A Birthright Trip for Photographers? 'This Place' at the Brooklyn Museum," Touching Photographs, May 12, 2016, https://touchingphoto-graphs.com/2016/05/12/a-birthright-trip-for-photographers-this-place-at-the-brooklyn-museum/. Accessed September 13, 2016.

Palestinian Campaign for the Academic and Cultural Boycott of Israel, "Guidelines for the International Academic Boycott of Israel," Palestinian BDS National Committee, 2014, https://bdsmovement.net/pacbi/academic-boycott-guidelines. Accessed May 6, 2018.

Eric Sandeen, *Picturing an Exhibition: The Family of Man and 1950s America* (Albuquerque: University of New Mexico Press, 1995).

Allan Sekula, "Dismantling Modernism, Reinventing Documentary (Notes on the Politics of Representation)" (1976/1978), in *Dismal Science: Photo Works 1972–1996* (Normal, IL: Illinois State University, 1999), 117–138.

Allan Sekula, "The Traffic in Photographs" (1981), in *Photography against the Grain* (Halifax: The Press of the Nova Scotia College of Art and Design, 1984), 77–101.

Allan Sekula, "The Body and the Archive," *October*, no. 39 (Winter 1986): 3–64.

Allan Sekula, "Photography and the Limits of National Identity" (1993/2006), *Grey Room*, no 55 (Spring 2014): 28–33.

Stephen Shore, *From the Galilee to the Negev* (London: Phaidon, 2014).

Roberta Smith, "Capturing Human Moments Amid Chaos in Israel and the West Bank," *New York Times*, February 18, 2016, https://www.nytimes.com/2016/02/19/arts/design/capturing-human-moments-amid-chaos-in-israel-and-the-west-bank.html. Accessed May 6, 2018.

Fred Turner, "*The Family of Man* and the Politics of Attention in Cold War America," *Public Culture* 24, no. 1 (2012): 55–84.

Jeff Wall, "Jeff Wall Interviewed by Charlotte Cotton," in *This Place*, exh. cat. (London: Mack, 2014), 170–172.

Nick Waplington, "Nick Waplington Interviewed by Charlotte Cotton," in *This Place*, exh. cat. (London: Mack, 2014), 185–186.

Regina Weinreich, "Frederic Brenner, the 'Jewish Christo,' Uses Photography To Challenge Israel Debate," *Forward*, June 7, 2014, https://forward.com/culture/199050/frederic-brenner-the-jewish-christo-uses-photograp/. Accessed May 6, 2018.

Eyal Weizman, "Holey Earth," in Stephen Shore,
From the Galilee to the Negev (London: Phaidon, 2014),
77–80.

Eyal Weizman and Fazal Sheikh, *The Conflict Shoreline:
Colonization as Climate Change in the Negev Desert*
(Göttingen, Germany: Steidl; Brooklyn, NY: Cabinet
Books, 2015).

Yesh Din, "Data Sheet, December 2017: Law
Enforcement on Israeli Civilians in the West Bank,"
2017, https://www.yesh-din.org/en/data-sheet-decem-
ber-2017-law-enforcement-israeli-civilians-west-bank/.
Accessed July 27, 2018.

About the authors

Anthony Abiragi received a PhD in French Literature from New York University (2008) and an MA in Philosophy from the New School (2004). He teaches in the Program for Writing and Rhetoric at the University of Colorado, Boulder, where his classes include "Writing in the Visual Arts." He has presented papers on Gordon Matta-Clark, Tehching Hsieh, Claire Fontaine, Thomas Hirschhorn, Abbas Kiarostami, and Claire Denis.

Barbara Baert is Professor of Art History at the University of Leuven (KU Leuven). Her research is situated in the field of Iconology, Art Theory, and Medieval Art. She published several books and articles, with emphasis on the role of the sensorium in the arts, on visual culture and new hermeneutical paradigms such as Echo and Kairos, and on the past, presence and future of visual anthropology. She is the founder of the series *Studies in Iconology* (Peeters Publishers) and of the annual *Recollection. Experimental Reflections on Texts, Images and Ideas* (Leuven University Press). In 2016 Barbara Baert was awarded with the Francqui Prize (www.francquifoundation.be) for her outstanding interdisciplinary achievements in the *Bildwissenschaften* in particular and for her international impact on the Human Sciences in general.

Edwin Carels is Senior Film Programmer and Curator for the International Film Festival of Rotterdam. As a writer Carels publishes essays on media-archaeology, visual arts, film and animation. As a teacher and researcher he is affiliated with the School of Arts KASK/HoGent (University College Ghent – Faculty of Fine Arts), from which he holds a PhD in the Arts. He is currently working on his post-doc project 'Counter-archives.' As a curator Carels has worked on exhibitions together with among others Dora Garcia, Luc Tuymans, Chris Marker, The Quay Brothers, Robert Breer, Jan Svankmajer, Zoe Beloff, Ken Jacobs, Peter Kubelka, and Apichatpong Weeraseethakul. Carels is also affiliated with the Museum of Contemporary Art in Antwerp, the M HKA, where he has curated thematic shows such as *El Hotel Eléctrico* (2014), *Graphology* (2011), *Animism* (2010) and *The Projection Project* (2006).

Bart De Baere is the Director of M HKA, Museum van Hedendaagse Kunst Antwerpen since 2002. De Baere served as chairman of the Flemish Council for Culture, where he advised the government on cultural policy. From 1999 until 2001 he also acted as advisor for the Flemish Minister of Culture concerning cultural heritage and contemporary art. De Baere has also been chairman of the Flemish Council for Museums. From 1986 until 2001 he was curator in S.M.A.K. Ghent, and also co-curated external projects, such as Documenta IX. In 2016 he was involved in the establishment of a biennial in South Africa, as a consultant for the City of Johannesburg. He was a member of the International Advisory Council for the network of Soros Centres for contemporary art in Eastern Europe.

Stefanie Diekmann is Professor of Media Studies and Image Theory at Hildesheim University. Her ongoing research interests are the intermedia relations of images (both photographic and filmic) and the representation of media in fiction and non-fiction film. Her current work focuses on documentary film, with a particular interest in interview situations and the uses of footage. Recent publications include: *Backstage* (Berlin: Kadmos 2013), *Six Feet Under* (Berlin: diaphanes 2014) and *Die andere Szene* (ed., Berlin: Theater der Zeit 2014).

Carles Guerra is the Director of the Fundació Antoni Tàpies. He received his PhD in Fine Arts from the University of Barcelona. His professional career has developed in the fields of curatorial practice, art criticism, visual production, teaching and academic research. In 2004 he was appointed Director of the Primavera Fotogràfica de Catalunya. From 2009 until 2011 he acted as Director of the Virreina Centre de la Imatge in Barcelona. Subsequently, he was appointed Chief Curator at MACBA Barcelona from 2011 until 2013. In his research, Guerra investigates the dialogical aspects of artistic practice and the cultural policies of Post-Fordism. He has taught at the Universitat Pompeu Fabra as associate professor and lectured at many other institutions.

Clara Masnatta is a writer, independent curator, and post-doctoral fellow at the ICI Berlin Institute of Cultural Inquiry. She holds a joint PhD degree in Comparative Literature from Harvard University and from the Humboldt-Universität zu Berlin. Her exhibition of Gisèle Freund photo portraits *Exhibición-espectáculo* will open in 2019 at the Sívori Museum in Buenos Aires, and is scheduled to travel to Paris and Berlin with its accompanying bilingual exhibition catalog. Her writing has appeared in books (*About Raymond Williams*, Routledge, 2010; *Los primeros modernos. Horacio Coppola, Grete Stern y la fotografía argentina*, La Marca/Interzona, 2018), periodicals (*Art in Translation; ExBerliner*), and the catalog for Rinko Kawauchi's retrospective at the Kunst Haus Wien in 2015. Masnatta's research focuses on women in photography, cinema, and the arts, as well as transnational flows across Europe and the Americas.

W.J.T. Mitchell is Gaylord Donnelley Distinguished Service Professor of English and Art History at the University of Chicago. He served as Chair of the English Department from 1988 to 1991, and has been the editor of *Critical Inquiry* since 1978. Professor Mitchell has received fellowships from the Guggenheim Foundation, the National Endowment for the Humanities, and the American Philosophical Society, as well as research conference grants from the Rockefeller Foundation and the Exxon Educational Foundation. His work is primarily focused on the interplay of vision and language in art, literature, and media, and the subjects of his articles range from general problems in the theory of representation, to specific issues in cultural politics and political culture. His books include *Blake's Composite Art* (Princeton, 1977), *Iconology* (Chicago, 1986), *Picture Theory* (Chicago, 1994), *The Last Dinosaur Book* (Chicago, 1998), *What Do Pictures Want?* (Chicago, 2005), *Cloning Terror: The War of Images, 9–11 to the Present* (Chicago, 2011), *Seeing Through Race* (Harvard, 2012), and *Image Science: Iconology, Media Aesthetics, and Art History* (Chicago, 2015).

Marco Poloni lives and works as an artist in Berlin. His work spans cinema, photography, text and installation. Over the past several years, Poloni has been building an index of plots, problems and tropes of the Mediterranean, www.theanalogueislandbureau.net. This archive of documents reformulates and expands a number of geopolitical scripts and anthropological narratives of this area, focusing on relationships between social invisibility and power, subjectivity and ideology, individual action and political change. His last large work, "Codename: Osvaldo," shown in 2016 at the Centre Culturel Suisse in Paris, provides a comprehensive synthesis of his research to date.

Anja Isabel Schneider studied American literature in Los Angeles (UCLA) and Tübingen (Eberhard Karls Universität), as well as art history and curating in London (The Courtauld Institute of Art; Goldsmiths College). She is currently a PhD candidate in Curatorial Research at the University of Leuven (KU Leuven, Lieven Gevaert Research Centre for Photography, Art and Visual Culture) and M HKA, Museum van Hedendaagse Kunst Antwerpen. She is a member of the research team *Art Against the Grain of "Collective Sisyphus": The Case of Allan Sekula's* Ship of Fools / The Dockers' Museum *(2010–2013).* In 2011, she was the laureate of the 4th edition of MARCO/Frac Lorraine Award for Young

Curators. Her writing has appeared in magazines, exhibition catalogs and artist monographs.

Stephanie Schwartz is a Lecturer in History of Art at University College London. Her writing on photography and film has appeared in *October*, *Oxford Art Journal* and *ARTMargins*. She was recently awarded a Creative Capital Warhol Foundation Arts Writers Grant to write 'Martha Rosler: Seeing the Screen', an essay on the politics of disclosure. Schwartz is also working on a related project on protest photography. Her initial consideration of subject appeared in her Tate Modern *In Focus* study of Allan Sekula's *Waiting for Tear Gas [White Globe to Black]* (1999–2000).

Jonathan Stafford is an interdisciplinary scholar of the sea, with a particular focus on maritime mobilities, landscape and culture. His PhD (2015) examined the heterodox narratives of modernity presented by nineteenth-century colonial steamship connections with the East. He is a Lecturer in Cultural Studies at the University of Nottingham.

Alexander Streitberger is Professor of Modern and Contemporary Art History at the Université catholique de Louvain (UCLouvain), and Director of the Lieven Gevaert Research Centre for Photography, Art and Visual Culture. He is editor of the Lieven Gevaert Series. His research interests are focused on the relationship between language theory and art in the 20th century, photographic art and the theory of photography since the 1960s, photography and the book, the encounter between the still (photographic) and the moving (filmic) image, and panoramic and dioramic images in contemporary art and visual culture. His publications include: *Ausdruck – Modell – Diskurs. Sprachreflexion in der Kunst des 20. Jahrhunderts* (Reimer, 2004), *Situational Aesthetics. Selected writings by Victor Burgin* (Leuven University Press, 2009), *Shifting Places: Peter Downsbrough, the Photographs* (Leuven University Press, 2011), *The Photofilmic. Entangled Images in Contemporary Art and Visual Culture* (Leuven University Press, 2016).

Hilde Van Gelder is Professor of Modern and Contemporary Art History at the University of Leuven (KU Leuven). She is director of the Lieven Gevaert Research Centre for Photography, Art and Visual Culture. She is editor of the Lieven Gevaert Series (Leuven University Press) and of *Image [&] Narrative*, a peer reviewed online journal, part of Open Humanities Press. Her research focuses on how photography within contemporary visual art and culture is an operative force for both re-legitimating and re-imagining fundamental rights. Occasionally she guest curates research exhibitions, such as *Inventer le possible* at

Jeu de Paume, Paris (2014) and *Allan Sekula. Collective Sisyphus* at the Fundació Antoni Tàpies, Barcelona (2017). She also writes as an art critic for artforum.com, and has held blogs for Jeu de Paume (2011) and for Fotomuseum Winterthur (2012).

Benjamin J. Young teaches the history of photography at Parsons School of Design, The New School. He is also managing editor of *Grey Room*, where he coedited, with Marie Muracciole, the special issue "Allan Sekula and the Traffic in Photographs" (Spring 2014). He completed a PhD in the Department of Rhetoric at the University of California, Berkeley, with a dissertation titled "Sympathetic Materialism: Allan Sekula's Photo-Works, 1971–2000," which he is currently turning into a book. His essay "Documents and Documentary: San Diego, c. 1973," on artists in San Diego including Sekula, David Antin, Eleanor Antin, John Baldessari, Fred Lonidier, Martha Rosler, Phel Steinmetz, and Carrie Mae Weems, appeared to the exhibition catalog *The Uses of Photography: Art, Politics, and the Reinvention of a Medium* (Museum of Contemporary Art San Diego, 2016).

A Note on Allan Sekula's Life

Allan Sekula (1951–2013) was an artist, writer, critic, and poet. Shortly after receiving his MFA from UCSD in 1974, he began publishing influential articles that probed the social uses of photography in *Artforum*. Sekula taught briefly at NYU in the School of Cinema Studies, then for five years at Ohio State University, before returning in 1985 to Los Angeles to join the faculty of California Institute of the Arts where he taught for nearly three decades. The essays collected in his first book, *Photography against the Grain: Essays and Photo Works 1973–1983* (Press of the Nova Scotia College of Art and Design, 1984 [reprint MACK, 2016]), significantly altered the way in which the documentary function of photography was conceptualized. His more recent volumes mobilize us through his visual art and writing to carefully consider the effects of capitalism, globalization, labor and class.

Sekula's other books include *Fish Story* (Richter Verlag, 1995 [reprint MACK, 2018]); *Geography Lesson: Canadian Notes* (MIT Press, 1996); *Dismal Science* (Illinois State University Galleries, 1999); *Performance under Working Conditions* (Generali Foundation, 2003); *TITANIC's wake* (Le Point du Jour, 2003); and *Polonia and Other Fables* (The Renaissance Society and Zachęta National Gallery of Art, 2009). These range thematically from critical investigations of the history of photography to studies of family life in the grip of the military-industrial complex, branching out into explorations of myths of national identity. Sekula also actively collaborated on *Constantin Meunier. A Dialogue with Allan Sekula* (ed. Hilde Van Gelder, Leuven University Press, 2005); and on *Critical Realism in Contemporary Art. Around Allan Sekula's Photography* (eds Jan Baetens and Hilde Van Gelder, Leuven University Press, 2006).

His longstanding interest in questions of maritime economies and their relation to globalization led to extended photographic works that were included in Documenta 11 (2002) and Documenta 12 (2007). Since the early 1970s, his works with photographic sequences, written texts, slide shows, and sound recordings have traveled a path close to cinema. In addition to *Gala* (2005), Sekula's other works in video and film include *Tsukiji* (2001), *Lottery of the Sea* (2006), and in collaboration with co-director Noël Burch, *The Forgotten Space* (2010), the latter having won the Special Jury Prize in the Orizzonti Competition at the 2010 Venice Film Festival. A collected edition of, mostly, his early writings has been published in Polish and French translations (by Karolina Lewandowska and Krzysztof Pijarski for the Zachęta National Gallery of Art, 2010; and by Marie Muracciole for Beaux-Arts de Paris, 2013).

Posthumous solo exhibitions of Sekula's work were organized by Johann Jacobs Museum, Zürich, Switzerland (2014), Galerie Michel Rein (2014), NTC CCA, Singapore (2015), TBA21, Vienna (2017), Beirut Art Center (2017), Fundació Antoni Tàpies, Barcelona (2017). Posthumous group exhibitions featuring his work were organized by Whitney Biennial (2014); Museo Nacional Centro de Arte Reina Sofía, Madrid (2015); Centre Pompidou, Paris (2015); MoMA, New York (2015); Museum Folkwang, Essen (2016); Museum of Contemporary Art, San Diego (2016), Documenta 14, Athens/Kassel (2017).

Posthumous publications either exclusively or largely featuring his visual art and critical writings include "Allan Sekula and the Traffic in Photographs," special issue of *Grey Room* (55) edited by Benjamin J. Young and Marie Muracciole: (MIT, 2014); *Facing the Music: Documenting Walt Disney Concert Hall and the Redevelopment of Downtown Los Angeles*, a Project by Allan Sekula edited by Edward Dimendberg (East of Borneo, 2015); *Allan Sekula.* Ship of Fools / The Dockers' Museum, edited by Hilde Van Gelder (Leuven University Press, 2015); and *Allan Sekula: Mining Section* (Bureau des mines), edited by Nicola Setari and Hilde Van Gelder (Ghent: MER Paper Kunsthalle, 2016). Posthumous symposia organized around Sekula's works and ongoing influence took place in Zurich (2014), Singapore (2015), Vienna (2017) and Antwerp (2017).

Allan Sekula's library was transferred to the Clark Art Institute in 2015; his archive to the Getty Research Institute in 2016. His art work is represented by Galerie Michel Rein, Paris-Brussels.

A Note on Allan Sekula's Works Discussed in the Present Volume

Gallery Voice Montage (1970) is part of the collection of the Generali Foundation, Vienna.

Untitled Slide Sequence (1972) was produced in an edition of 5 plus 1 AP. It is part of the collections of CNAP, Paris; MOCA, Los Angeles; Generali Foundation, Vienna; Museo Nacional Centro de Arte Reina Sofía, Madrid, amongst others.

Aerospace Folktales (1973) was produced in an edition of 2. It is part of the collections of the John Paul Getty Museum, Los Angeles, and the Generali Foundation, Vienna.

Fish Story (1990–1993), chapter 1 from *Fish Story* (1989–1995), was originally envisioned as an edition of 5 of which only 3 were produced. It is part of the collections of MOMA, NY; Walker Art Center, Minneapolis and Frac Bretagne, Rennes.

Loaves and Fishes (1992), chapter 2 from *Fish Story* (1989–1995), was originally envisioned as an edition of 5 of which only 4 were produced. It is part of the collections of Michel Rein, Paris and Walker Art Center, Minneapolis, amongst others.

Message in a Bottle (1992/1994), chapter 5 from *Fish Story* (1989–1995), was originally envisioned as an edition of 5 of which only 2 were produced. It is part of the collections of TBA 21, Vienna and the Walker Art Center, Minneapolis.

Dear Bill Gates (1999) was produced in an edition of 5 plus 1 AP. It is part of the collections of SFMOMA, amongst others.

Waiting for Tear Gas [white globe to black] (1999/2000) was produced in an edition of 5. It is part of the collections of FRAC Rhone Alps, Lyon; MACBA, Barcelona; Fotomuseum, Winterthur; Tate Modern, London and MOMA, NY.

Black Tide/Marea negra (2002–03) was produced in an edition of 5. It is part of the collections of MUSAC, Spain and TBA21, Vienna, amongst others.

All items from *Ship of Fools | The Dockers' Museum* (2010–2013) are in the collection of M HKA, Antwerp / Collection Flemish Community of Belgium.

Allan Sekula's notebooks are part of the Allan Sekula Archive at the Getty Research Institute in Los Angeles.

Plates

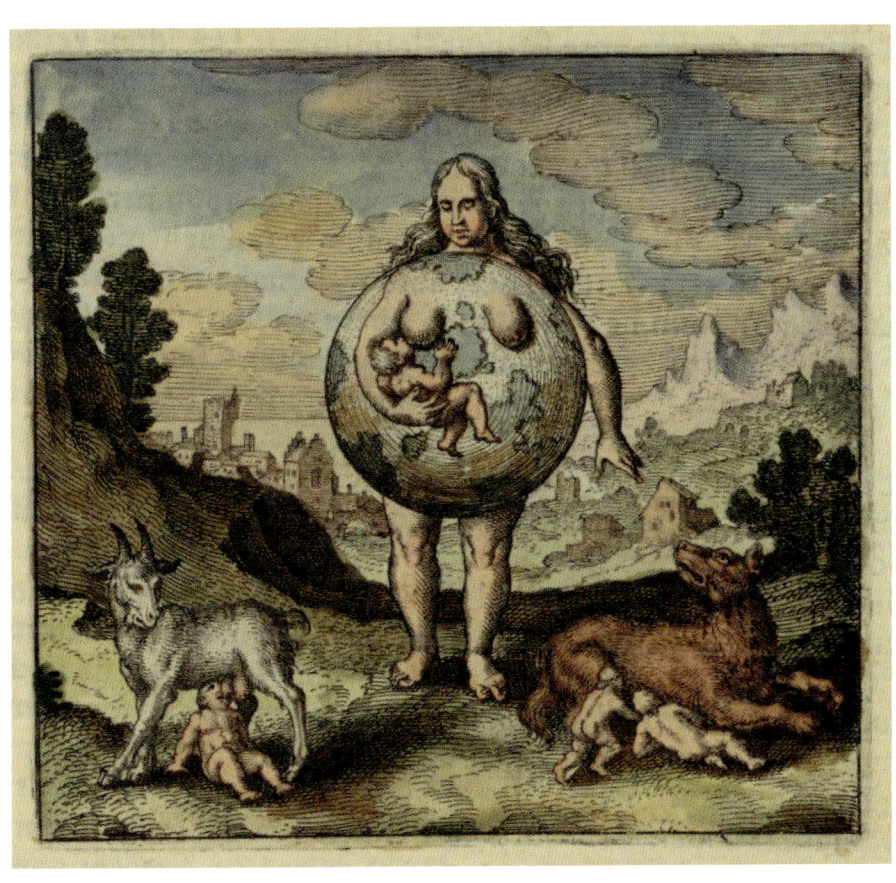

Plate 1

Michael Maier, *Atalanta Fugiens*, published by Johann Theodor de Bry in Oppenheim, 1617, p. 17.

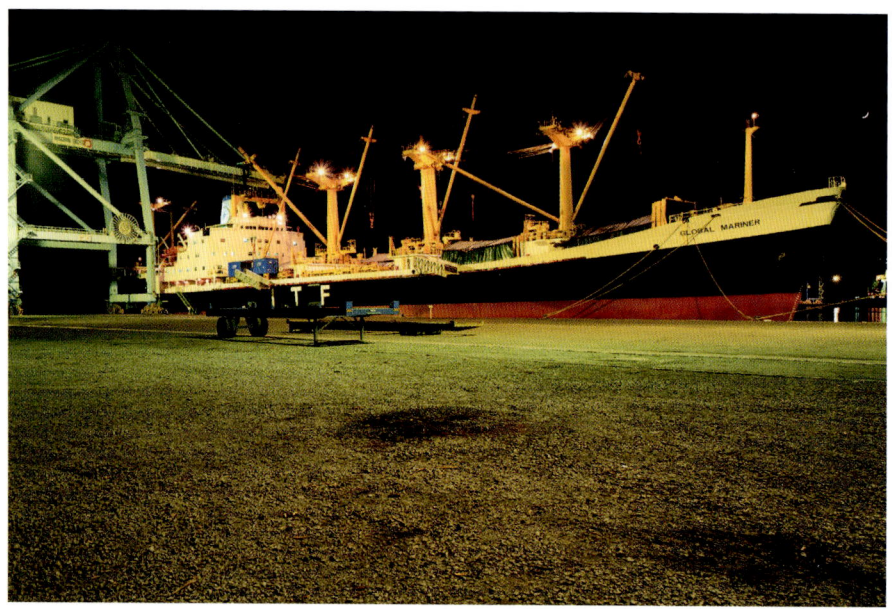

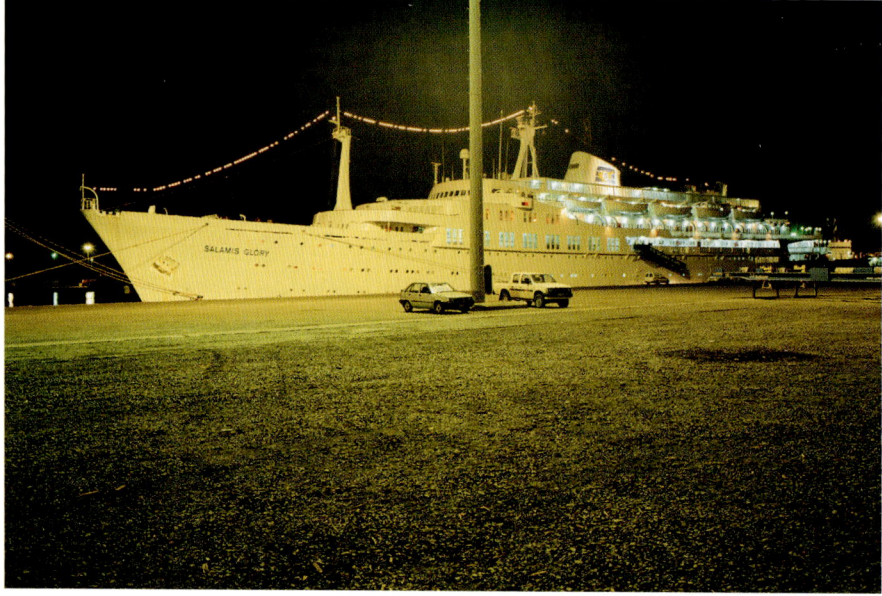

Plate 2 (above)

Allan Sekula, *Good Ship (Limassol) 1*, 1999/2010. Framed chromogenic print mounted on alu-dibond, part of *Ship of Fools* (2010), 101,6 × 154,9 cm. Collection м нка / Collection Flemish Community of Belgium. © Allan Sekula Studio.

Plate 3 (below)

Allan Sekula, *Bad Ship (Limassol) 2*, 1999/2010. Framed chromogenic print mounted on alu-dibond, part of *Ship of Fools* (2010), 101,6 × 154,9 cm. Collection м нка / Collection Flemish Community of Belgium. © Allan Sekula Studio.

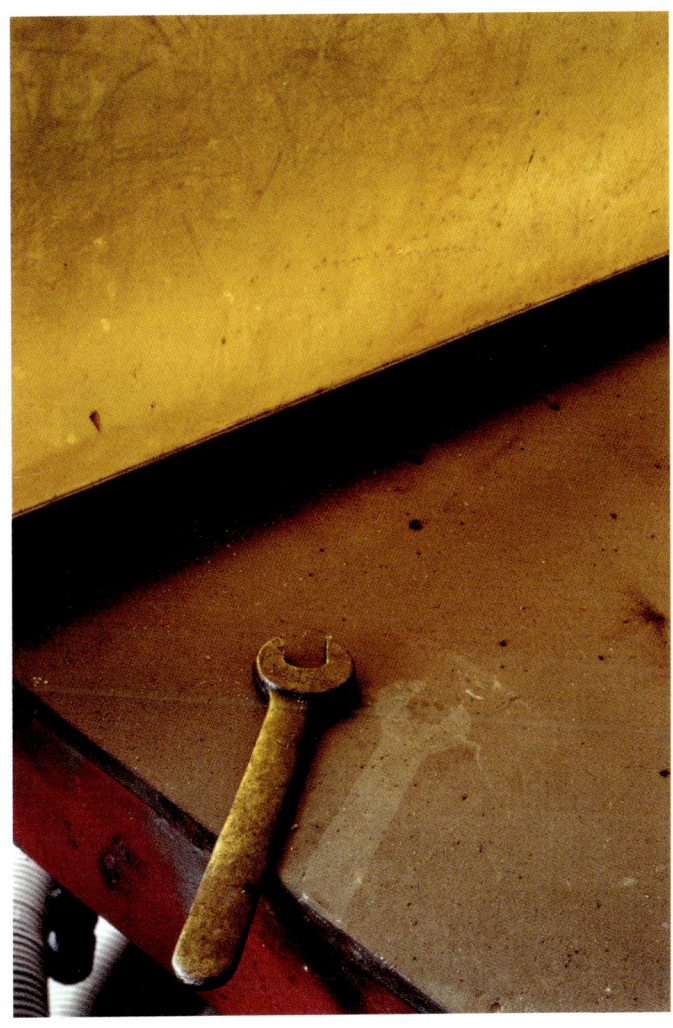

Plate 4

Allan Sekula, *Welder's booth in bankrupt Todd Shipyard. Two years after closing. Los Angeles harbor. San Pedro, California. July 1991*. Cibachrome print, 83,18 × 59 × 4,45 cm (framed). Part of *Fish Story* (1990–1993), chapter 1 of *Fish Story* (1989–1995), 18 Cibachrome prints and 2 text panels, various dimensions. © Allan Sekula Studio.

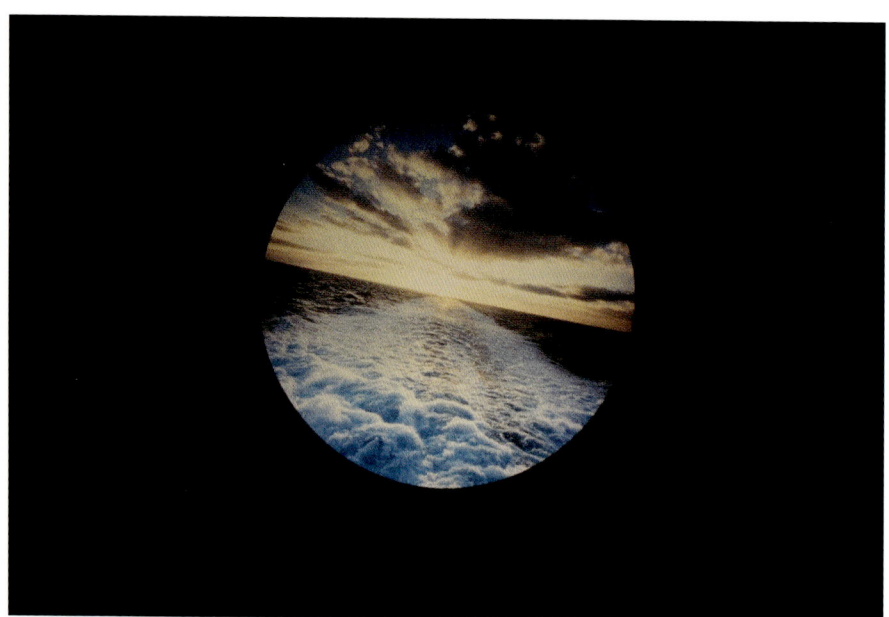

Plate 5

Allan Sekula, *Churn Clockwise 1 rpm*, 2009/2010. Circular color slide in a single rotary projector for planetaria, aided by two projectors with a syncing system, part of *Ship of Fools* (2010). Projected dimensions: 113,03 × 132,08 cm. Installation view at м нка, Antwerp, Spring 2010 Collection м нка / Collection Flemish Community of Belgium. © Photo: м нка, Christine Clinckx, 2010. Courtesy Allan Sekula Studio.

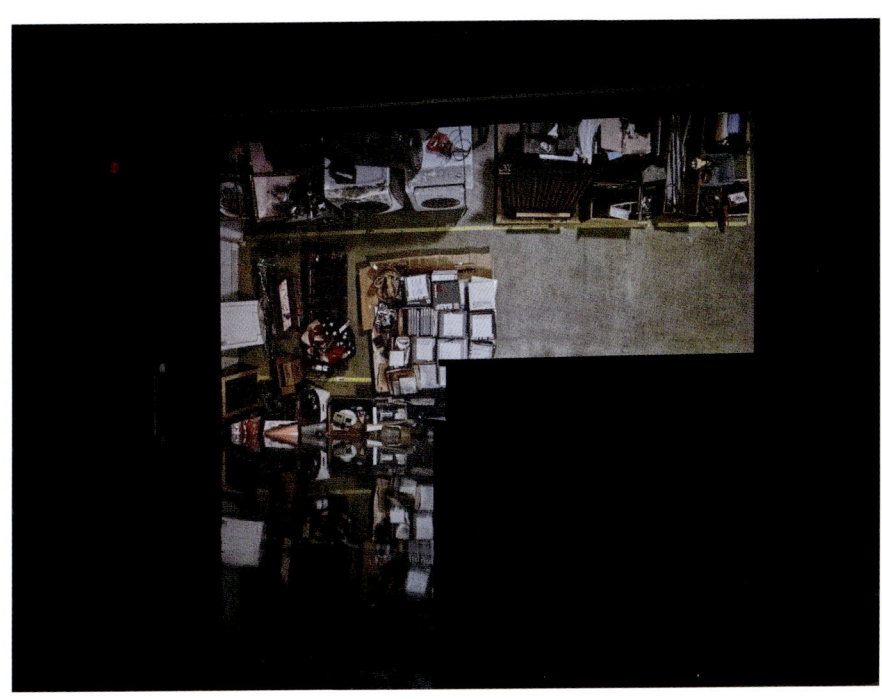

Plate 6
Installation view of *Chris Larson: Land Speed Record*, 2016. © Walker Art Center.

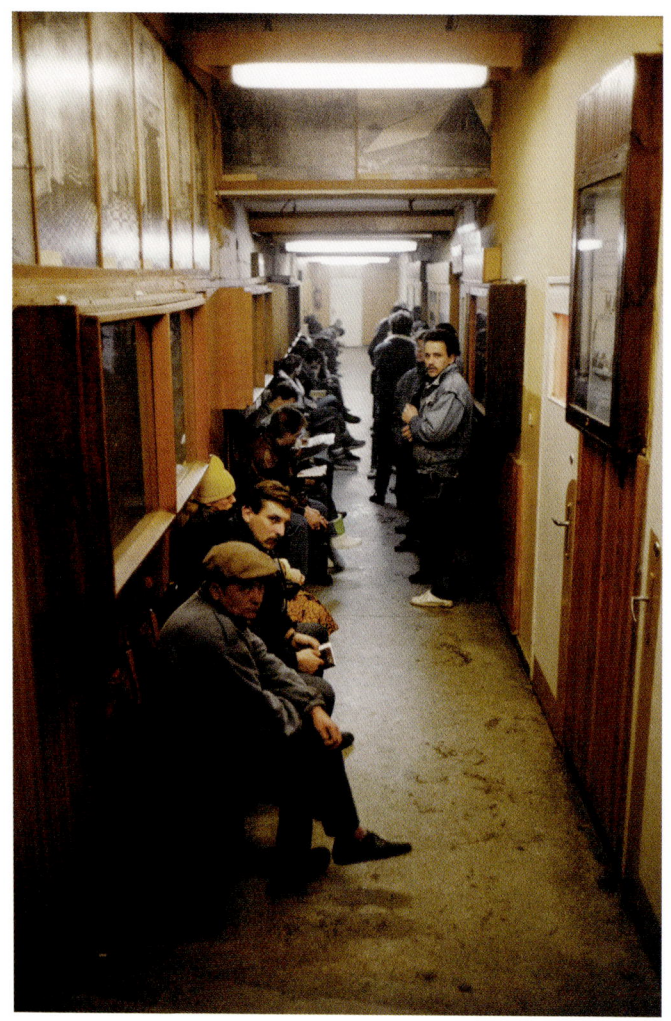

Plate 7

Allan Sekula, *Unemployment office. Gdańsk, Poland. November 1990*. Cibachrome print, 83,2 × 59,2 × 4,5 cm (framed). Part of *Loaves and Fishes* (1992), chapter 2 of *Fish Story* (1989–1995), 8 Cibachrome prints and 2 text panels, various dimensions. © Allan Sekula Studio.

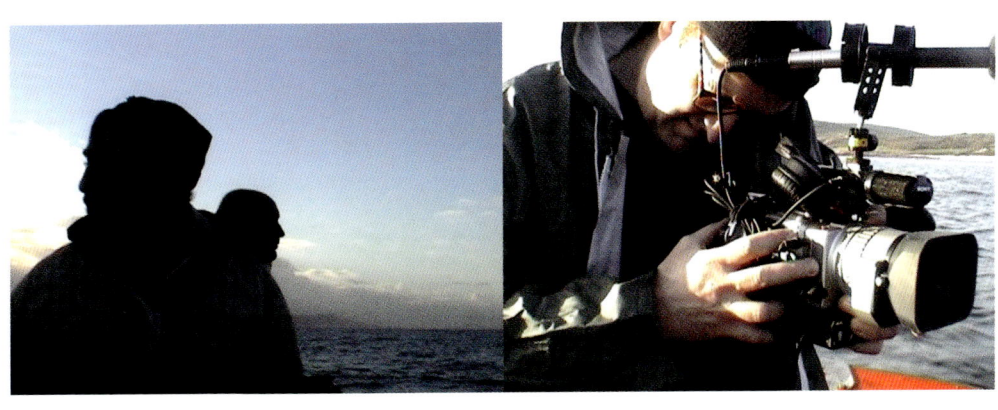

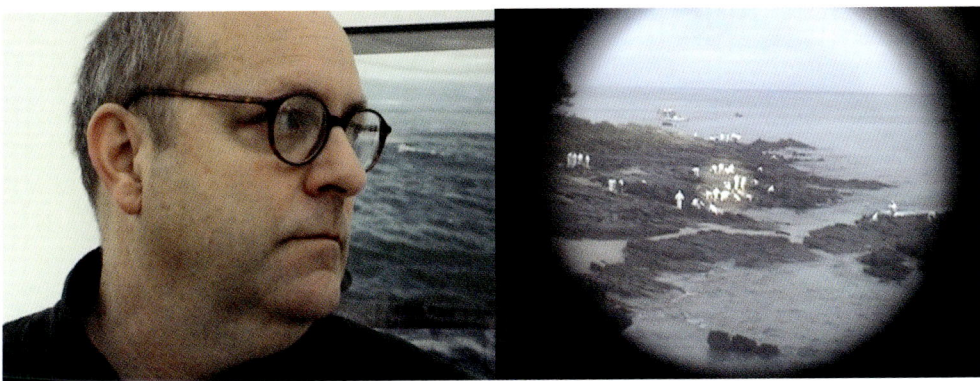

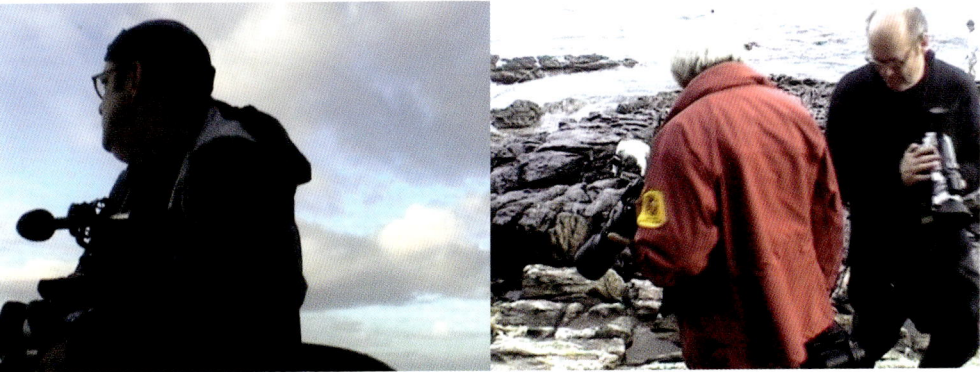

Plate 8

Sequence of stills from *The Last Days of December with Allan Sekula*, 2003, documentary filmed and produced by Carles Guerra with the support of Hangar, 2003. © and courtesy Carles Guerra.

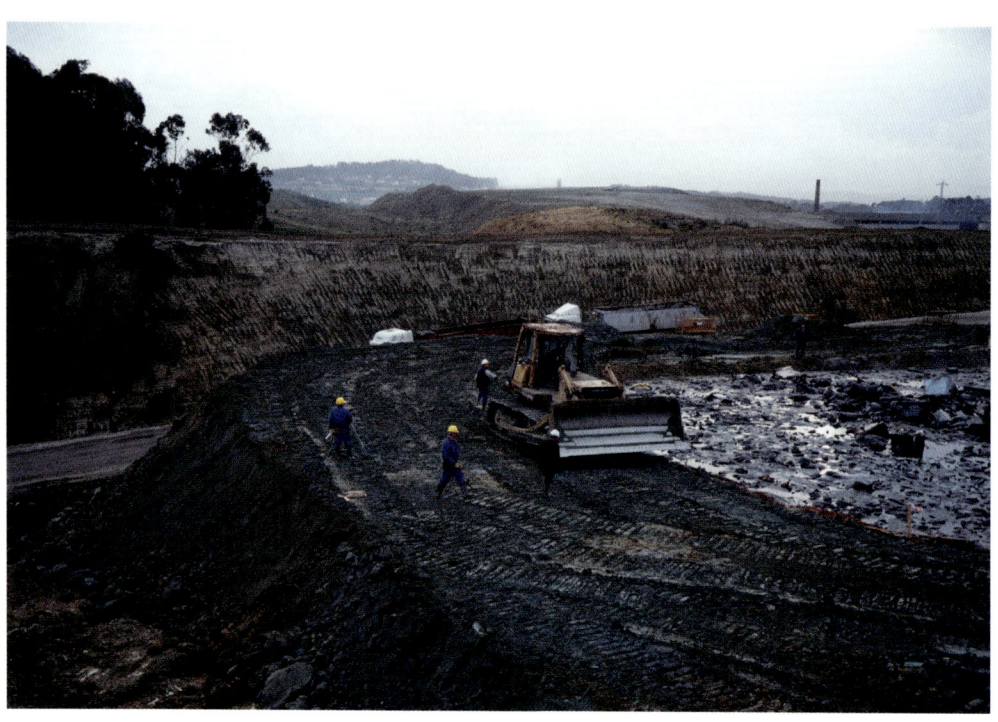

Plates 9–10

Allan Sekula, *Disposal Pit (Lendo, 12/23/02)*, part of *Black Tide/*Marea negra (2002–03). Horizontal diptych, Cibachrome print, 37,2 × 113,7 cm / 51,9 × 125,7 cm (framed). © Allan Sekula Studio.

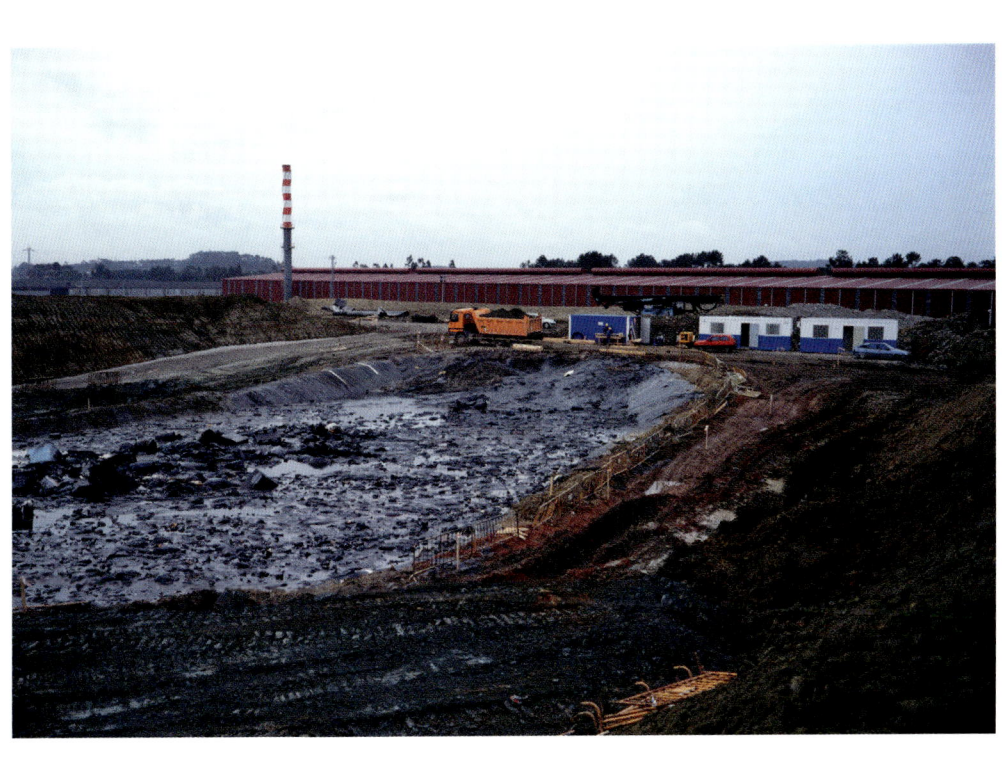

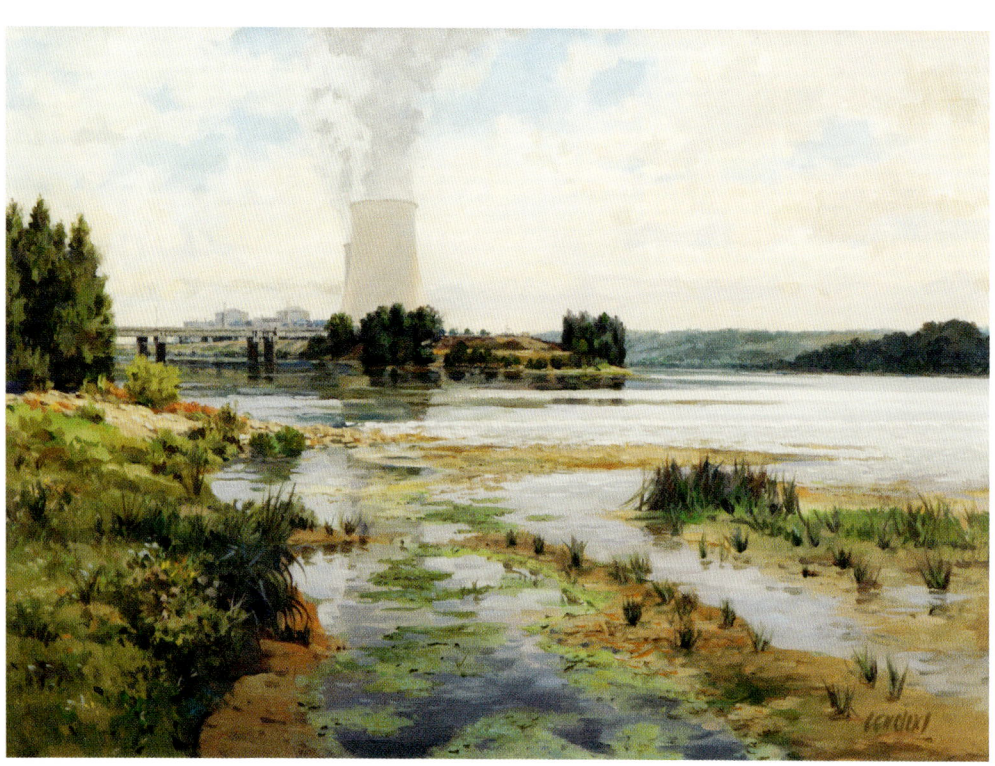

Plate 11

Romantic Landscape Painting of Three Mile Island Nuclear Reactor, Made Before 1979 Partial Meltdown, Artist Name Indecipherable [title given by Allan Sekula], oil on canvas, 1974–1975, 61 × 76,2 cm. Part of Allan Sekula, *Ship of Fools / The Dockers' Museum* (2010–2013) [TDM 57]. Purchased by Allan Sekula through eBay on 10 April 2011. © Photo: Ina Steiner. Collection M HKA, Antwerp /Flemish Community of Belgium. Courtesy Allan Sekula Studio.

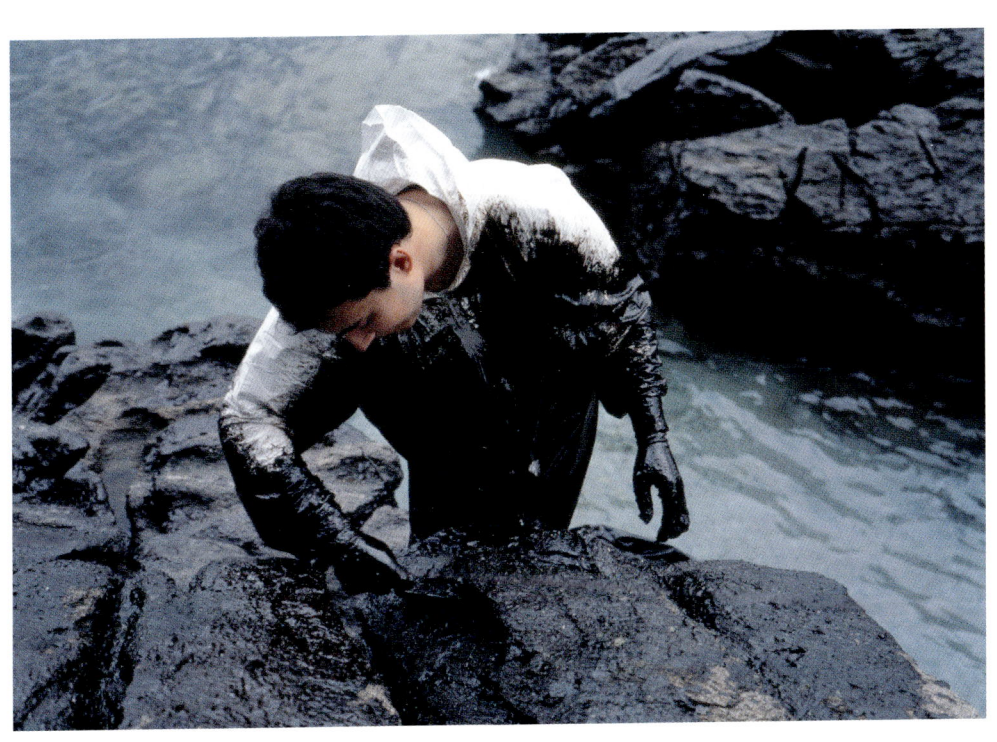

Plate 12

Allan Sekula, *Volunteer on the edge (Islas Cíes, 12/20/02)*, part of *Black Tide/*Marea negra (2002–03). Cibachrome print, 60,5 × 86,1 cm / 75,2 × 107,3 cm (framed). © Allan Sekula Studio.

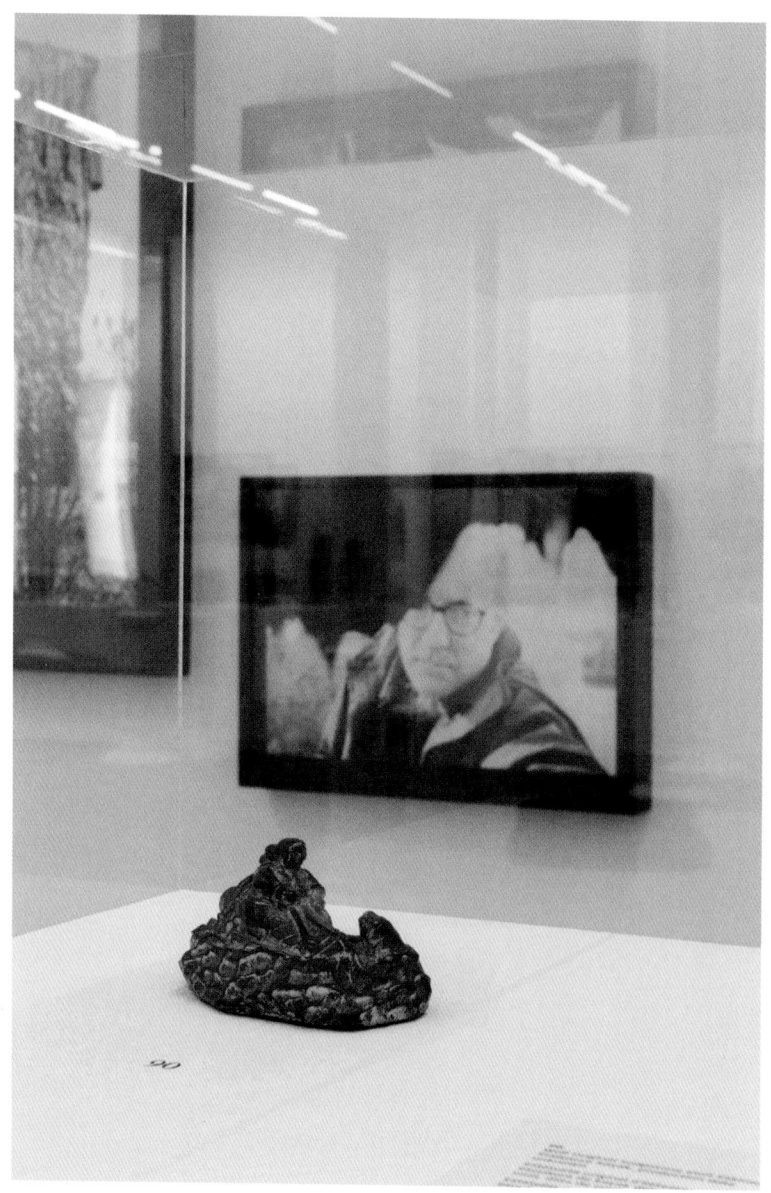

Plate 13

Allan Sekula, *Self-portrait (Lendo, 12/22/02)*, part of *Black Tide/*Marea negra (2002–03). Cibachrome print, 42,7 × 52,7 cm (framed). Installation view during the exhibition *Allan Sekula. Collective Sisyphus*, Fundació Antoni Tàpies, 2017. Private collection. Hung next to *Wolf Original Soapstone Inuit Eskimo Sculpture Kayak* [as indicated on PayPal document]. Soapstone, felt, labelled: "A WOLF ORIGINAL. Fait à la main au Canada. Hand made in Canada. The Wolf Sculptures," 7,6 × 5,1 × 5,1 cm. Production date unknown. Purchased by Allan Sekula through eBay on 14 July 2010. Part of Allan Sekula, *Ship of Fools / The Dockers' Museum* (2010–2013). Collection M HKA, Antwerp / Collection Flemish Community. © Photo: Roberto Ruiz. Courtesy Allan Sekula Studio.

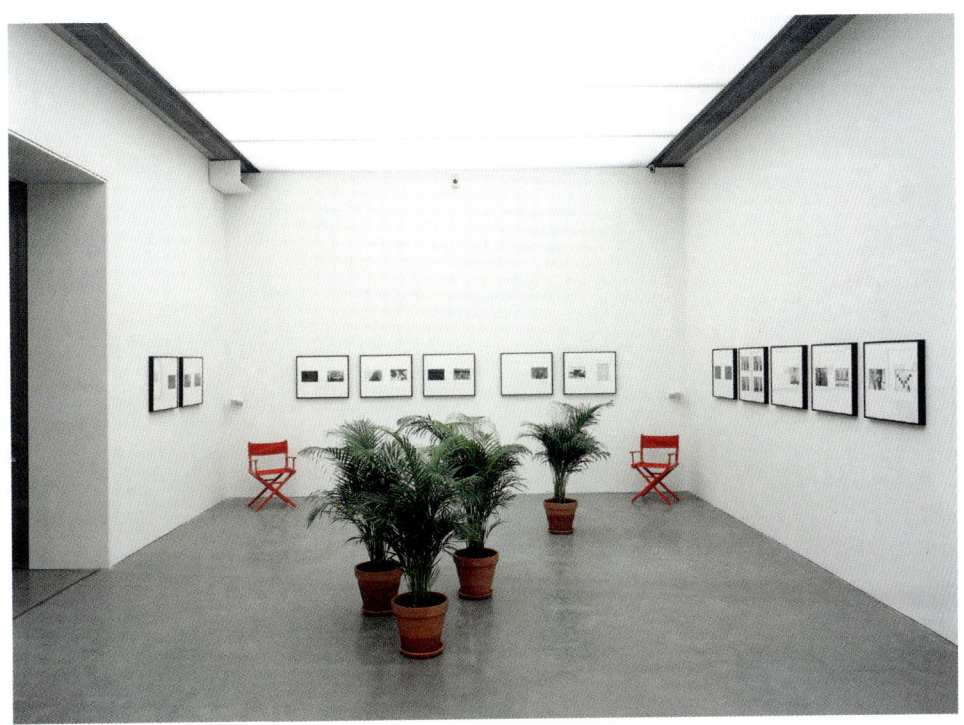

Plate 14

Allan Sekula, *Aerospace Folktales*, 1973. 51 b&w photographs in 23 frames. Three red canvases director's chairs, six potted fan palms, three CD players, three speakers, three simultaneous, unsynchronized CD recordings. Each frame 55,9 × 71,5 cm. CD total play time 17 min, 21 min, and 23 min. Installation view. © Allan Sekula Studio.

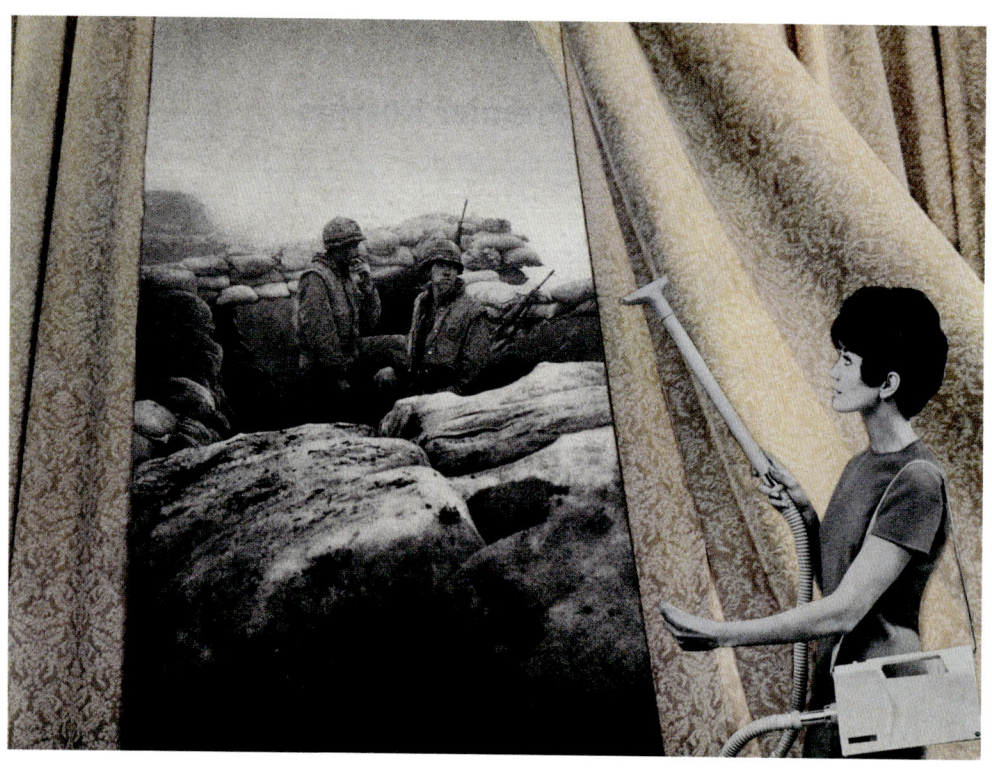

Plate 15

Martha Rosler, *Cleaning the Drapes*, from the series *House Beautiful: Bringing the War Home*, ca. 1967–72, photomontage. © Martha Rosler.

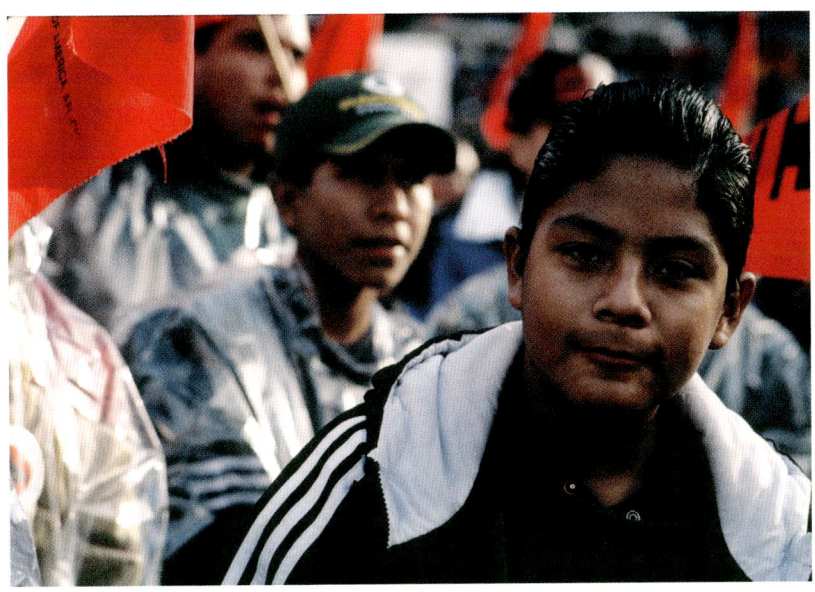

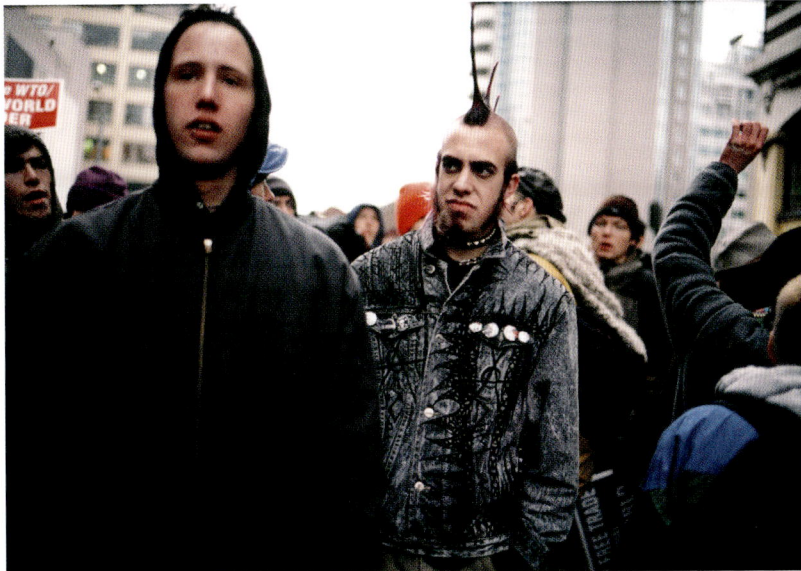

Plate 16

From Allan Sekula, *Waiting for Tear Gas [white globe to black]*, 1999/2000. 81 slides, 35 mm, color, and wall text, 13–16 minutes (depending on the selected interval within the allowed range of 10–12 seconds), looped. Sequence coeditor: Sally Stein © Allan Sekula Studio.

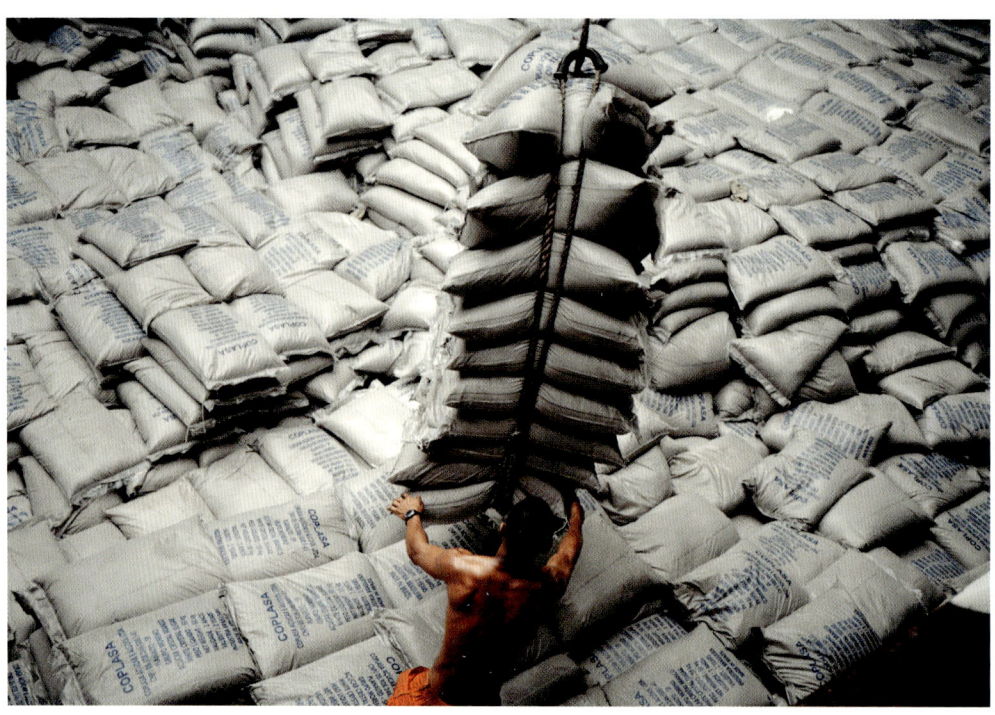

Plate 17

Allan Sekula, *Working (Santos)*, 2010. Framed chromogenic print mounted on alu-dibond, part of *Ship of Fools* (2010), 101,6 × 149,9 cm. Collection м нка / Collection Flemish Community of Belgium. © Allan Sekula Studio.

Colophon

Every effort has been made to contact all holders of the copyright to the visual material contained in this publication. Any copyright-holders who believe that illustrations have been reproduced without their knowledge are asked to contact the Lieven Gevaert Research Centre for Photography, Art and Visual Culture.

Lieven Gevaert Research Centre for Photography, Art and Visual Culture
Arts Faculty KU Leuven
Blijde-Inkomststraat 21 box 3313
B-3000 Leuven
Belgium

Editors: Alexander Streitberger, Hilde Van Gelder
Asisstant Editor: Federica Mantoan
Language Revision: Ton Brouwers
Lay-out and cover design: DOGMA

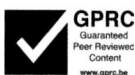

ISBN 978 94 6270 1717
D/2019/1869/12
NUR: 652

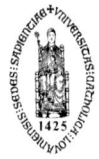
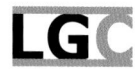
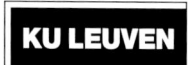
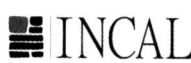
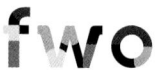

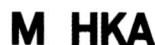
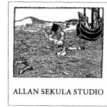
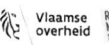
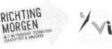
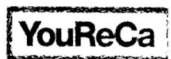